Magical
Girl Site

VOLUME 5

AUTHOR
KENTARO SATO

SUMMARY AND CHARACTER INTROS

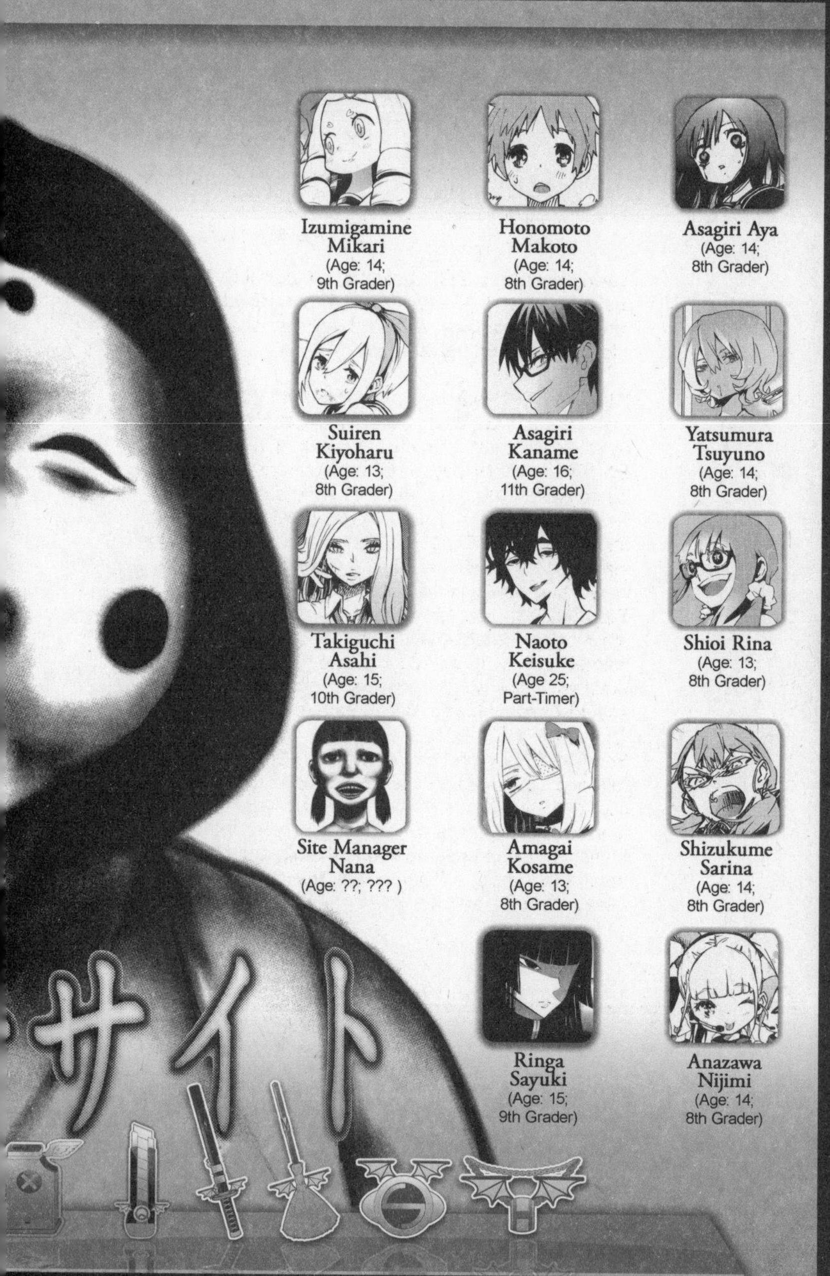
Izumigamine Mikari
(Age: 14; 9th Grader)
Honomoto Makoto
(Age: 14; 8th Grader)
Asagiri Aya
(Age: 14; 8th Grader)
Suiren Kiyoharu
(Age: 13; 8th Grader)
Asagiri Kaname
(Age: 16; 11th Grader)
Yatsumura Tsuyuno
(Age: 14; 8th Grader)
Takiguchi Asahi
(Age: 15; 10th Grader)
Naoto Keisuke
(Age 25; Part-Timer)
Shioi Rina
(Age: 13; 8th Grader)
Site Manager Nana
(Age: ??; ???)
Amagai Kosame
(Age: 13; 8th Grader)
Shizukume Sarina
(Age: 14; 8th Grader)
Ringa Sayuki
(Age: 15; 9th Grader)
Anazawa Nijimi
(Age: 14; 8th Grader)
サイト

Magical Girl Site

Magical Girl Site 4

Display Images

Summary

Having been revived by Kosame, a Magical Girl from a different site, Aya, Tsuyuno, and Rina joined forces with her to capture a Site Manager and obtain information about the Tempest.

When Aya and Tsuyuno returned to Aya's home, they were struck with dread when they discovered that Aya's older brother, Kaname, knew about Magical Girl Site. Then, a few days later, a new transfer student joined Aya's class. That student turned out to be Shioi Rina! Upon seeing her, Anazawa Nijimi instantly attempted to kill Rina with her wand, but Tsuyuno managed to contain her while Aya stole Nijimi's panty wand. Afterwards, in the park behind the school, Aya, Tsuyuno, Rina, and Nijimi met with three girls from the other site: Kosame, Kiyoharu, and Sayuki. They learned that there are countless other Magical Girls like them in the world, and were also told more details about Kosame's plan to capture a Site Manager.

Soon after they part ways, Aya, Tsuyuno, and Rina returned to Aya's home. Once there, Kiyoharu informed them that the Site Managers were assassinating Magical Girls. Not long after that, Site Manager Nana appeared before the trio and attacked them. Meanwhile, a different Site Manager appeared before Kiyoharu and Kosame...

SEVEN SEAS ENTERTAINMENT PRESENTS

MAGICAL GIRL SITE

story and art by **KENTARO SATO**

VOLUME 5

TRANSLATION
Wesley Bridges

ADAPTATION
Janet Houck

LETTERING AND LAYOUT
Meaghan Tucker

COVER DESIGN
Nicky Lim

PROOFREADER
Brett Hallahan

ASSISTANT EDITOR
Jenn Grunigen

PRODUCTION ASSISTANT
CK Russell

PRODUCTION MANAGER
Lissa Pattillo

EDITOR-IN-CHIEF
Adam Arnold

PUBLISHER
Jason DeAngelis

MAHO SYOJYO SITE Volume 5
© Kentaro Sato 2016
Originally published in Japan in 2016 by Akita Publishing Co., Ltd..
English translation rights arranged with Akita Publishing Co., Ltd. through
TOHAN CORPORATION, Tokyo.

Seven Seas books may be purchased in bulk for promotional, educational, or
business use. Please contact your local bookseller or the Macmillan Corporate
and Premium Sales Department at 1-800-221-7945, extension 5442, or by
e-mail at MacmillanSpecialMarkets@macmillan.com.

Seven Seas and the Seven Seas logo are trademarks of
Seven Seas Entertainment, LLC. All rights reserved.

ISBN: 978-1-626926-90-5

Printed in Canada

First Printing: February 2018

10 9 8 7 6 5 4 3 2 1

FOLLOW US ONLINE: *www.gomanga.com*

READING DIRECTIONS

This book reads from *right to left*, Japanese style.
If this is your first time reading manga, you start
reading from the top right panel on each page and
take it from there. If you get lost, just follow the
numbered diagram here. It may seem backwards at
first, but you'll get the hang of it! Have fun!!

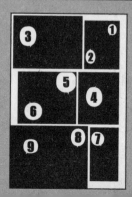

ENTER. 29 DEBT

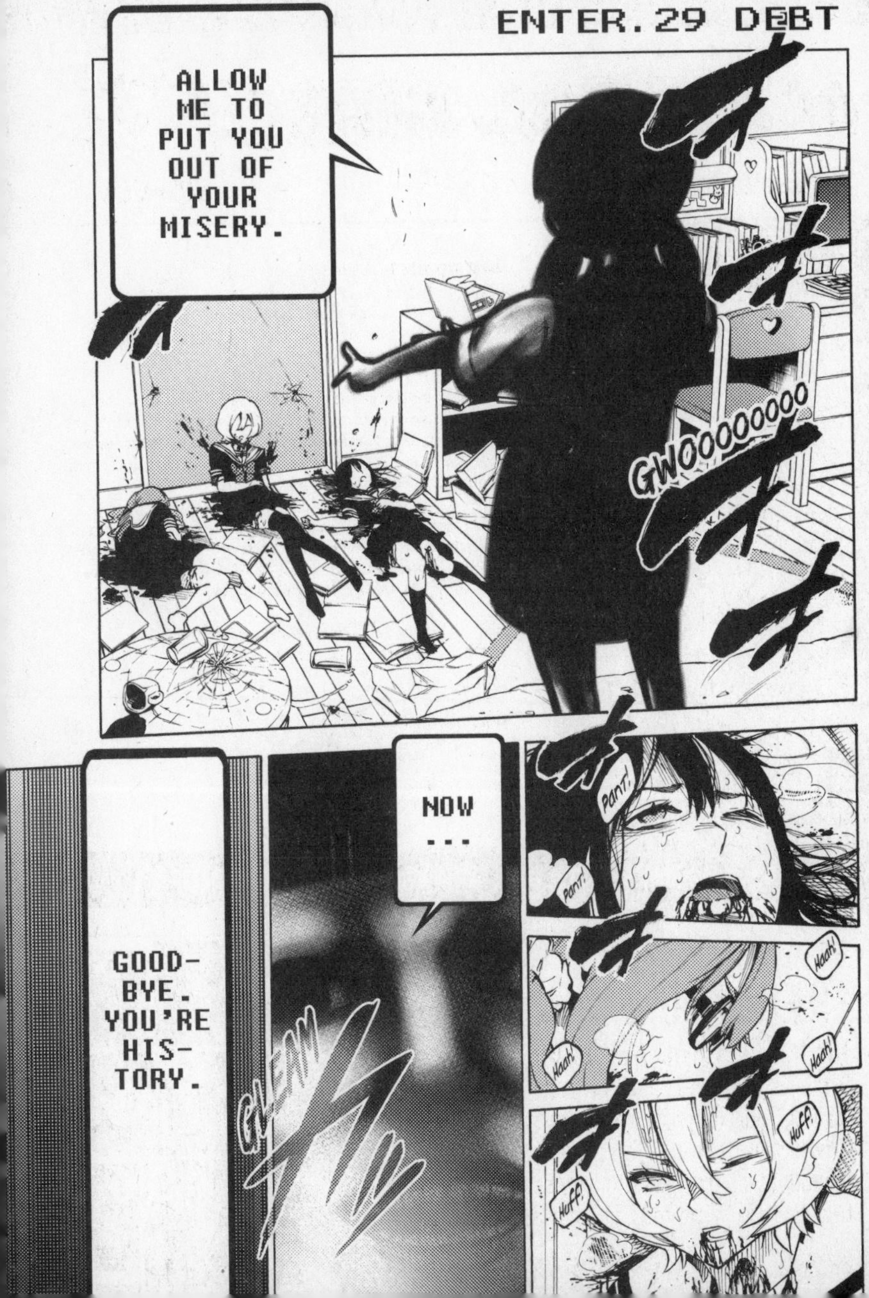
ALLOW ME TO PUT YOU OUT OF YOUR MISERY.
GWOOOOOOOO
PANT!
PANT!
HAAH!
HAAH!
HAAH!
HUFF!
HUFF!
NOW ...
GLEAM
GOOD-BYE. YOU'RE HIS-TORY.

ENTER. 29 DEBT

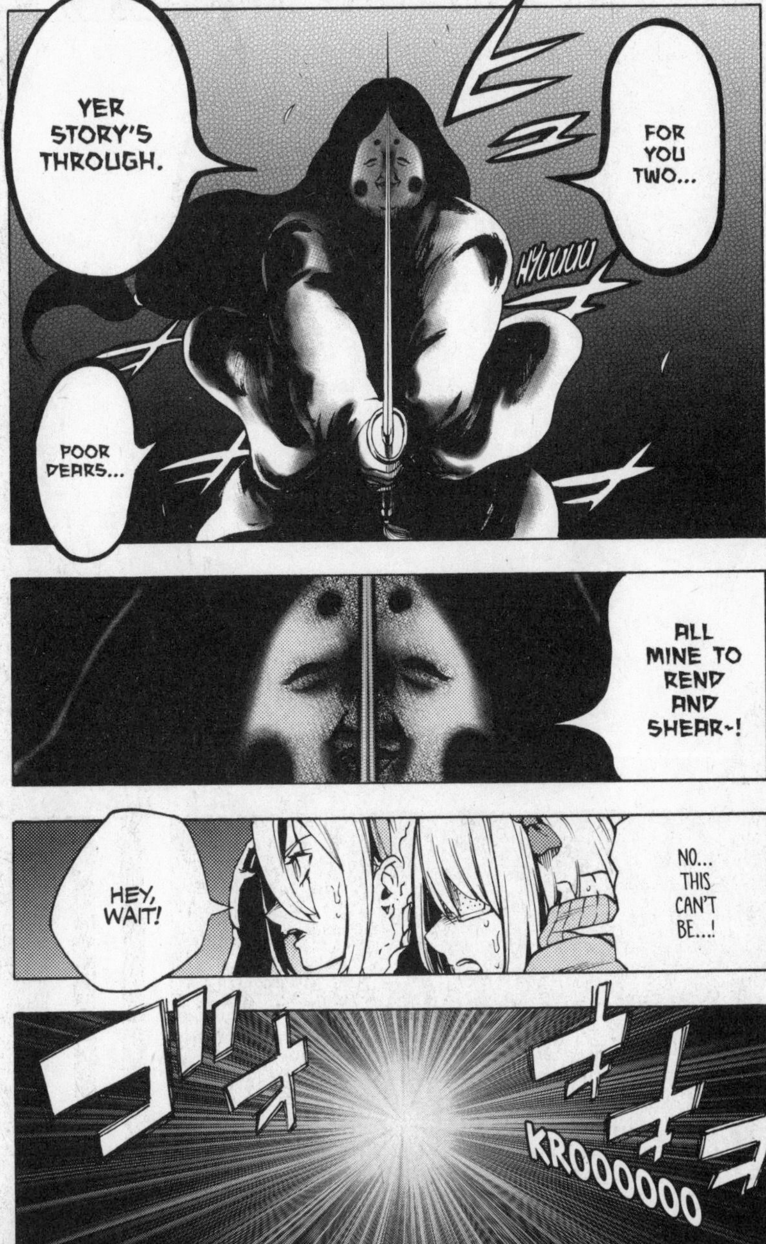
FOR YOU TWO...
HYUUUU
YER STORY'S THROUGH.
POOR DEARS...
ALL MINE TO REND AND SHEAR~!
NO... THIS CAN'T BE...!
HEY, WAIT!
KROOOOOO

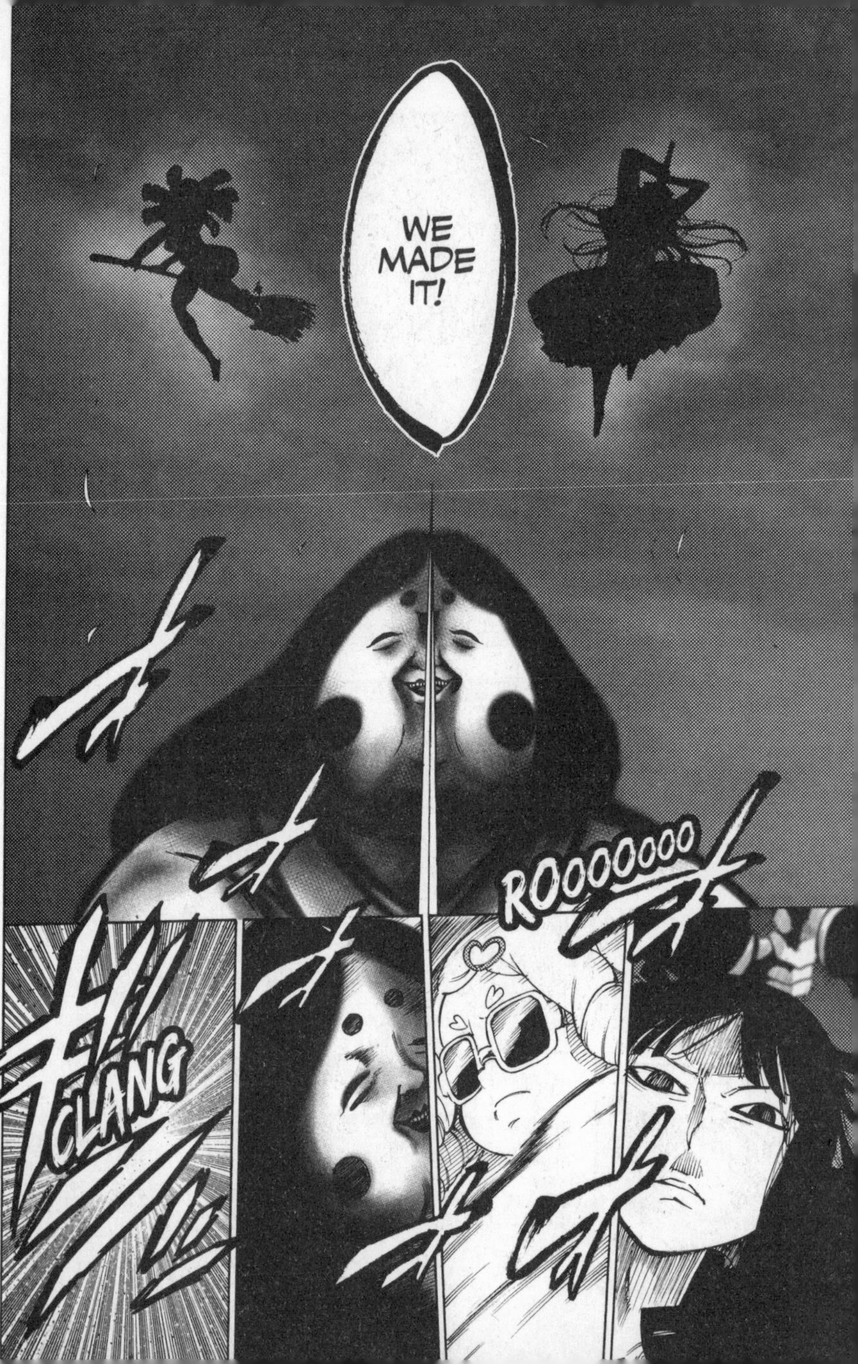
WE MADE IT!
ROOOOOOO
CLANG

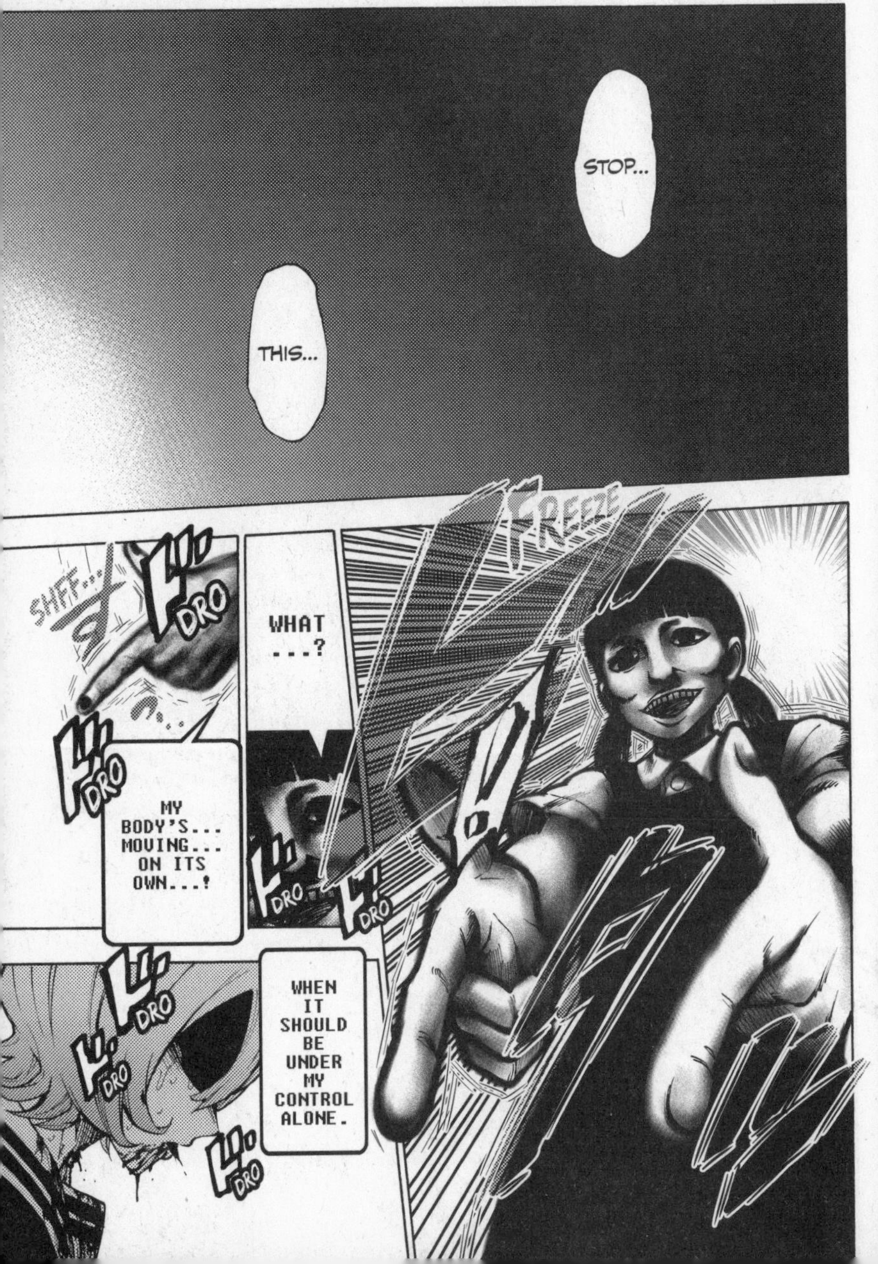
STOP...
THIS...
FREEZE
WHAT ...?
DRO
DRO
SHFF...
DRO
DRO
MY BODY'S... MOVING... ON ITS OWN...!
DRO
DRO
WHEN IT SHOULD BE UNDER MY CONTROL ALONE.
DRO

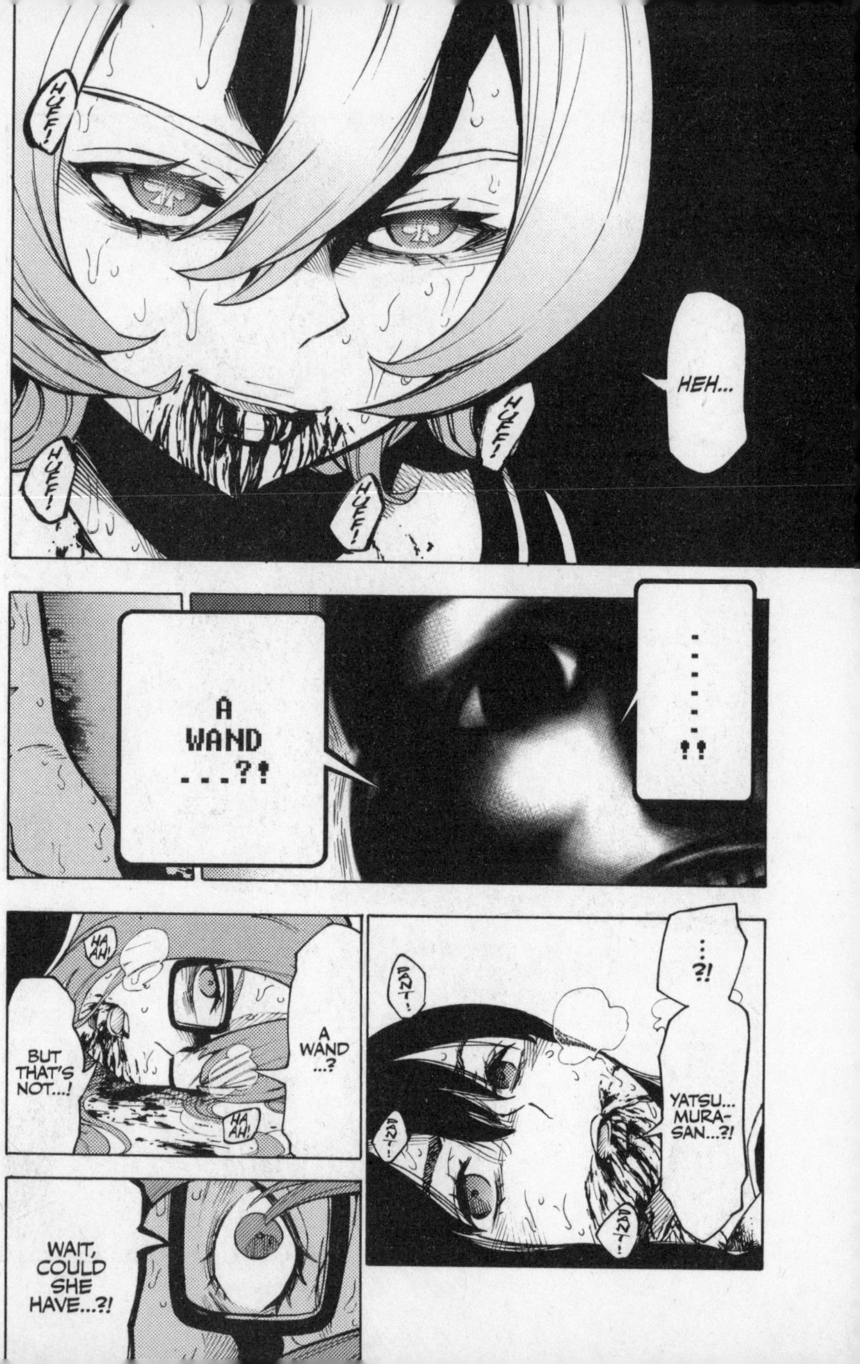
HEH...
HUFF!
HUFF!
HUFF!
HUFF!
HUFF!
......!!
A WAND ...?!
...?!
PANT!
YATSU... MURA-SAN...?!
PANT!
PANT!
HA AH!
A WAND ...?
BUT THAT'S NOT...!
HA AH!
WAIT, COULD SHE HAVE...?!

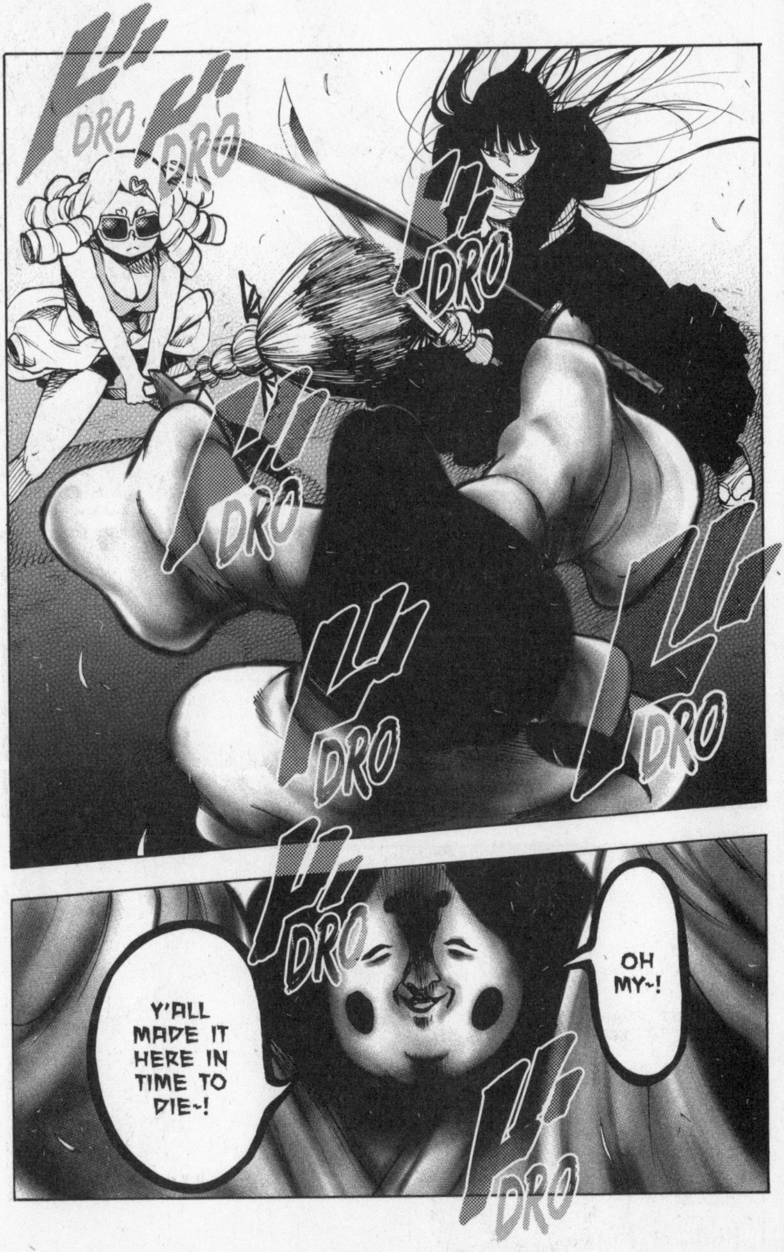
DRO
DRO
DRO
DRO
DRO
DRO
DRO
OH MY~!
Y'ALL MADE IT HERE IN TIME TO DIE~!
DRO
DRO

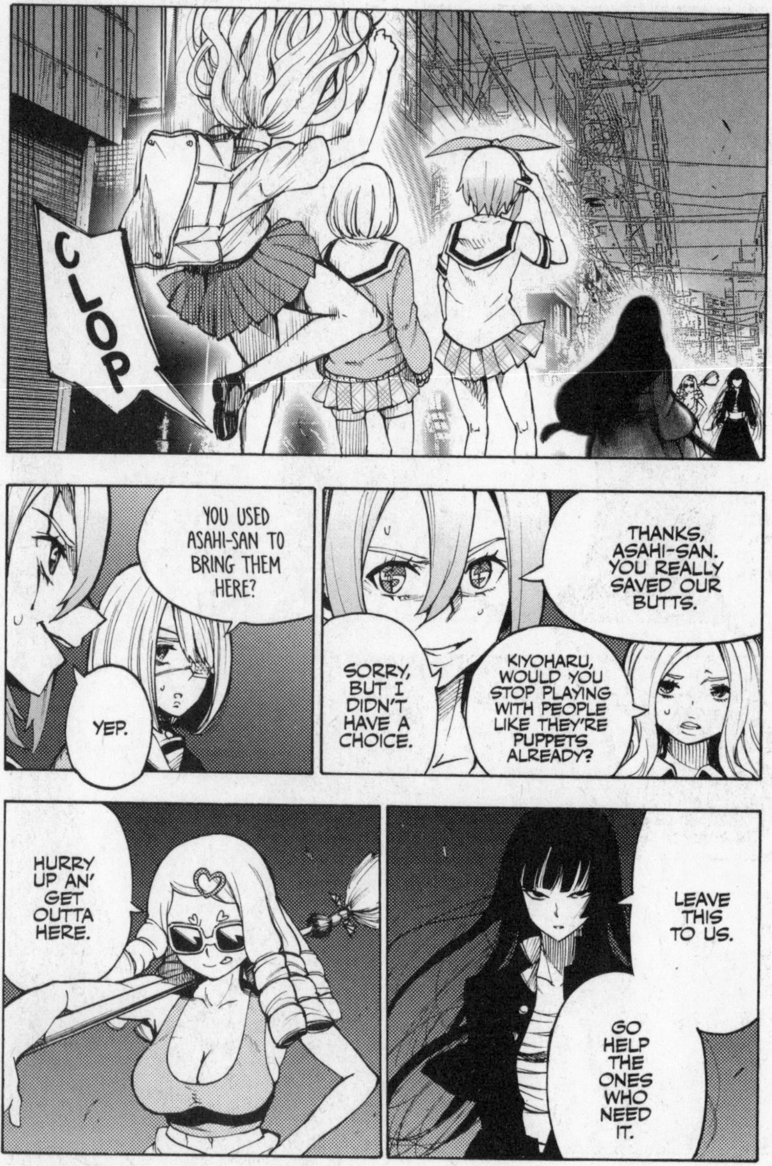
CLOP
THANKS, ASAHI-SAN. YOU REALLY SAVED OUR BUTTS.
KIYOHARU, WOULD YOU STOP PLAYING WITH PEOPLE LIKE THEY'RE PUPPETS ALREADY?
SORRY, BUT I DIDN'T HAVE A CHOICE.
YOU USED ASAHI-SAN TO BRING THEM HERE?
YEP.
LEAVE THIS TO US.
GO HELP THE ONES WHO NEED IT.
HURRY UP AN' GET OUTTA HERE.

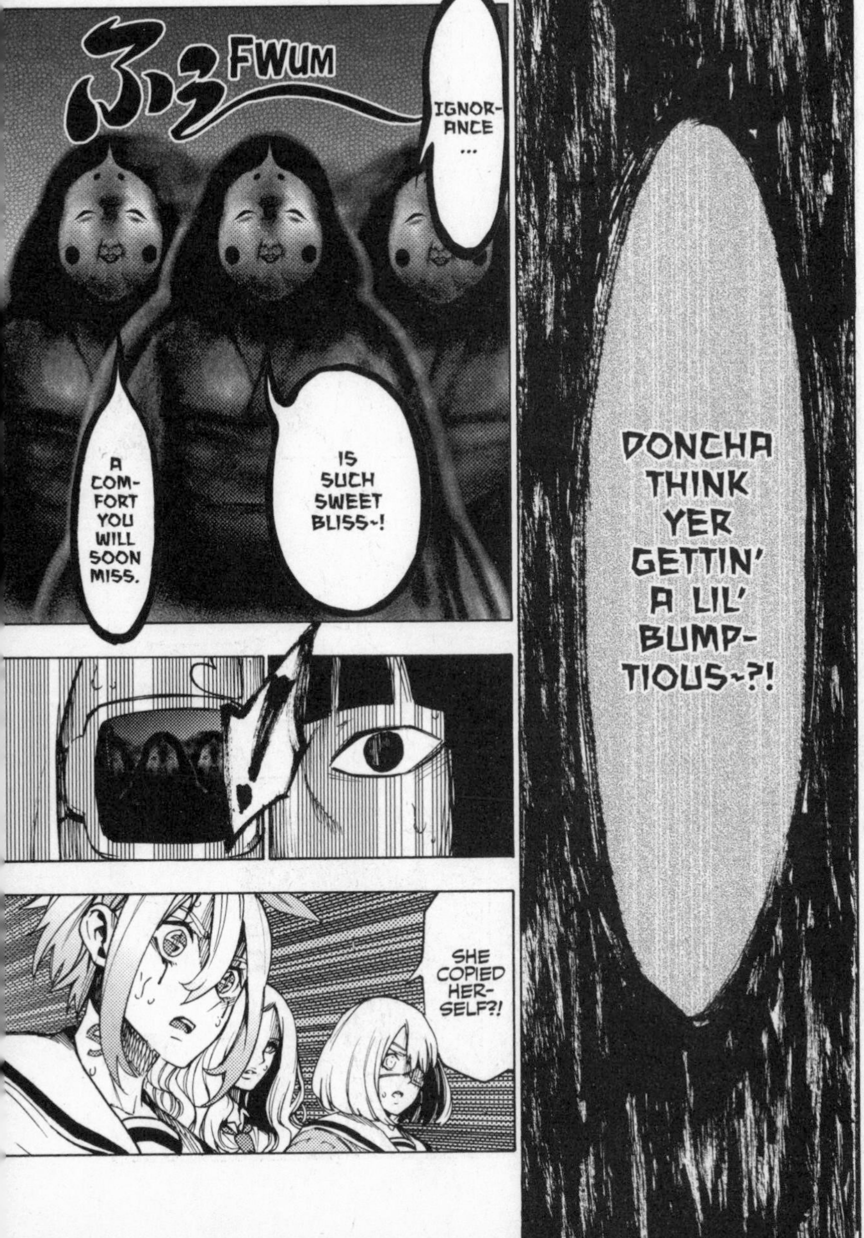
DONCHA THINK YER GETTIN' A LIL' BUMPTIOUS~?!
IGNORANCE...
FWUM
IS SUCH SWEET BLISS~!
A COMFORT YOU WILL SOON MISS.
SHE COPIED HERSELF?!

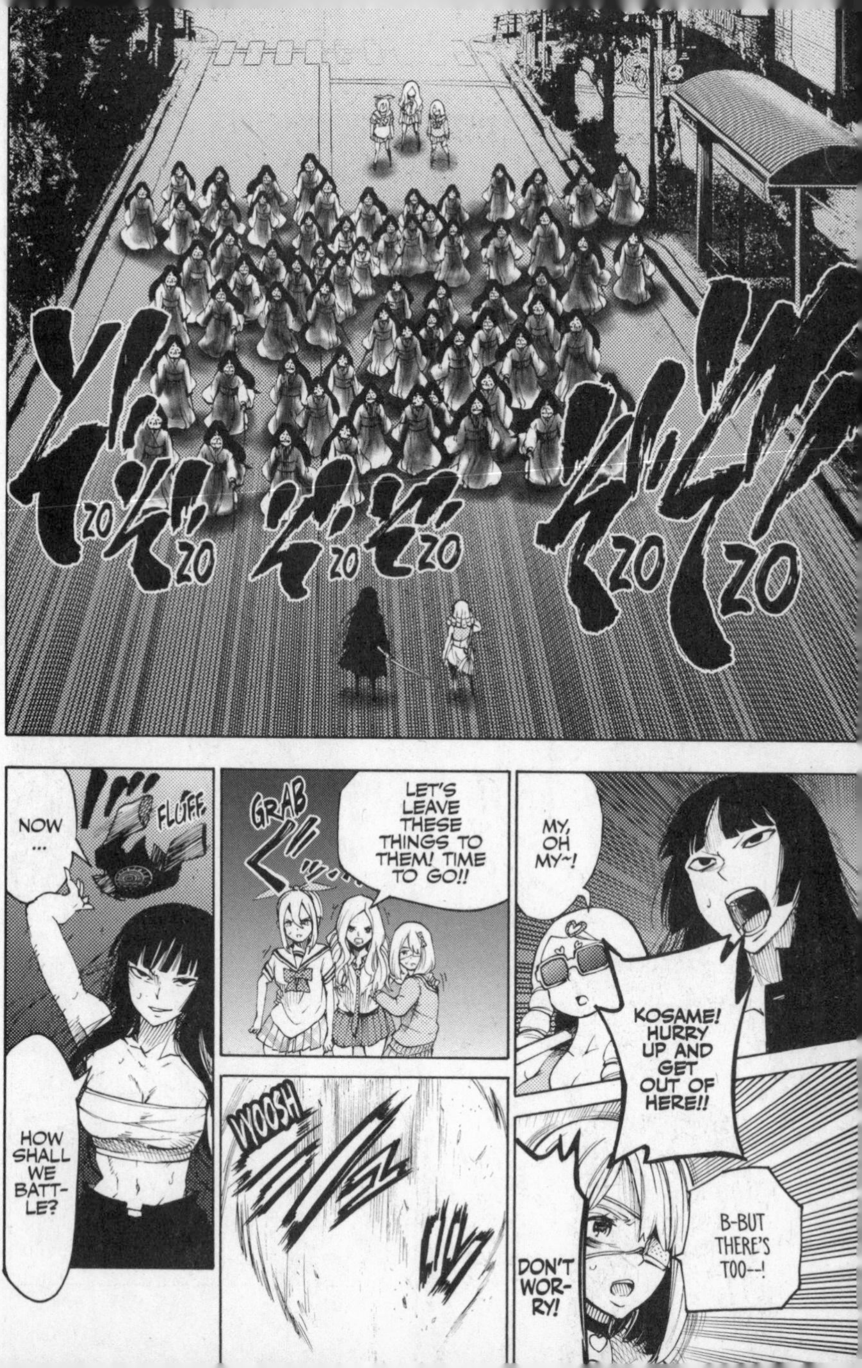
ZO
ZO
ZO
ZO
ZO
ZO
MY, OH MY~!
KOSAME! HURRY UP AND GET OUT OF HERE!!
LET'S LEAVE THESE THINGS TO THEM! TIME TO GO!!
GRAB
B-BUT THERE'S TOO--!
DON'T WORRY!
WOOSH
NOW ...
FLUFF
HOW SHALL WE BATTLE?

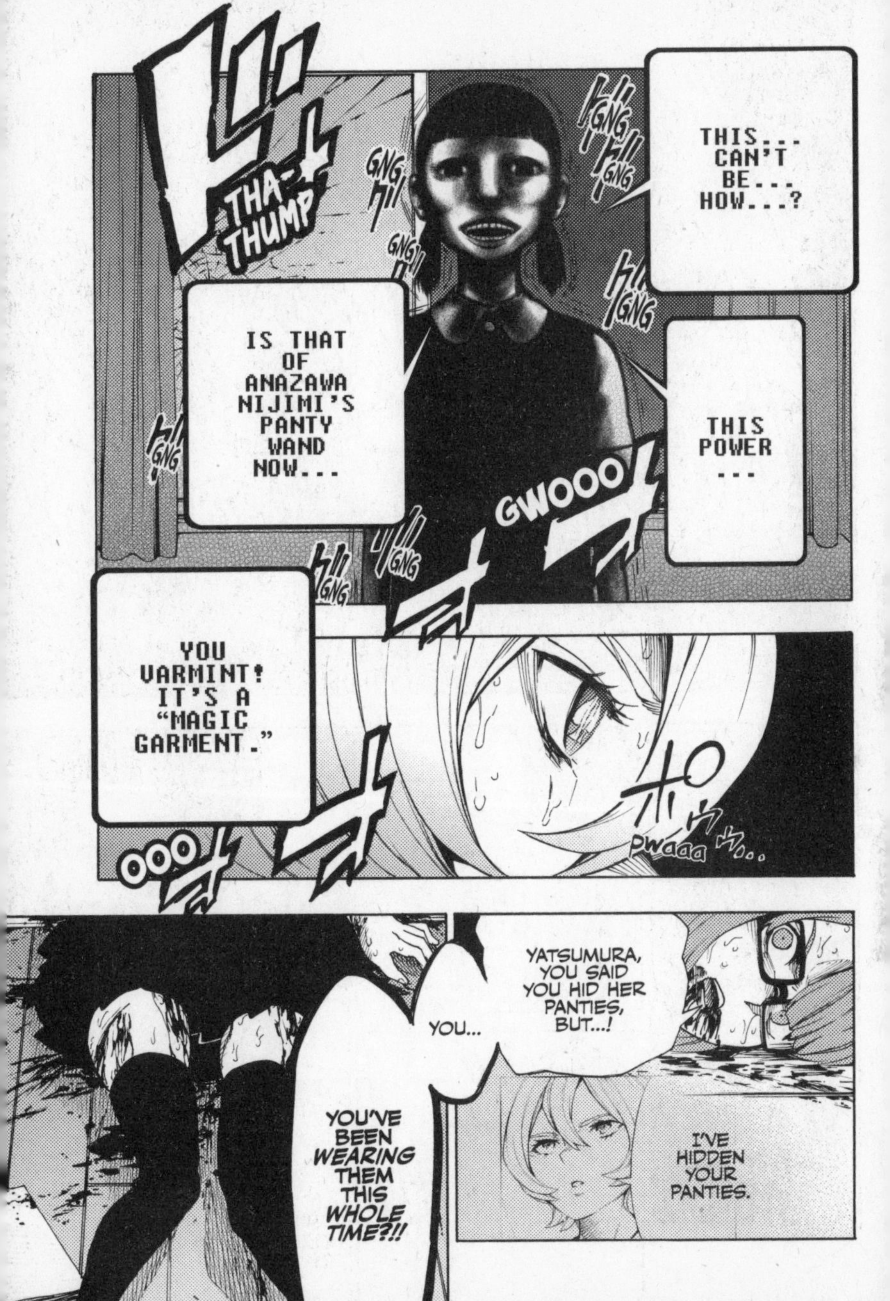
THA-THUMP
GNG
THIS... CAN'T BE... HOW...?
THIS POWER ...
IS THAT OF ANAZAWA NIJIMI'S PANTY WAND NOW...
GWOOO
YOU VARMINT! IT'S A "MAGIC GARMENT."
OOO
Pwaaa
YATSUMURA, YOU SAID YOU HID HER PANTIES, BUT...!
YOU...
I'VE HIDDEN YOUR PANTIES.
YOU'VE BEEN WEARING THEM THIS WHOLE TIME?!!

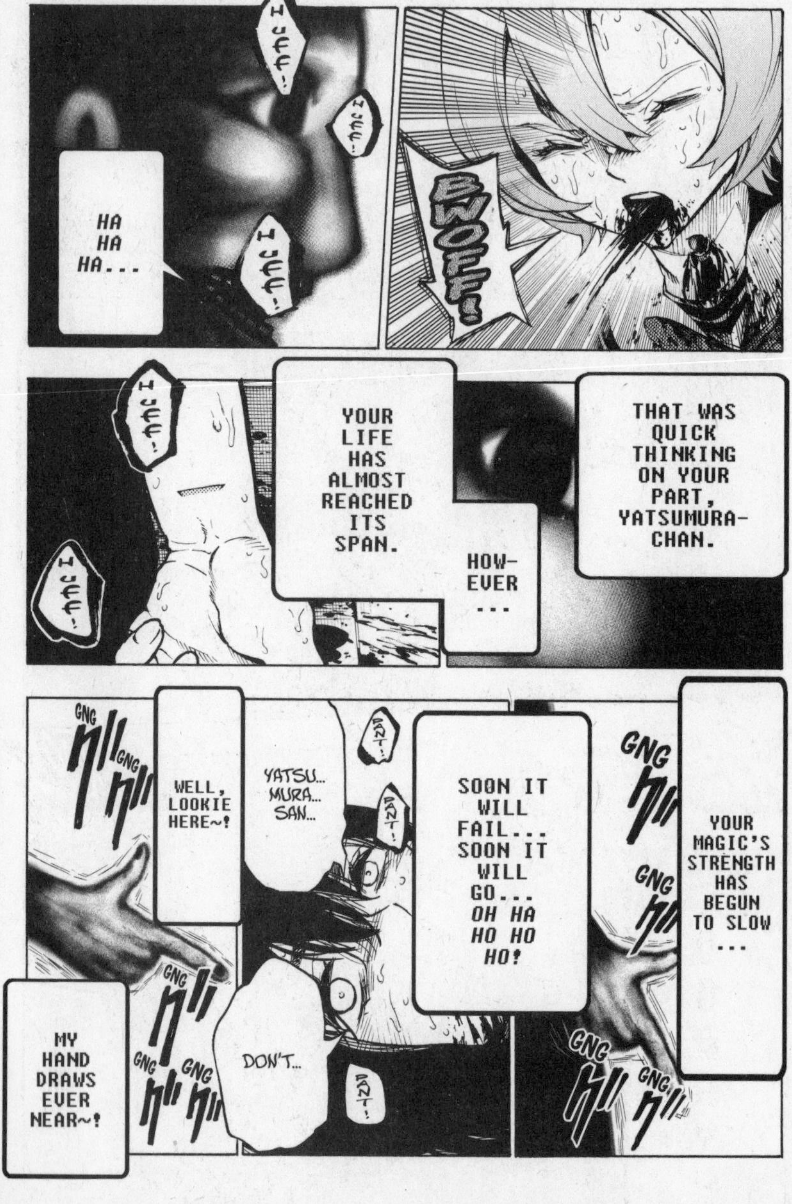
BWOFF!
HUFF!
HUFF!
HA HA HA...
HUFF!
THAT WAS QUICK THINKING ON YOUR PART, YATSUMURA-CHAN.
HOW-EVER...
YOUR LIFE HAS ALMOST REACHED ITS SPAN.
HUFF!
HUFF!
YOUR MAGIC'S STRENGTH HAS BEGUN TO SLOW...
GNG
GNG
SOON IT WILL FAIL... SOON IT WILL GO... OH HA HO HO HO!
GNG
GNG
PANT!
PANT!
YATSU... MURA... SAN...
DON'T...
PANT!
GNG
GNG
WELL, LOOKIE HERE~!
GNG
GNG
GNG
MY HAND DRAWS EVER NEAR~!

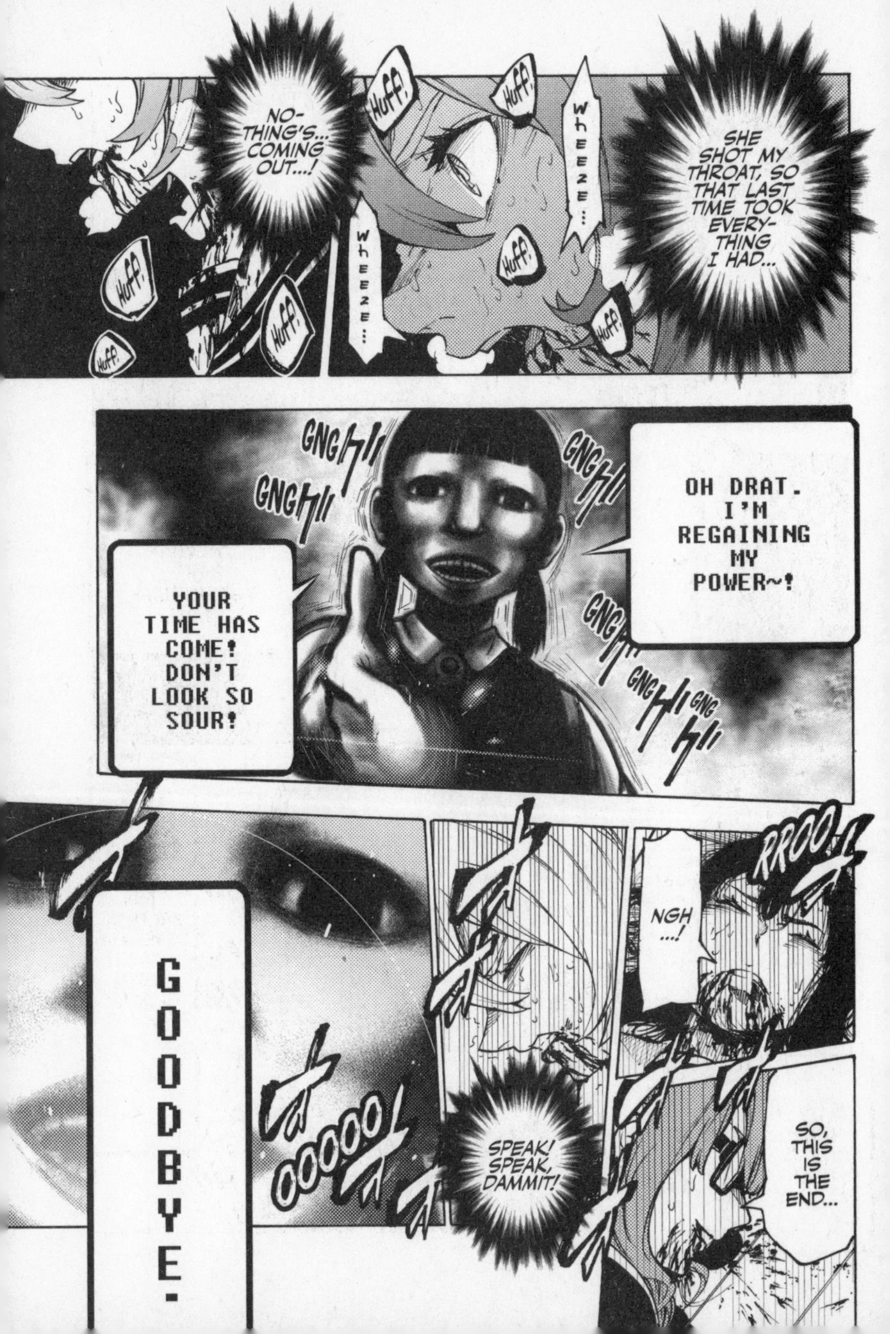
SHE SHOT MY THROAT, SO THAT LAST TIME TOOK EVERY-THING I HAD...
HUFF!
HUFF!
WHEEZE...
HUFF!
HUFF!
WHEEZE...
NO-THING'S... COMING OUT...!
HUFF!
HUFF!
HUFF!
OH DRAT. I'M REGAINING MY POWER~!
GNG
GNG
GNG
GNG
GNG
GNG
YOUR TIME HAS COME! DON'T LOOK SO SOUR!
RROO...
NGH ...!
SO, THIS IS THE END...
SPEAK! SPEAK, DAMMIT!
OOOOO
GOODBYE.

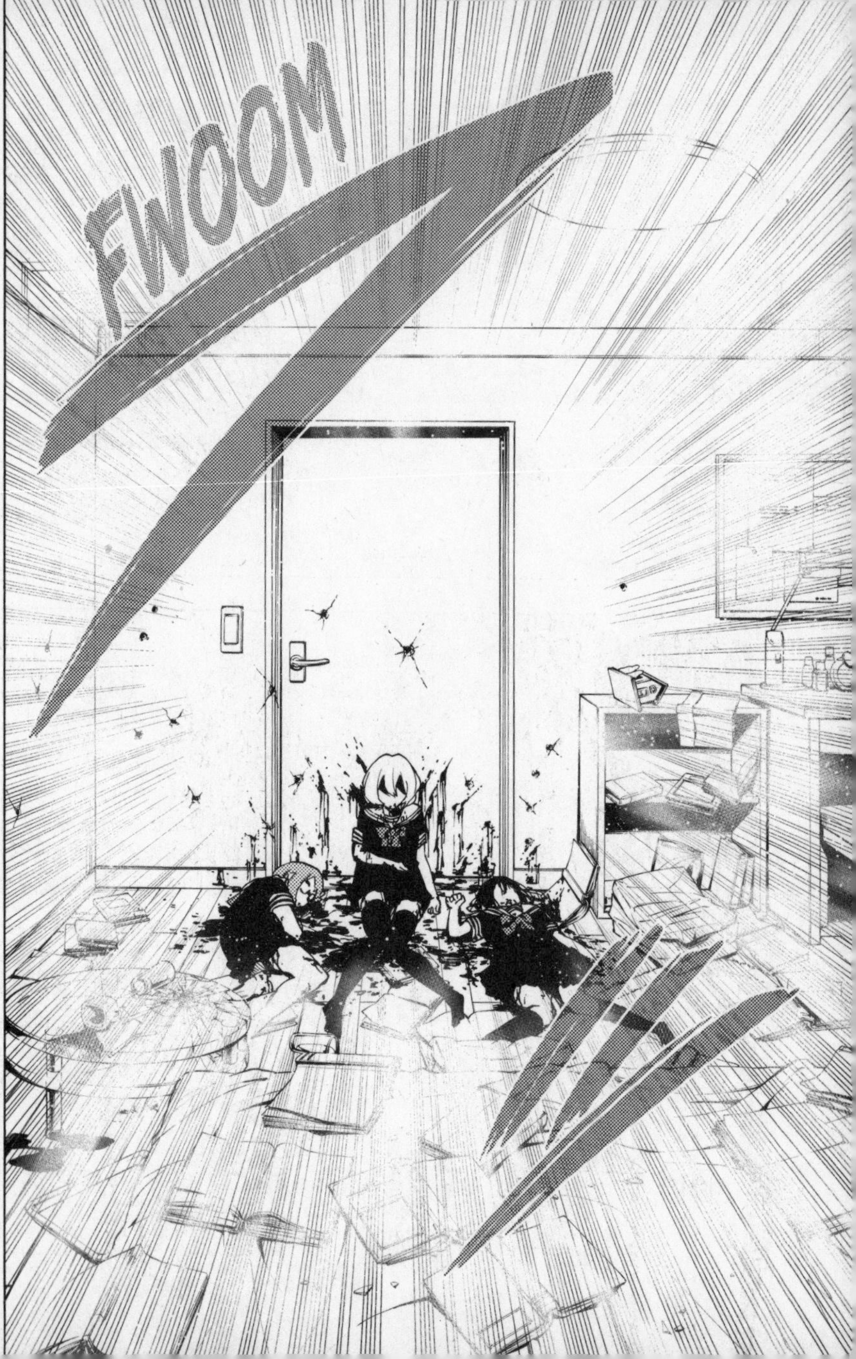
FWOOM

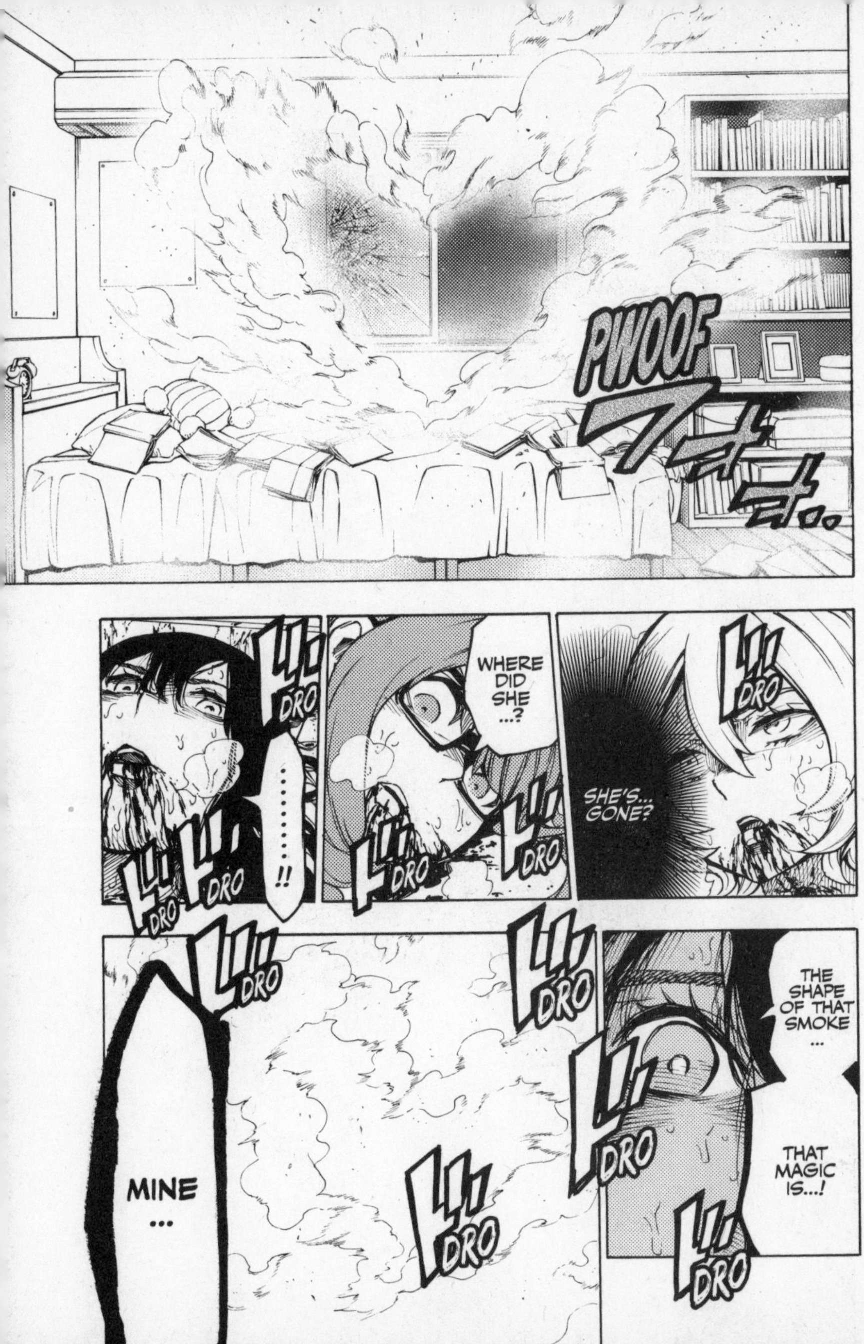
PWOOF
フォォォ
DRO
SHE'S... GONE?
WHERE DID SHE ...?
DRO
DRO
DRO
......!!
DRO
DRO
THE SHAPE OF THAT SMOKE ...
THAT MAGIC IS...!
DRO
DRO
DRO
DRO
DRO
MINE ...

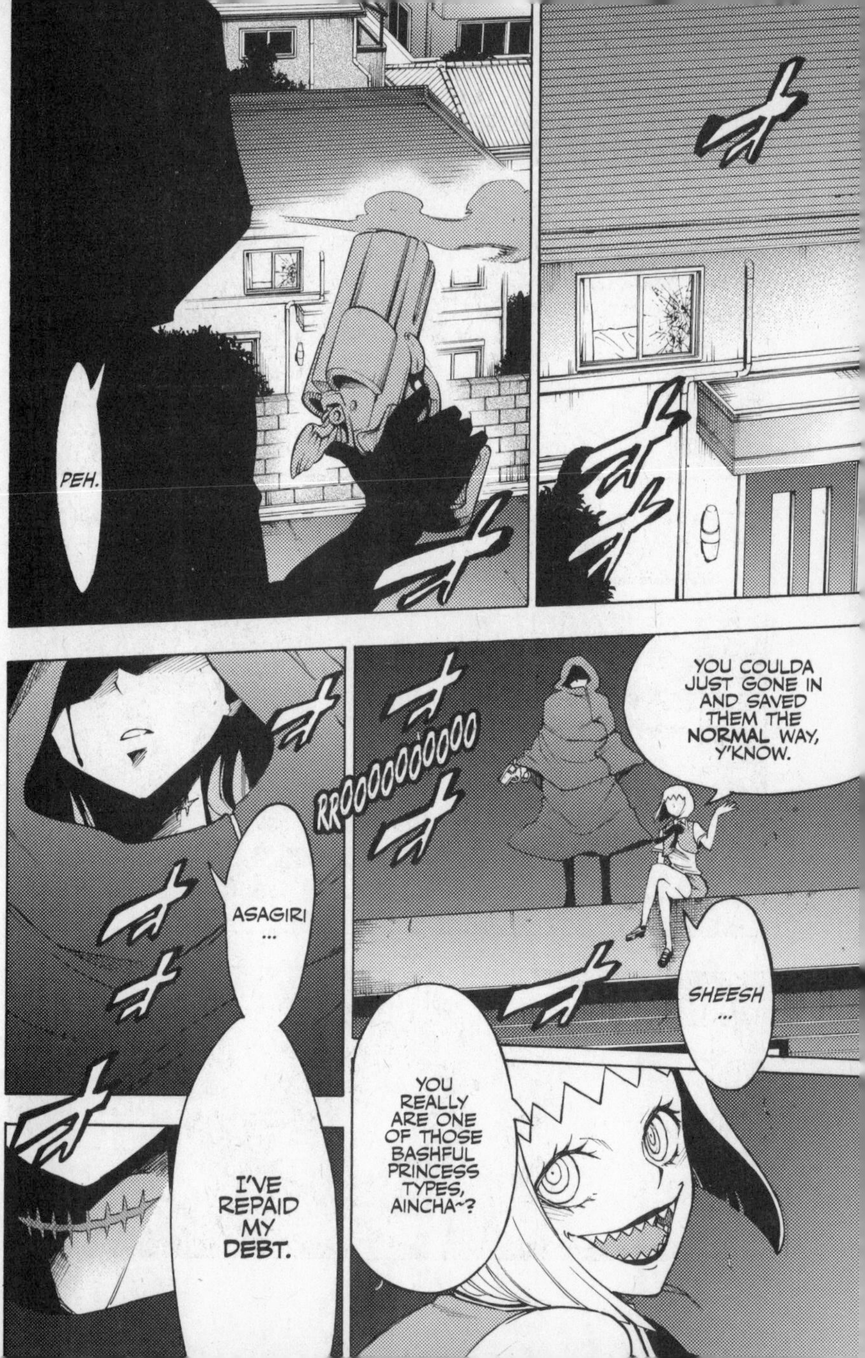
PEH.
YOU COULDA JUST GONE IN AND SAVED THEM THE NORMAL WAY, Y'KNOW.
RROOOOOOOOOO
SHEESH ...
ASAGIRI ...
YOU REALLY ARE ONE OF THOSE BASHFUL PRINCESS TYPES, AINCHA~?
I'VE REPAID MY DEBT.

ENTER.30 COME BACK HERE~!

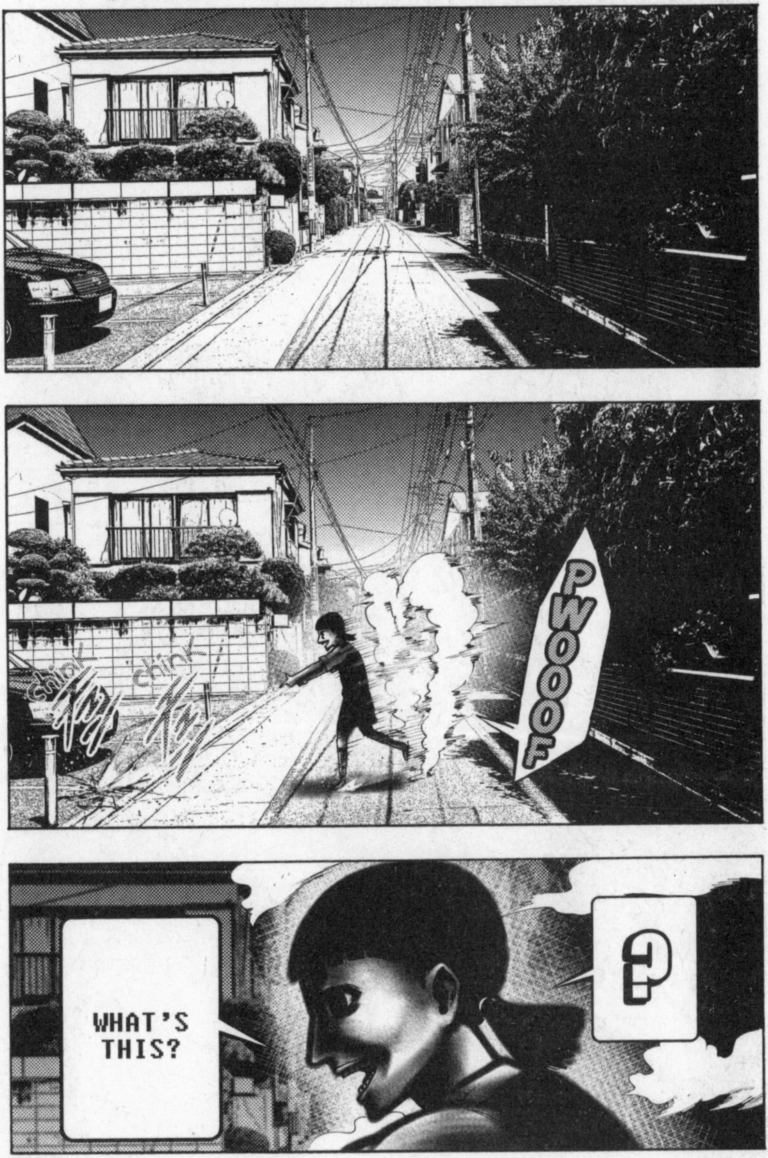
PWOOOF
chink
chink
?
WHAT'S THIS?

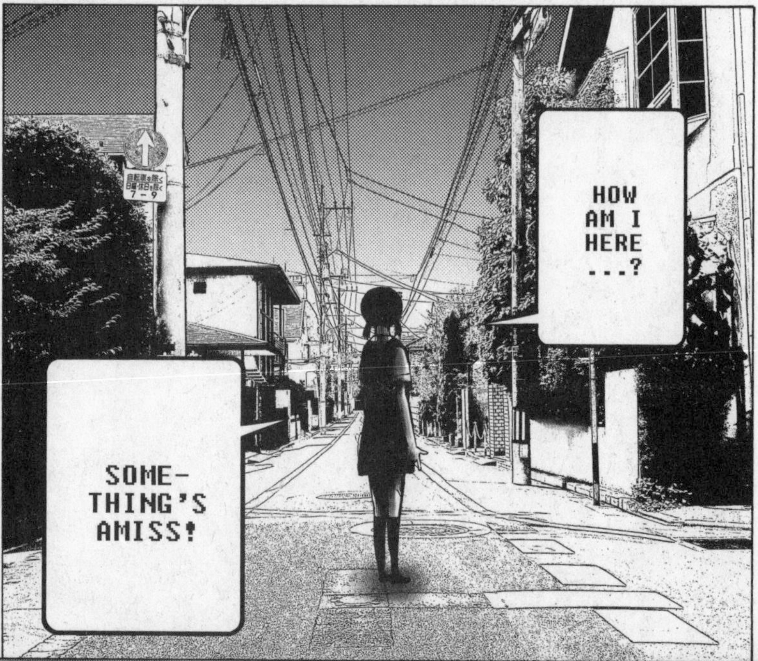
HOW AM I HERE ...?
SOME-THING'S AMISS!

ENTER. 30
COME BACK HERE~!

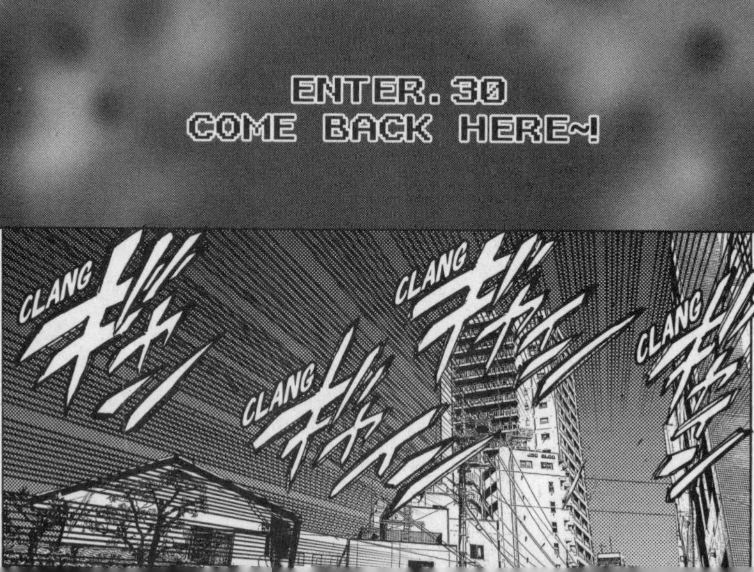
CLANG
CLANG
CLANG
CLANG

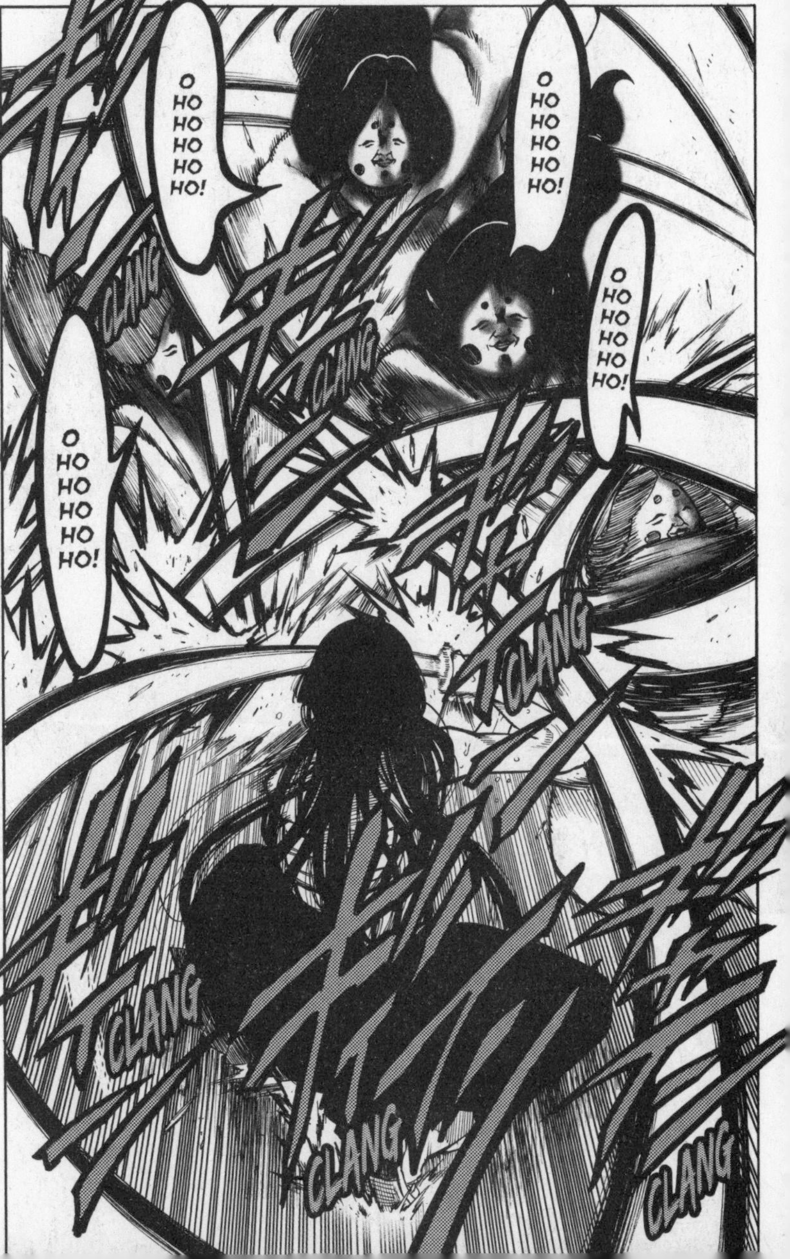
O HO HO HO HO HO!
O HO HO HO HO HO!
O HO HO HO HO HO HO!
CLANG
CLANG
O HO HO HO HO HO HO!
CLANG
CLANG
CLANG
CLANG

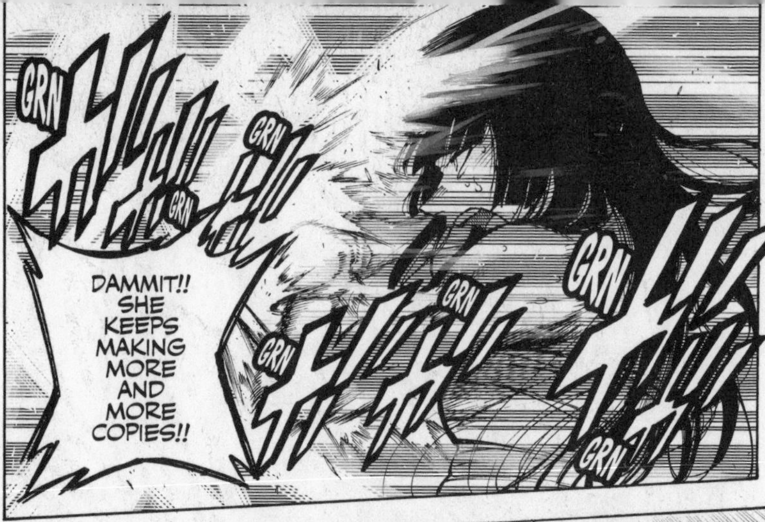
GRN
GRN
GRN
GRN
GRN
GRN
GRN
DAMMIT!! SHE KEEPS MAKING MORE AND MORE COPIES!!

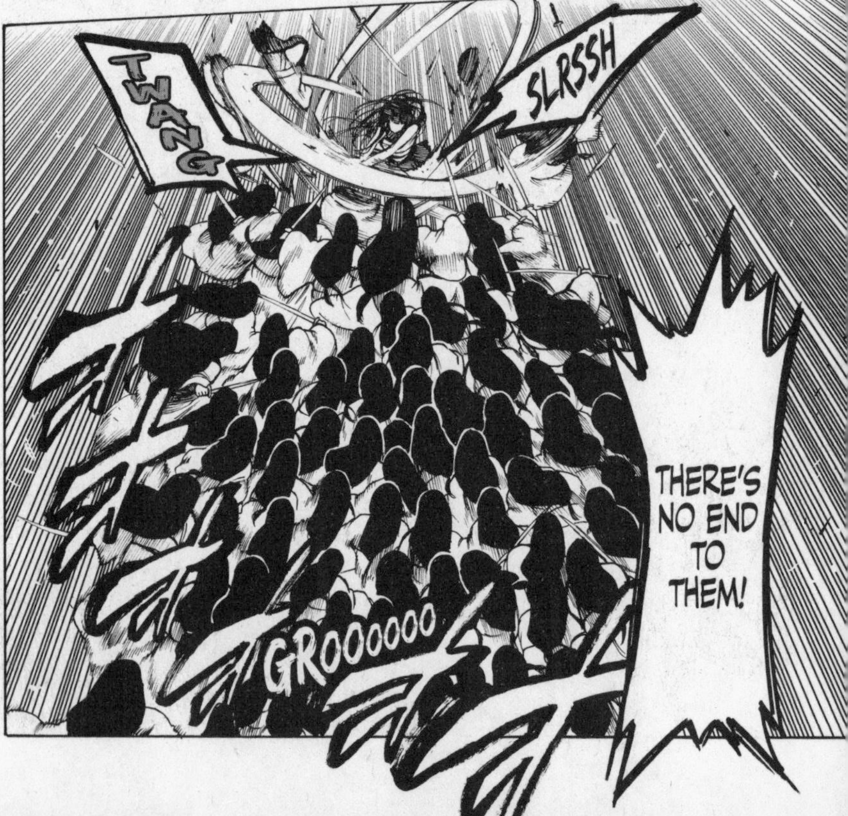
SLRSSH
TWANG
THERE'S NO END TO THEM!
GROOOOOO

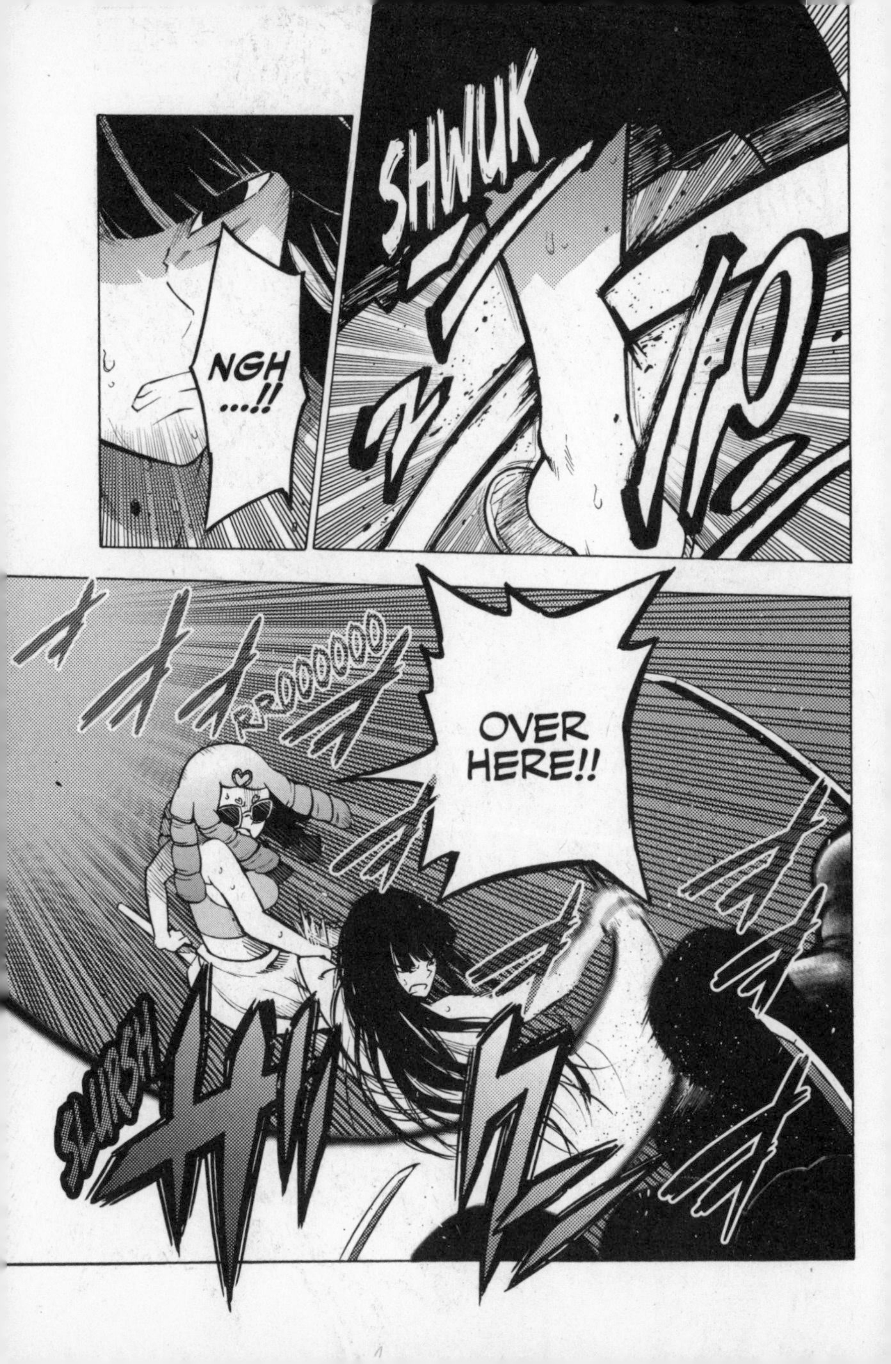
SHWUK
NGH ...!!
OVER HERE!!
RROOOOOO
SLURSH

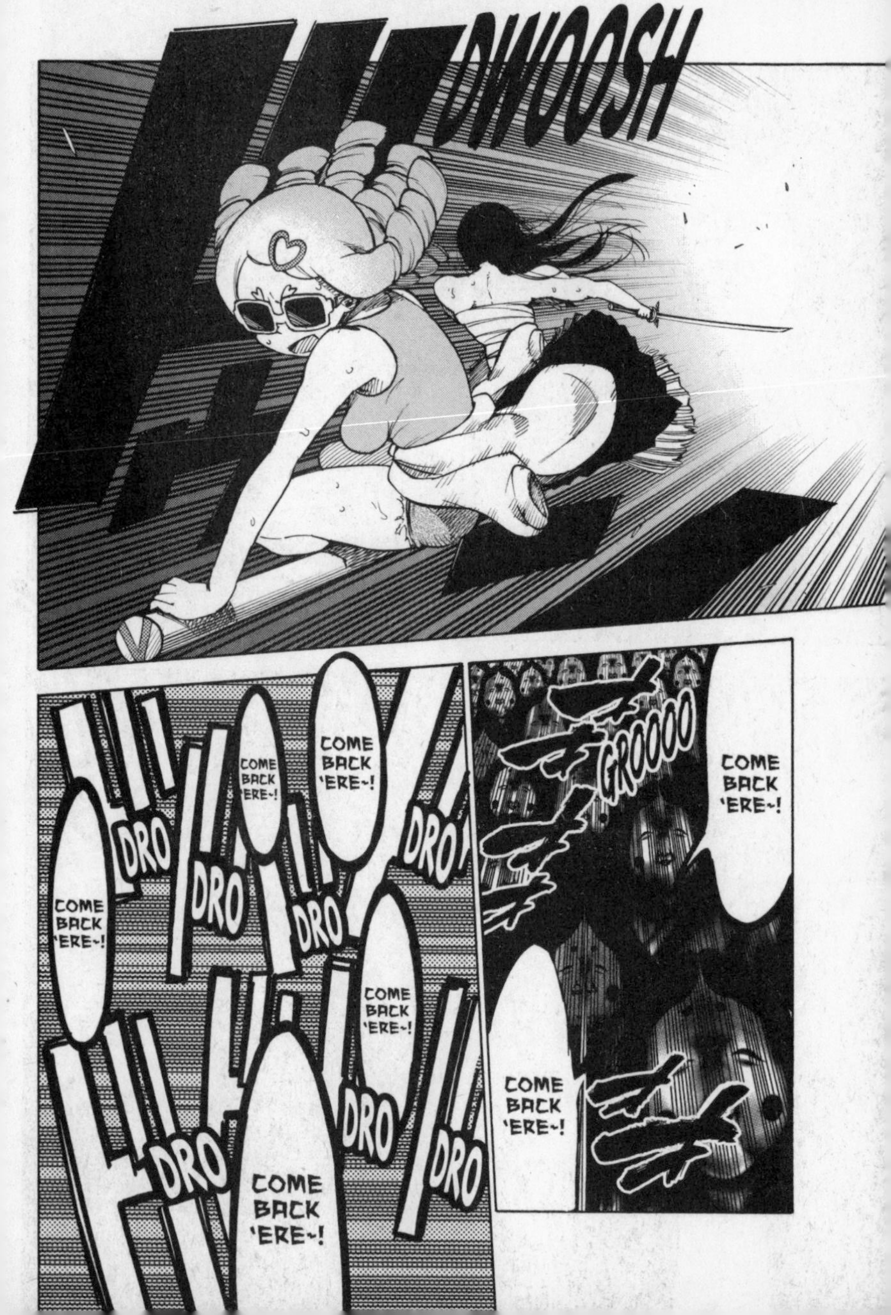
DWOOSH
GROOOO
COME BACK 'ERE~!
COME BACK 'ERE~!
DRO
COME BACK 'ERE~!
COME BACK 'ERE~!
DRO
DRO
DRO
DRO
COME BACK 'ERE~!
COME BACK 'ERE~!
DRO
DRO
DRO
COME BACK 'ERE~!

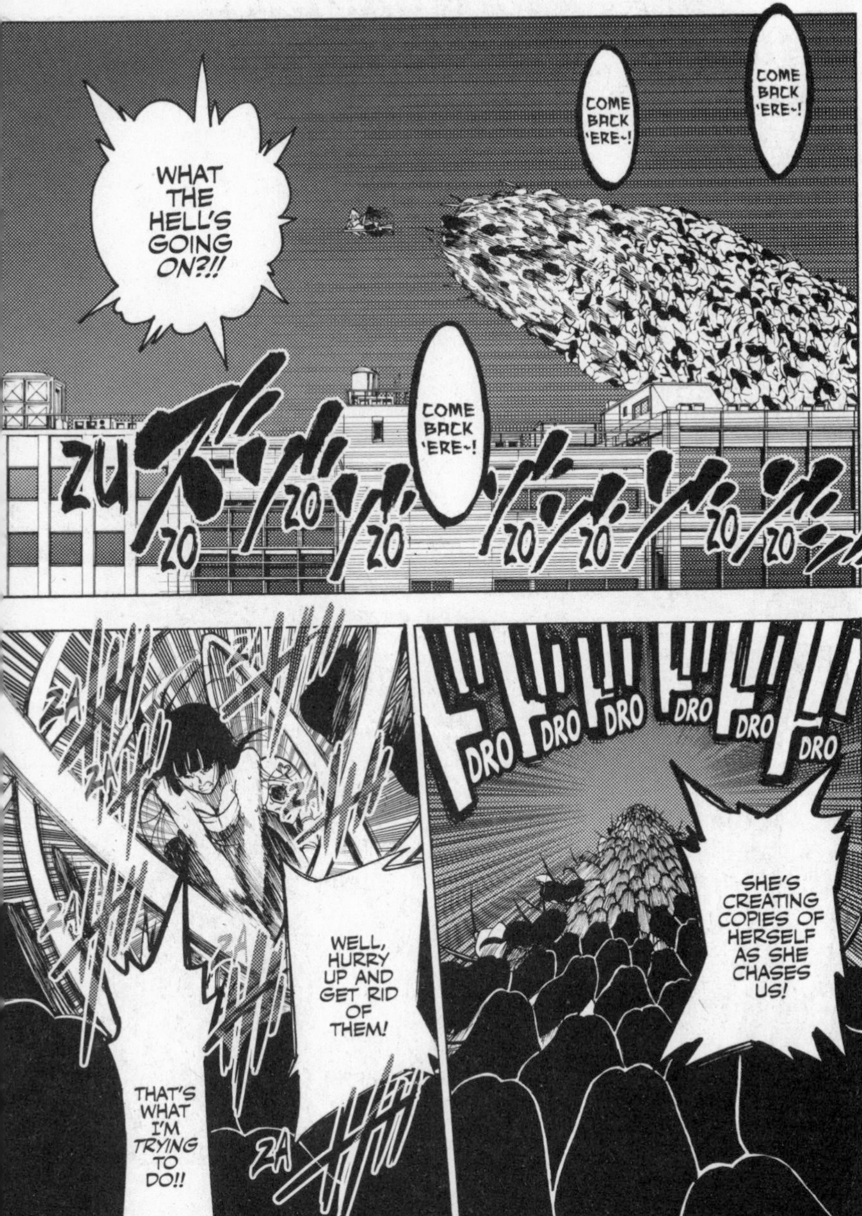

COME BACK 'ERE~!
COME BACK 'ERE~!
WHAT THE HELL'S GOING ON?!!
COME BACK 'ERE~!
ZU ZO ZO ZO ZO ZO ZO ZO
DRO DRO DRO DRO DRO DRO
SHE'S CREATING COPIES OF HERSELF AS SHE CHASES US!
ZA ZA ZA
WELL, HURRY UP AND GET RID OF THEM!
THAT'S WHAT I'M *TRYING* TO DO!!
ZA

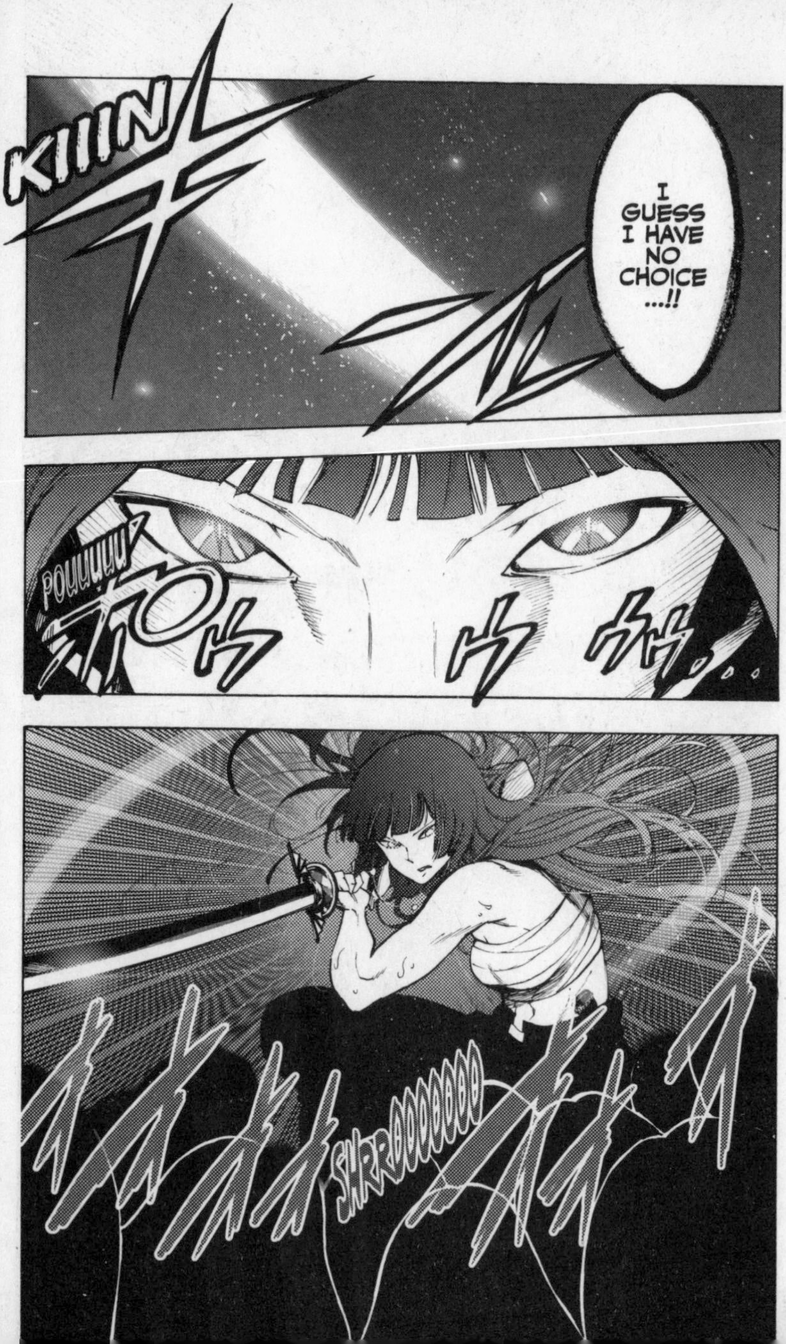
KIIIN
I GUESS I HAVE NO CHOICE ...!!
POUUUUU
SHRROOOOOOO

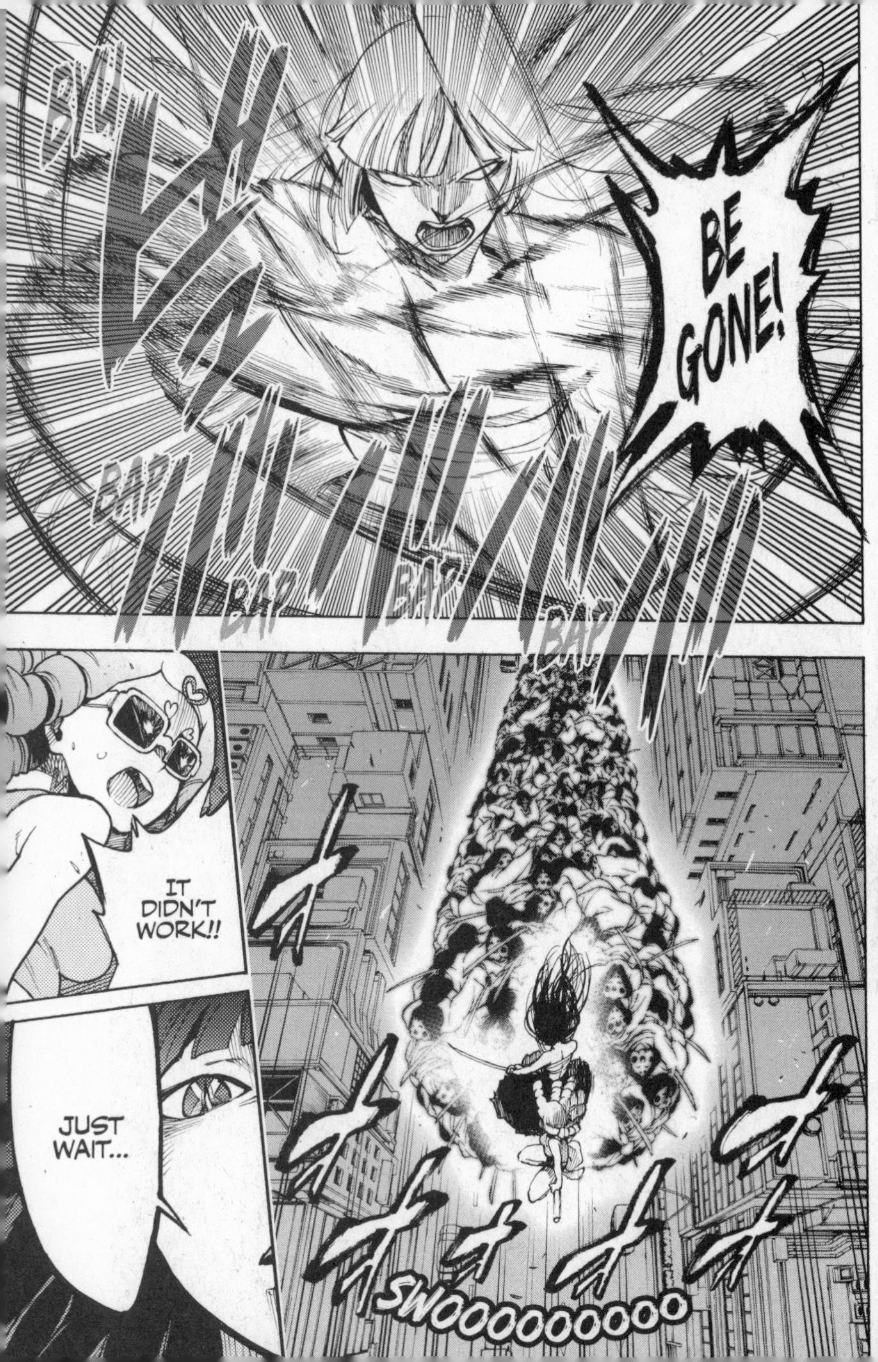

BE GONE!
BAP
BAP
BAP
BAP
SWOOOOOOOOOO
IT DIDN'T WORK!!
JUST WAIT...

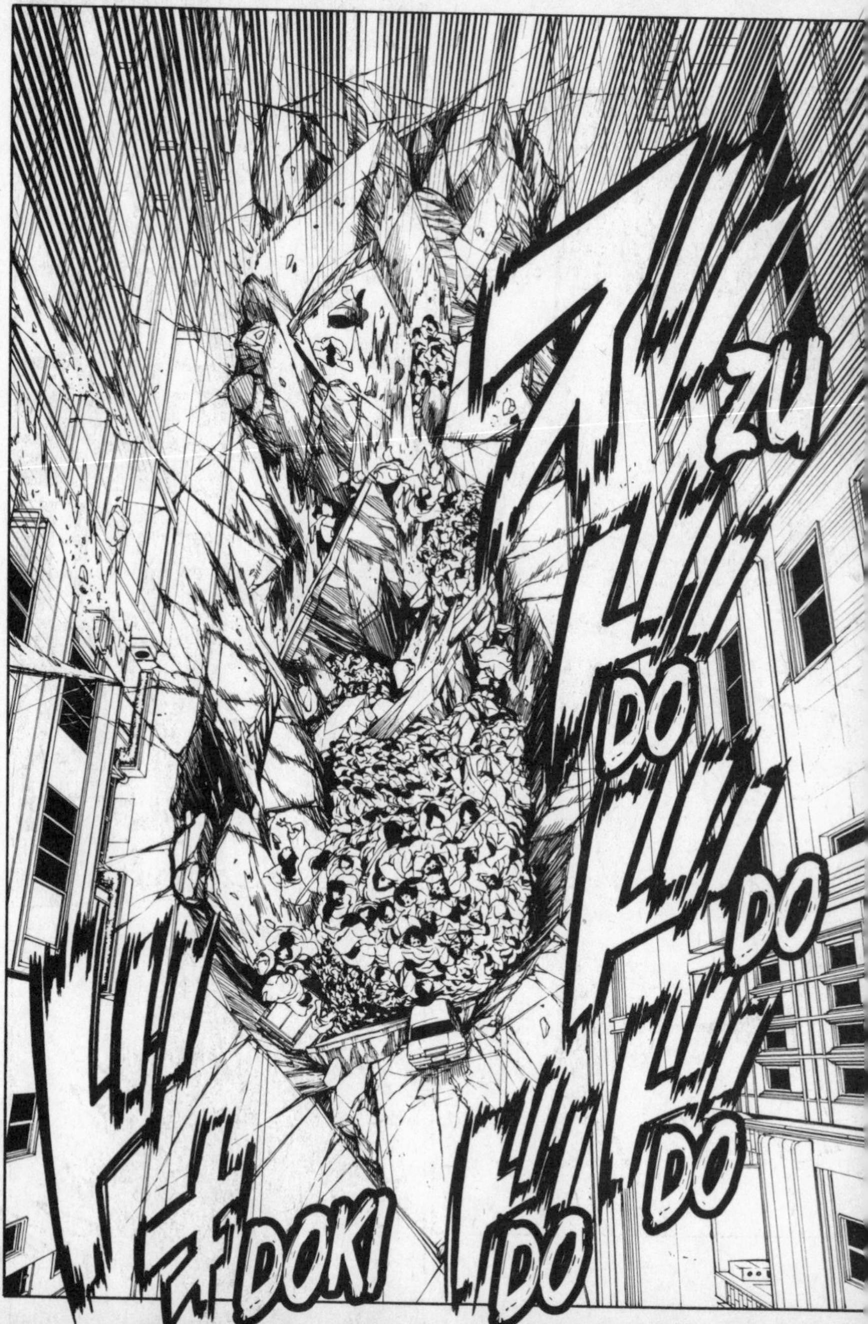
ZU
DO
DO
DO
DO
DOKI

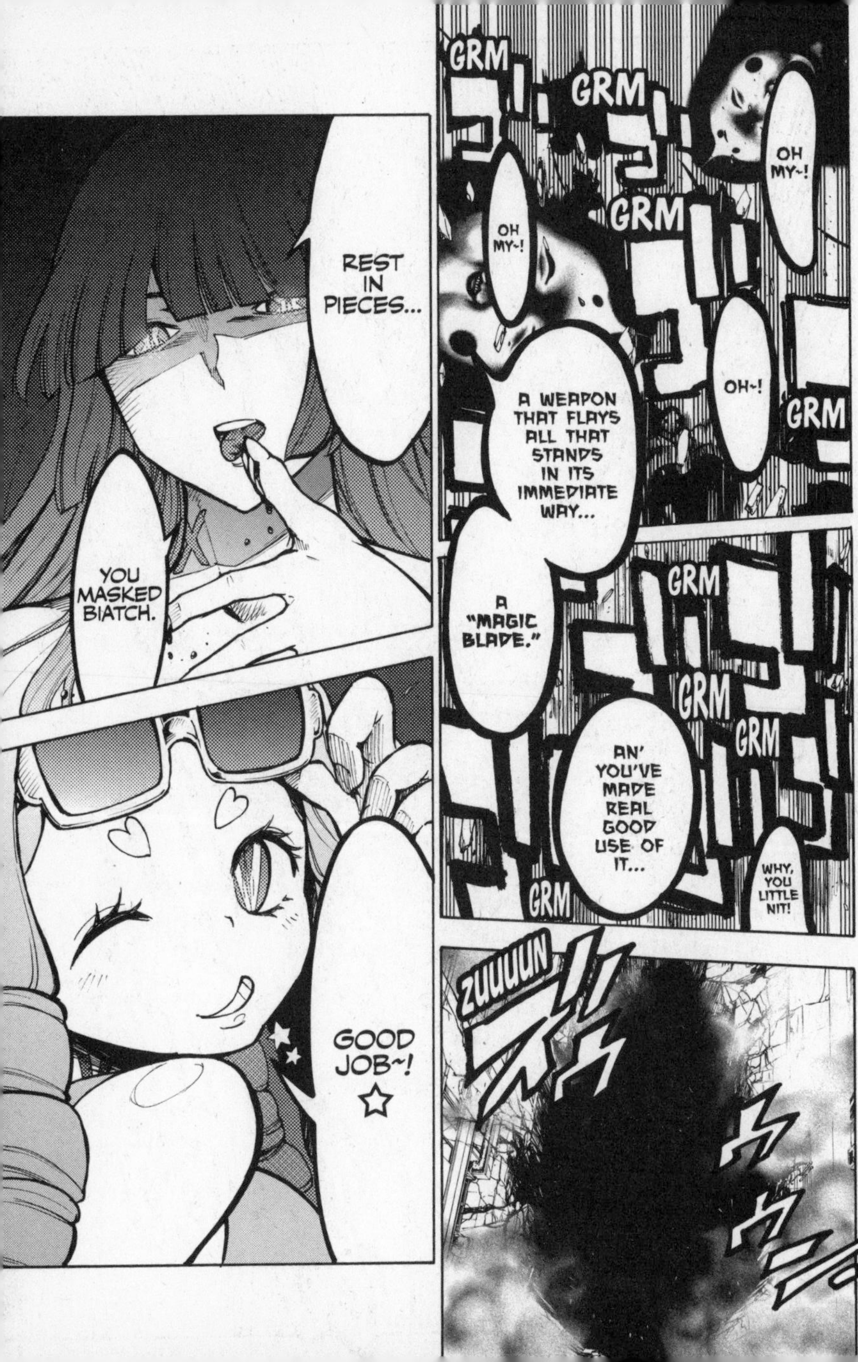
GRM
GRM
GRM
OH MY~!
OH MY~!
OH~!
GRM
A WEAPON THAT FLAYS ALL THAT STANDS IN ITS IMMEDIATE WAY...
A "MAGIC BLADE."
GRM
GRM
GRM
AN' YOU'VE MADE REAL GOOD USE OF IT...
WHY, YOU LITTLE NIT!
GRM
ZUUUUN
REST IN PIECES...
YOU MASKED BIATCH.
GOOD JOB~! ☆

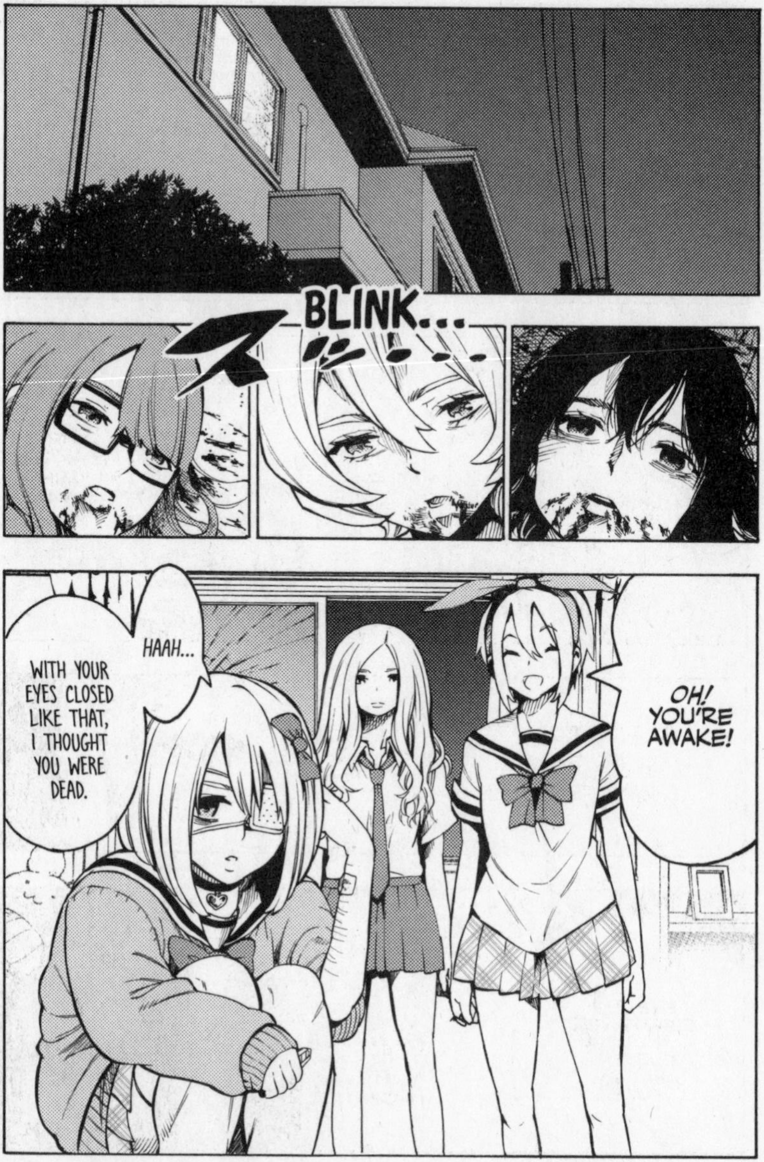
BLINK...
OH! YOU'RE AWAKE!
HAAH...
WITH YOUR EYES CLOSED LIKE THAT, I THOUGHT YOU WERE DEAD.

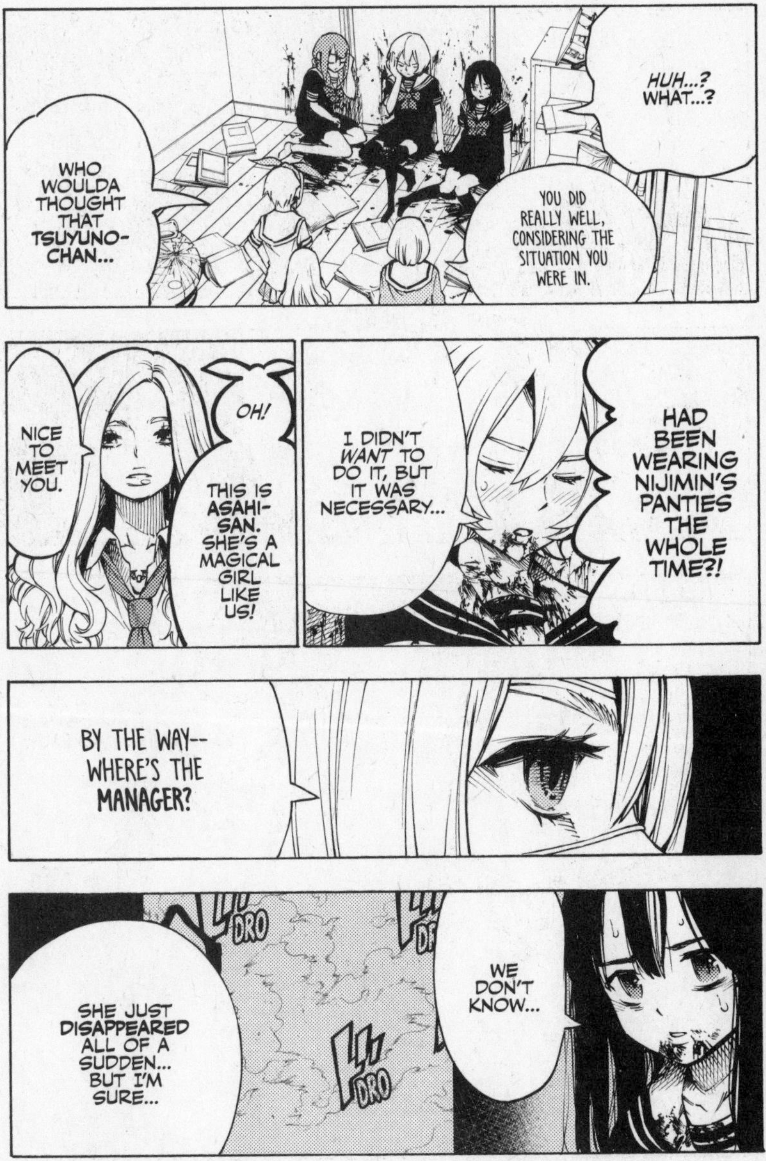
HUH...? WHAT...?
YOU DID REALLY WELL, CONSIDERING THE SITUATION YOU WERE IN.
WHO WOULDA THOUGHT THAT TSUYUNO-CHAN...
HAD BEEN WEARING NIJIMIN'S PANTIES THE WHOLE TIME?!
I DIDN'T *WANT* TO DO IT, BUT IT WAS NECESSARY...
OH!
THIS IS ASAHI-SAN. SHE'S A MAGICAL GIRL LIKE US!
NICE TO MEET YOU.
BY THE WAY-- WHERE'S THE MANAGER?
WE DON'T KNOW...
DRO
DRO
DRO
SHE JUST DISAPPEARED ALL OF A SUDDEN... BUT I'M SURE...

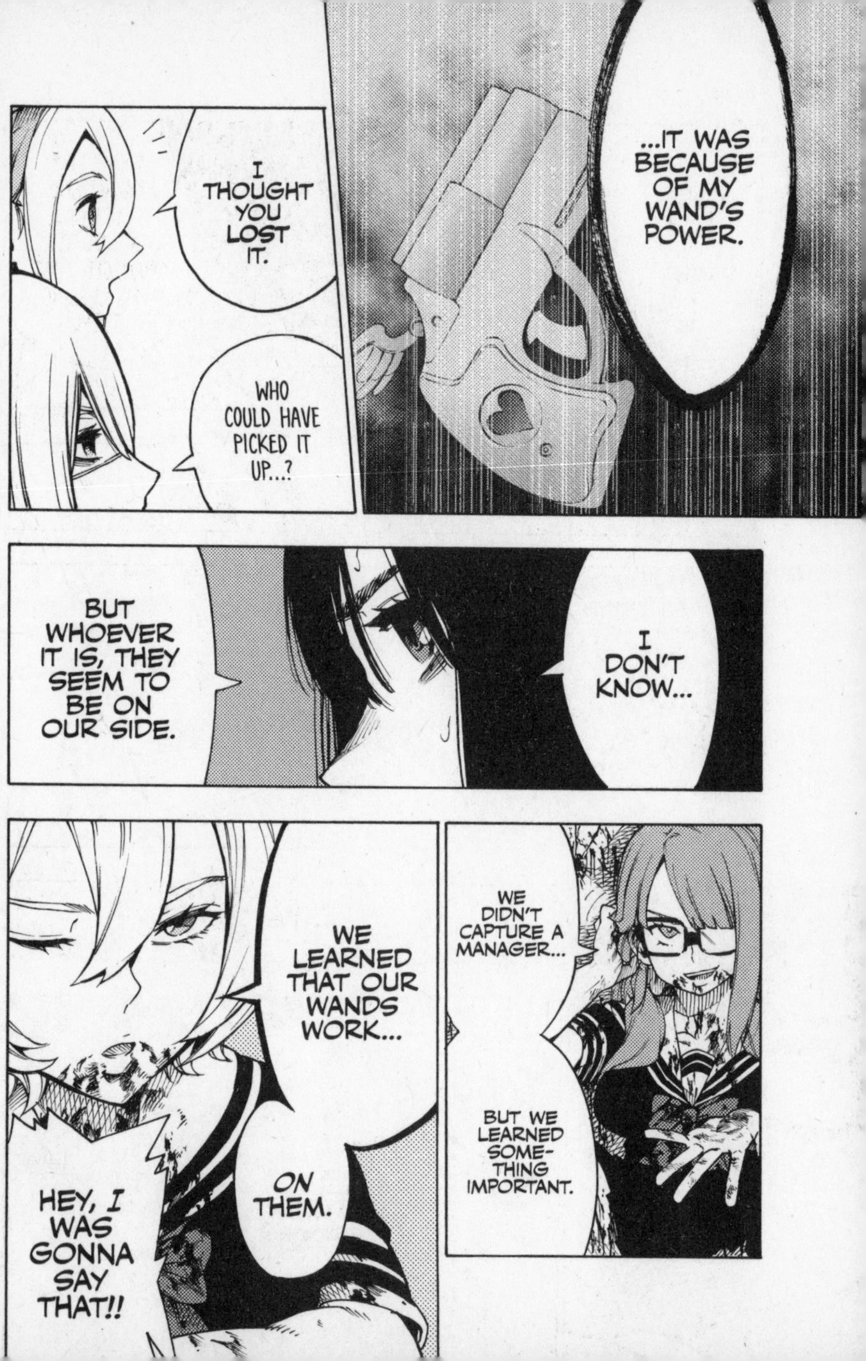
...IT WAS BECAUSE OF MY WAND'S POWER.
I THOUGHT YOU LOST IT.
WHO COULD HAVE PICKED IT UP...?
I DON'T KNOW...
BUT WHOEVER IT IS, THEY SEEM TO BE ON OUR SIDE.
WE DIDN'T CAPTURE A MANAGER...
BUT WE LEARNED SOME-THING IMPORTANT.
WE LEARNED THAT OUR WANDS WORK...
ON THEM.
HEY, I WAS GONNA SAY THAT!!

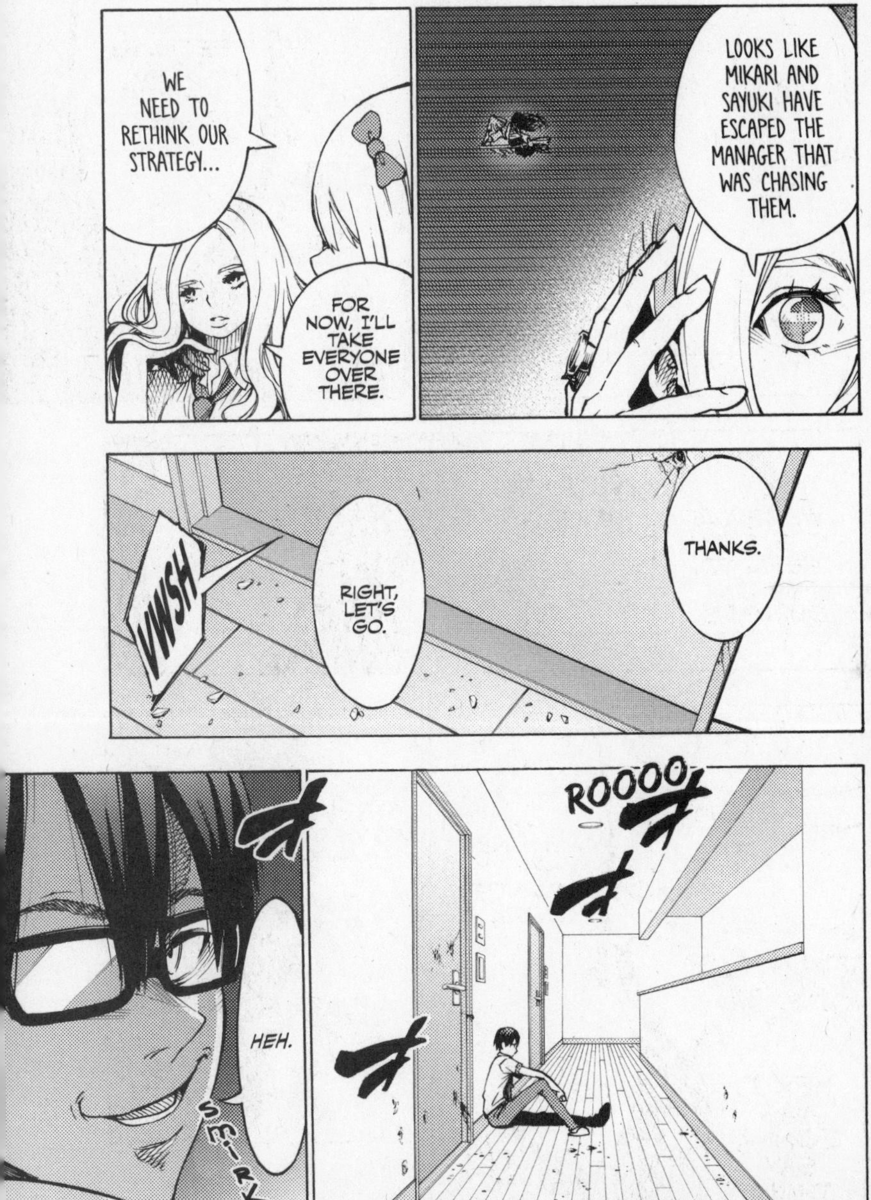
LOOKS LIKE MIKARI AND SAYUKI HAVE ESCAPED THE MANAGER THAT WAS CHASING THEM.
WE NEED TO RETHINK OUR STRATEGY...
FOR NOW, I'LL TAKE EVERYONE OVER THERE.
THANKS.
RIGHT, LET'S GO.
VWSH
ROOOO
HEH.
SMIRK

I gotta
do what
I gotta
do...

ENTER. 31 GRADUATION

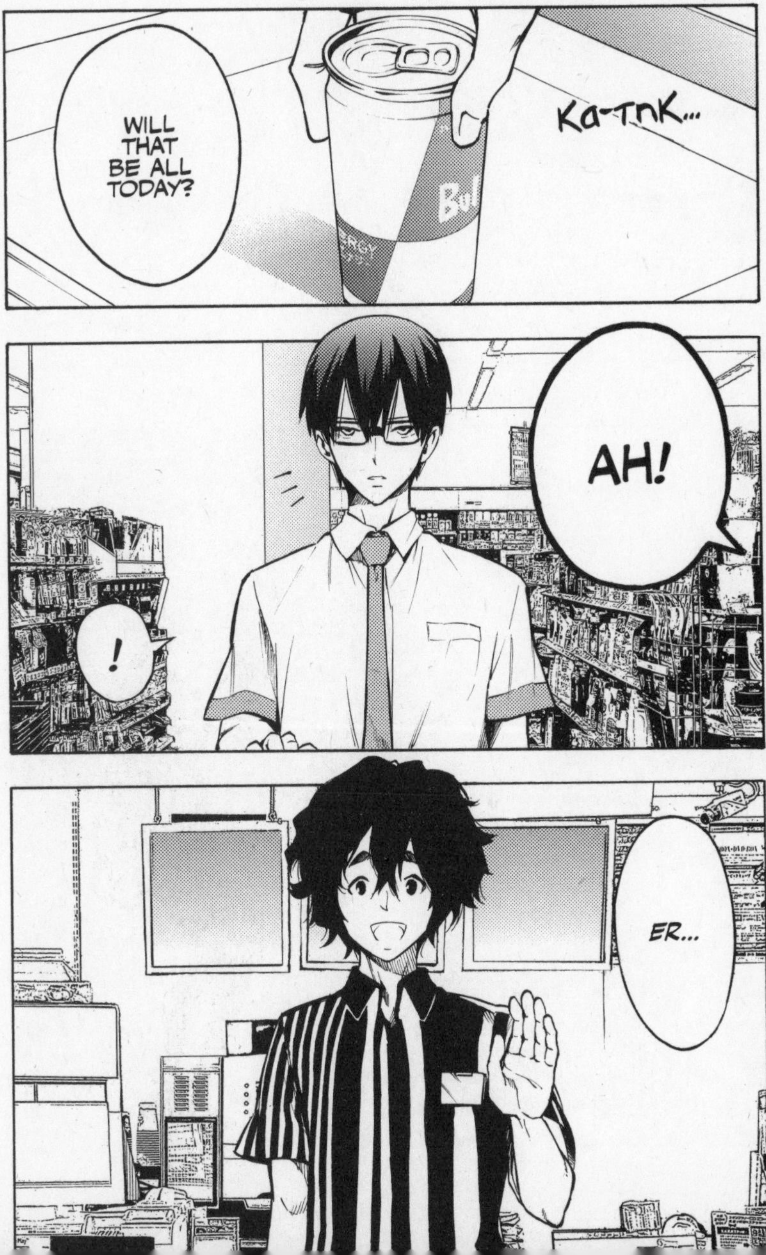
Ka-TnK...
WILL THAT BE ALL TODAY?
AH!
!
ER...

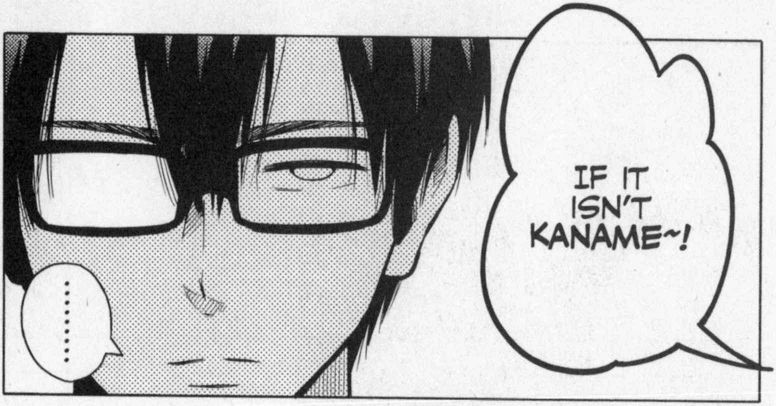
IF IT ISN'T KANAME~!
......
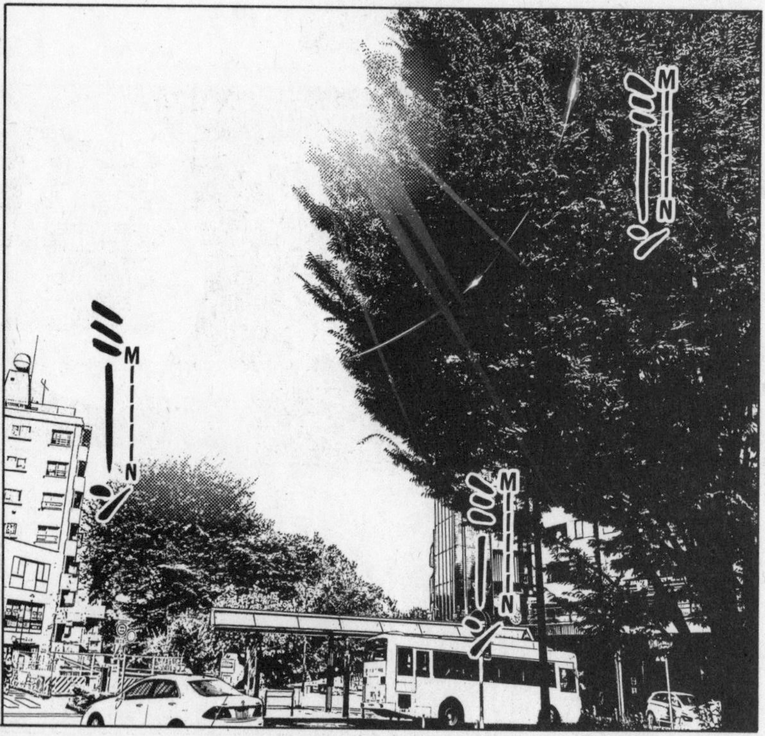
MIIIIIN
MIIIIIN
MIIIIIN

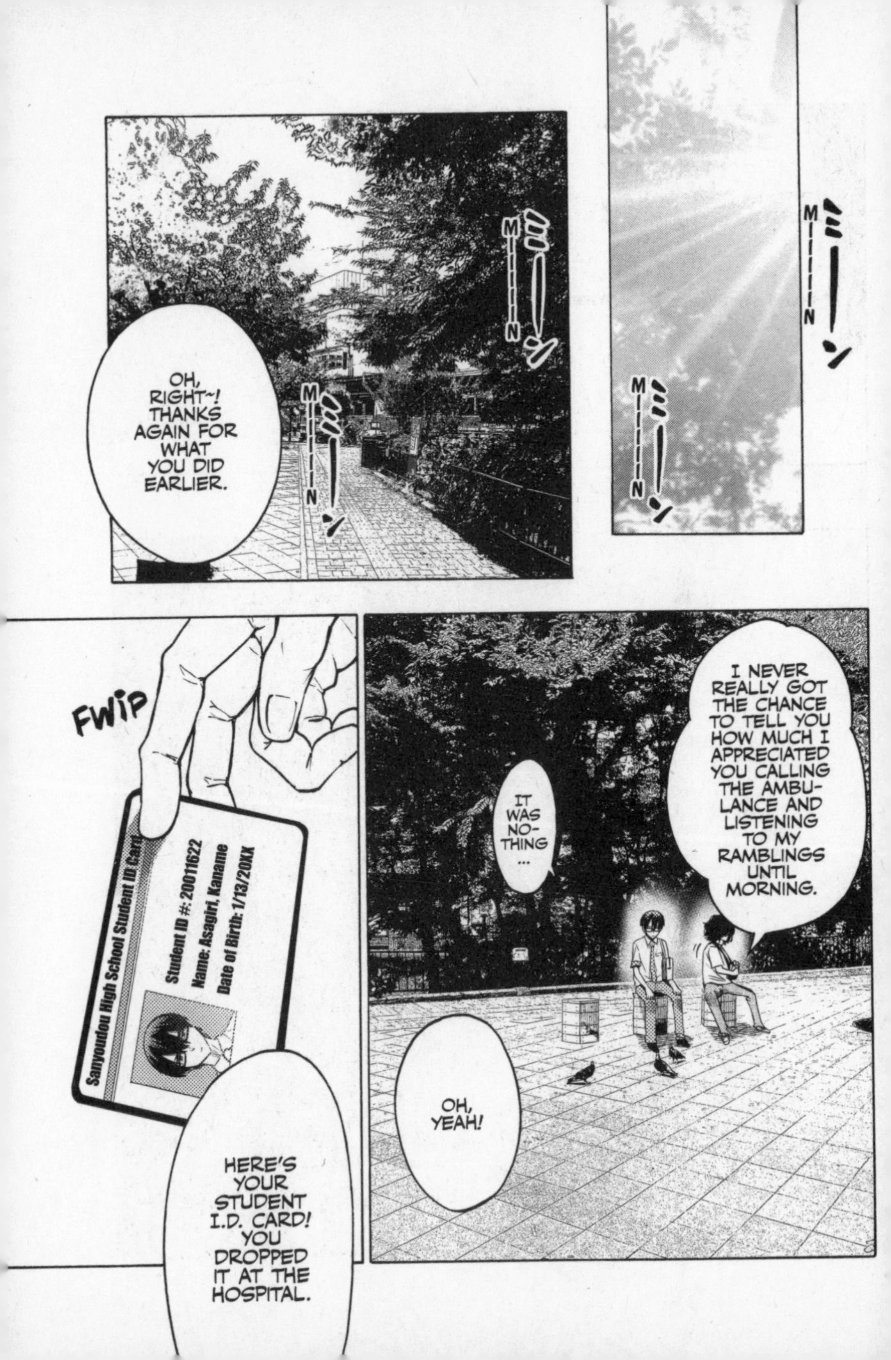
MIIIN
MIIIN
MIIIN
MIIIN
OH, RIGHT~! THANKS AGAIN FOR WHAT YOU DID EARLIER.
I NEVER REALLY GOT THE CHANCE TO TELL YOU HOW MUCH I APPRECIATED YOU CALLING THE AMBU-LANCE AND LISTENING TO MY RAMBLINGS UNTIL MORNING.
IT WAS NO-THING ...
OH, YEAH!
FWIP
Sanyoudou High School Student ID Car
Student ID #: 20011622
Name: Asagiri, Kaname
Date of Birth: 1/13/20KK
HERE'S YOUR STUDENT I.D. CARD! YOU DROPPED IT AT THE HOSPITAL.

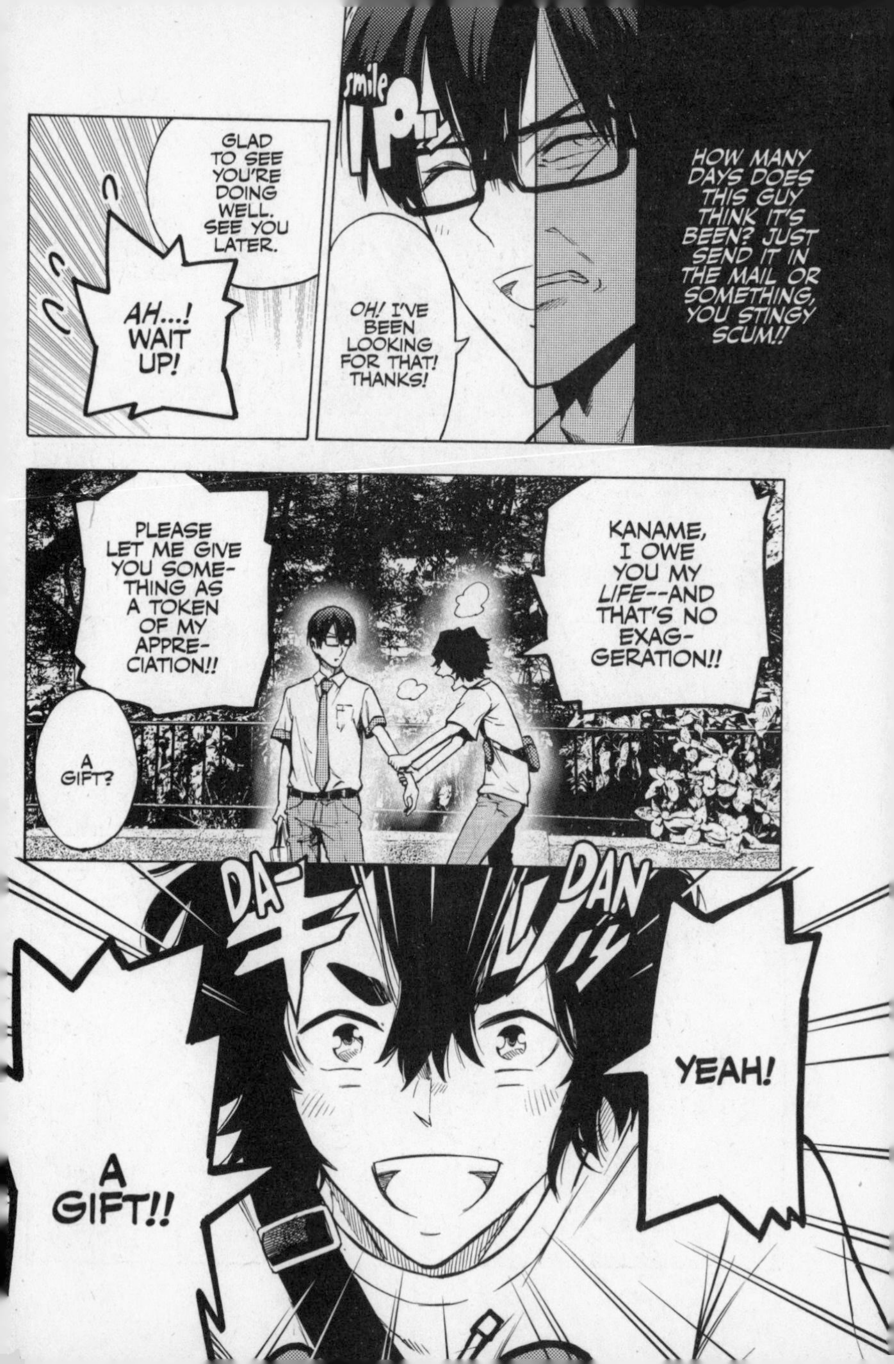
HOW MANY DAYS DOES THIS GUY THINK IT'S BEEN? JUST SEND IT IN THE MAIL OR SOMETHING, YOU STINGY SCUM!!
smile
OH! I'VE BEEN LOOKING FOR THAT! THANKS!
GLAD TO SEE YOU'RE DOING WELL. SEE YOU LATER.
AH...! WAIT UP!
KANAME, I OWE YOU MY LIFE--AND THAT'S NO EXAG-GERATION!!
PLEASE LET ME GIVE YOU SOME-THING AS A TOKEN OF MY APPRE-CIATION!!
A GIFT?
DA-
DAN
YEAH!
A GIFT!!

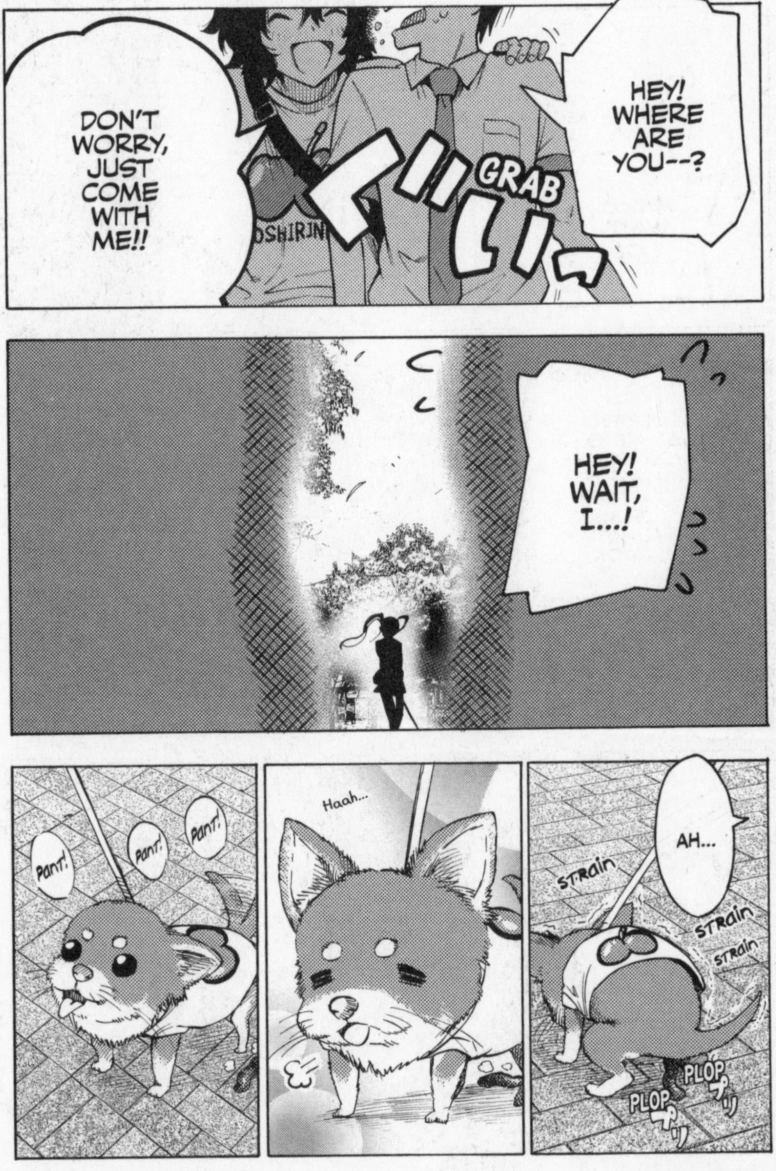
HEY! WHERE ARE YOU--?
GRAB
DON'T WORRY, JUST COME WITH ME!!
HEY! WAIT, I...!
AH...
STRAIN
STRAIN
STRAIN
PLOP
PLOP
Haah...
Pant!
Pant!
Pant!

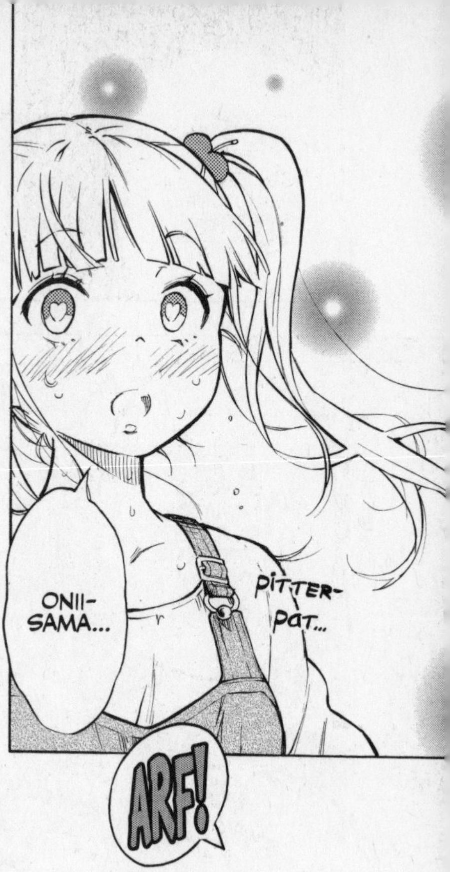
ONII-SAMA...
PIT-TER-PAT...
ARF!

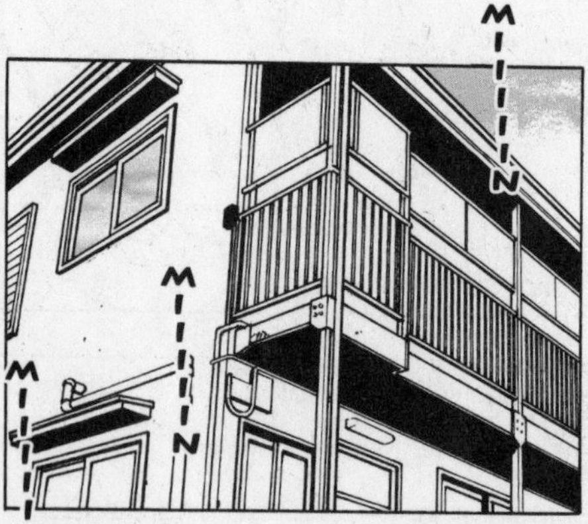
MIIIIN
MIIIIN
MIIIIN

ENTER. 31 GRADUATION

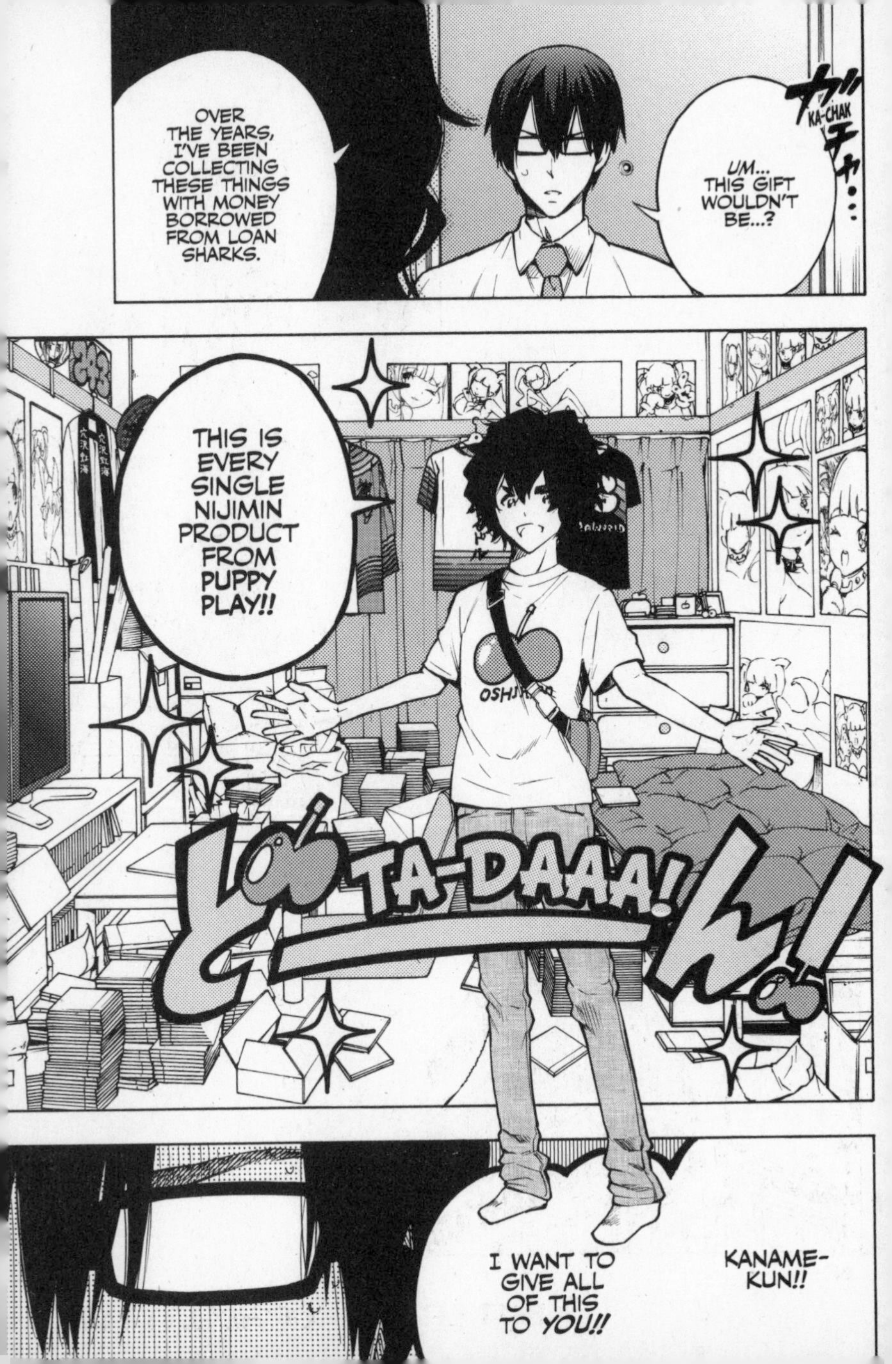
KA-CHAK
UM... THIS GIFT WOULDN'T BE...?
OVER THE YEARS, I'VE BEEN COLLECTING THESE THINGS WITH MONEY BORROWED FROM LOAN SHARKS.
THIS IS EVERY SINGLE NIJIMIN PRODUCT FROM PUPPY PLAY!!
TA-DAAA!
KANAME-KUN!!
I WANT TO GIVE ALL OF THIS TO *YOU*!!

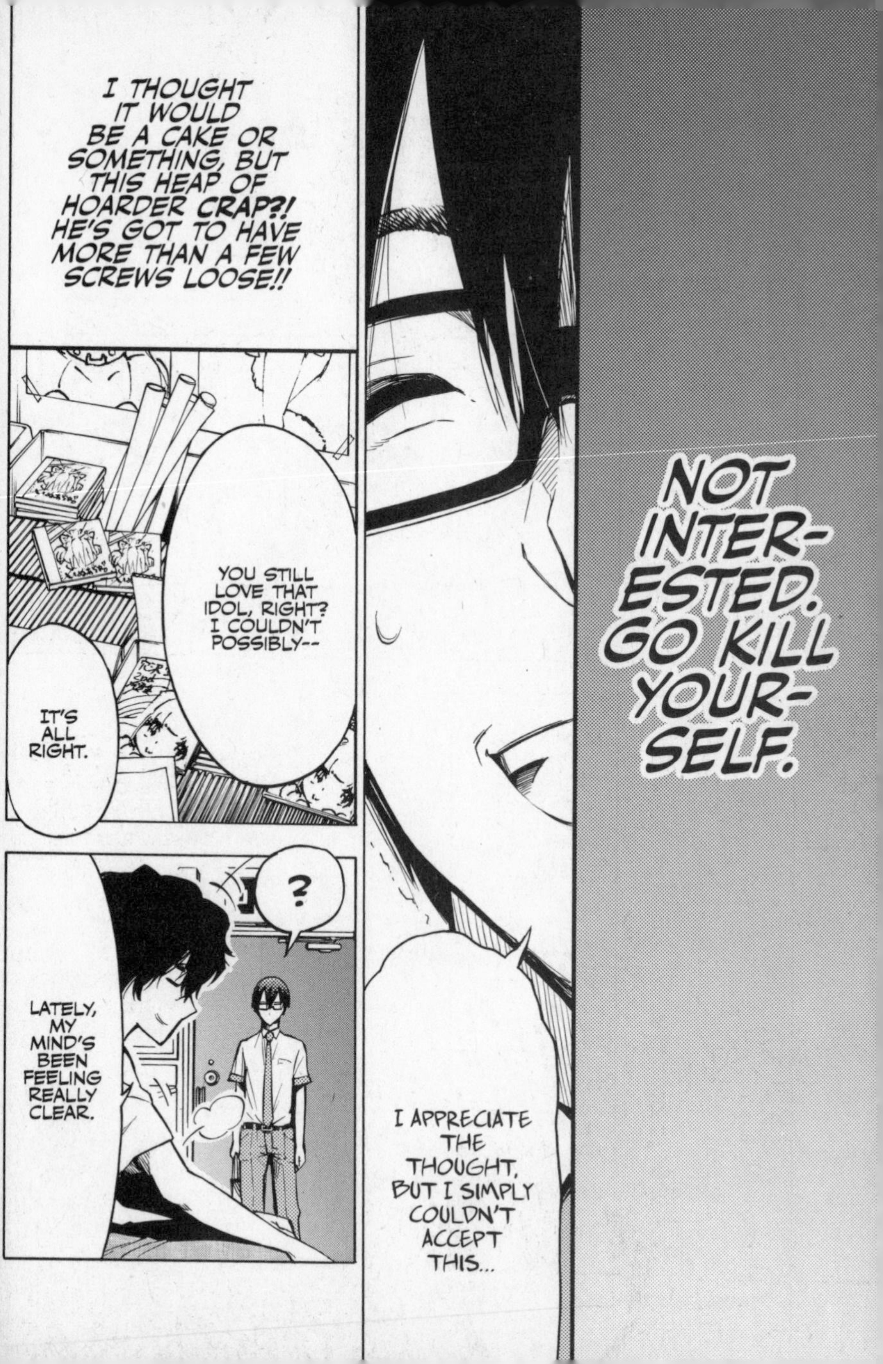
NOT INTER-ESTED. GO KILL YOUR-SELF.
I APPRECIATE THE THOUGHT, BUT I SIMPLY COULDN'T ACCEPT THIS...
I THOUGHT IT WOULD BE A CAKE OR SOMETHING, BUT THIS HEAP OF HOARDER CRAP?! HE'S GOT TO HAVE MORE THAN A FEW SCREWS LOOSE!!
YOU STILL LOVE THAT IDOL, RIGHT? I COULDN'T POSSIBLY--
IT'S ALL RIGHT.
?
LATELY, MY MIND'S BEEN FEELING REALLY CLEAR.

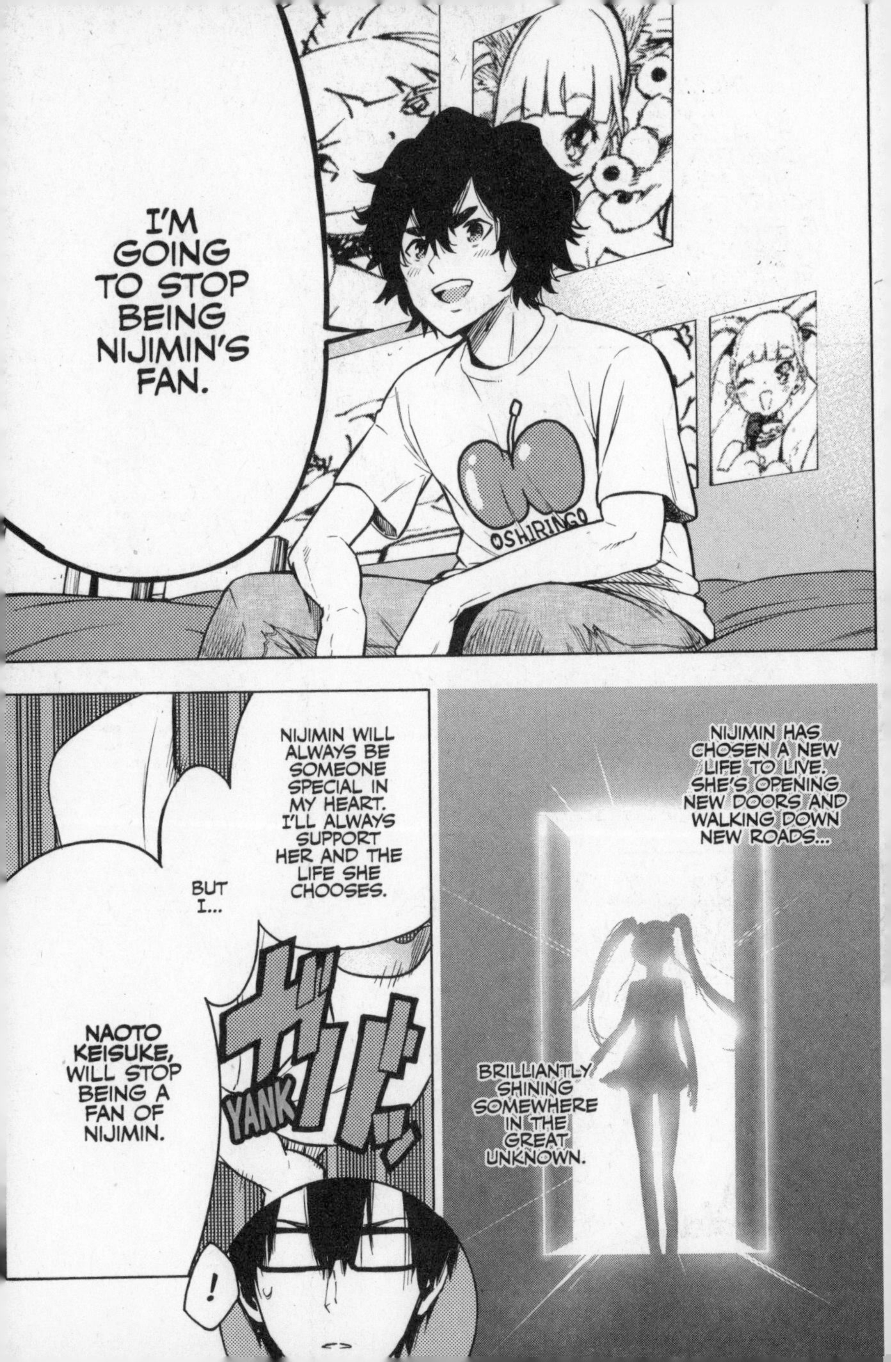
I'M GOING TO STOP BEING NIJIMIN'S FAN.
OSHIRINGO
NIJIMIN HAS CHOSEN A NEW LIFE TO LIVE. SHE'S OPENING NEW DOORS AND WALKING DOWN NEW ROADS...
BRILLIANTLY SHINING SOMEWHERE IN THE GREAT UNKNOWN.
NIJIMIN WILL ALWAYS BE SOMEONE SPECIAL IN MY HEART. I'LL ALWAYS SUPPORT HER AND THE LIFE SHE CHOOSES.
BUT I...
NAOTO KEISUKE, WILL STOP BEING A FAN OF NIJIMIN.
YANK
!

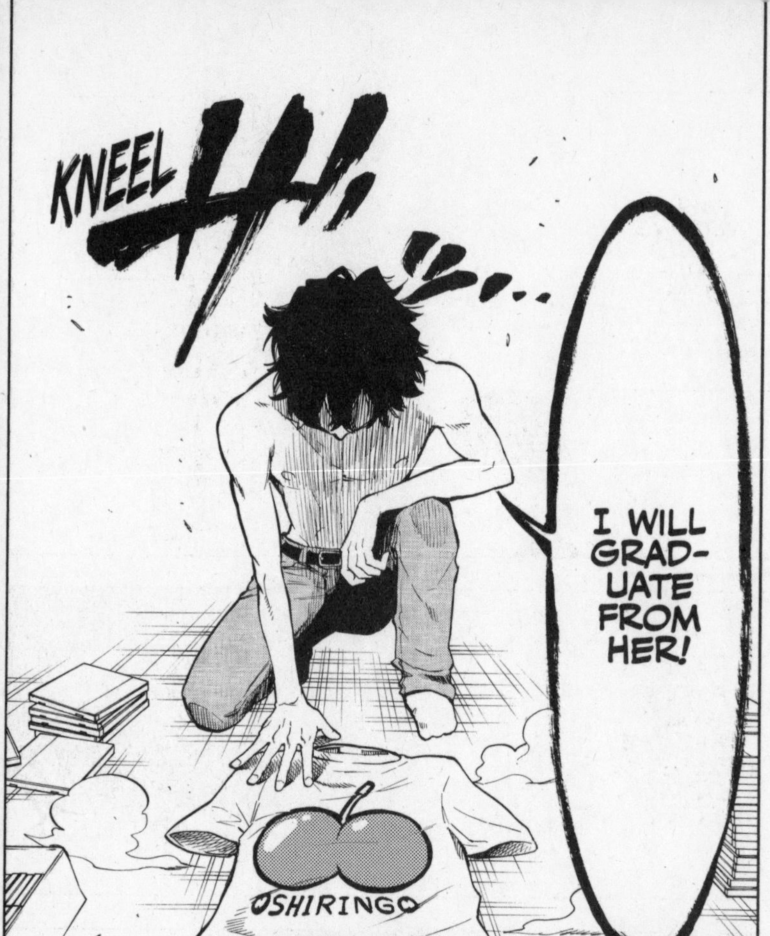
KNEEL
I WILL GRADUATE FROM HER!
OSHIRINGO
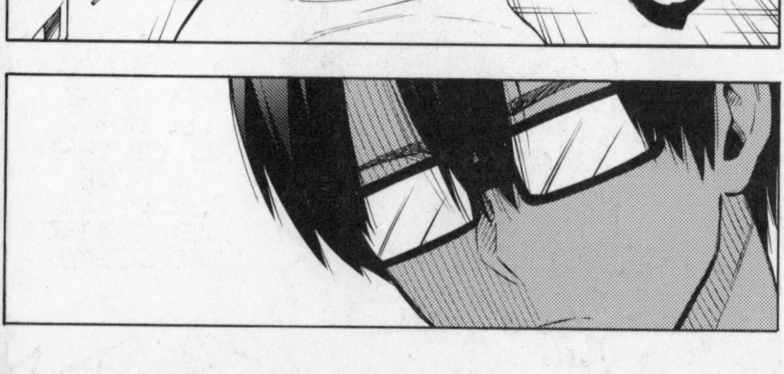

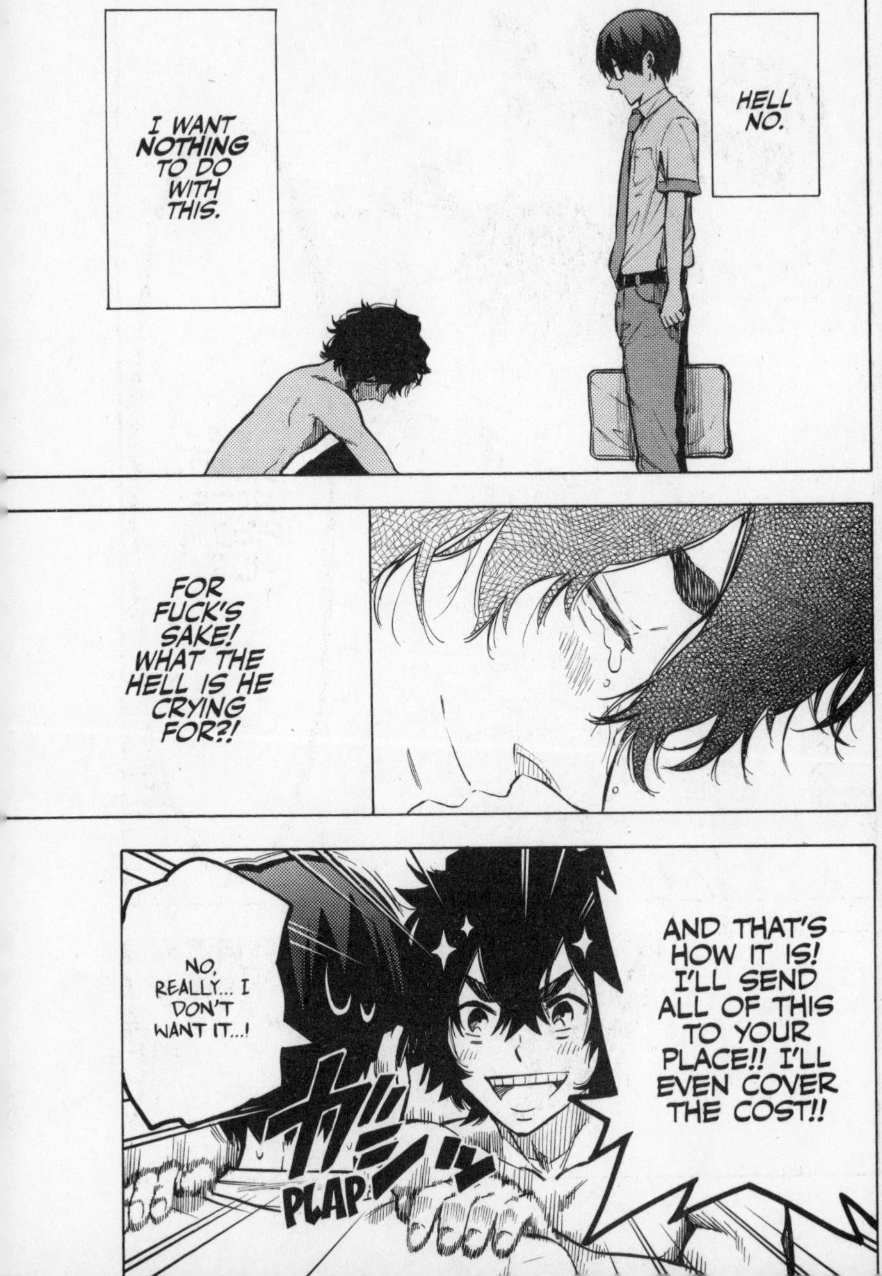
HELL NO.
I WANT NOTHING TO DO WITH THIS.
FOR FUCK'S SAKE! WHAT THE HELL IS HE CRYING FOR?!
AND THAT'S HOW IT IS! I'LL SEND ALL OF THIS TO YOUR PLACE!! I'LL EVEN COVER THE COST!!
NO, REALLY... I DON'T WANT IT...!
PLAP

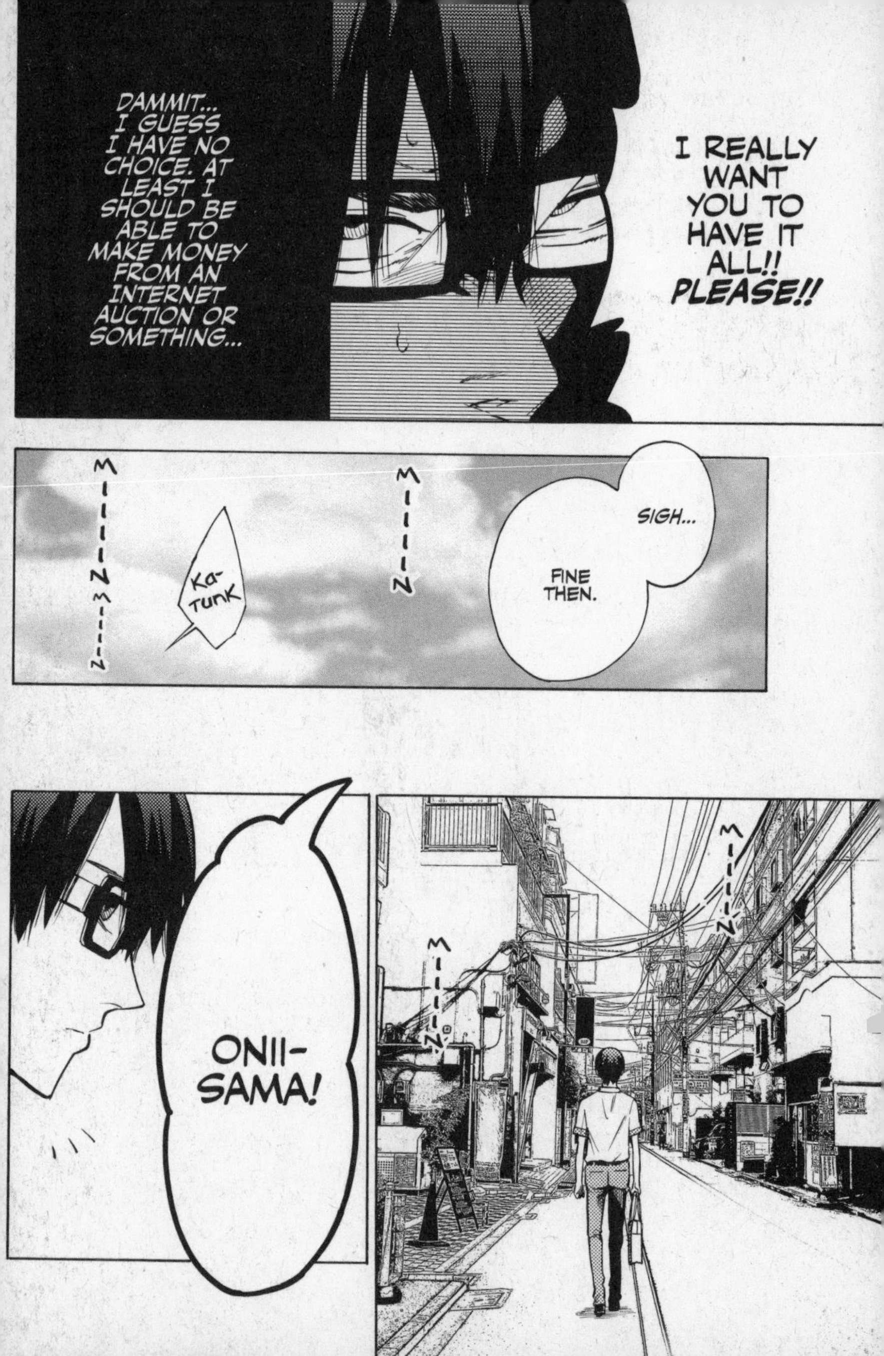
I REALLY WANT YOU TO HAVE IT ALL!! PLEASE!!
DAMMIT... I GUESS I HAVE NO CHOICE. AT LEAST I SHOULD BE ABLE TO MAKE MONEY FROM AN INTERNET AUCTION OR SOMETHING...
SIGH...
FINE THEN.
MIIIN
Ka-tunk
MIIIN
MIIIN
MIIIN
MIIIN
ONII-SAMA!

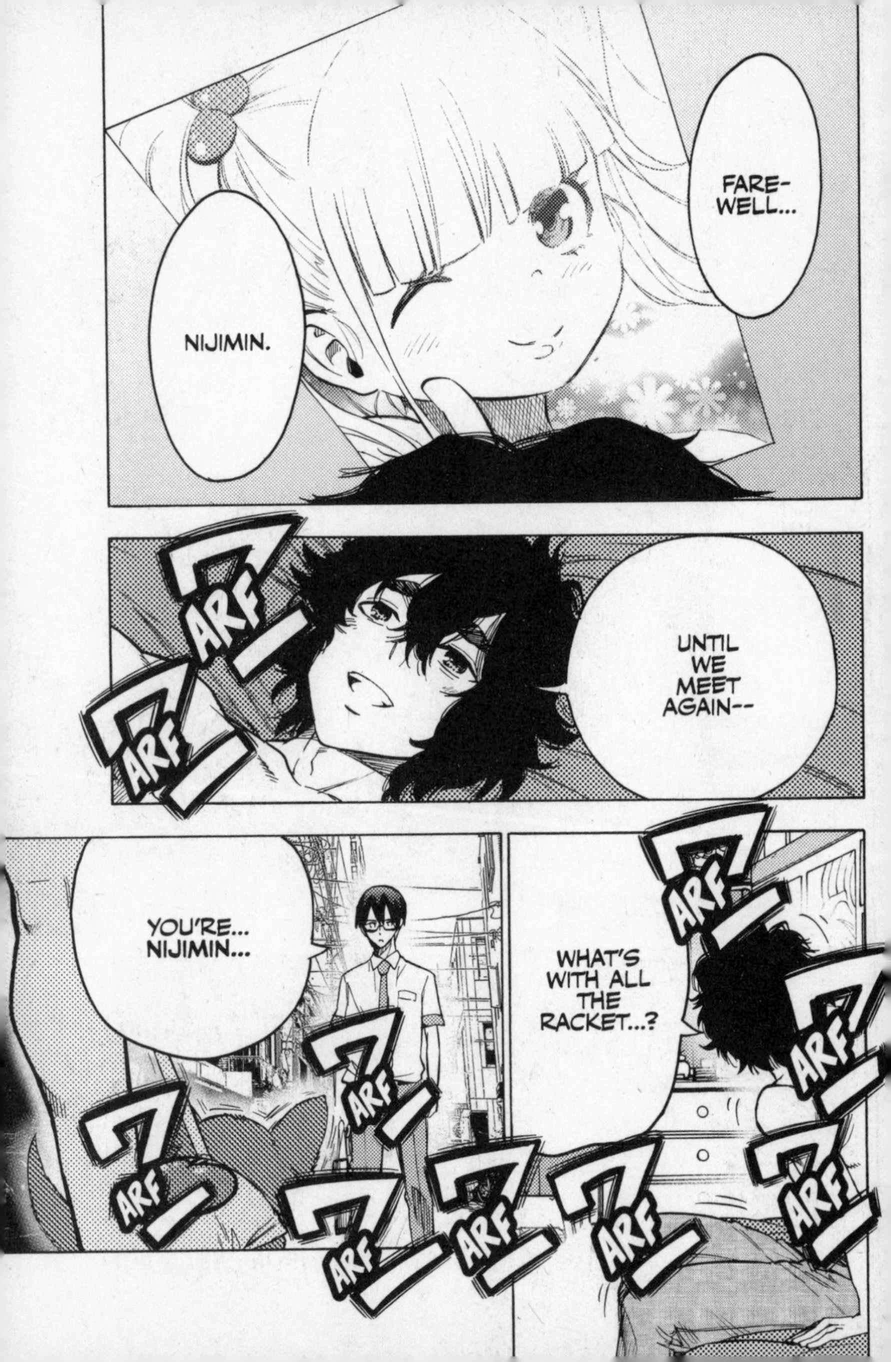
FARE-WELL...
NIJIMIN.
UNTIL WE MEET AGAIN--
ARF
ARF
WHAT'S WITH ALL THE RACKET...?
ARF
ARF
ARF
ARF
YOU'RE... NIJIMIN...
ARF
ARF
ARF
ARF

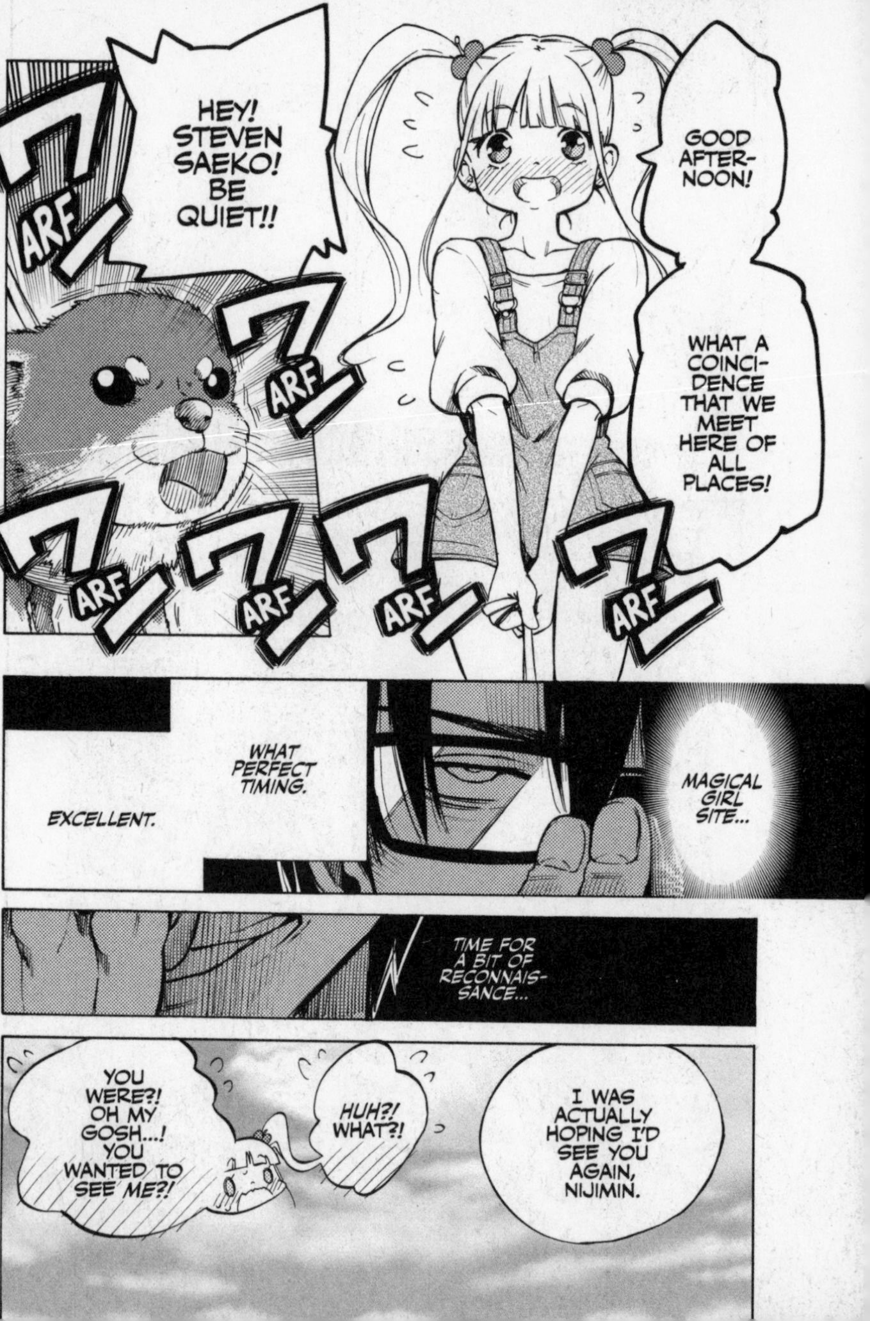
GOOD AFTERNOON!
WHAT A COINCIDENCE THAT WE MEET HERE OF ALL PLACES!
HEY! STEVEN SAEKO! BE QUIET!!
ARF
ARF
ARF
ARF
ARF
ARF
ARF
MAGICAL GIRL SITE...
WHAT PERFECT TIMING.
EXCELLENT.
TIME FOR A BIT OF RECONNAISSANCE...
I WAS ACTUALLY HOPING I'D SEE YOU AGAIN, NIJIMIN.
HUH?! WHAT?!
YOU WERE?! OH MY GOSH...! YOU WANTED TO SEE ME?!

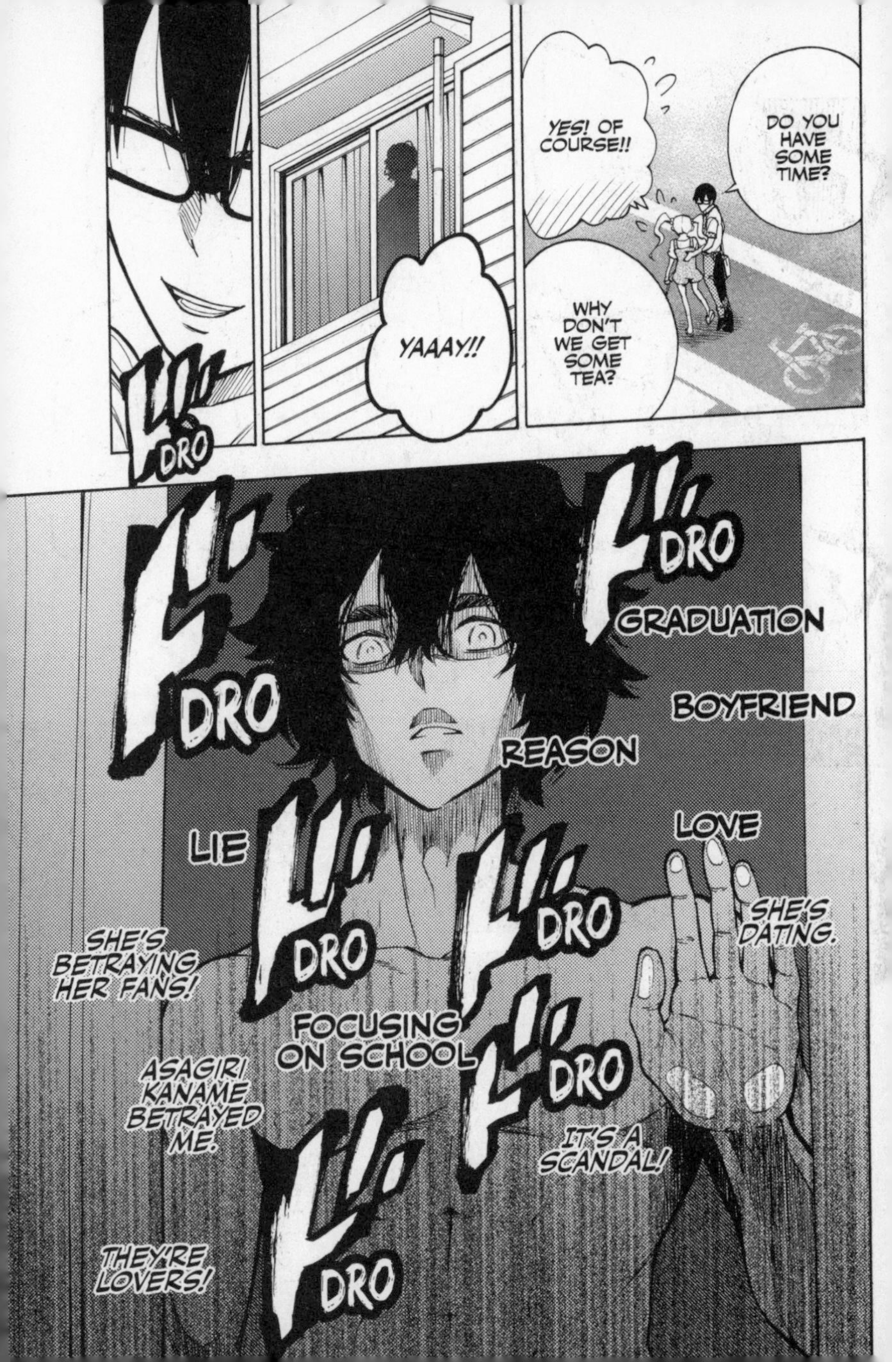

DO YOU HAVE SOME TIME?
YES! OF COURSE!!
WHY DON'T WE GET SOME TEA?
YAAAY!!
DRO
DRO
GRADUATION
BOYFRIEND
REASON
DRO
LOVE
LIE
SHE'S DATING.
DRO
DRO
SHE'S BETRAYING HER FANS!
FOCUSING ON SCHOOL
DRO
IT'S A SCANDAL!
ASAGIRI KANAME BETRAYED ME.
THEY'RE LOVERS!
DRO

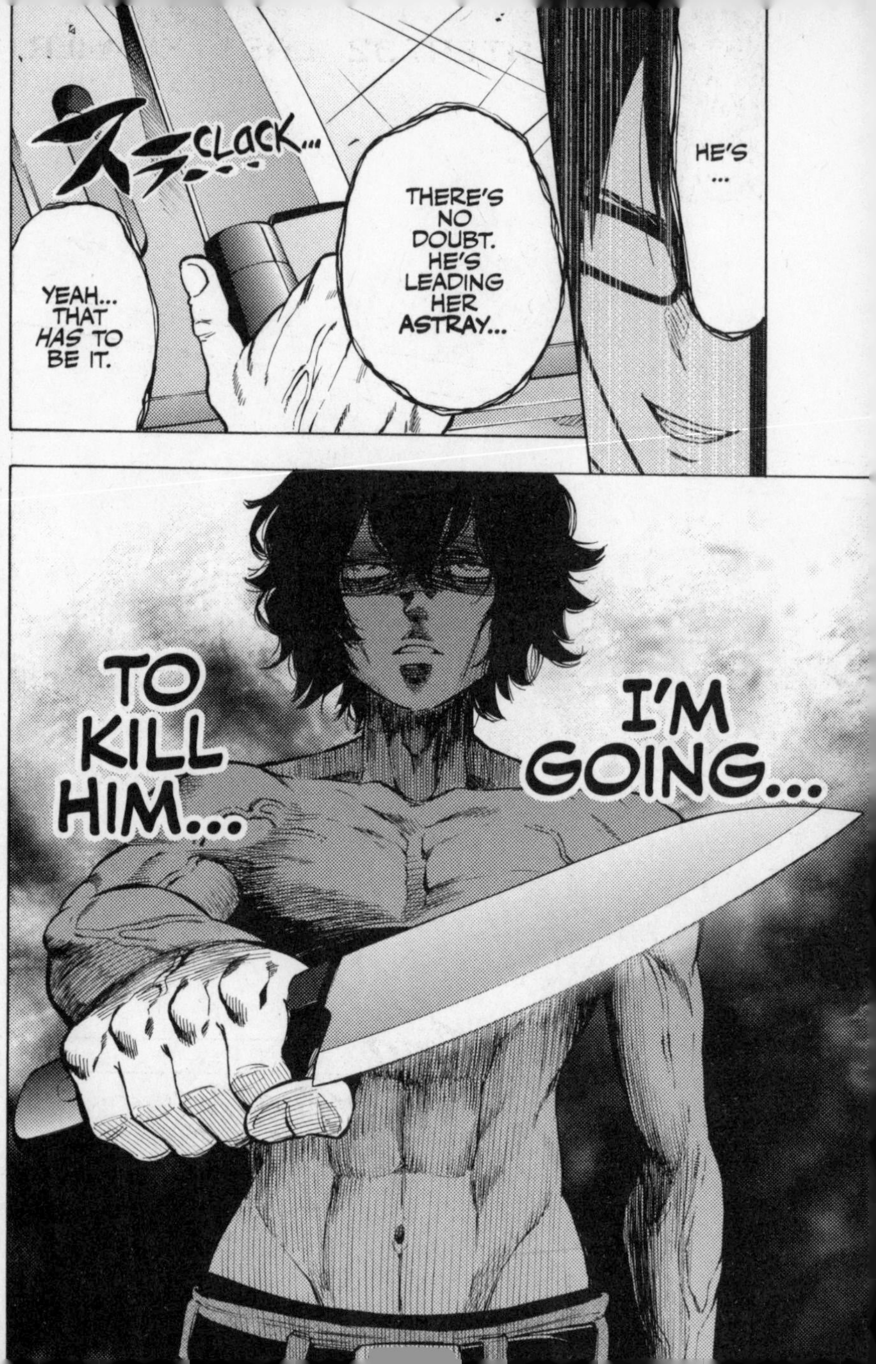
HE'S ...
THERE'S NO DOUBT. HE'S LEADING HER ASTRAY...
CLACK...
YEAH... THAT HAS TO BE IT.
I'M GOING...
TO KILL HIM...

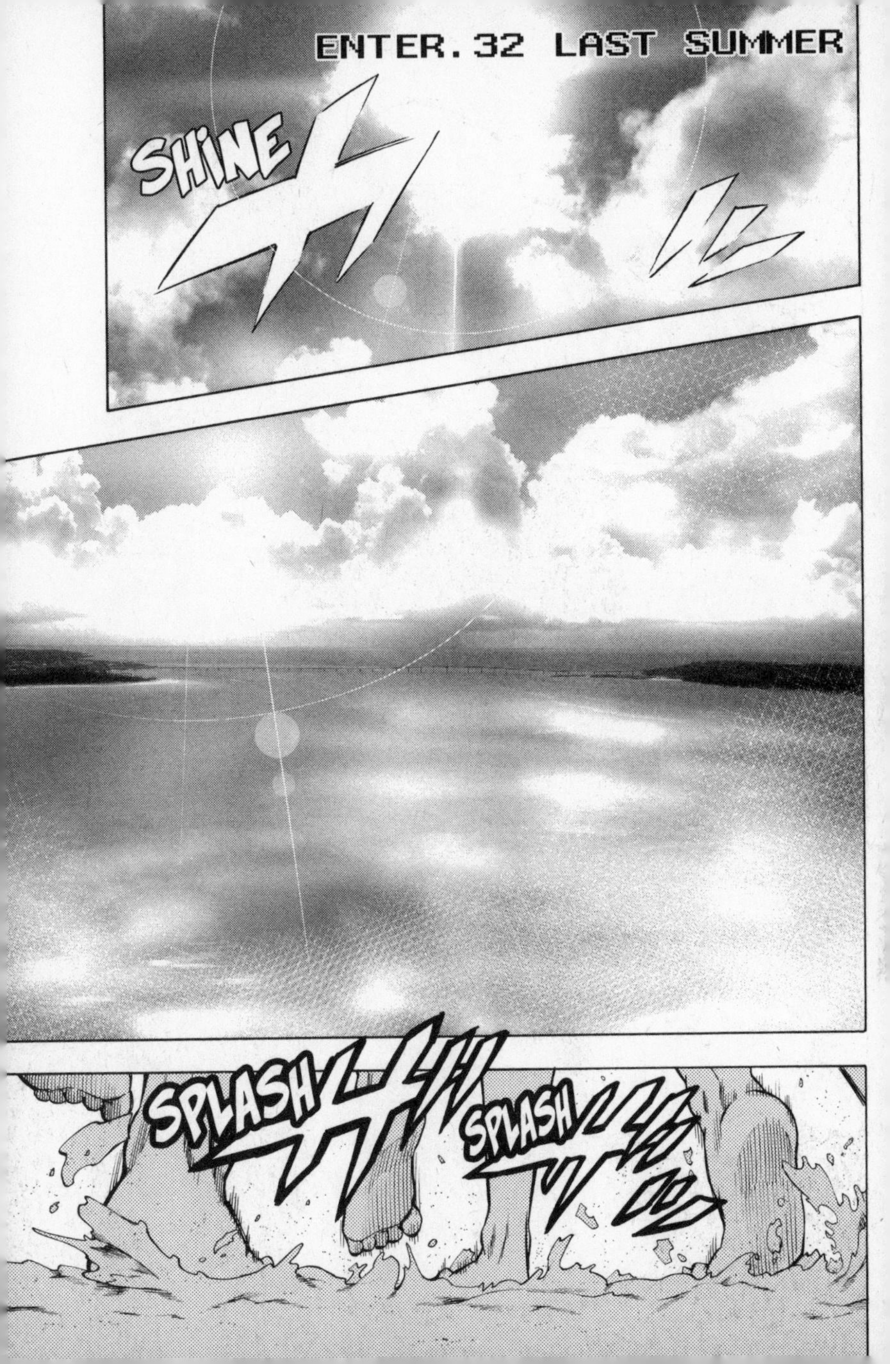
ENTER.32 LAST SUMMER
SHINE
SPLASH
SPLASH

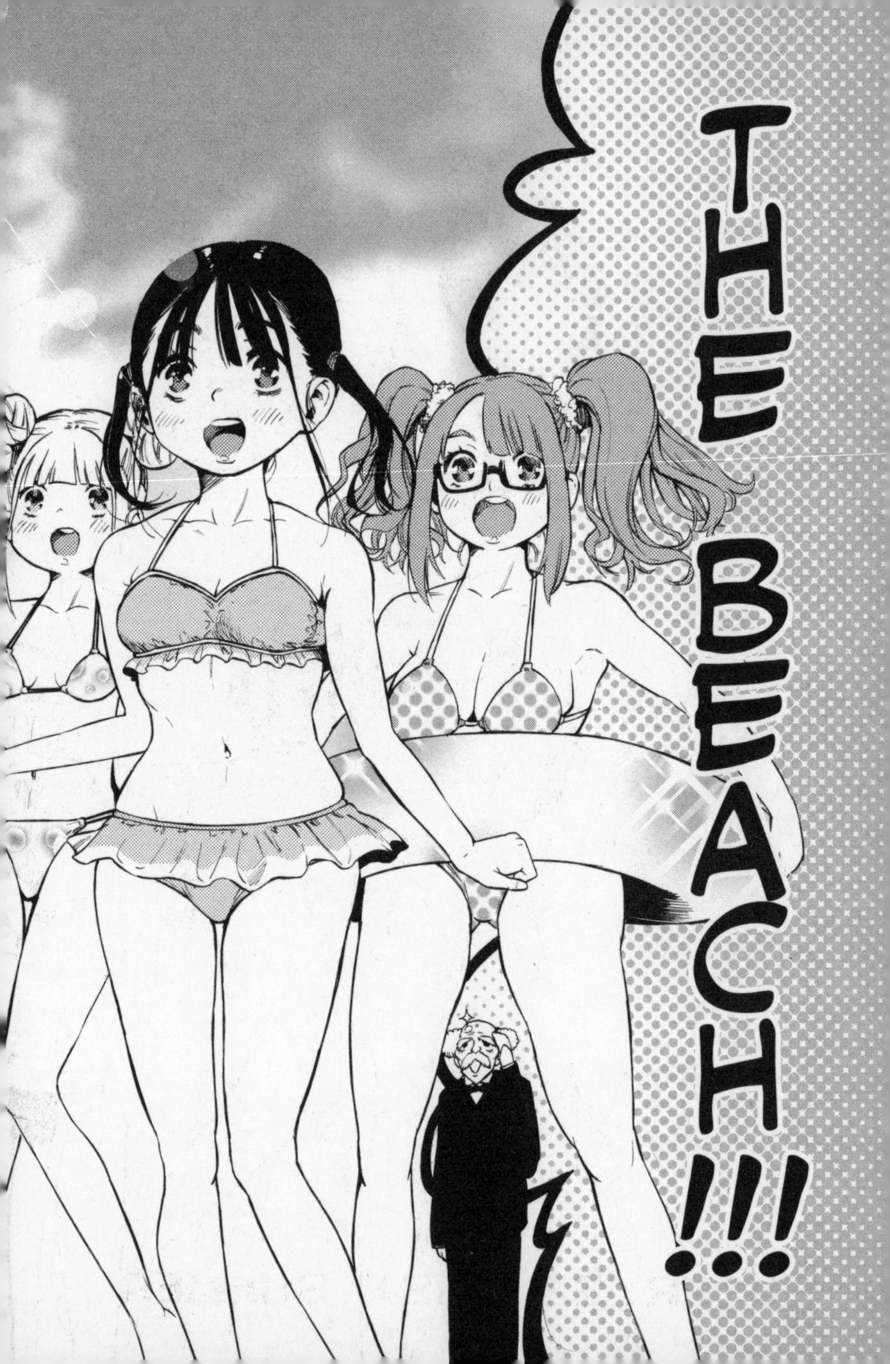
THE BEACH!!!

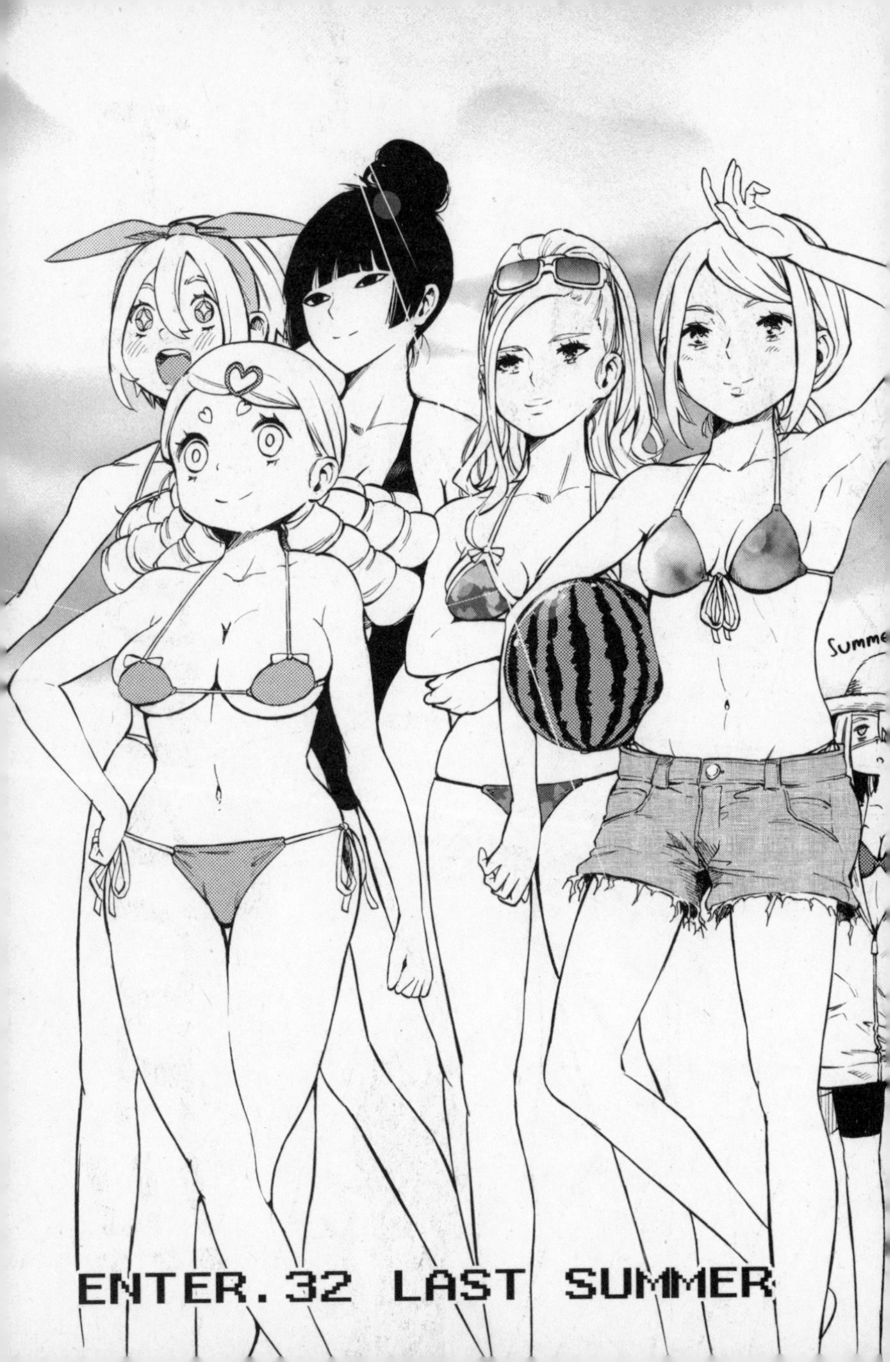
ENTER. 32 LAST SUMMER

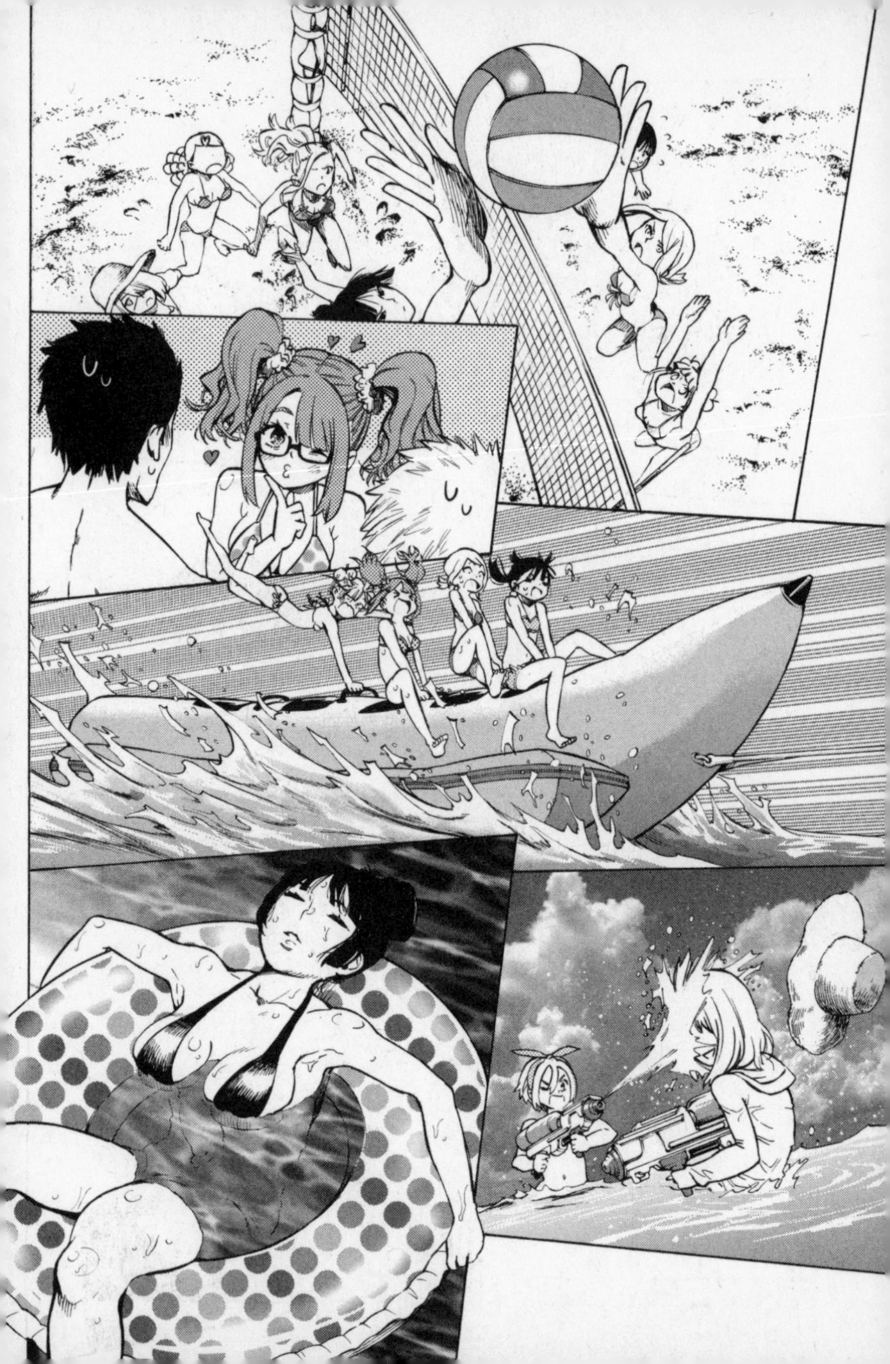

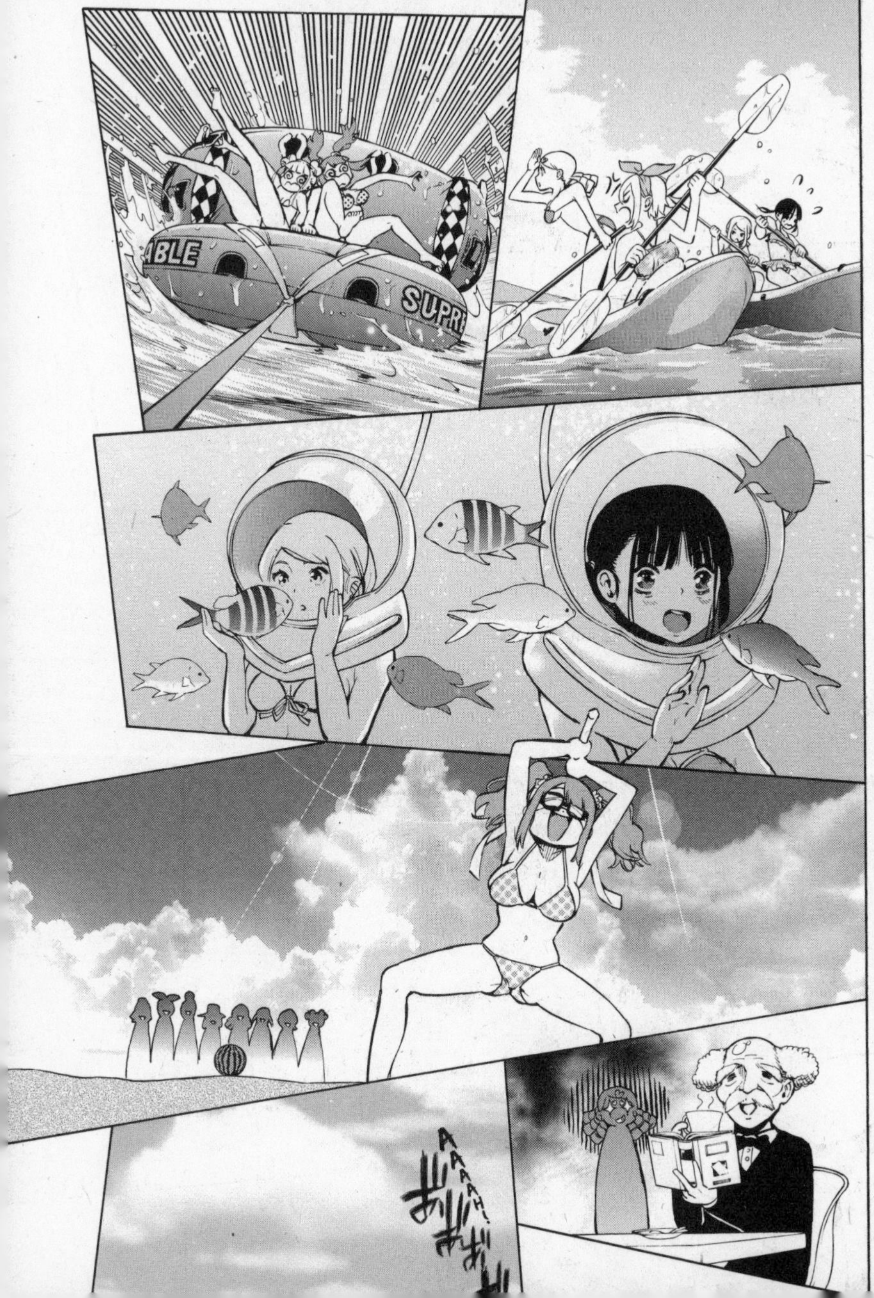
ABLE
SUPRE
AAAAH!

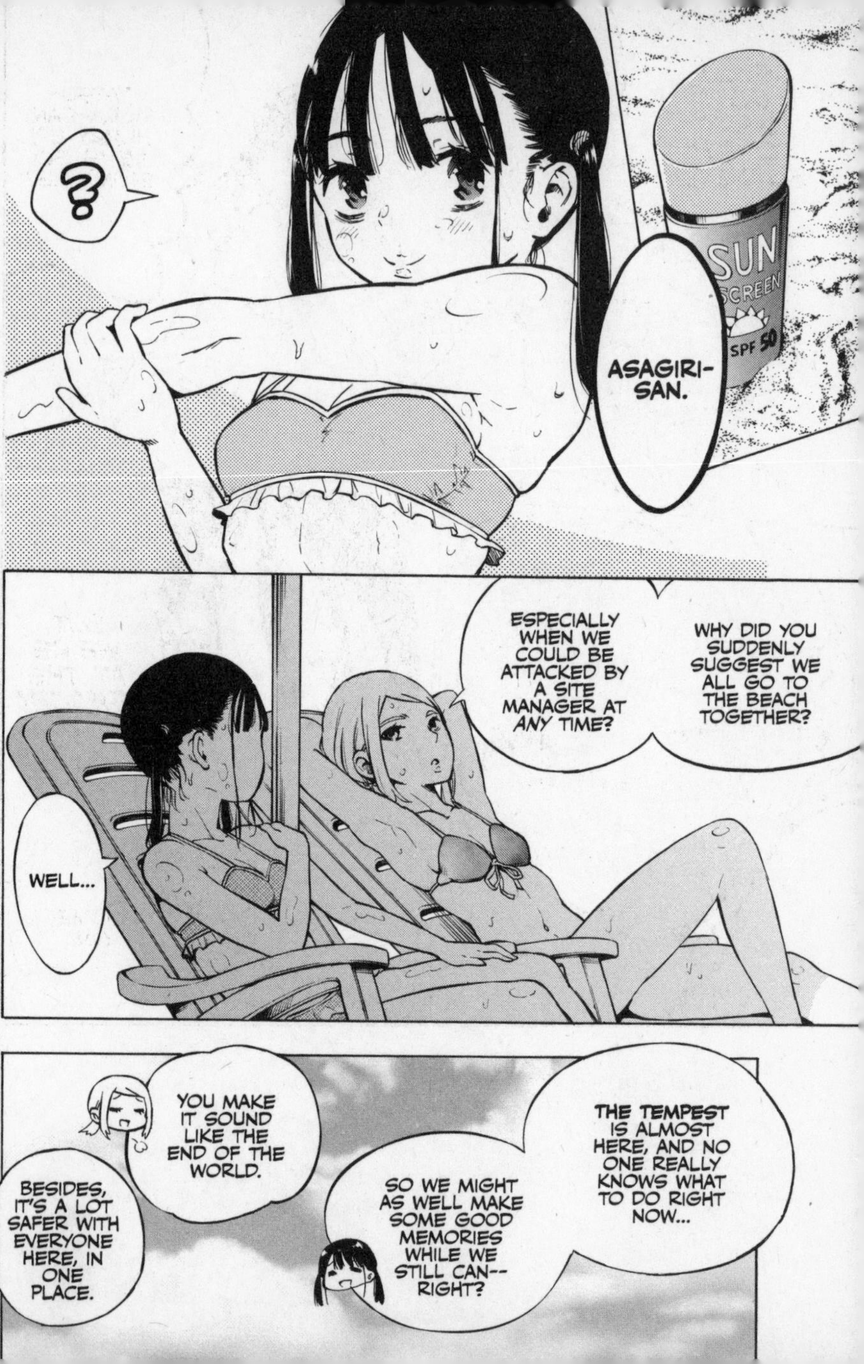
SUN SCREEN SPF 50
ASAGIRI-SAN.
?
WHY DID YOU SUDDENLY SUGGEST WE ALL GO TO THE BEACH TOGETHER?
ESPECIALLY WHEN WE COULD BE ATTACKED BY A SITE MANAGER AT *ANY* TIME?
WELL...
THE TEMPEST IS ALMOST HERE, AND NO ONE REALLY KNOWS WHAT TO DO RIGHT NOW...
SO WE MIGHT AS WELL MAKE SOME GOOD MEMORIES WHILE WE STILL CAN--RIGHT?
YOU MAKE IT SOUND LIKE THE END OF THE WORLD.
BESIDES, IT'S A LOT SAFER WITH EVERYONE HERE, IN ONE PLACE.

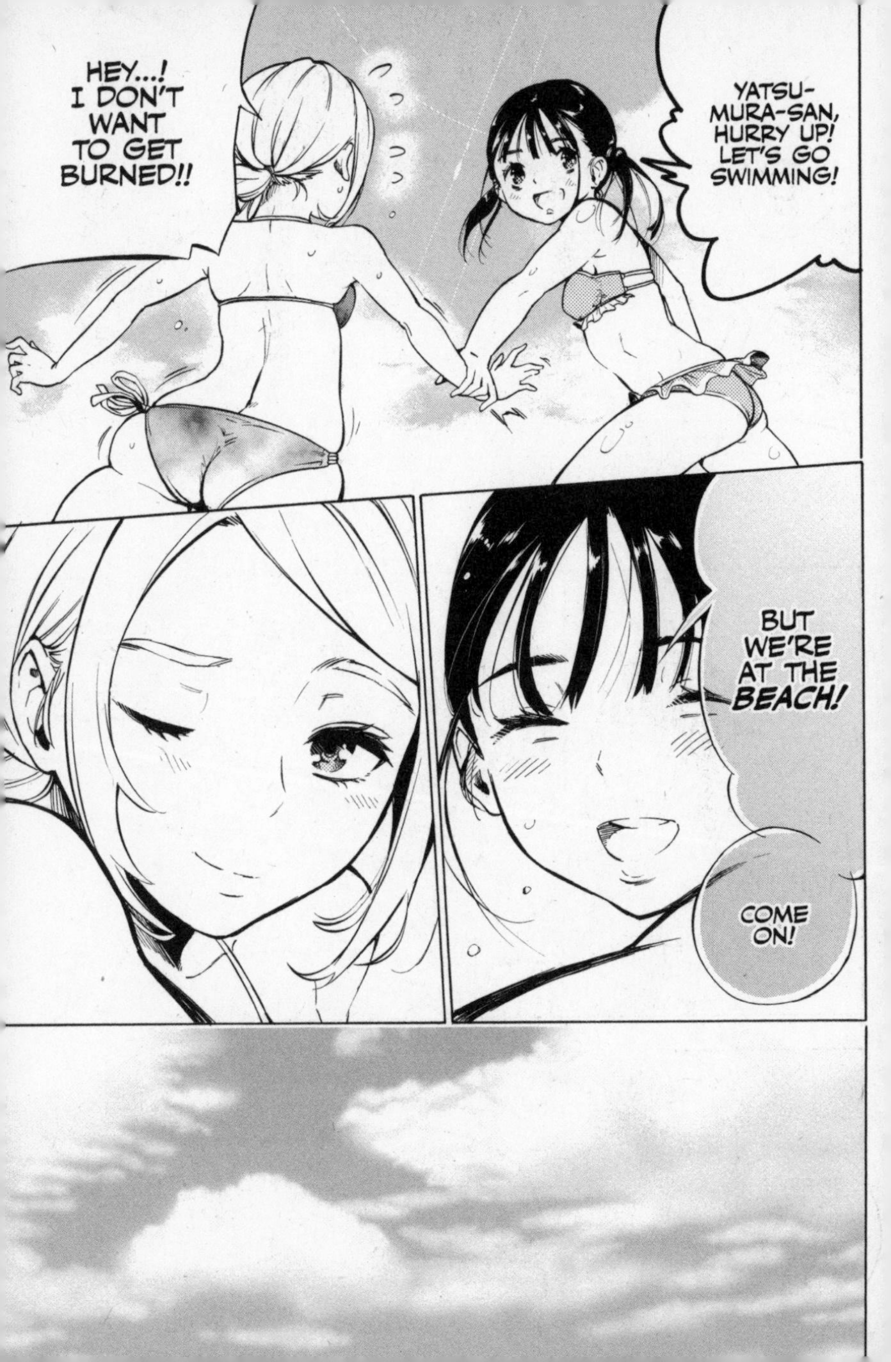
YATSU-MURA-SAN, HURRY UP! LET'S GO SWIMMING!
HEY...! I DON'T WANT TO GET BURNED!!
BUT WE'RE AT THE *BEACH!*
COME ON!

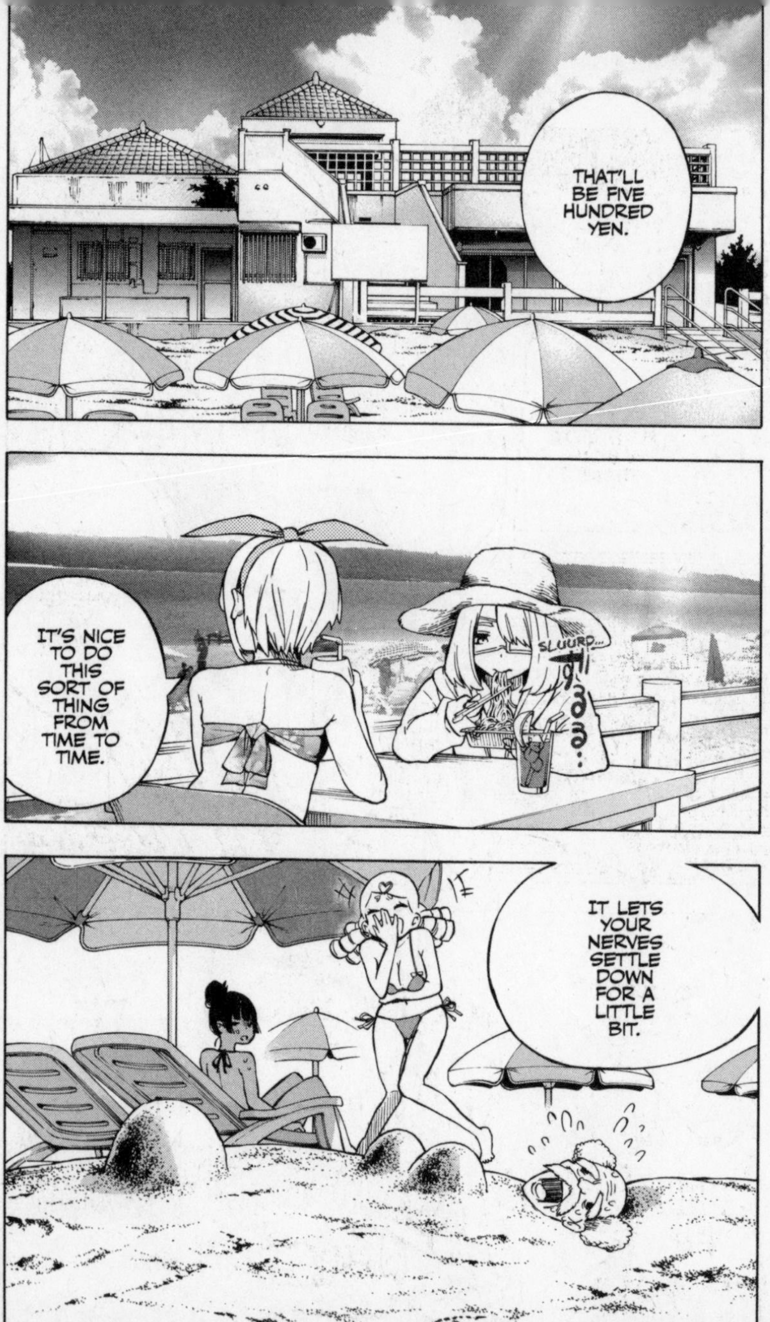
THAT'LL BE FIVE HUNDRED YEN.
IT'S NICE TO DO THIS SORT OF THING FROM TIME TO TIME.
SLUURP...
IT LETS YOUR NERVES SETTLE DOWN FOR A LITTLE BIT.

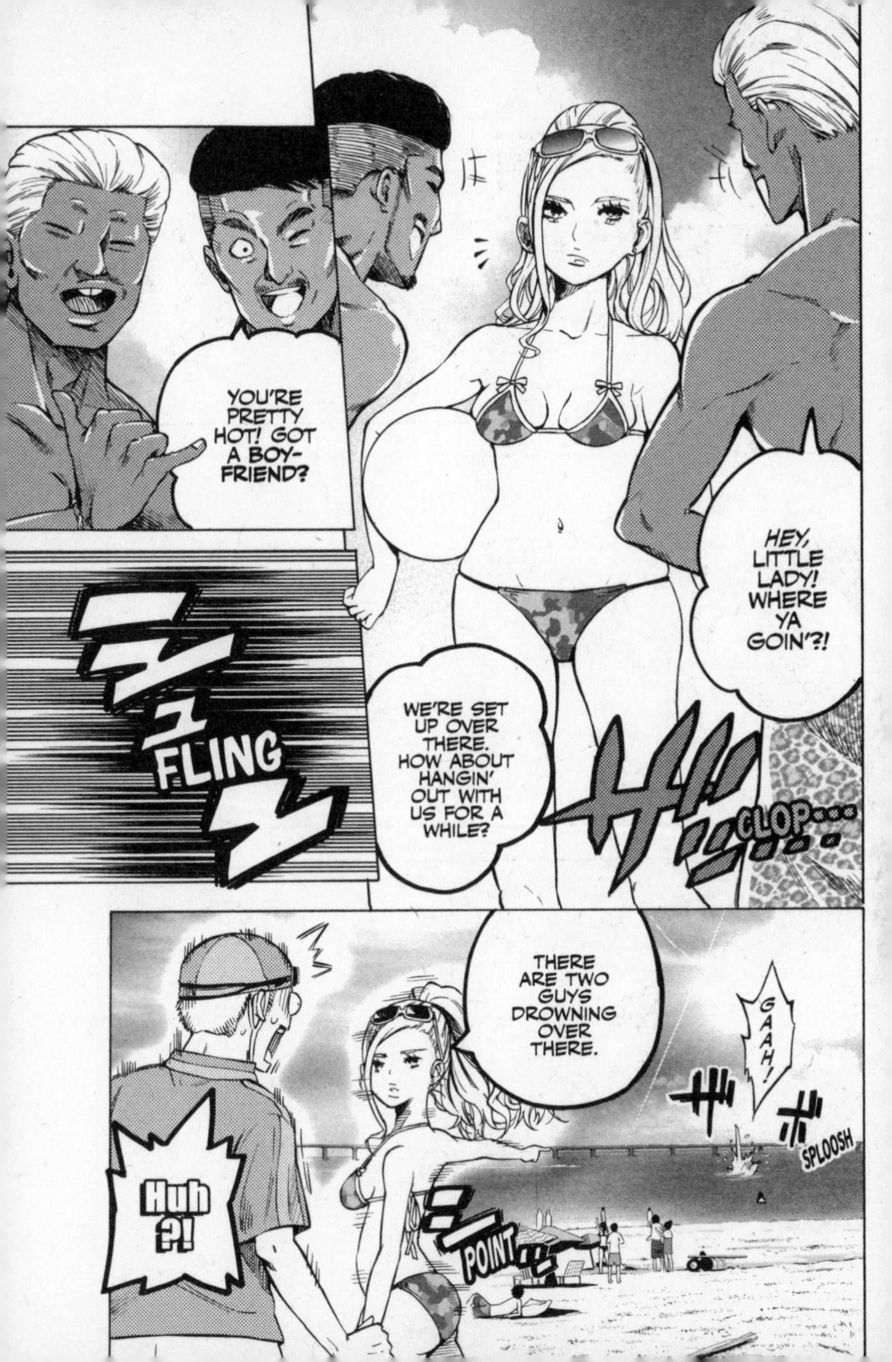
HEY, LITTLE LADY! WHERE YA GOIN'?!
CLOP...
WE'RE SET UP OVER THERE. HOW ABOUT HANGIN' OUT WITH US FOR A WHILE?
YOU'RE PRETTY HOT! GOT A BOY-FRIEND?
FLING
THERE ARE TWO GUYS DROWNING OVER THERE.
GAAH!
SPLOOSH
POINT
Huh?!

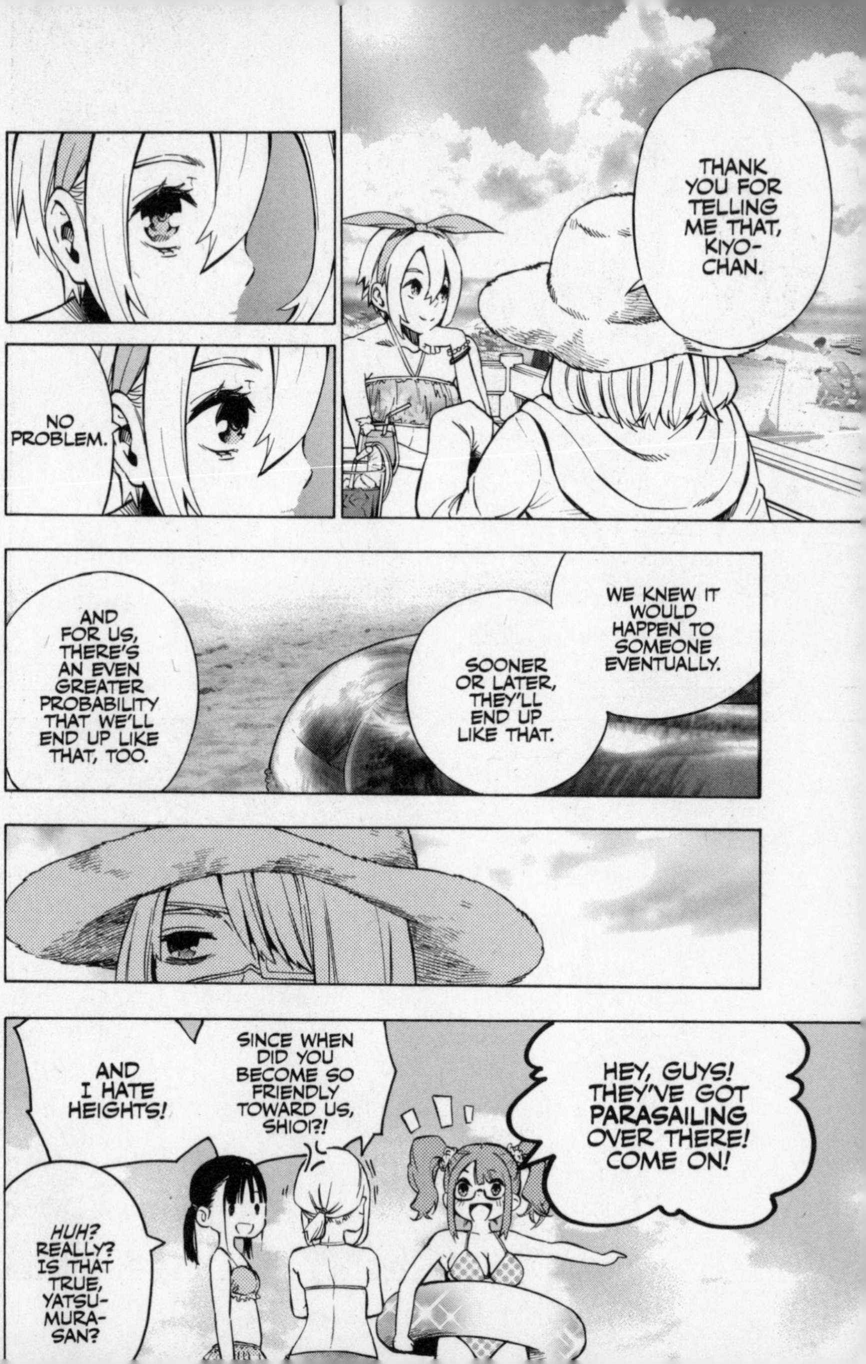
THANK YOU FOR TELLING ME THAT, KIYO-CHAN.
NO PROBLEM.
WE KNEW IT WOULD HAPPEN TO SOMEONE EVENTUALLY.
SOONER OR LATER, THEY'LL END UP LIKE THAT.
AND FOR US, THERE'S AN EVEN GREATER PROBABILITY THAT WE'LL END UP LIKE THAT, TOO.
HEY, GUYS! THEY'VE GOT PARASAILING OVER THERE! COME ON!
SINCE WHEN DID YOU BECOME SO FRIENDLY TOWARD US, SHIOI?!
AND I HATE HEIGHTS!
HUH? REALLY? IS THAT TRUE, YATSU-MURA-SAN?

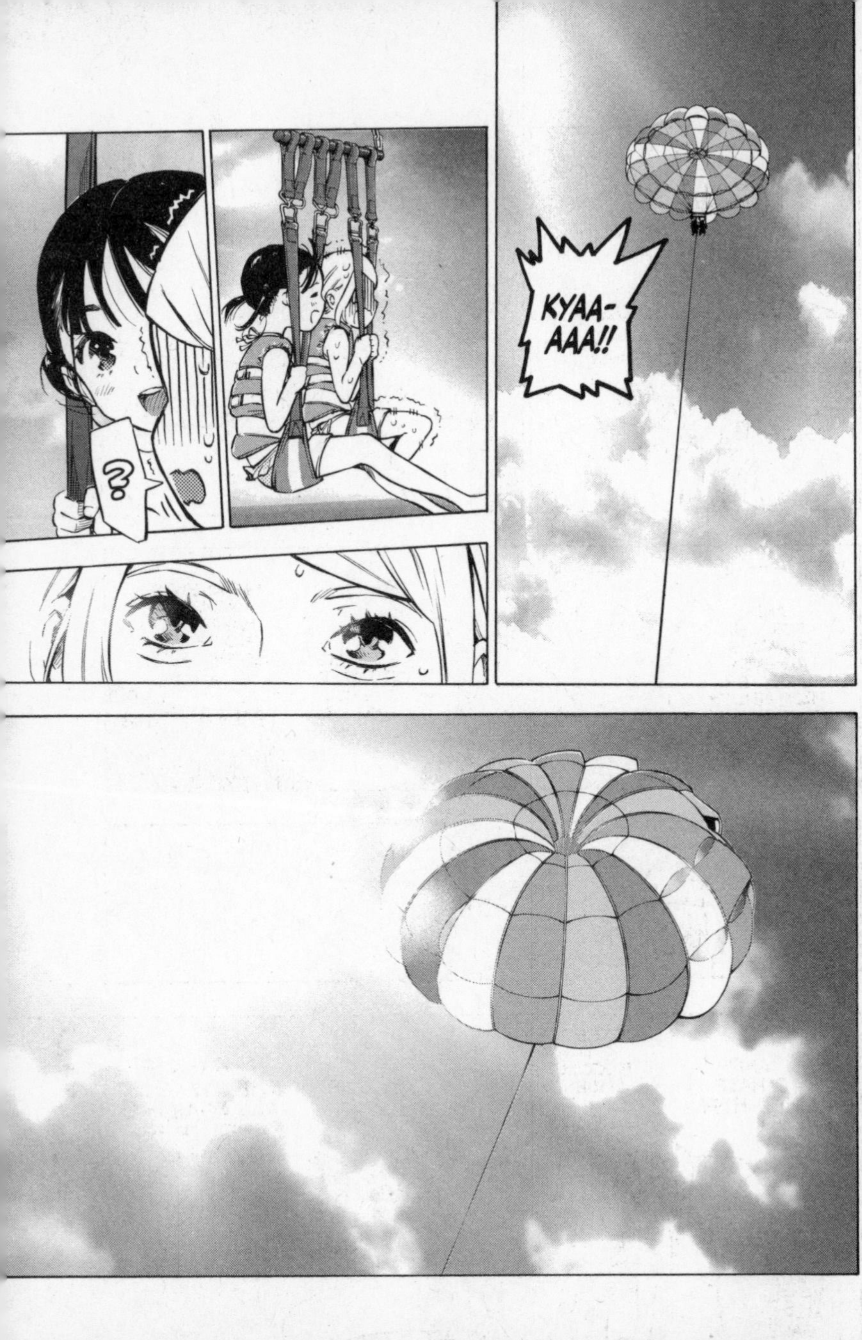
KYAA-AAA!!
?

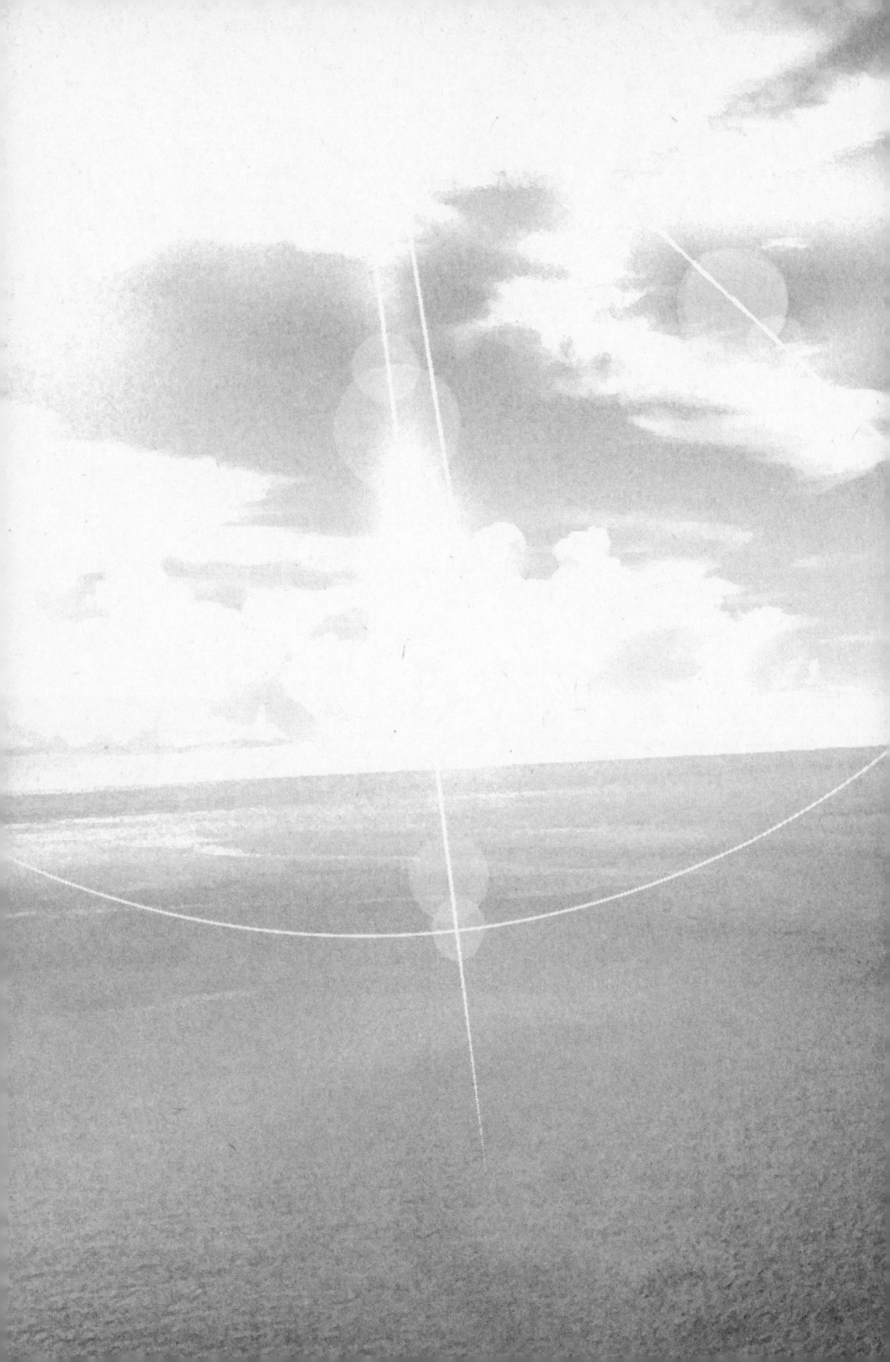

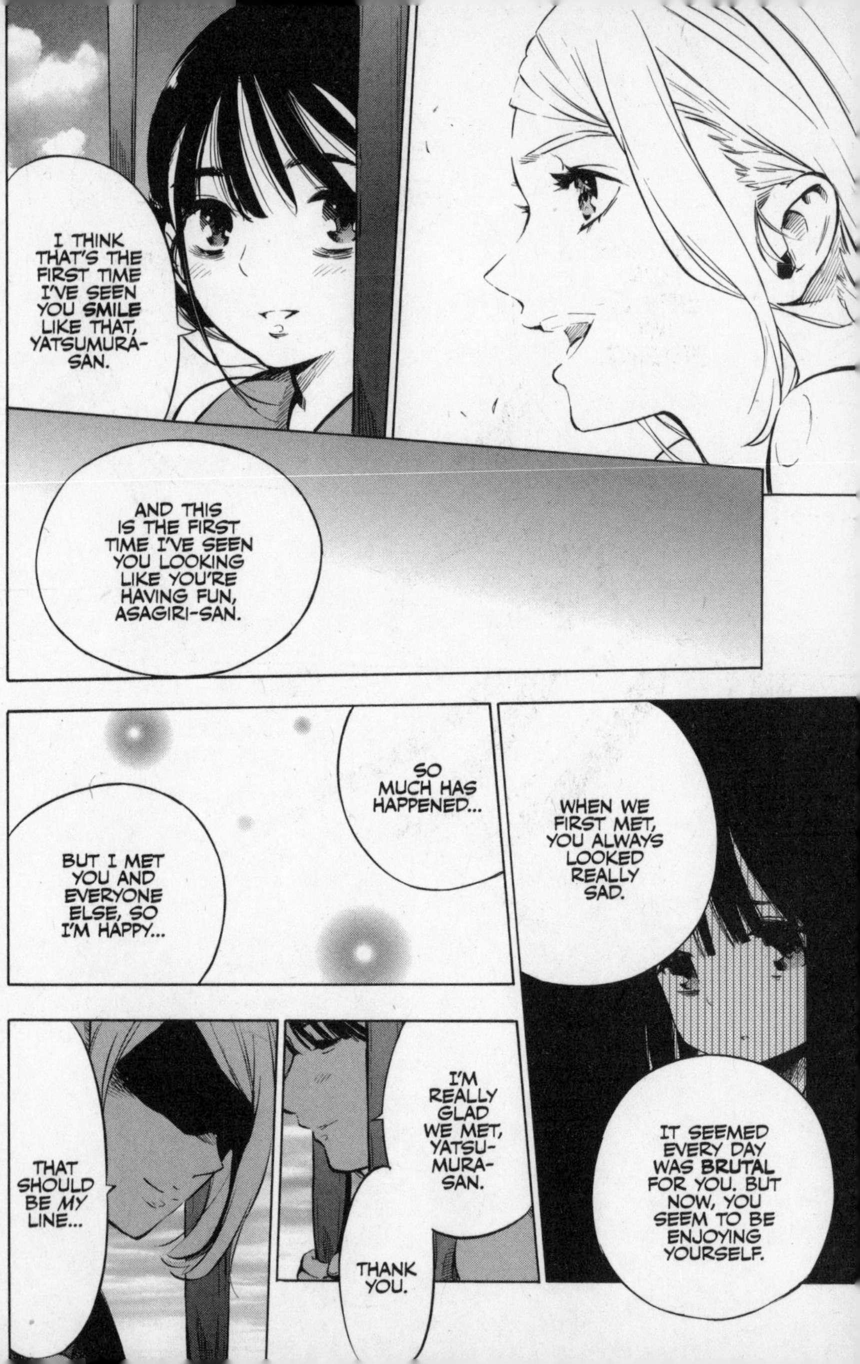
I THINK THAT'S THE FIRST TIME I'VE SEEN YOU SMILE LIKE THAT, YATSUMURA-SAN.
AND THIS IS THE FIRST TIME I'VE SEEN YOU LOOKING LIKE YOU'RE HAVING FUN, ASAGIRI-SAN.
WHEN WE FIRST MET, YOU ALWAYS LOOKED REALLY SAD.
IT SEEMED EVERY DAY WAS BRUTAL FOR YOU. BUT NOW, YOU SEEM TO BE ENJOYING YOURSELF.
SO MUCH HAS HAPPENED...
BUT I MET YOU AND EVERYONE ELSE, SO I'M HAPPY...
I'M REALLY GLAD WE MET, YATSUMURA-SAN.
THANK YOU.
THAT SHOULD BE *MY* LINE...

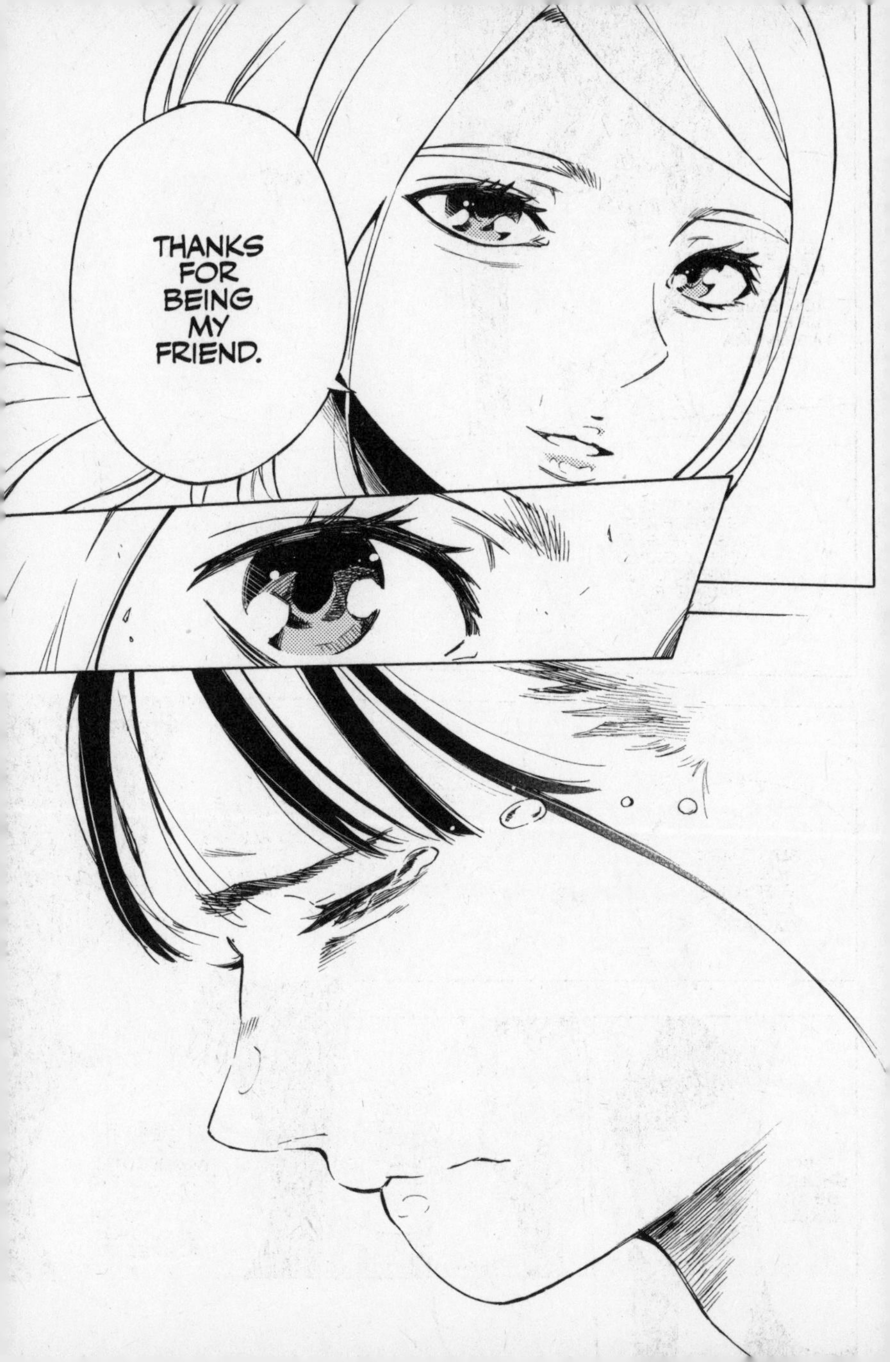
THANKS FOR BEING MY FRIEND.

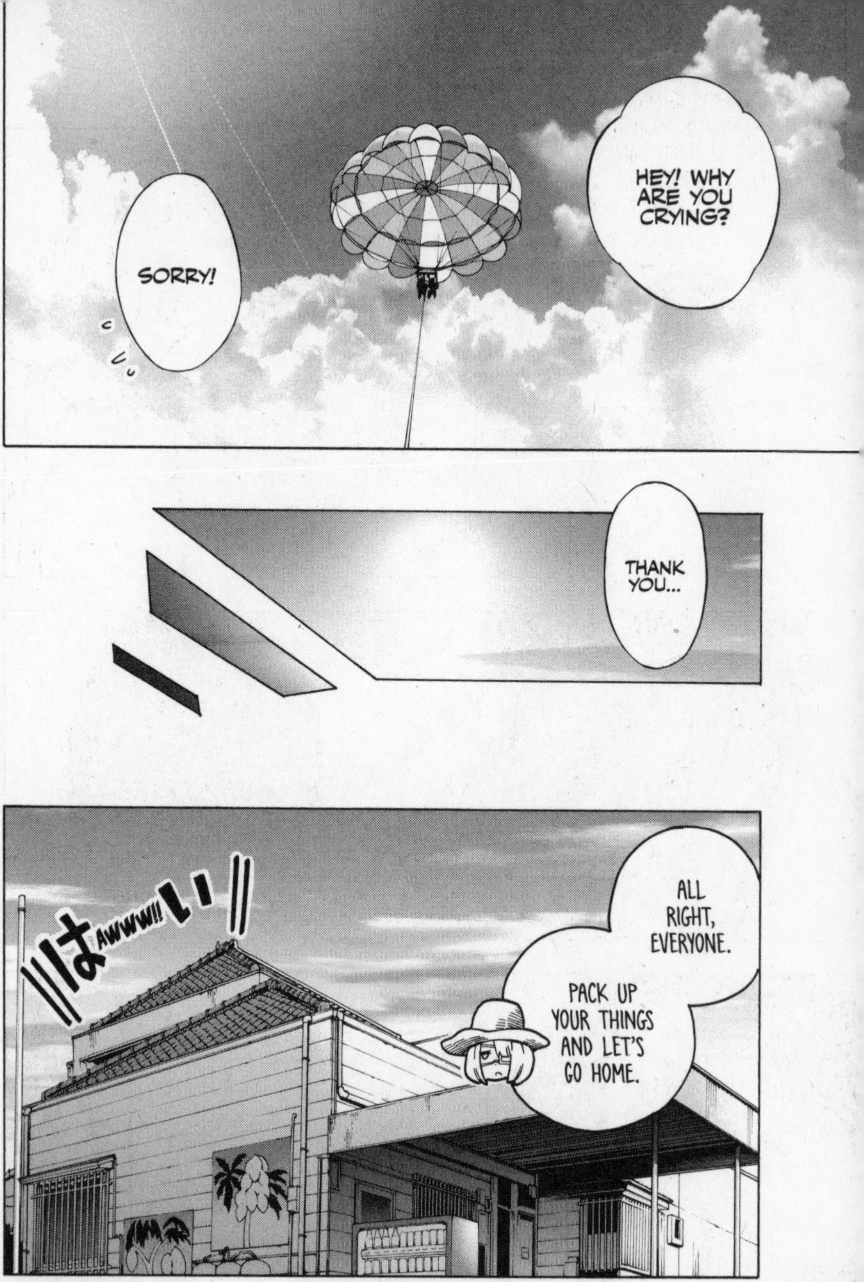
HEY! WHY ARE YOU CRYING?
SORRY!
THANK YOU...
ALL RIGHT, EVERYONE.
PACK UP YOUR THINGS AND LET'S GO HOME.
はAWWW!!い

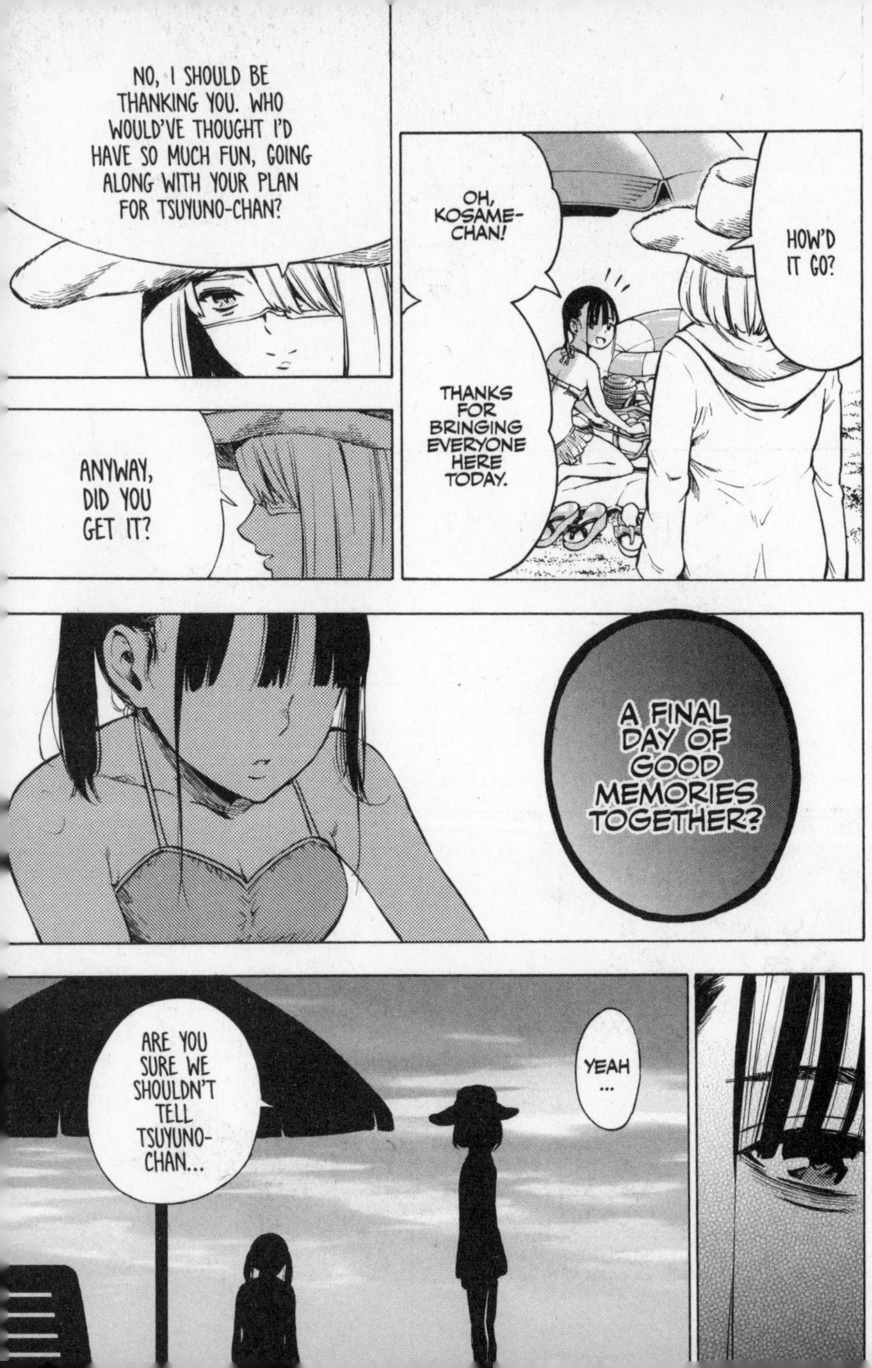
HOW'D IT GO?
OH, KOSAME-CHAN!
THANKS FOR BRINGING EVERYONE HERE TODAY.
NO, I SHOULD BE THANKING YOU. WHO WOULD'VE THOUGHT I'D HAVE SO MUCH FUN, GOING ALONG WITH YOUR PLAN FOR TSUYUNO-CHAN?
ANYWAY, DID YOU GET IT?
A FINAL DAY OF GOOD MEMORIES TOGETHER?
YEAH ...
ARE YOU SURE WE SHOULDN'T TELL TSUYUNO-CHAN...

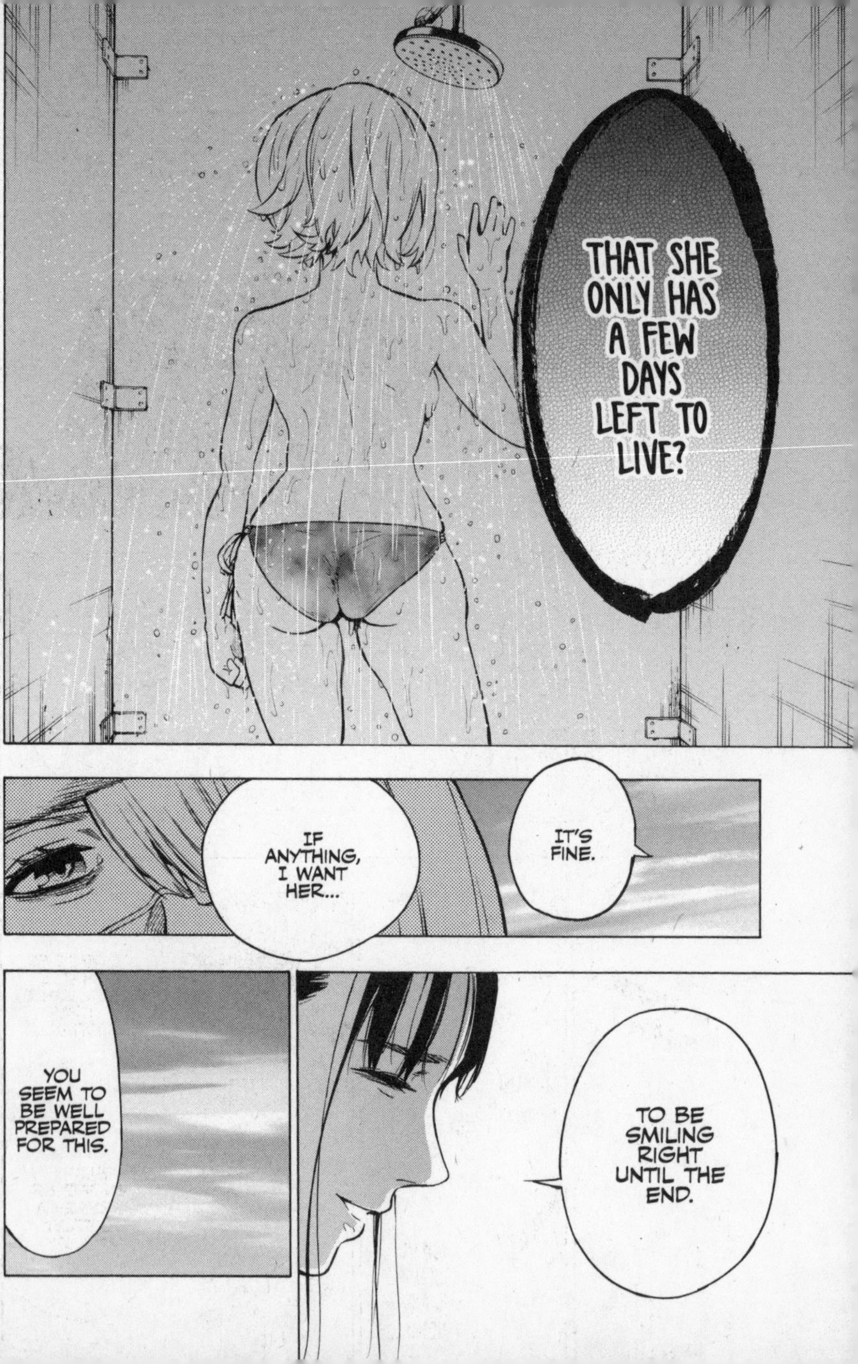

THAT SHE ONLY HAS A FEW DAYS LEFT TO LIVE?
IT'S FINE.
IF ANYTHING, I WANT HER...
TO BE SMILING RIGHT UNTIL THE END.
YOU SEEM TO BE WELL PREPARED FOR THIS.

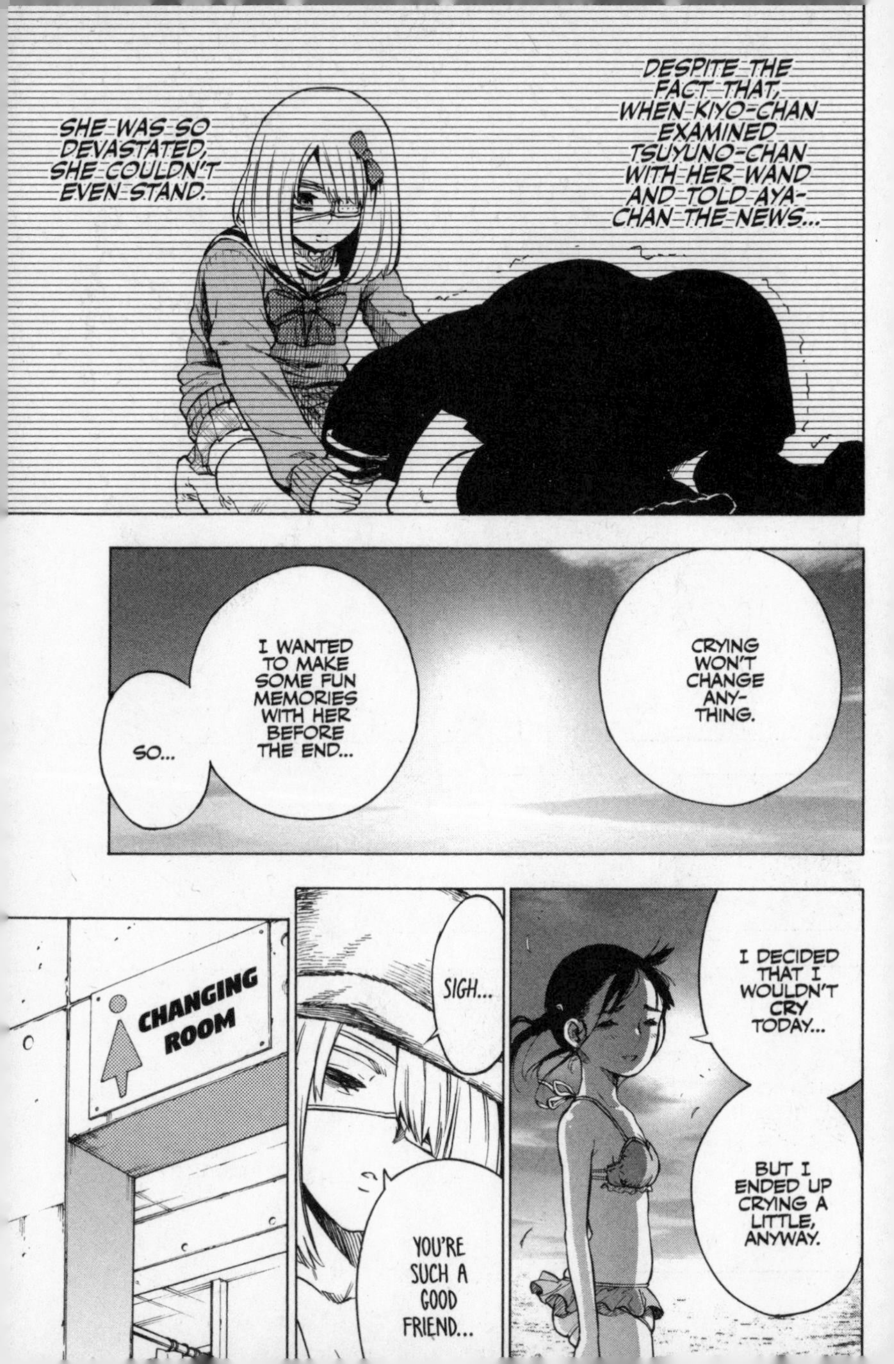
DESPITE THE FACT THAT, WHEN KIYO-CHAN EXAMINED TSUYUNO-CHAN WITH HER WAND AND TOLD AYA-CHAN THE NEWS...
SHE WAS SO DEVASTATED, SHE COULDN'T EVEN STAND.
CRYING WON'T CHANGE ANY-THING.
I WANTED TO MAKE SOME FUN MEMORIES WITH HER BEFORE THE END...
SO...
I DECIDED THAT I WOULDN'T CRY TODAY...
BUT I ENDED UP CRYING A LITTLE, ANYWAY.
SIGH...
YOU'RE SUCH A GOOD FRIEND...
CHANGING ROOM

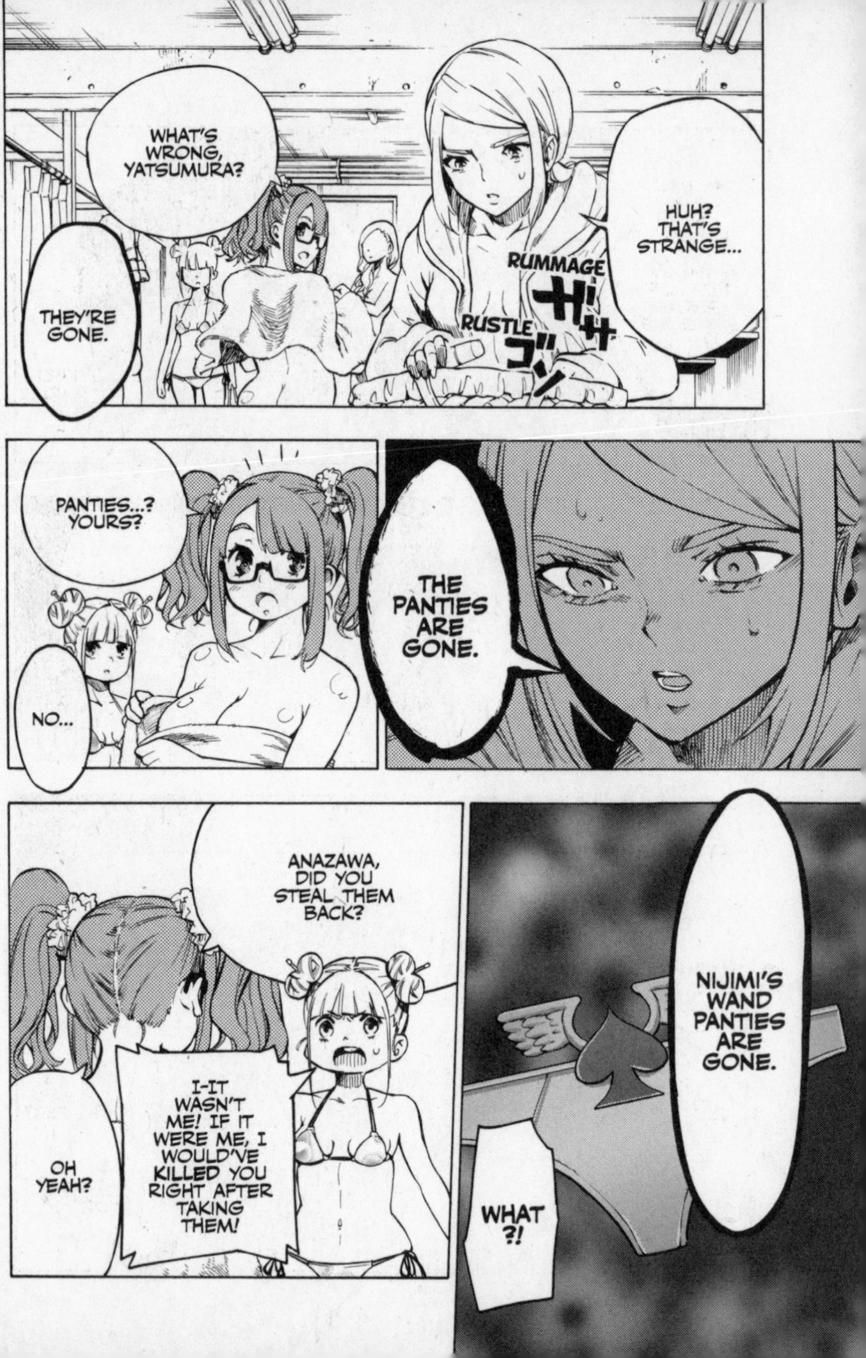
HUH? THAT'S STRANGE...
RUMMAGE
RUSTLE
WHAT'S WRONG, YATSUMURA?
THEY'RE GONE.
THE PANTIES ARE GONE.
PANTIES...? YOURS?
NO...
NIJIMI'S WAND PANTIES ARE GONE.
WHAT?!
ANAZAWA, DID YOU STEAL THEM BACK?
I-IT WASN'T ME! IF IT WERE ME, I WOULD'VE KILLED YOU RIGHT AFTER TAKING THEM!
OH YEAH?

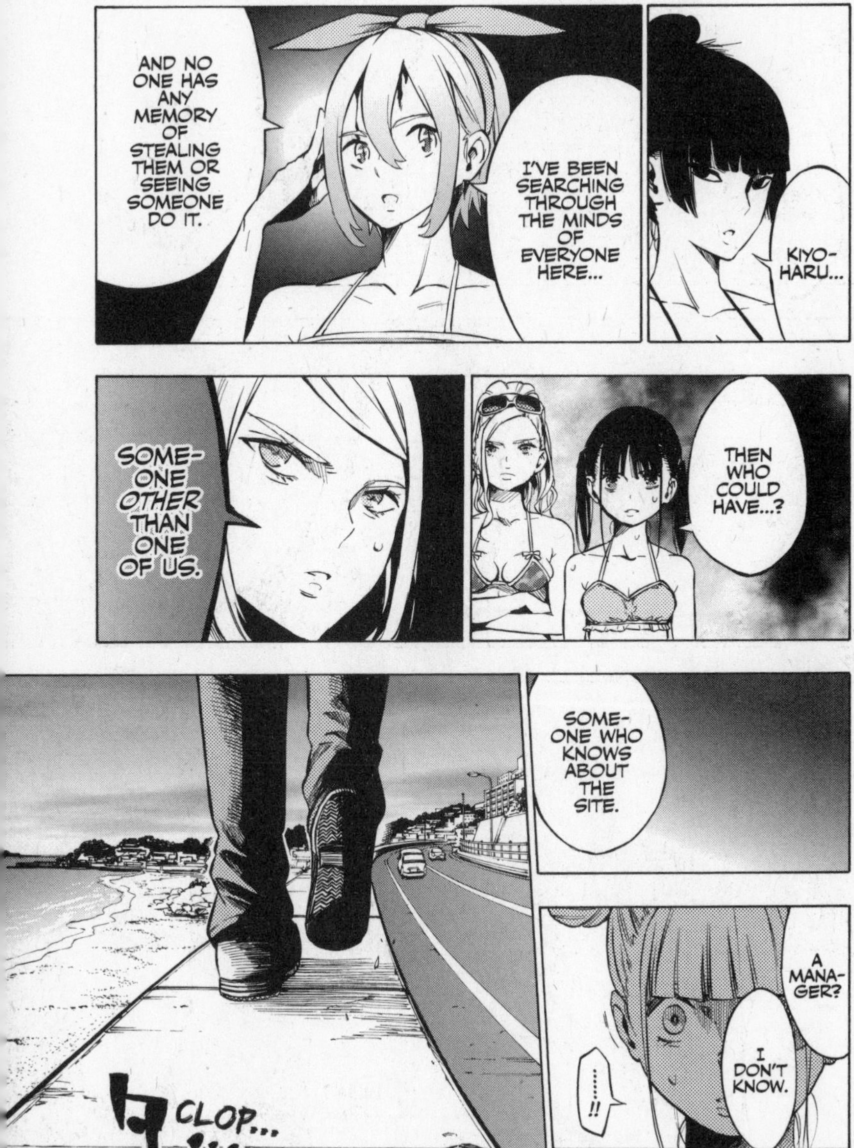
KIYO-HARU...
I'VE BEEN SEARCHING THROUGH THE MINDS OF EVERYONE HERE...
AND NO ONE HAS ANY MEMORY OF STEALING THEM OR SEEING SOMEONE DO IT.
THEN WHO COULD HAVE...?
SOME-ONE *OTHER* THAN ONE OF US.
SOME-ONE WHO KNOWS ABOUT THE SITE.
A MANA-GER?
I DON'T KNOW.
......!!
CLOP...

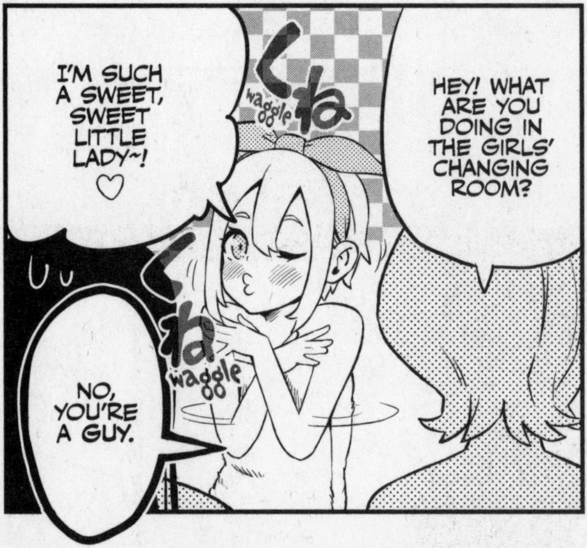
HEY! WHAT ARE YOU DOING IN THE GIRLS' CHANGING ROOM?
くね waggle
I'M SUCH A SWEET, SWEET LITTLE LADY~! ♡
くね waggle
NO, YOU'RE A GUY.

ENTER. 33 PFFT!

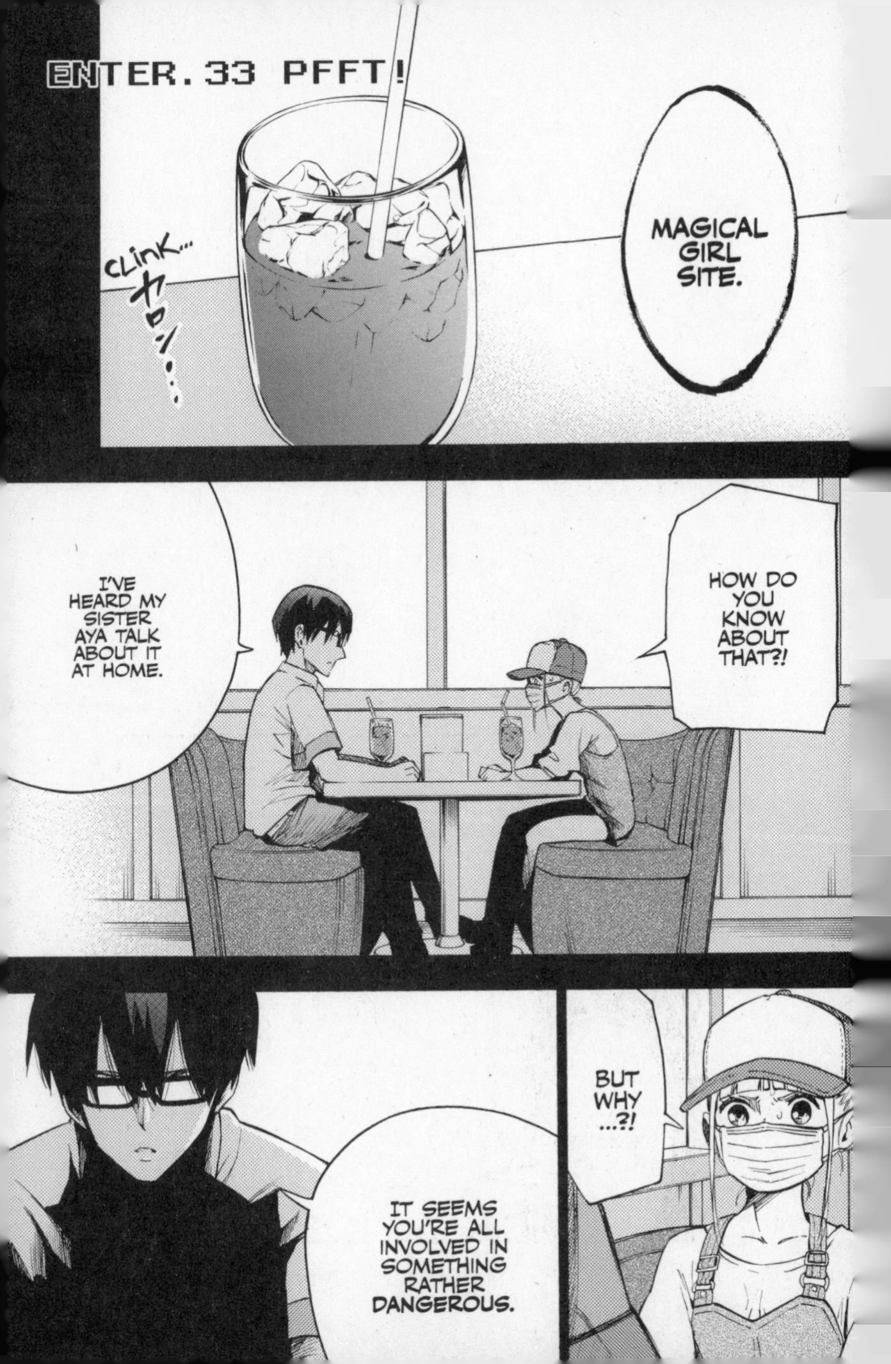
MAGICAL GIRL SITE.
CLINK...
カロン...
HOW DO YOU KNOW ABOUT THAT?!
I'VE HEARD MY SISTER AYA TALK ABOUT IT AT HOME.
BUT WHY ...?!
IT SEEMS YOU'RE ALL INVOLVED IN SOMETHING RATHER DANGEROUS.

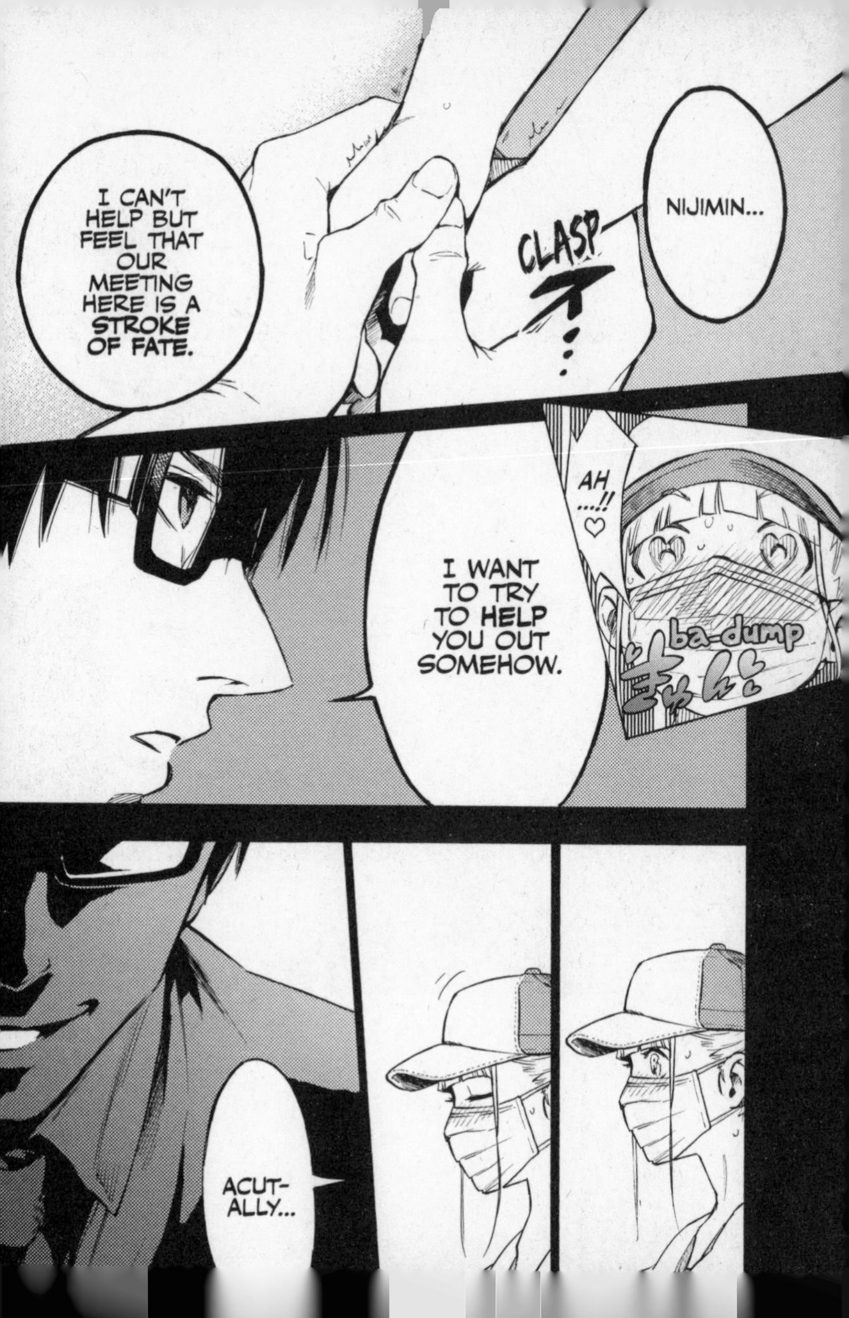
NIJIMIN...
CLASP
I CAN'T HELP BUT FEEL THAT OUR MEETING HERE IS A STROKE OF FATE.
AH ...!! ♥
ba-dump
I WANT TO TRY TO HELP YOU OUT SOMEHOW.
ACUT-ALLY...

ENTER. 33 PFFT!

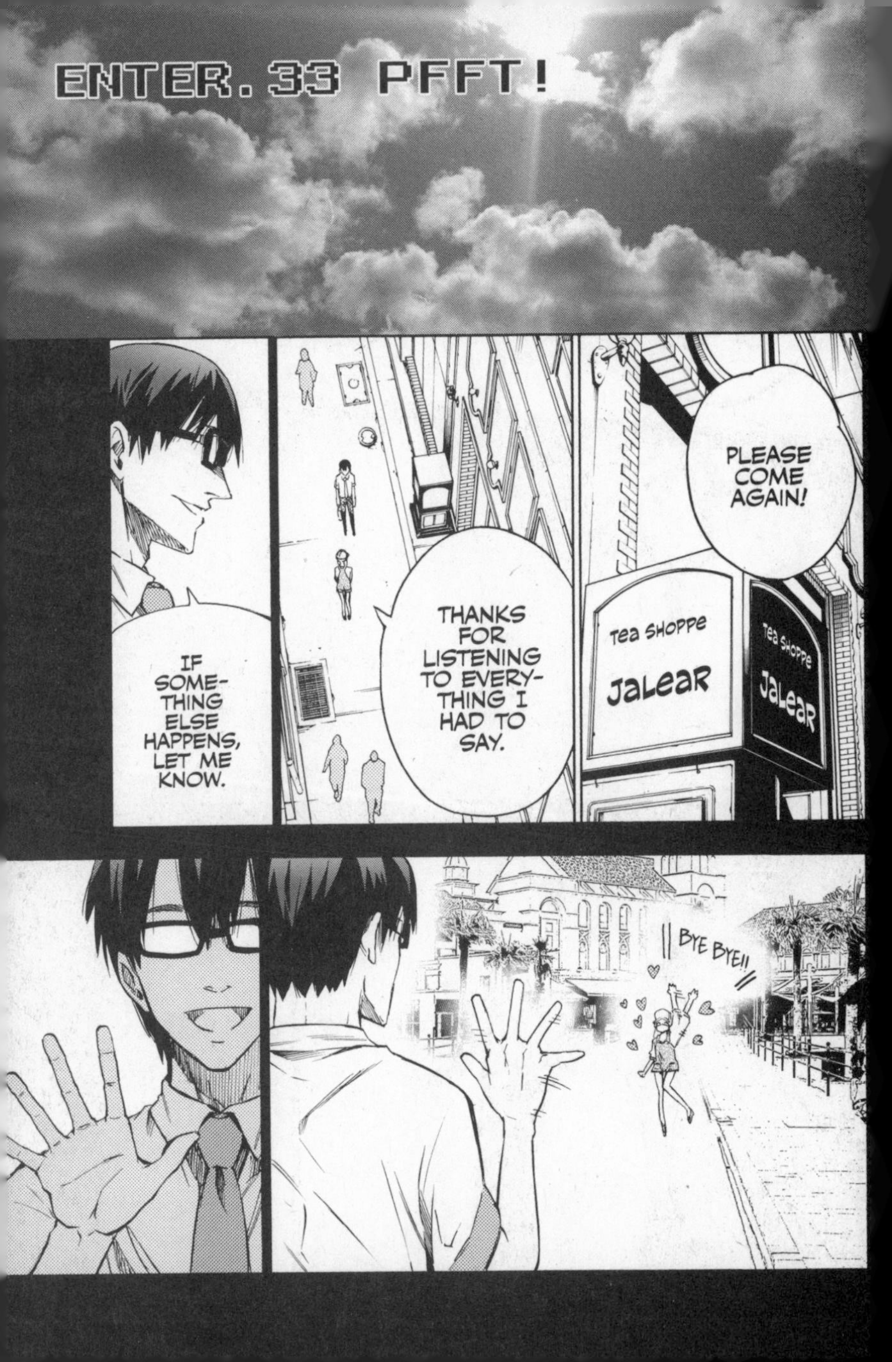

PLEASE COME AGAIN!
Tea SHOPPE JaLeaR
Tea SHOPPE JaLeaR
THANKS FOR LISTENING TO EVERY-THING I HAD TO SAY.
IF SOME-THING ELSE HAPPENS, LET ME KNOW.
BYE BYE!!

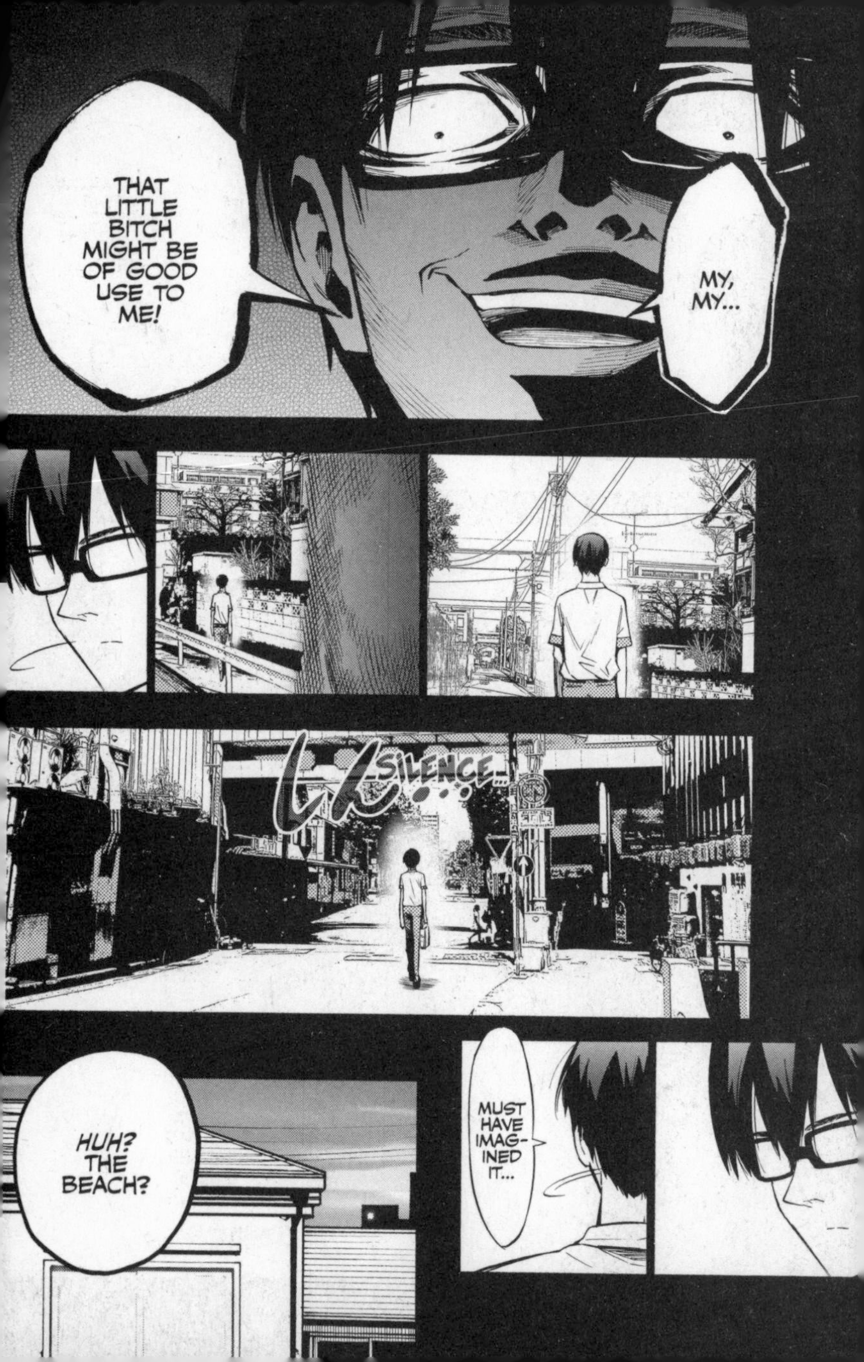
MY, MY...
THAT LITTLE BITCH MIGHT BE OF GOOD USE TO ME!
SILENCE...
MUST HAVE IMAG-INED IT...
HUH? THE BEACH?

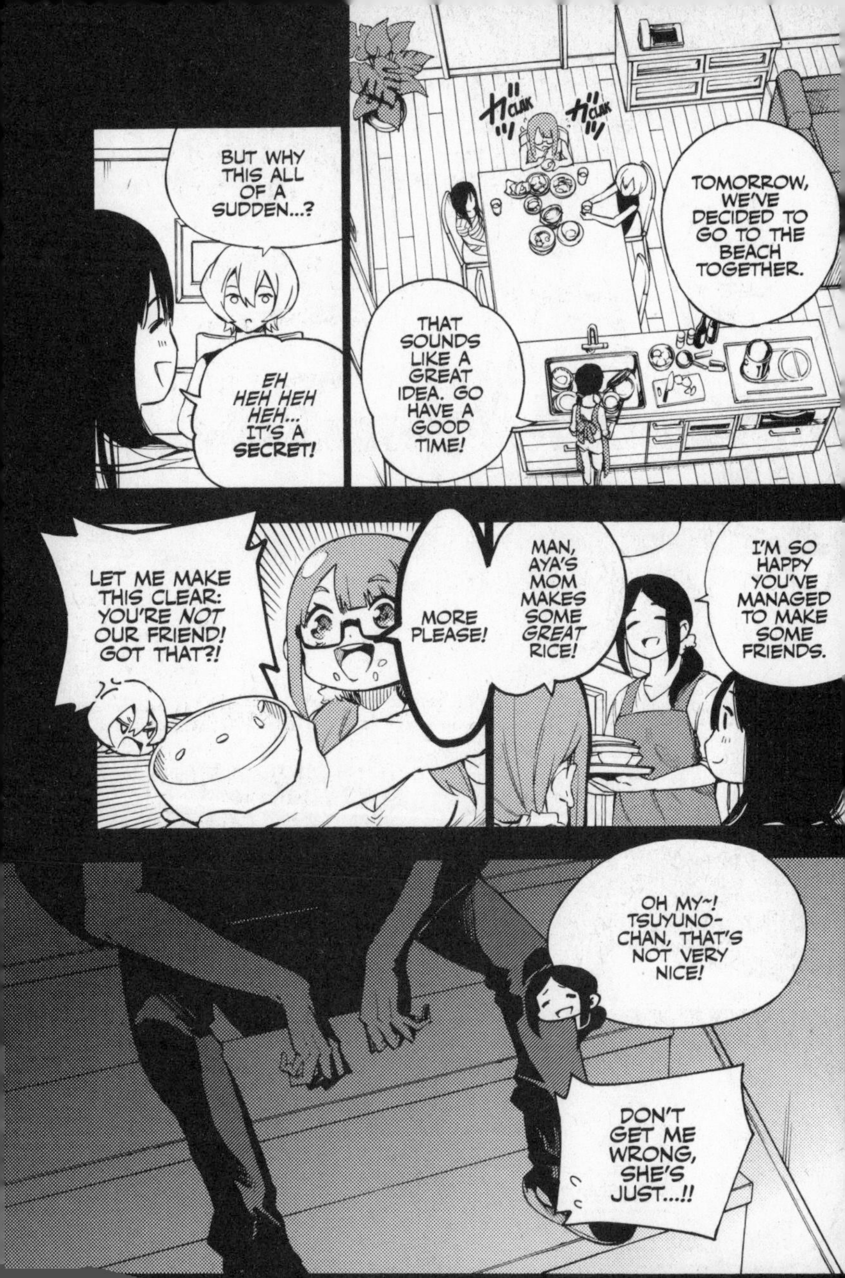
CLAK
CLAK
TOMORROW, WE'VE DECIDED TO GO TO THE BEACH TOGETHER.
THAT SOUNDS LIKE A GREAT IDEA. GO HAVE A GOOD TIME!
BUT WHY THIS ALL OF A SUDDEN...?
EH HEH HEH HEH... IT'S A SECRET!
I'M SO HAPPY YOU'VE MANAGED TO MAKE SOME FRIENDS.
MAN, AYA'S MOM MAKES SOME *GREAT* RICE!
MORE PLEASE!
LET ME MAKE THIS CLEAR: YOU'RE *NOT* OUR FRIEND! GOT THAT?!
OH MY~! TSUYUNO-CHAN, THAT'S NOT VERY NICE!
DON'T GET ME WRONG, SHE'S JUST...!!

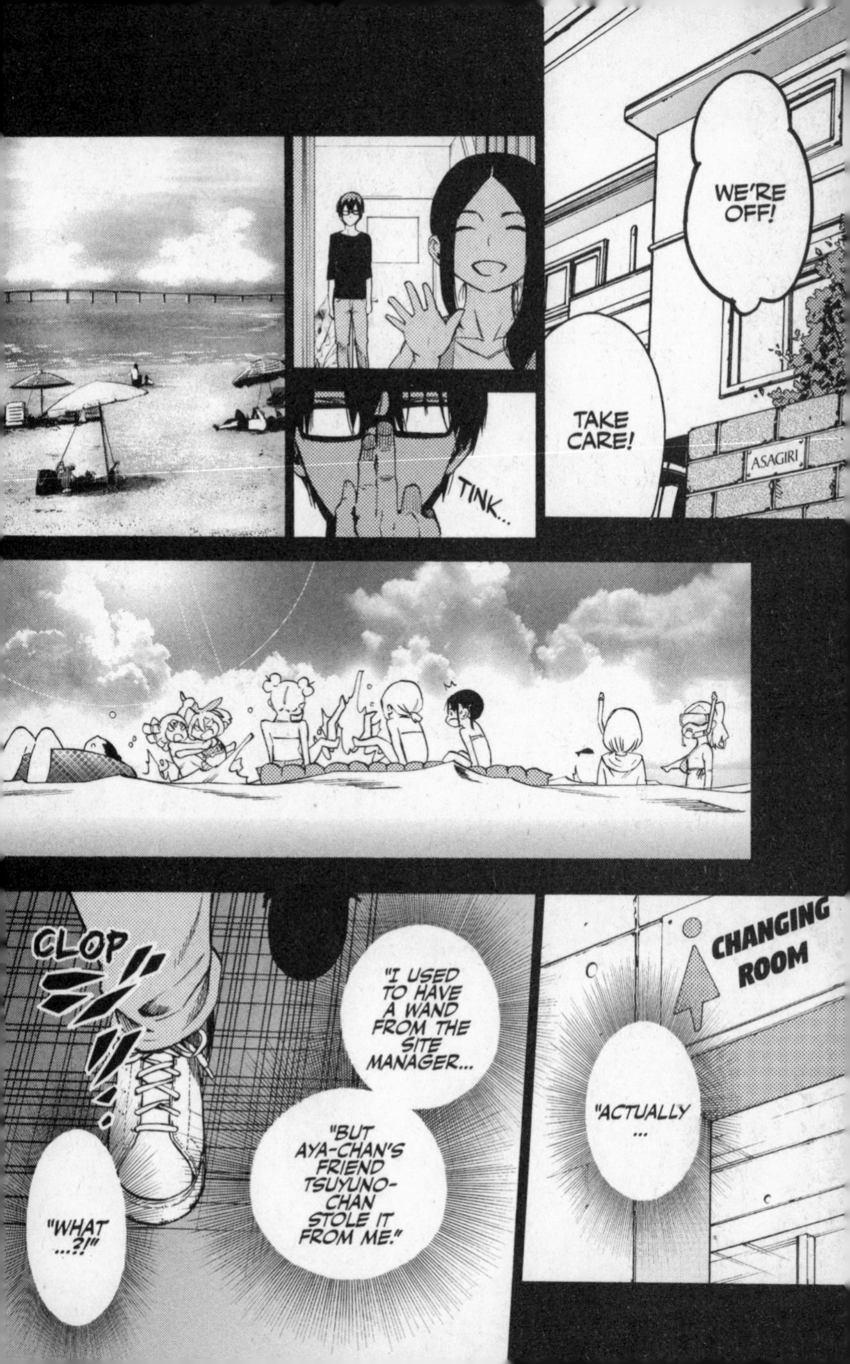
WE'RE OFF!
TAKE CARE!
ASAGIRI
TINK...
CHANGING ROOM
"ACTUALLY ...
"I USED TO HAVE A WAND FROM THE SITE MANAGER...
"BUT AYA-CHAN'S FRIEND TSUYUNO-CHAN STOLE IT FROM ME."
CLOP
"WHAT ...?!"

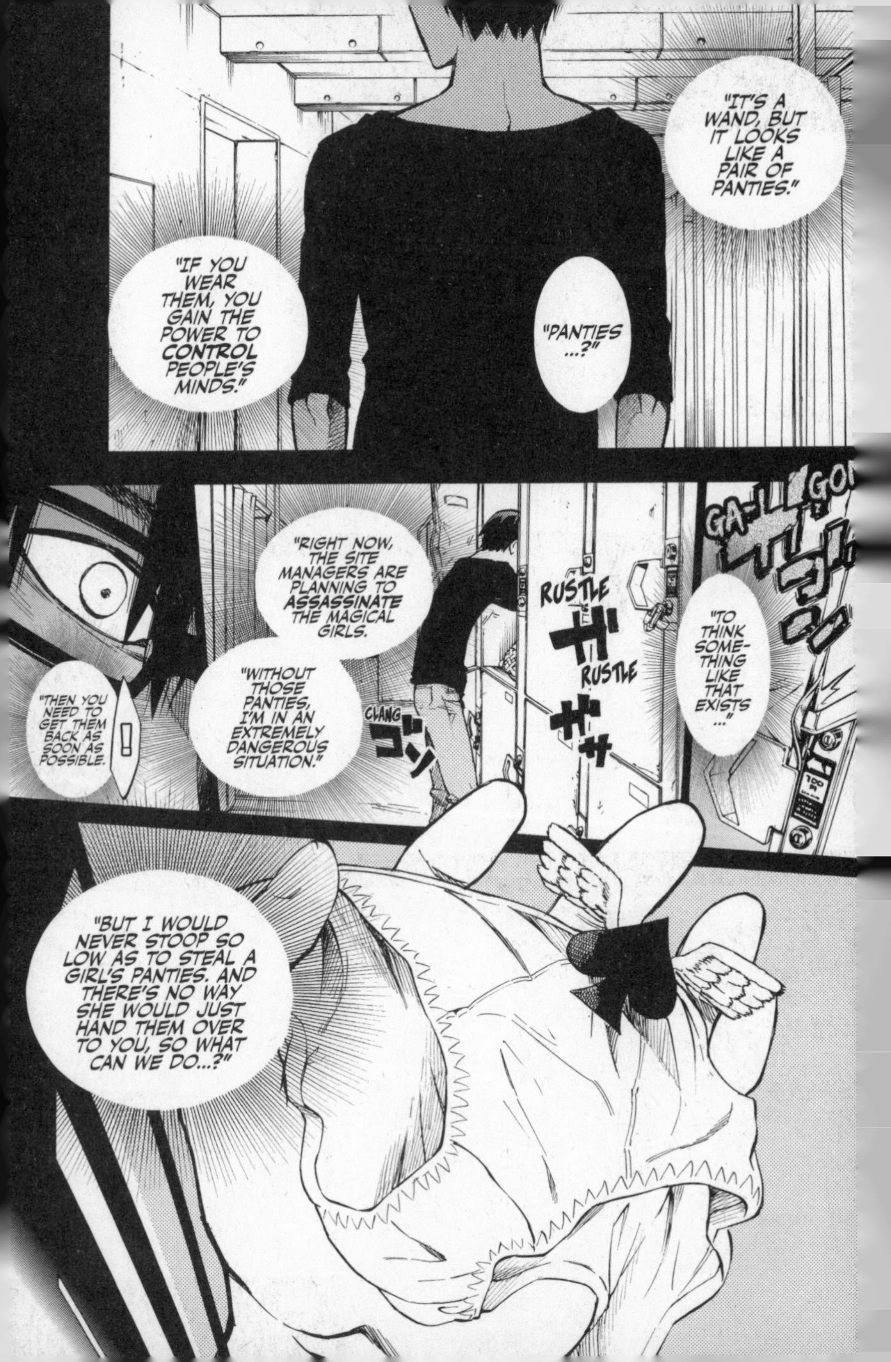
"IT'S A WAND, BUT IT LOOKS LIKE A PAIR OF PANTIES."
"PANTIES ...?"
"IF YOU WEAR THEM, YOU GAIN THE POWER TO CONTROL PEOPLE'S MINDS."
GA-L GO
"TO THINK SOME-THING LIKE THAT EXISTS ..."
RUSTLE
RUSTLE
"RIGHT NOW, THE SITE MANAGERS ARE PLANNING TO ASSASSINATE THE MAGICAL GIRLS.
"WITHOUT THOSE PANTIES, I'M IN AN EXTREMELY DANGEROUS SITUATION."
CLANG
!
"THEN YOU NEED TO GET THEM BACK AS SOON AS POSSIBLE.
"BUT I WOULD NEVER STOOP SO LOW AS TO STEAL A GIRL'S PANTIES. AND THERE'S NO WAY SHE WOULD JUST HAND THEM OVER TO YOU, SO WHAT CAN WE DO...?"

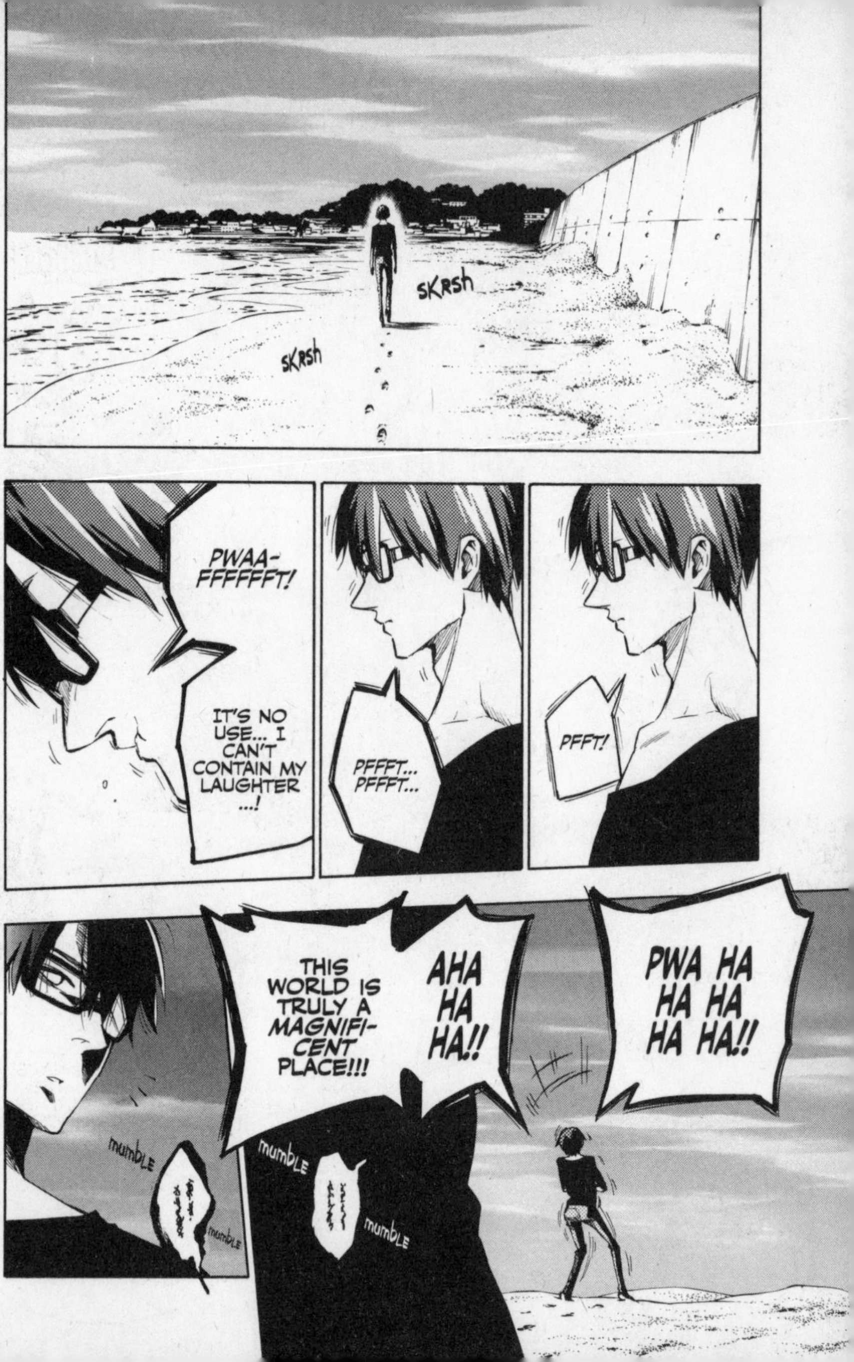
SKRSH
SKRSH
PFFT!
PFFFT... PFFFT...
PWAA-FFFFFFT!
IT'S NO USE... I CAN'T CONTAIN MY LAUGHTER ...!
PWA HA HA HA HA HA!!
AHA HA HA!!
THIS WORLD IS TRULY A MAGNIFI-CENT PLACE!!!
mumble
mumble
mumble
mumble

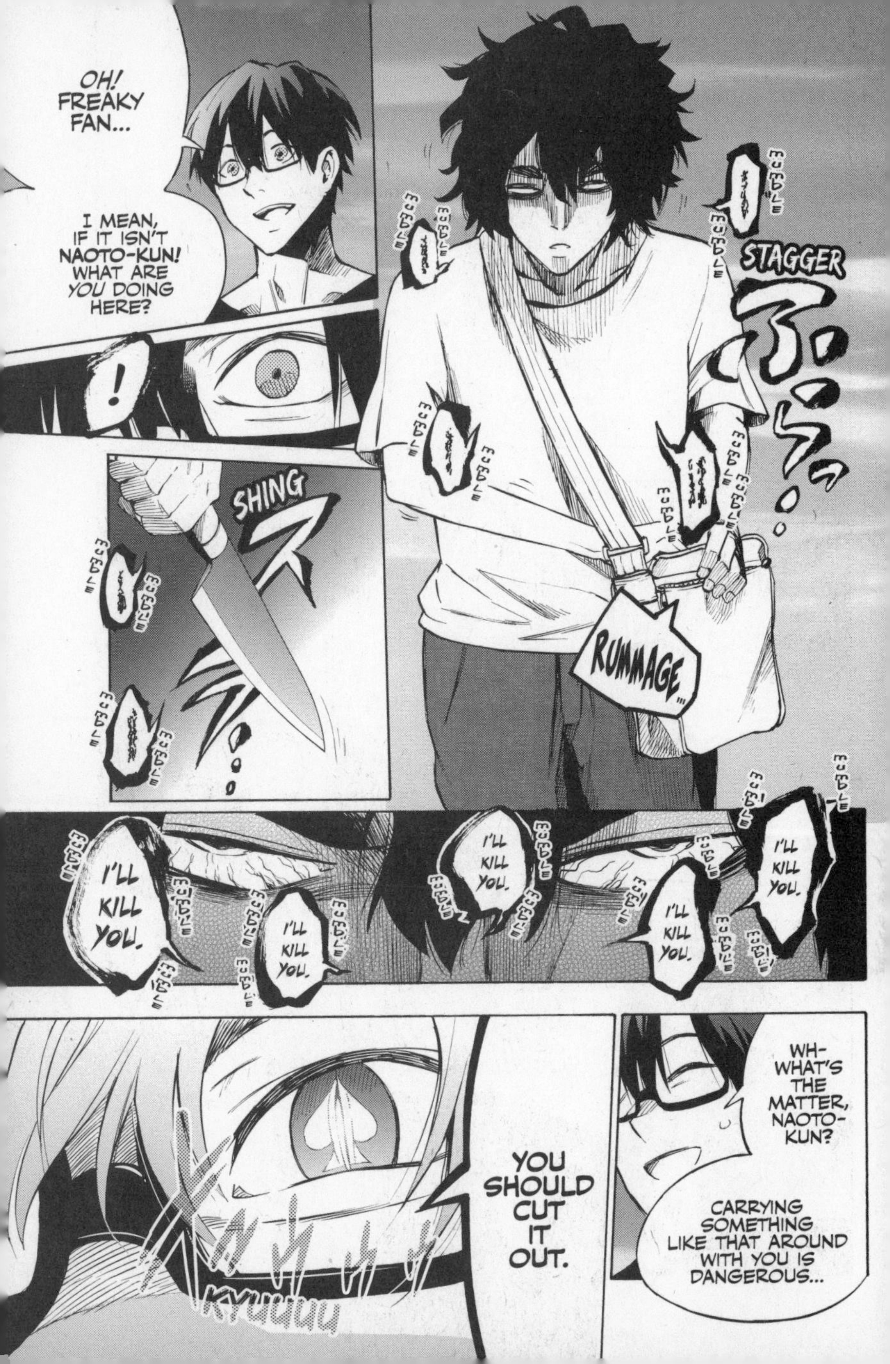

MUMBLE MUMBLE
STAGGER
MUMBLE MUMBLE
MUMBLE MUMBLE
RUMMAGE...
OH! FREAKY FAN...
I MEAN, IF IT ISN'T NAOTO-KUN! WHAT ARE YOU DOING HERE?
!
SHING
MUMBLE MUMBLE
MUMBLE MUMBLE
I'LL KILL YOU.
I'LL KILL YOU.
I'LL KILL YOU.
I'LL KILL YOU.
I'LL KILL YOU.
MUMBLE MUMBLE
WH-WHAT'S THE MATTER, NAOTO-KUN?
CARRYING SOMETHING LIKE THAT AROUND WITH YOU IS DANGEROUS...
YOU SHOULD CUT IT OUT.
KYUUUU

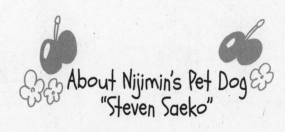

About Nijimin's Pet Dog "Steven Saeko"

A mysterious dog that suddenly appeared in the story.

Because Nijimi is usually busy with her idol career, it was being cared for at her family home.

This is why it was not there when Aya and Tsuyuno visited Nijimi in her penthouse suite.

Steven Saeko (3)
Chihuahua ♀
(Smooth Coat)

Pant
Pant

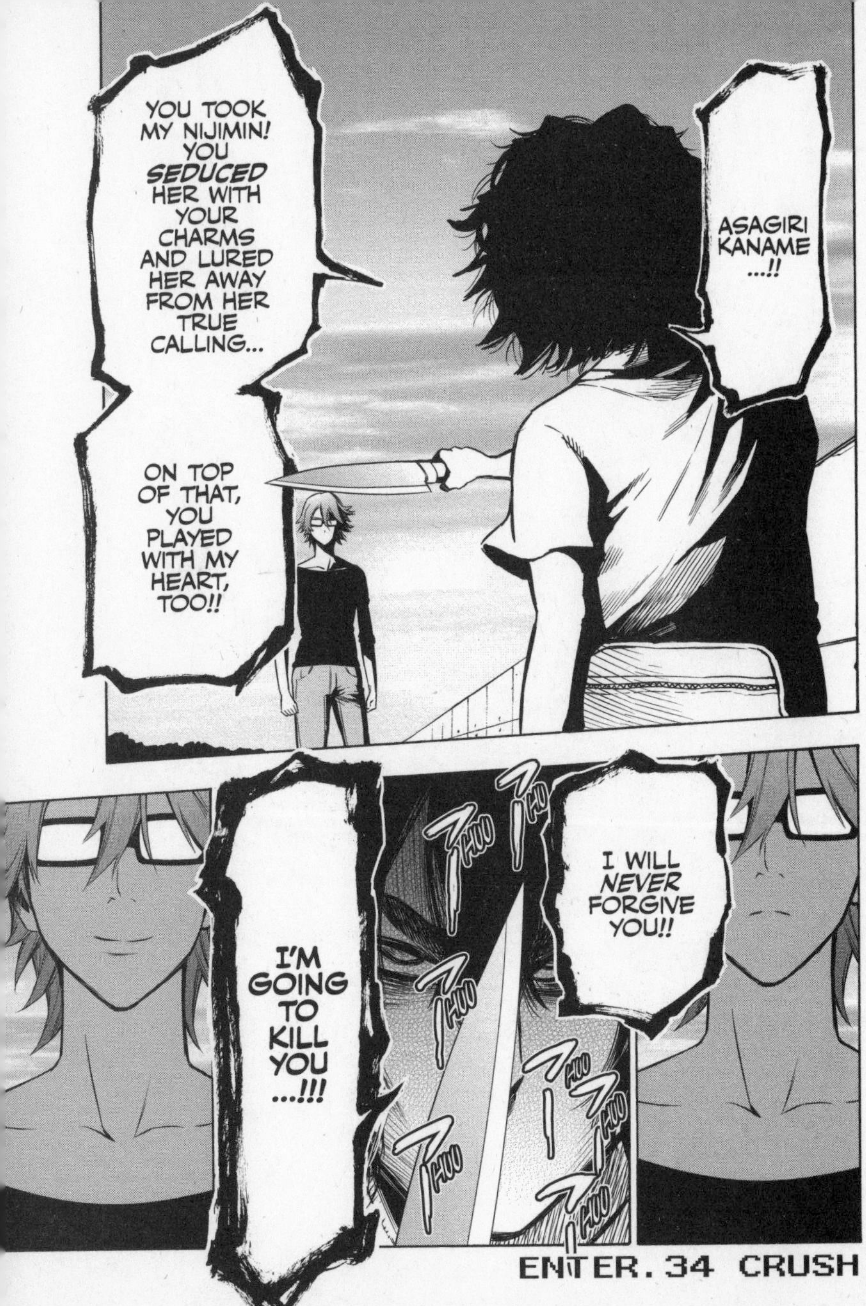
ASAGIRI KANAME ...!!
YOU TOOK MY NIJIMIN! YOU SEDUCED HER WITH YOUR CHARMS AND LURED HER AWAY FROM HER TRUE CALLING...
ON TOP OF THAT, YOU PLAYED WITH MY HEART, TOO!!
I WILL NEVER FORGIVE YOU!!
HOO
HOO
HOO
HOO
HOO
HOO
HOO
HOO
I'M GOING TO KILL YOU ...!!!

ENTER. 34 CRUSH

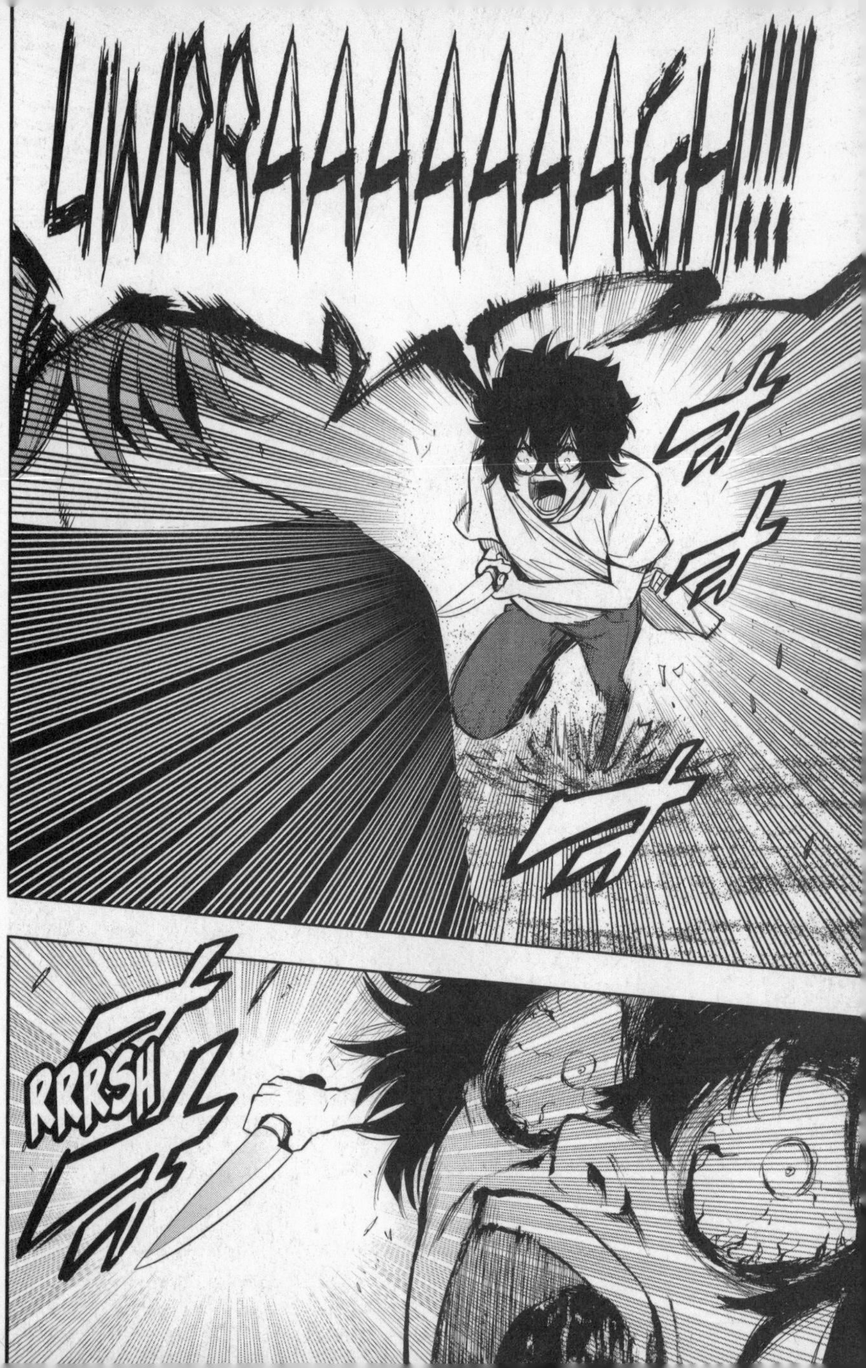
UWRRAAAAAAAGH!!!
RRRSH

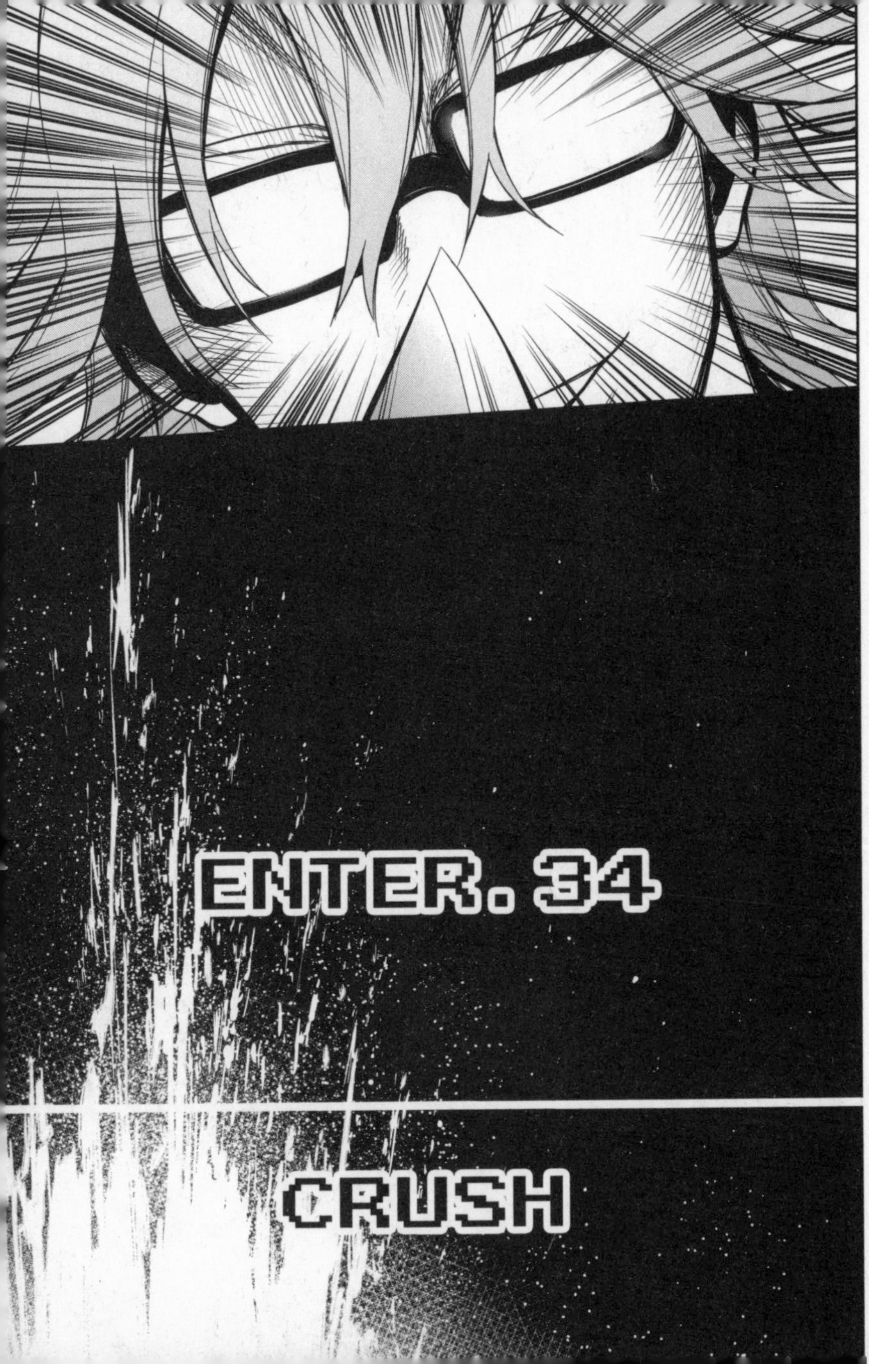
ENTER. 34
CRUSH

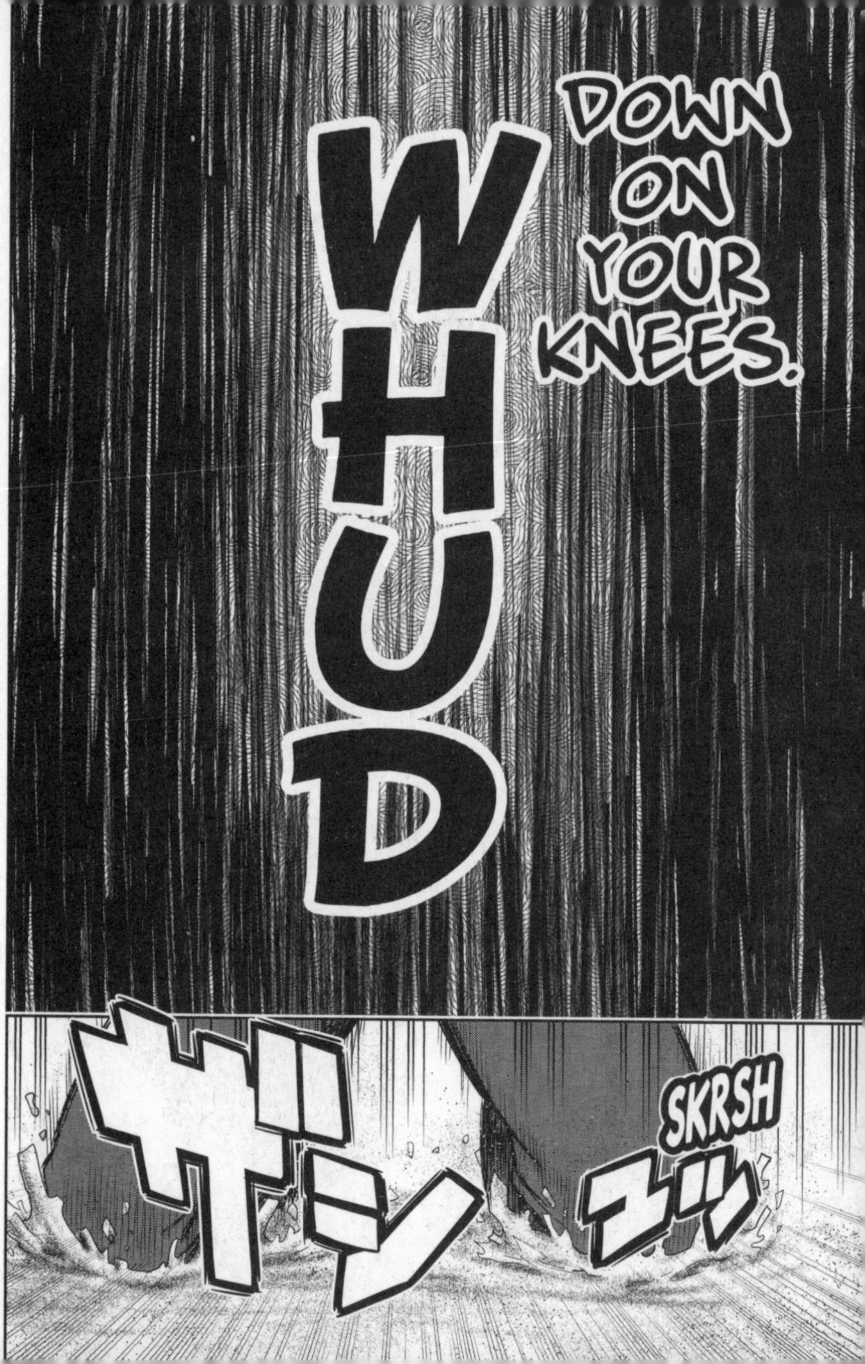
DOWN ON YOUR KNEES.
WHUD
SKRSH

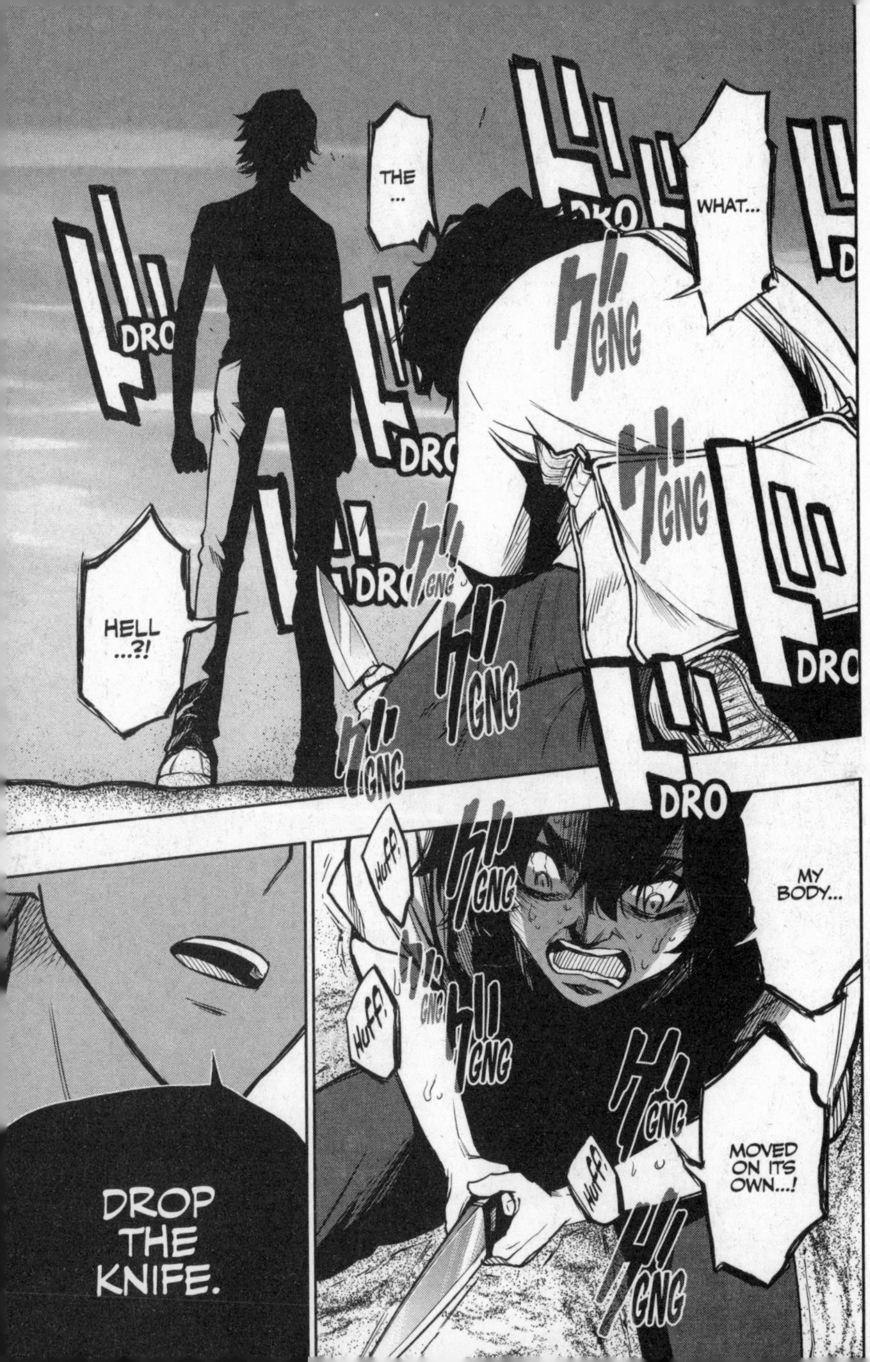

DRO
WHAT...
GNG
GNG
DRO
THE ...
DRO
DRO
GNG
HELL ...?!
GNG
GNG
DRO
MY BODY...
HUFF!
GNG
HUFF!
GNG
GNG
MOVED ON ITS OWN...!
HUFF!
GNG
DROP THE KNIFE.

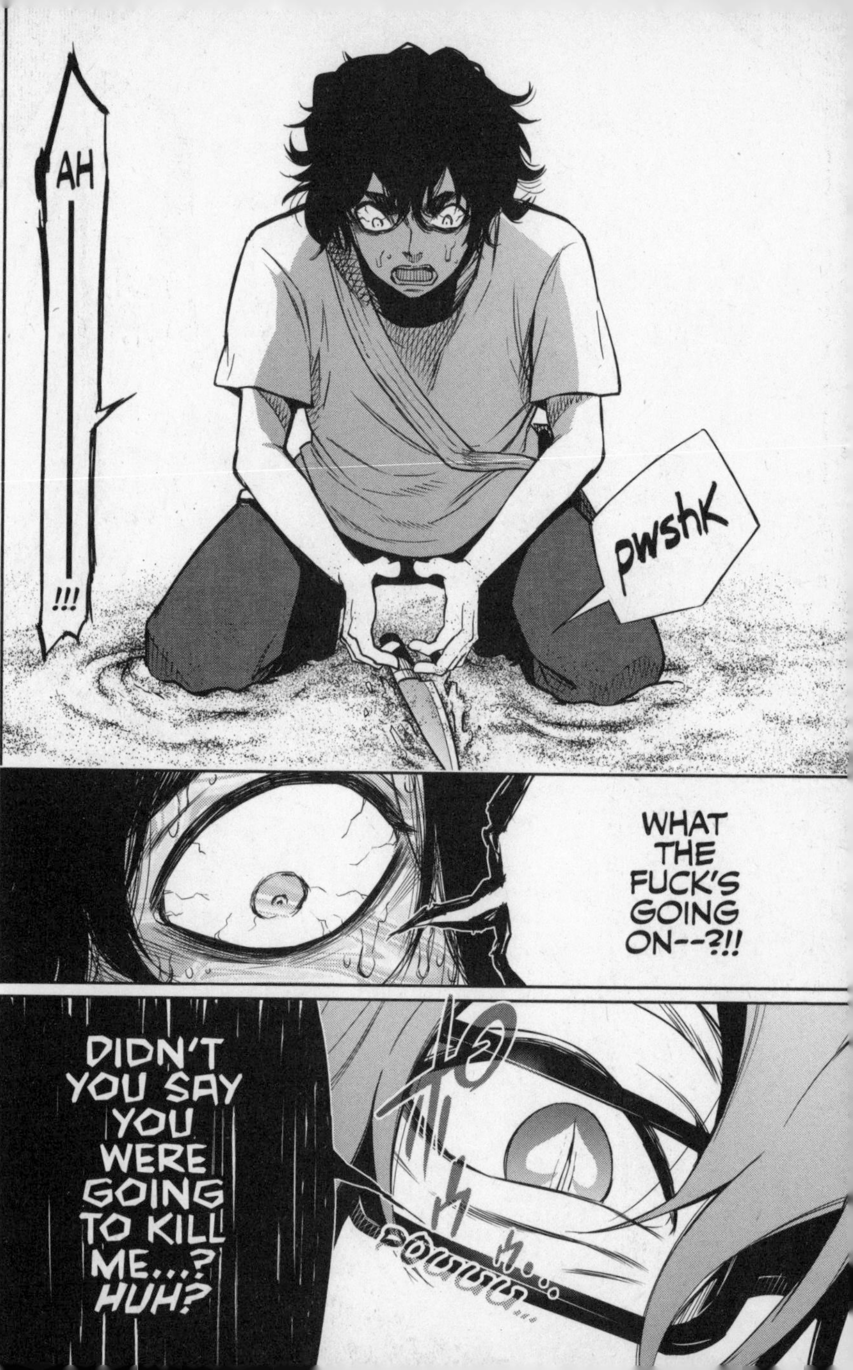
pwshK
AH ——!!!
WHAT THE FUCK'S GOING ON--?!!
DIDN'T YOU SAY YOU WERE GOING TO KILL ME...? HUH?

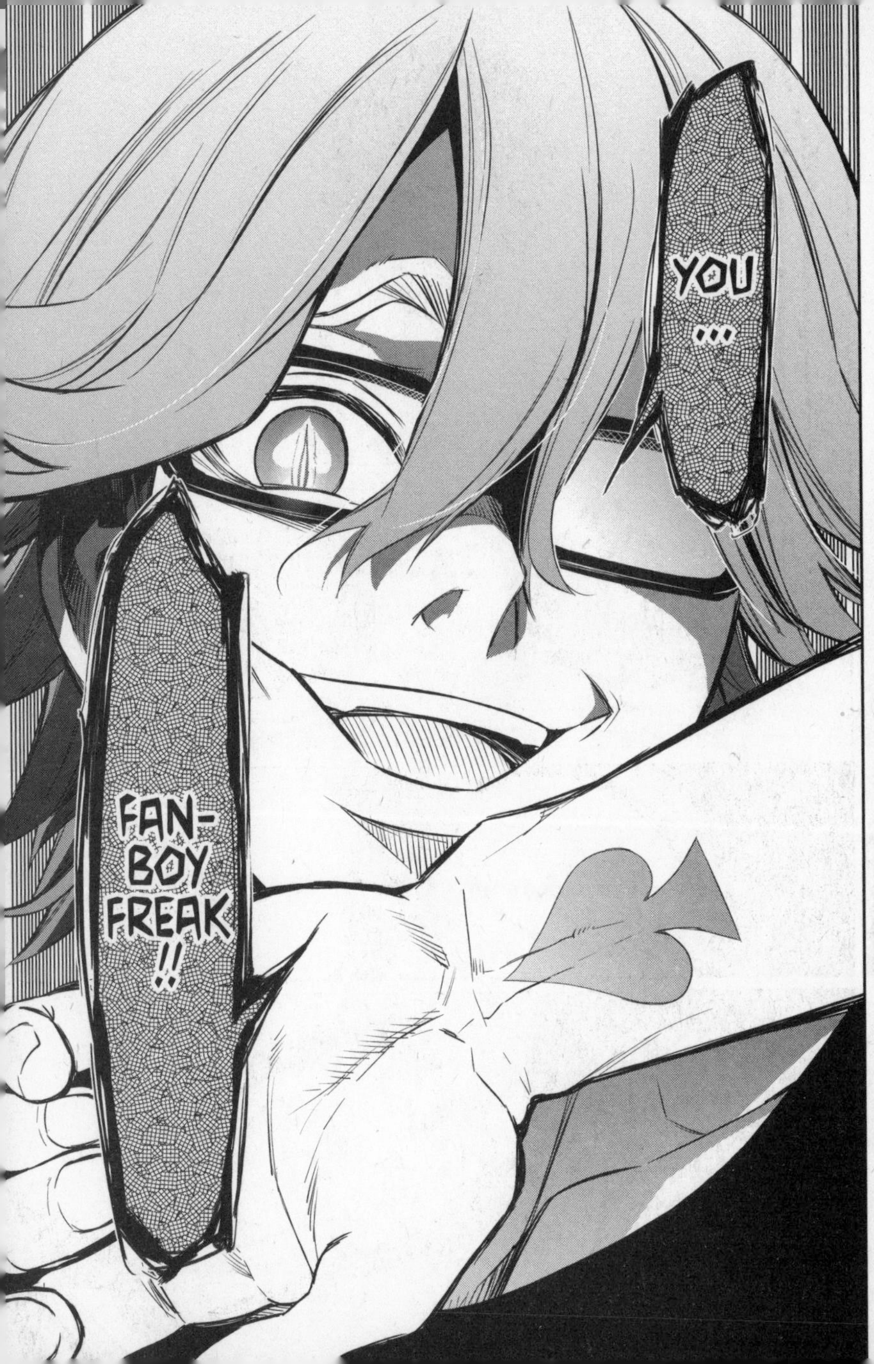
YOU ...
FAN-BOY FREAK!!

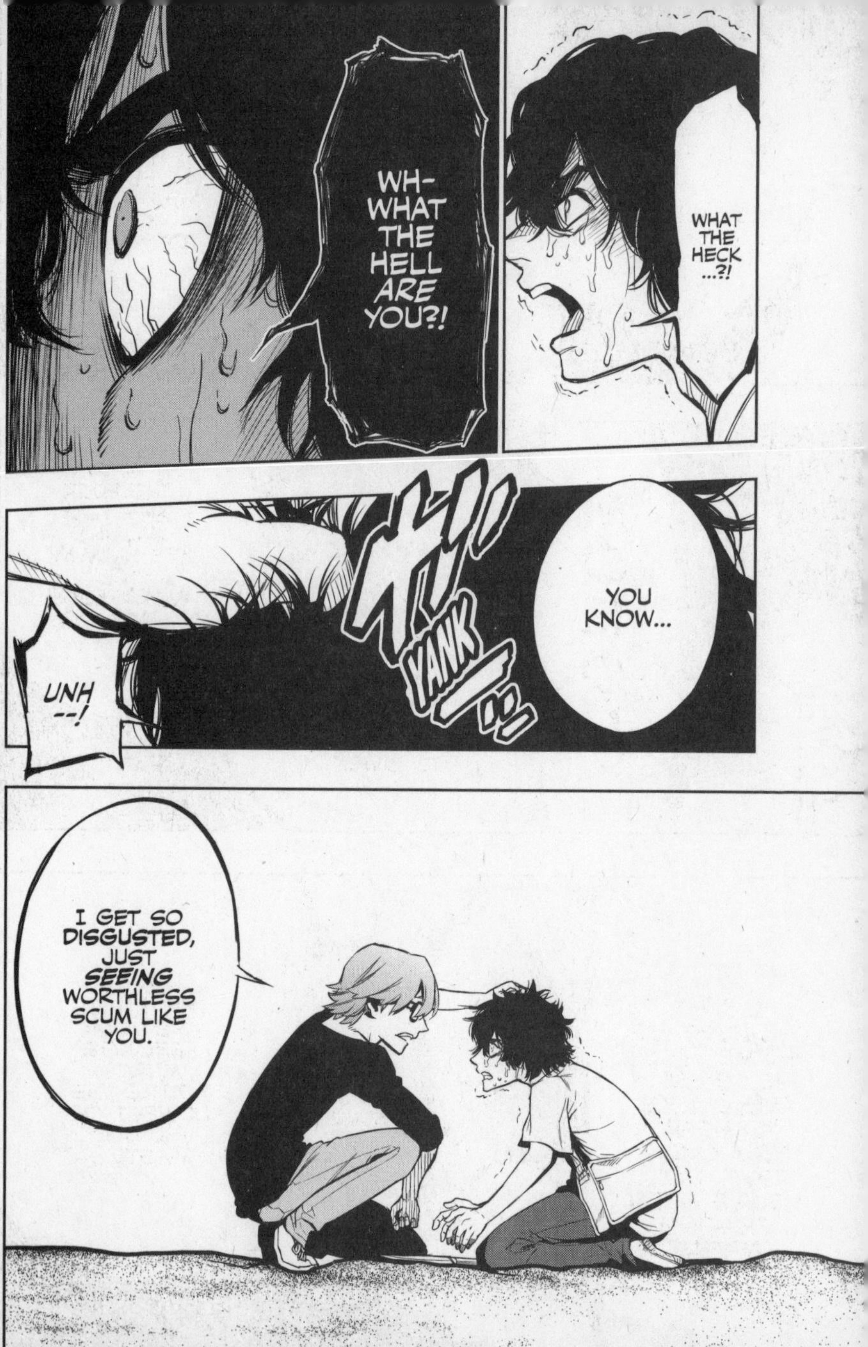
WHAT THE HECK ...?!
WH- WHAT THE HELL ARE YOU?!
YOU KNOW...
YANK
UNH --!
I GET SO DISGUSTED, JUST SEEING WORTHLESS SCUM LIKE YOU.

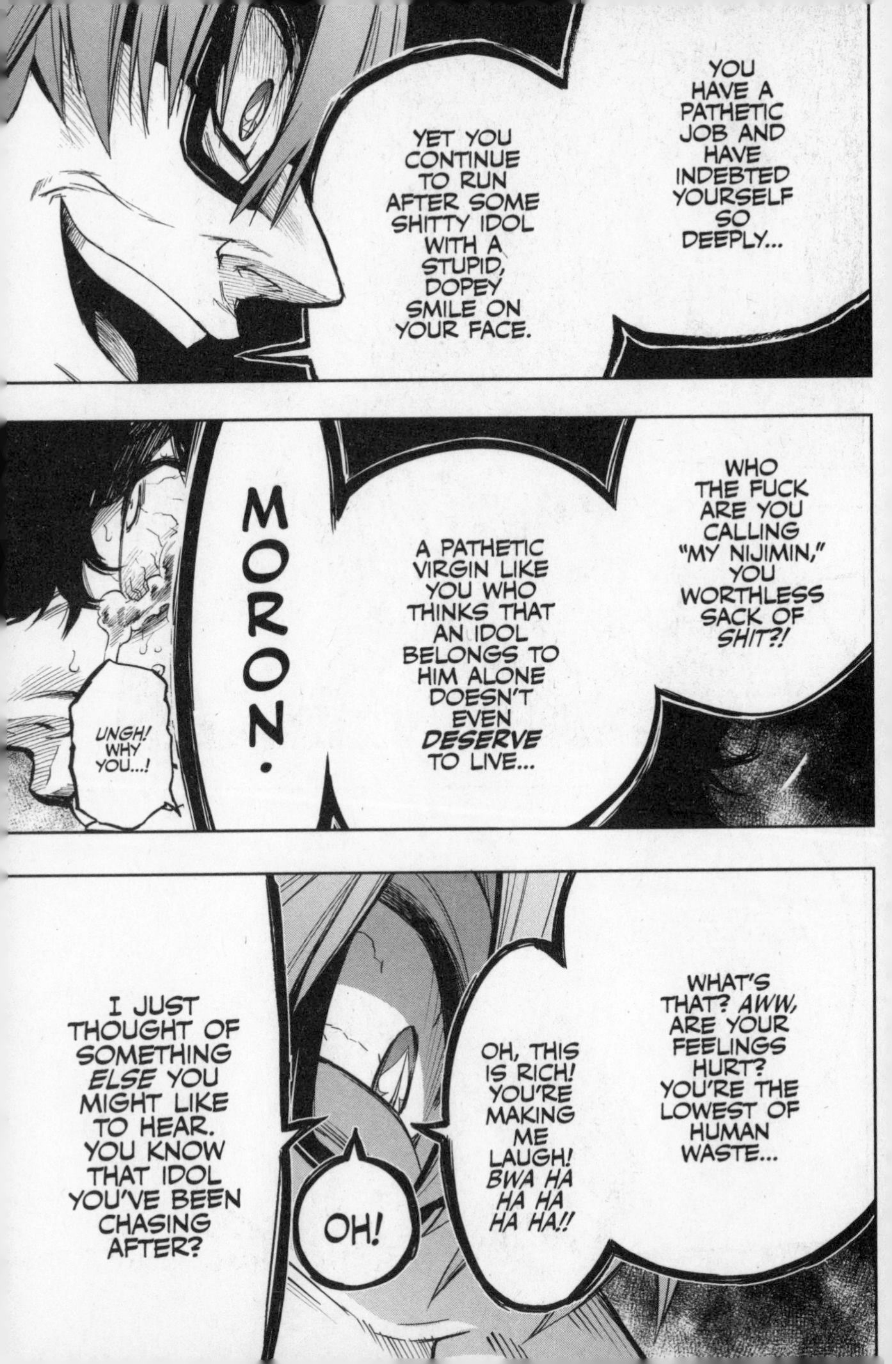
YOU HAVE A PATHETIC JOB AND HAVE INDEBTED YOURSELF SO DEEPLY...
YET YOU CONTINUE TO RUN AFTER SOME SHITTY IDOL WITH A STUPID, DOPEY SMILE ON YOUR FACE.
WHO THE FUCK ARE YOU CALLING "MY NIJIMIN," YOU WORTHLESS SACK OF *SHIT*?!
A PATHETIC VIRGIN LIKE YOU WHO THINKS THAT AN IDOL BELONGS TO HIM ALONE DOESN'T EVEN *DESERVE* TO LIVE...
MORON.
UNGH! WHY YOU...!
WHAT'S THAT? *AWW,* ARE YOUR FEELINGS HURT? YOU'RE THE LOWEST OF HUMAN WASTE...
OH, THIS IS RICH! YOU'RE MAKING ME LAUGH! *BWA HA HA HA HA HA!!*
OH!
I JUST THOUGHT OF SOMETHING *ELSE* YOU MIGHT LIKE TO HEAR. YOU KNOW THAT IDOL YOU'VE BEEN CHASING AFTER?

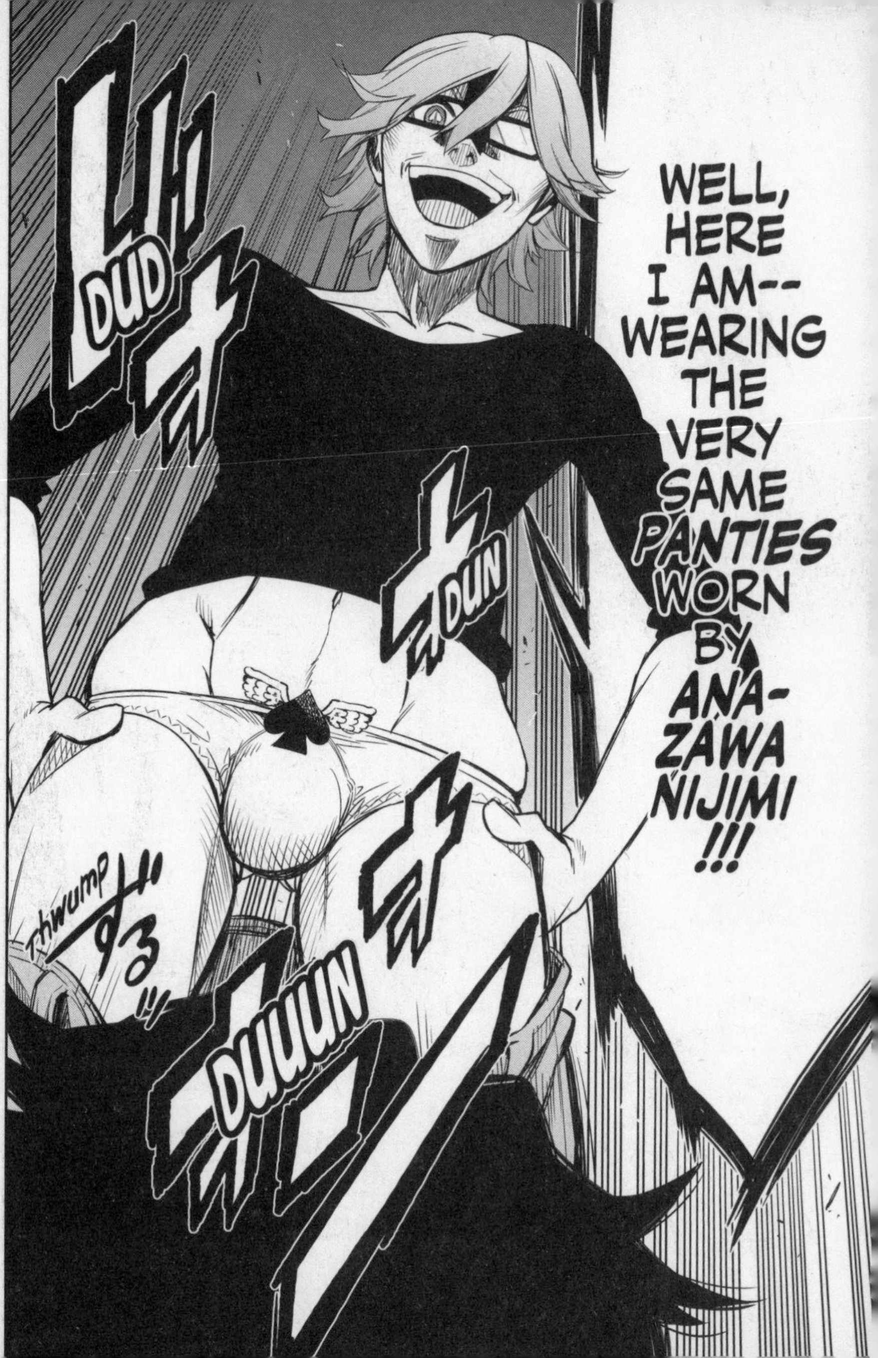
WELL, HERE I AM-- WEARING THE VERY SAME PANTIES WORN BY ANAZAWA NIJIMI!!!
DUD
DUN
thwump
DUUUN

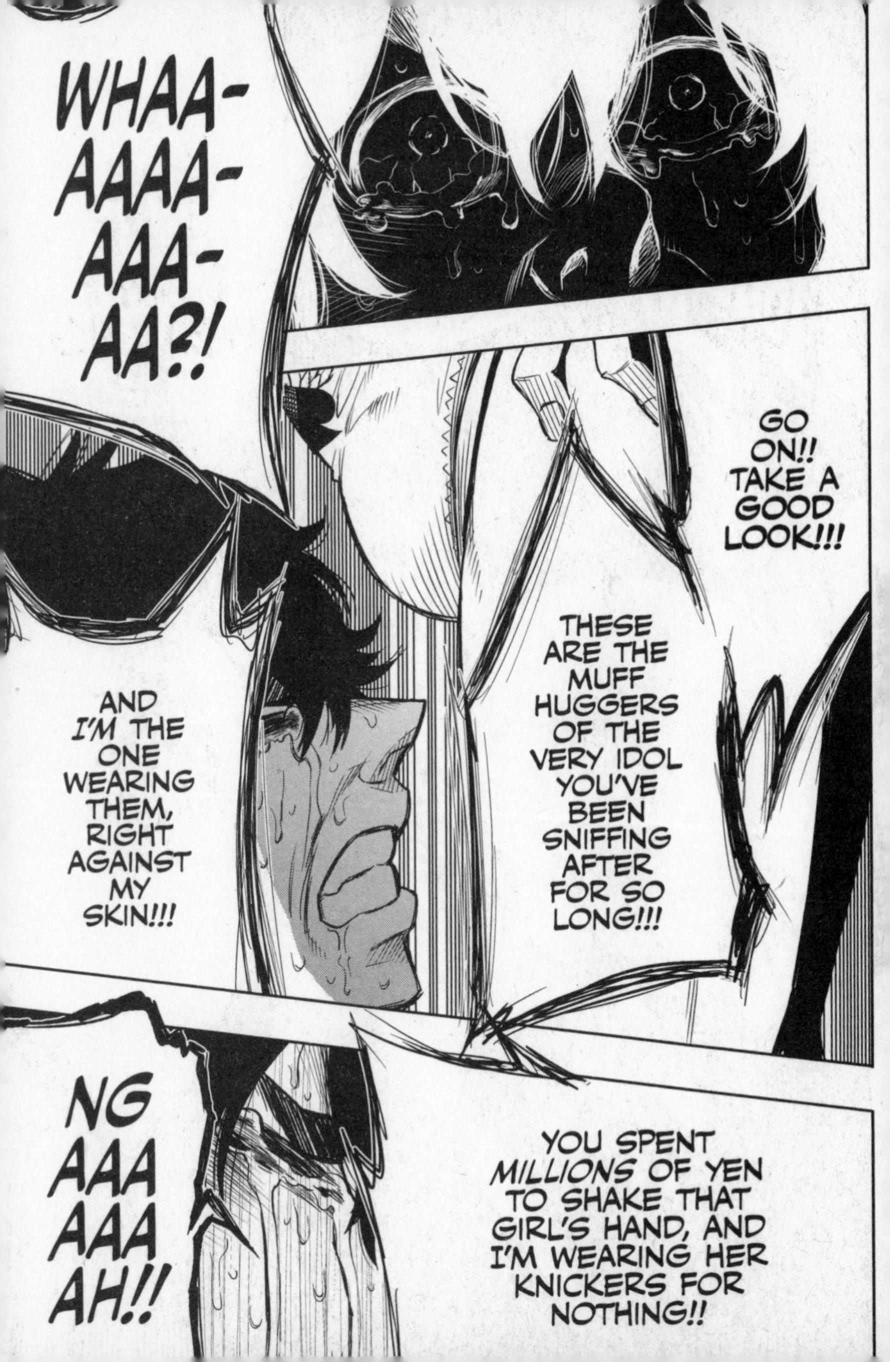

WHAA-AAAA-AAA-AA?!
GO ON!! TAKE A GOOD LOOK!!!
THESE ARE THE MUFF HUGGERS OF THE VERY IDOL YOU'VE BEEN SNIFFING AFTER FOR SO LONG!!!
AND *I'M* THE ONE WEARING THEM, RIGHT AGAINST MY SKIN!!!
YOU SPENT *MILLIONS* OF YEN TO SHAKE THAT GIRL'S HAND, AND I'M WEARING HER KNICKERS FOR NOTHING!!
NG AAA AAA AH!!

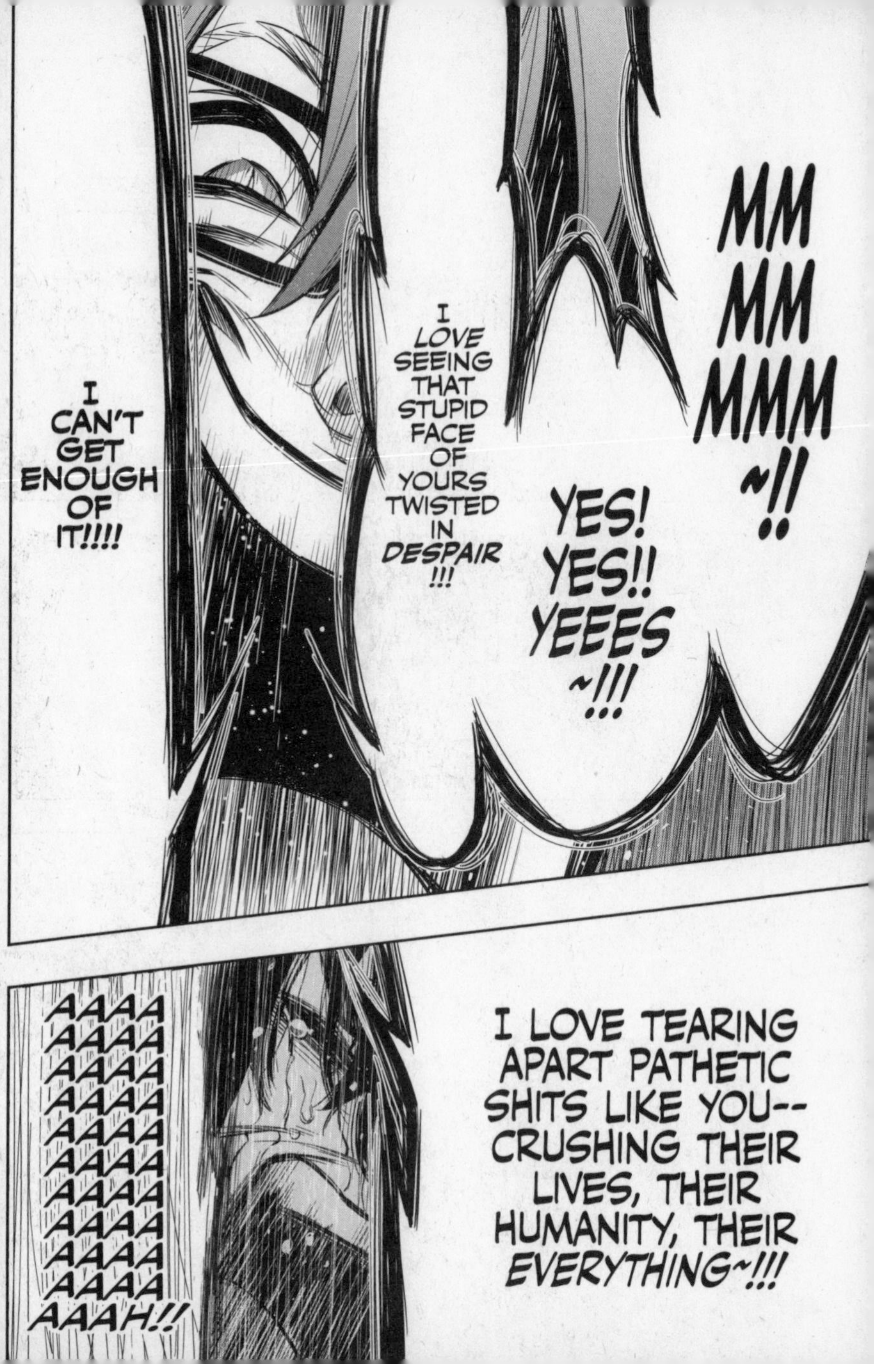
MMMMMMM~!!
YES! YES!! YEEES~!!!
I LOVE SEEING THAT STUPID FACE OF YOURS TWISTED IN DESPAIR!!!
I CAN'T GET ENOUGH OF IT!!!!
I LOVE TEARING APART PATHETIC SHITS LIKE YOU-- CRUSHING THEIR LIVES, THEIR HUMANITY, THEIR EVERYTHING~!!!
AAAAAAAAAAAAAAAAAAAAAAAAAAAAAAAAAAAAAAAAAAAAAAAAAH!!

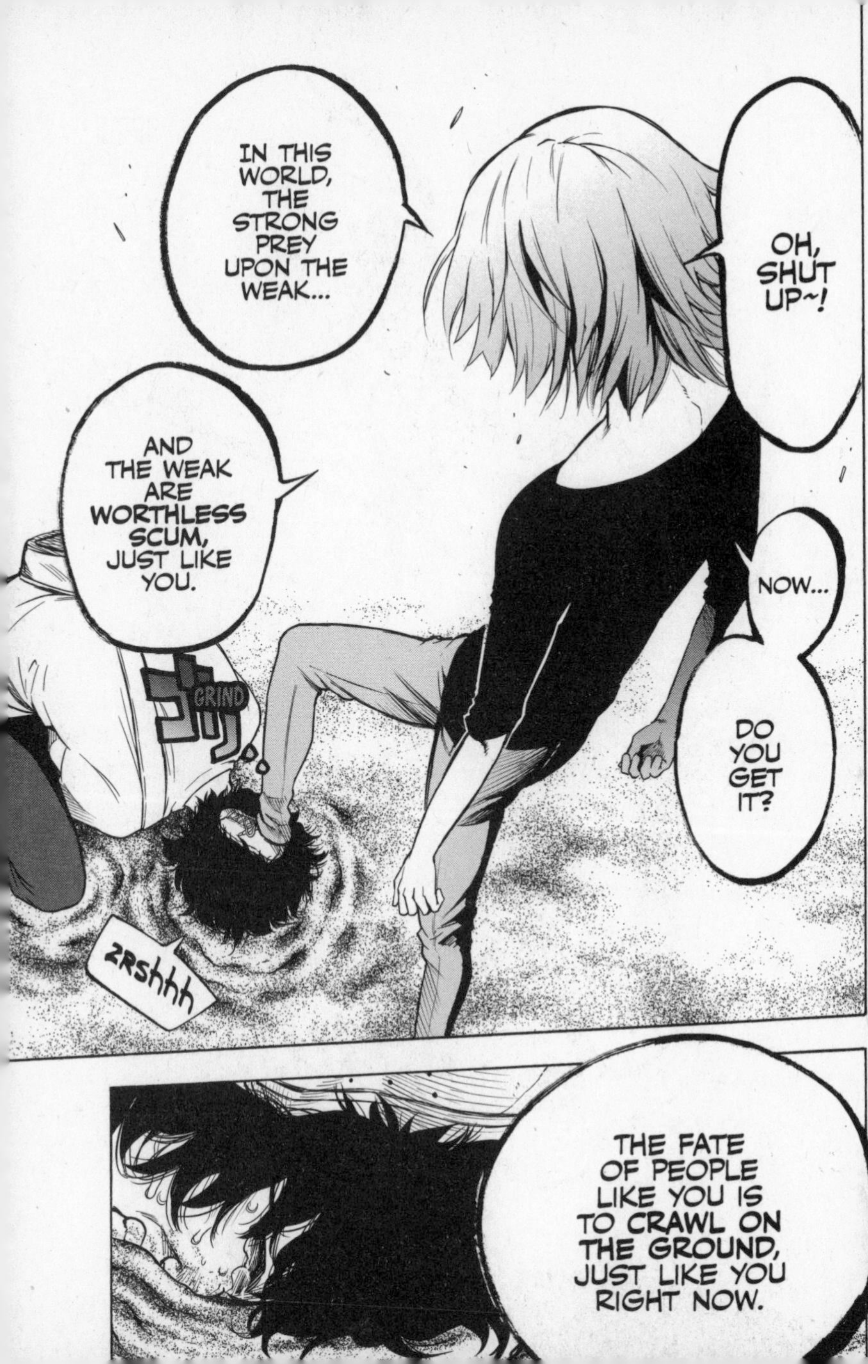
OH, SHUT UP~!
NOW...
DO YOU GET IT?
IN THIS WORLD, THE STRONG PREY UPON THE WEAK...
AND THE WEAK ARE WORTHLESS SCUM, JUST LIKE YOU.
GRIND
zrshhh
THE FATE OF PEOPLE LIKE YOU IS TO CRAWL ON THE GROUND, JUST LIKE YOU RIGHT NOW.

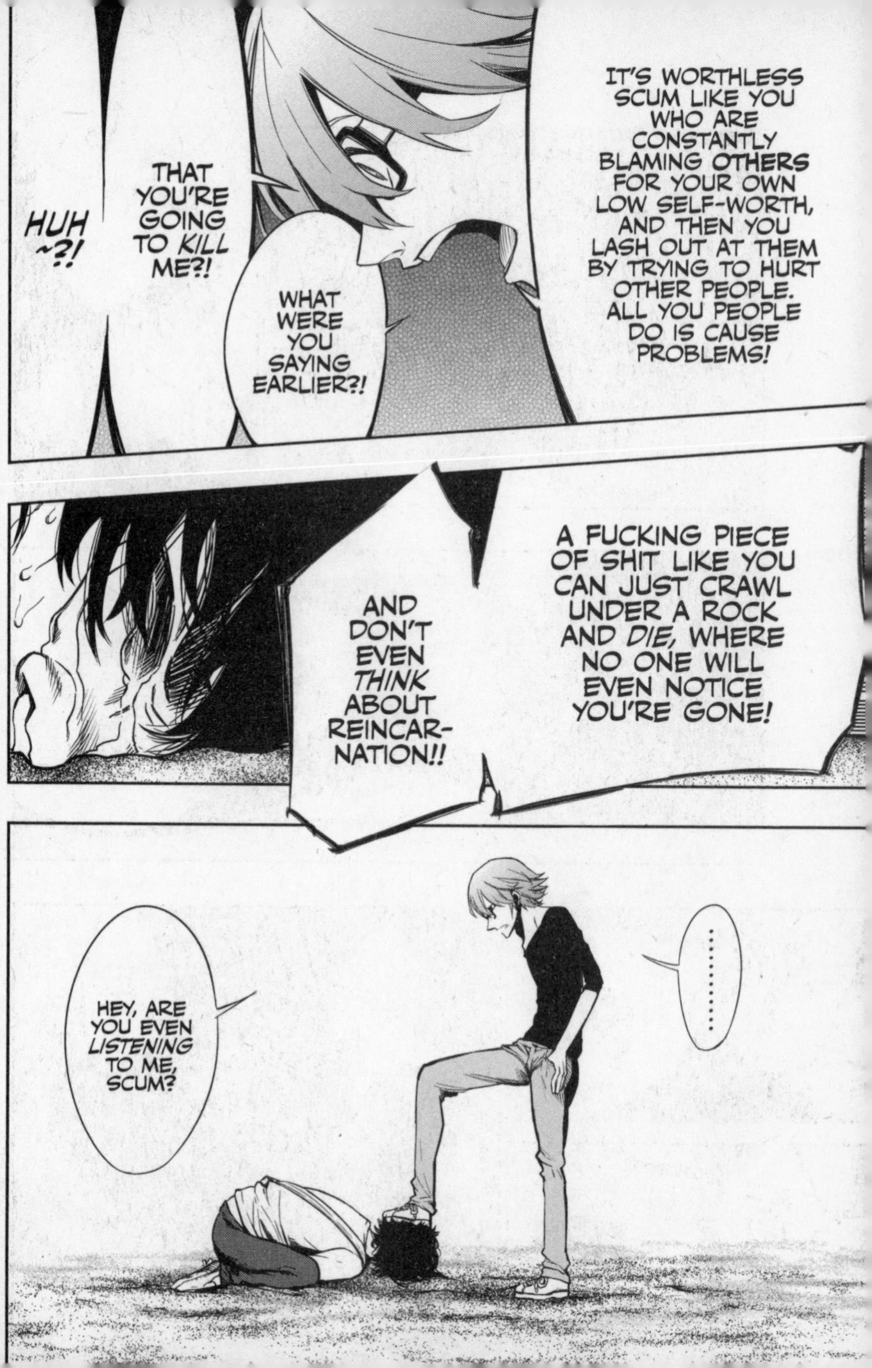
IT'S WORTHLESS SCUM LIKE YOU WHO ARE CONSTANTLY BLAMING OTHERS FOR YOUR OWN LOW SELF-WORTH, AND THEN YOU LASH OUT AT THEM BY TRYING TO HURT OTHER PEOPLE. ALL YOU PEOPLE DO IS CAUSE PROBLEMS!
WHAT WERE YOU SAYING EARLIER?!
THAT YOU'RE GOING TO KILL ME?!
HUH~?!
A FUCKING PIECE OF SHIT LIKE YOU CAN JUST CRAWL UNDER A ROCK AND DIE, WHERE NO ONE WILL EVEN NOTICE YOU'RE GONE!
AND DON'T EVEN THINK ABOUT REINCAR-NATION!!
....
HEY, ARE YOU EVEN LISTENING TO ME, SCUM?

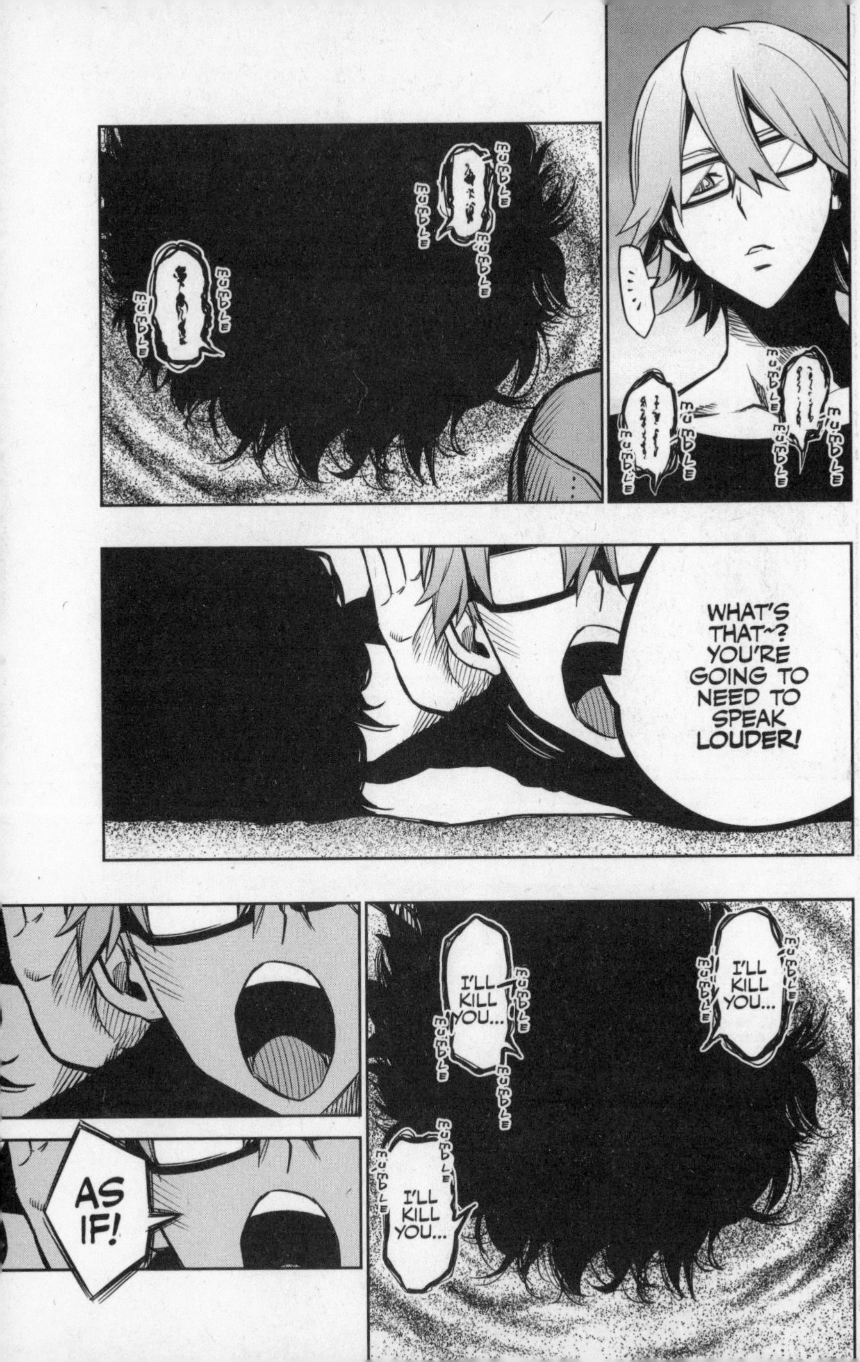

...
MUMBLE MUMBLE
MUMBLE MUMBLE
MUMBLE MUMBLE
MUMBLE MUMBLE
WHAT'S THAT~? YOU'RE GOING TO NEED TO SPEAK LOUDER!
MUMBLE MUMBLE
I'LL KILL YOU...
MUMBLE MUMBLE
I'LL KILL YOU...
MUMBLE MUMBLE
I'LL KILL YOU...
AS IF!

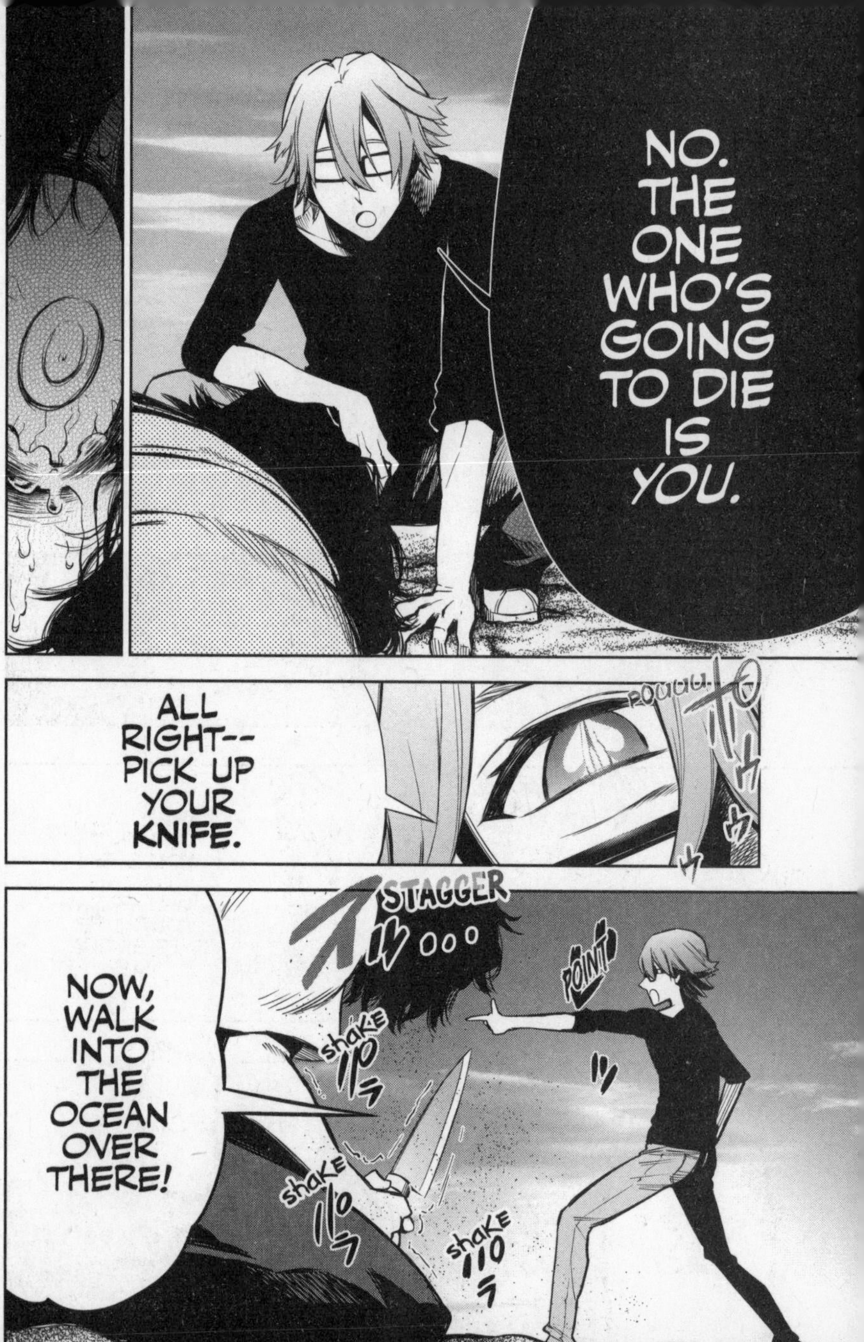
NO. THE ONE WHO'S GOING TO DIE IS YOU.
POUUU...
ALL RIGHT-- PICK UP YOUR KNIFE.
STAGGER
POINT
NOW, WALK INTO THE OCEAN OVER THERE!
shake
shake
shake

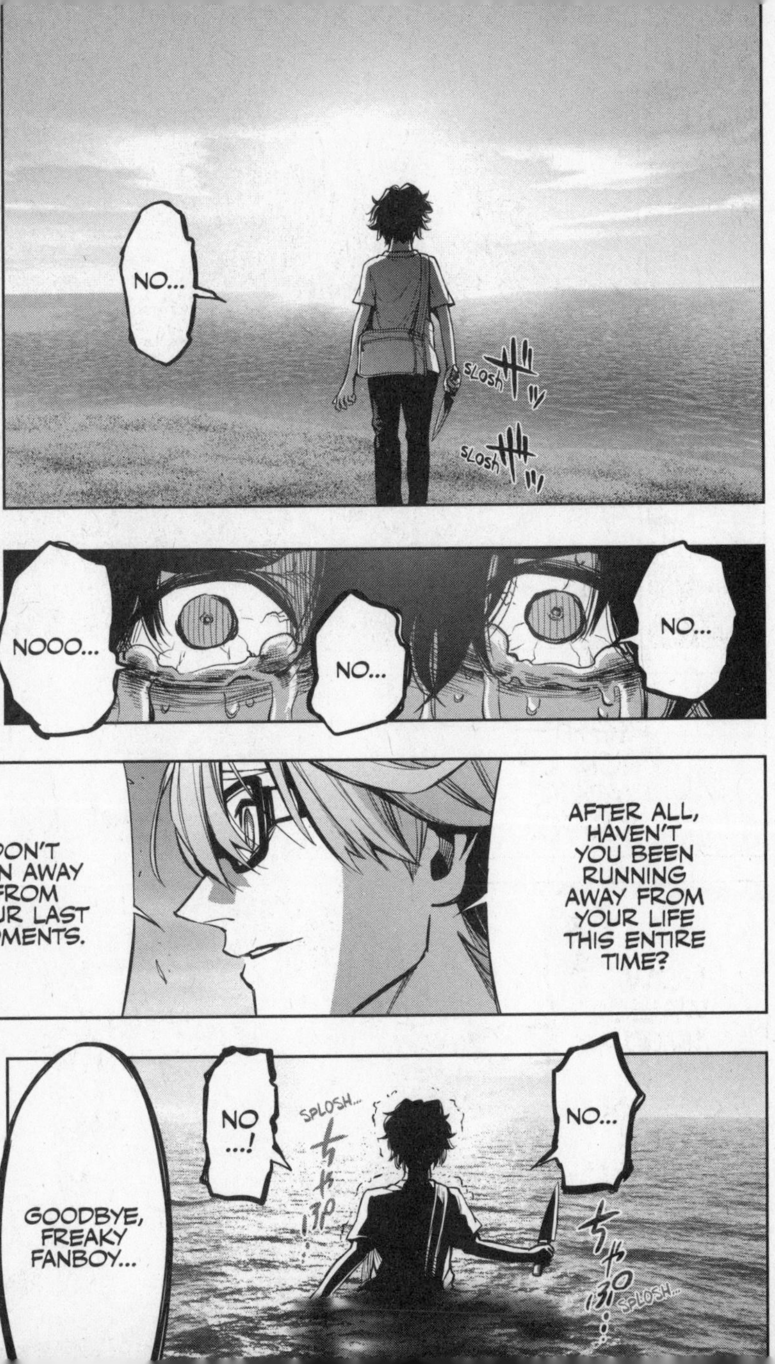

NO...
SLOSH
SLOSH
NO...
NO...
NOOO...
AFTER ALL, HAVEN'T YOU BEEN RUNNING AWAY FROM YOUR LIFE THIS ENTIRE TIME?
DON'T RUN AWAY FROM YOUR LAST MOMENTS.
NO...
SPLOSH...
SPLOSH...
NO ...!
GOODBYE, FREAKY FANBOY...

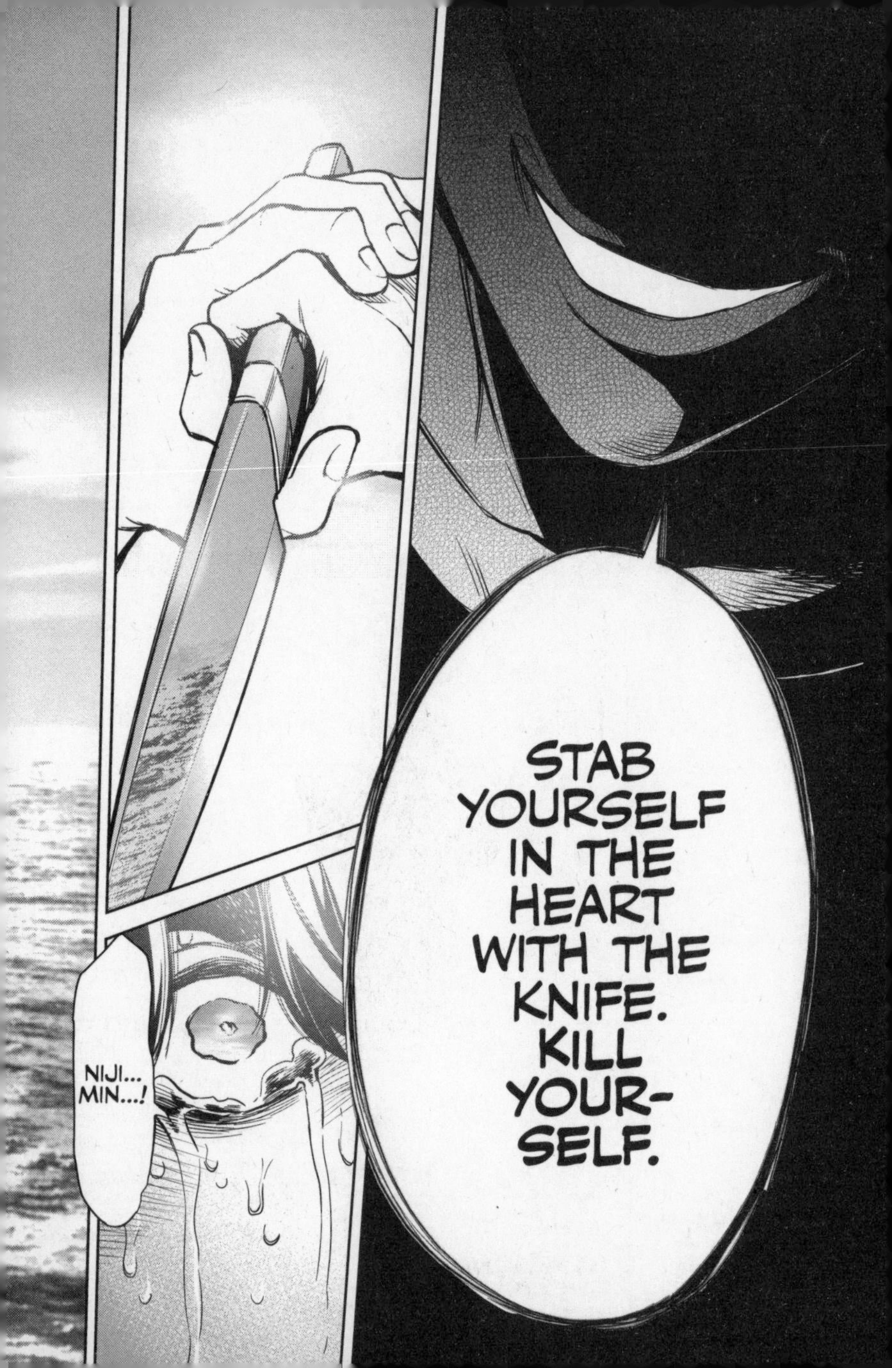
STAB YOURSELF IN THE HEART WITH THE KNIFE. KILL YOUR-SELF.
NIJI... MIN...!

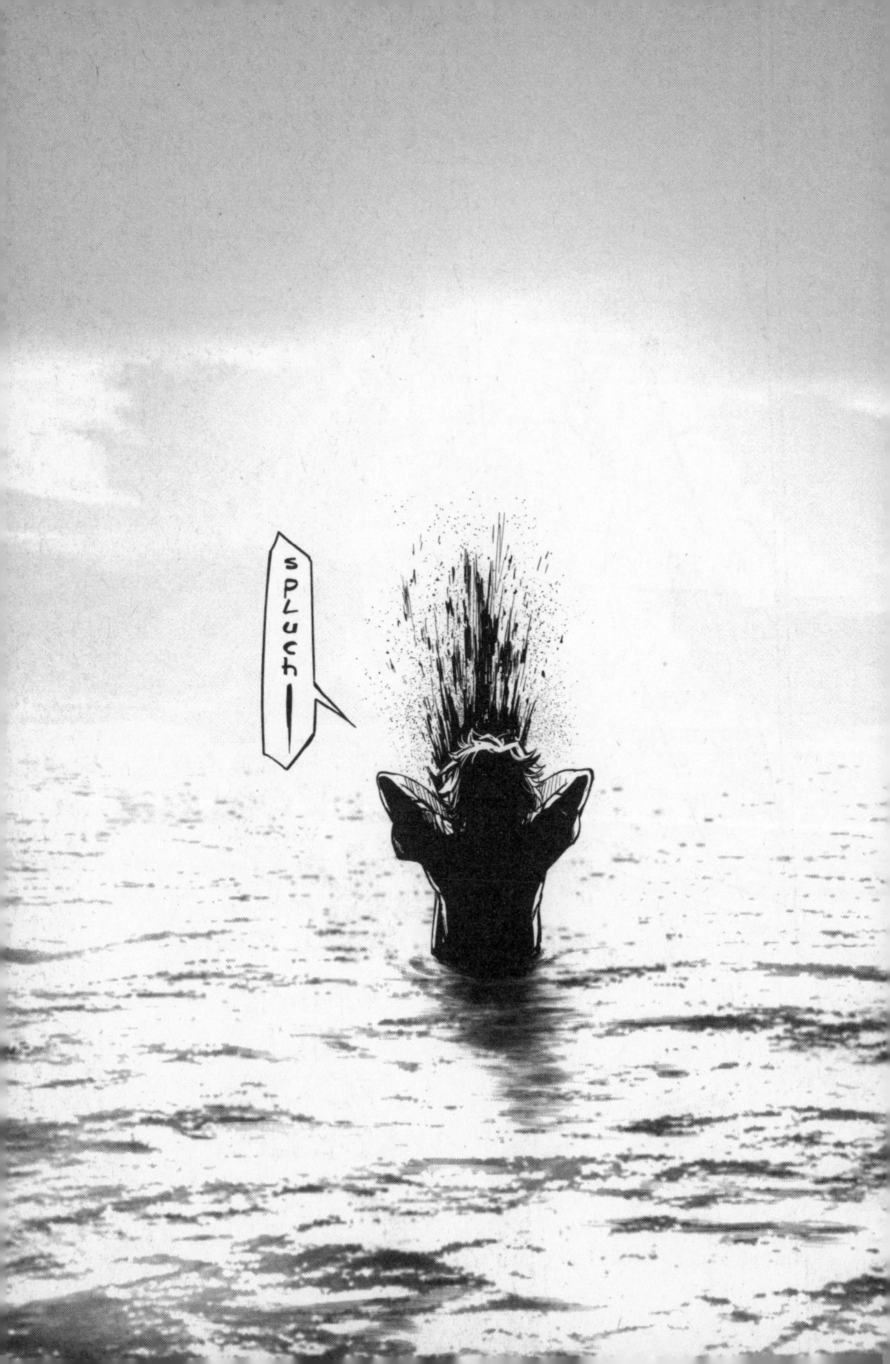
sPLuch!

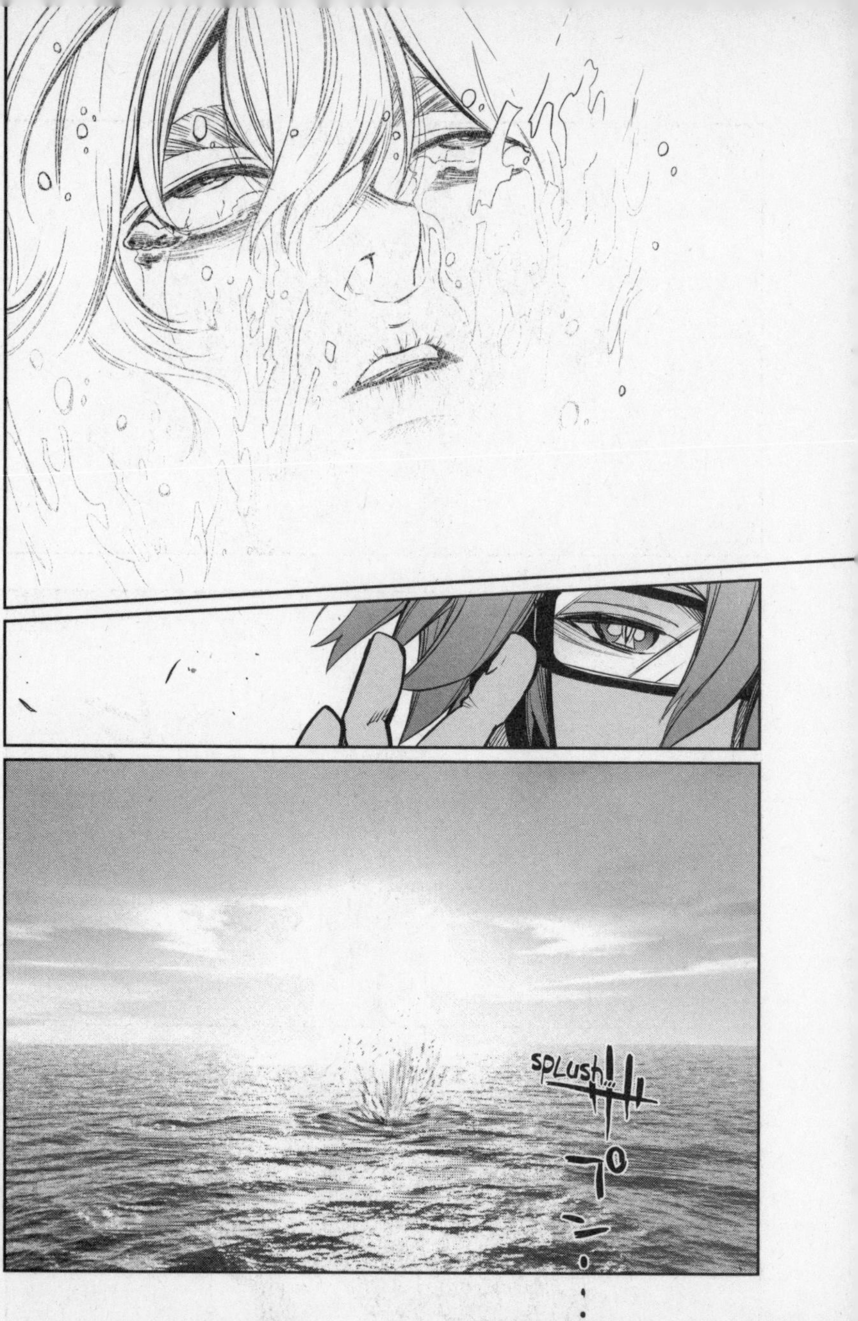
splush...

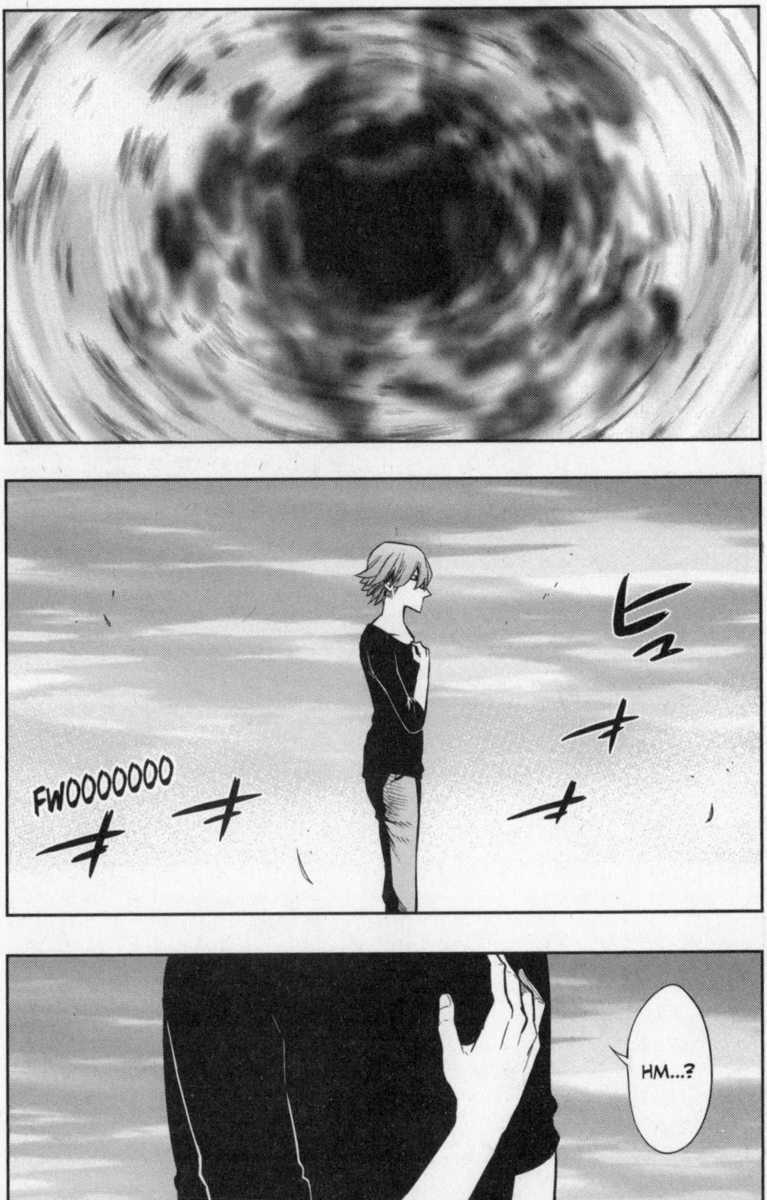
ヒュ
FWOOOOOOO
HM...?

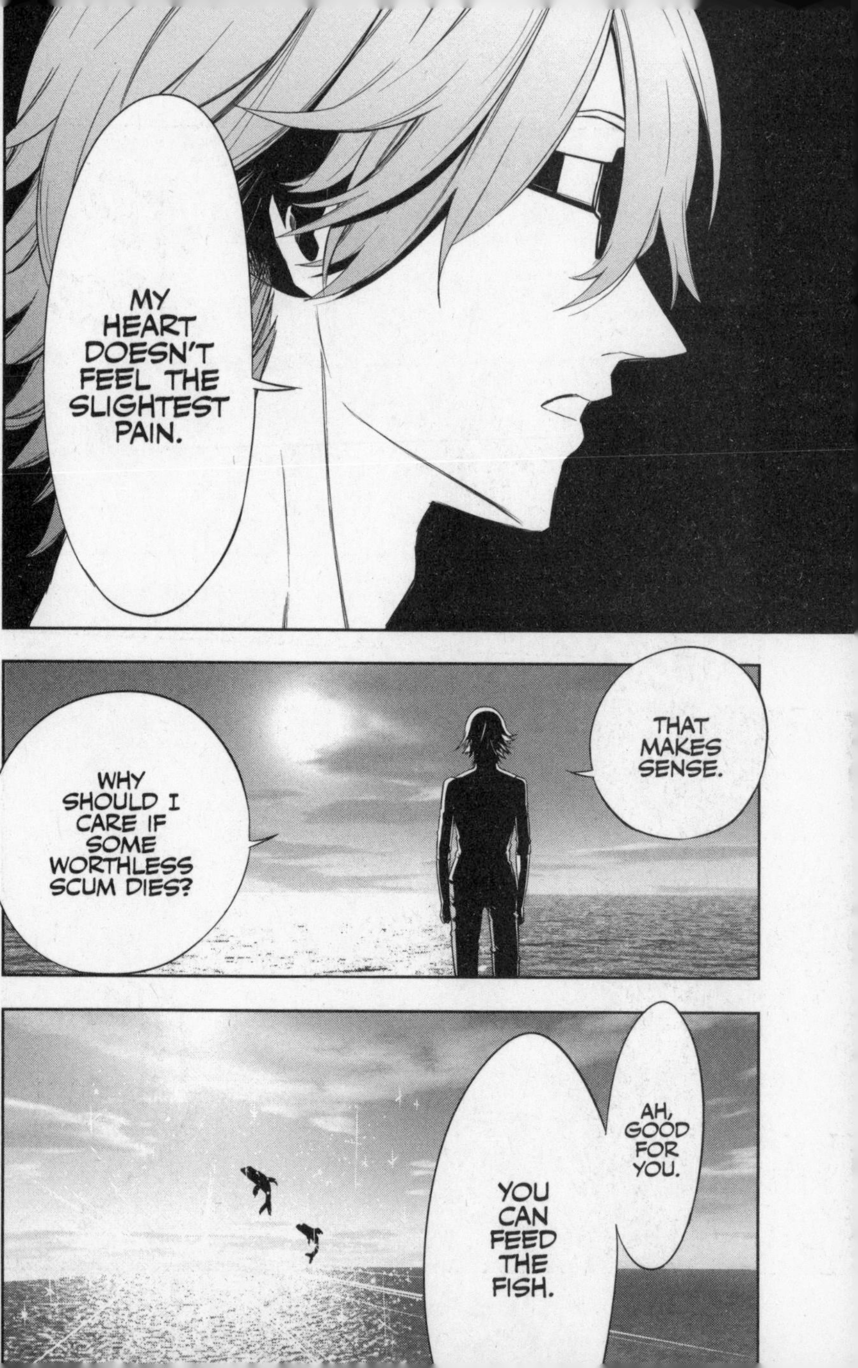
MY HEART DOESN'T FEEL THE SLIGHTEST PAIN.
THAT MAKES SENSE.
WHY SHOULD I CARE IF SOME WORTHLESS SCUM DIES?
AH, GOOD FOR YOU.
YOU CAN FEED THE FISH.

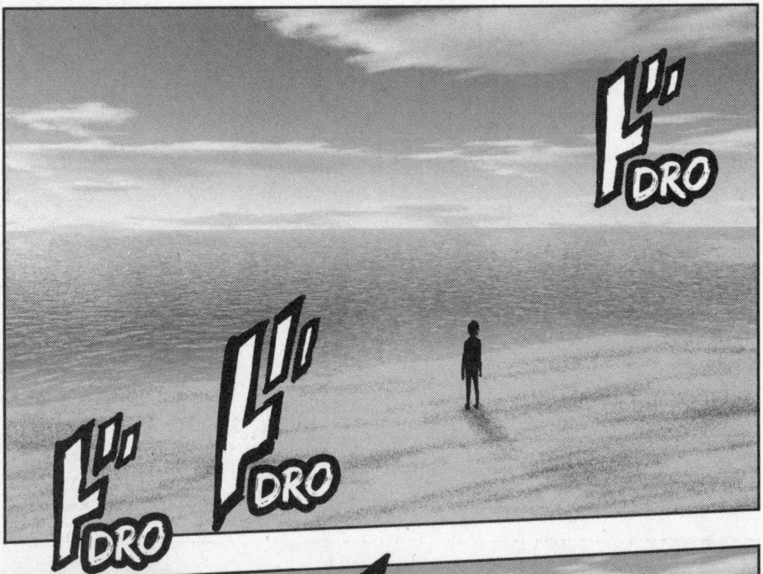
DRO
DRO
DRO

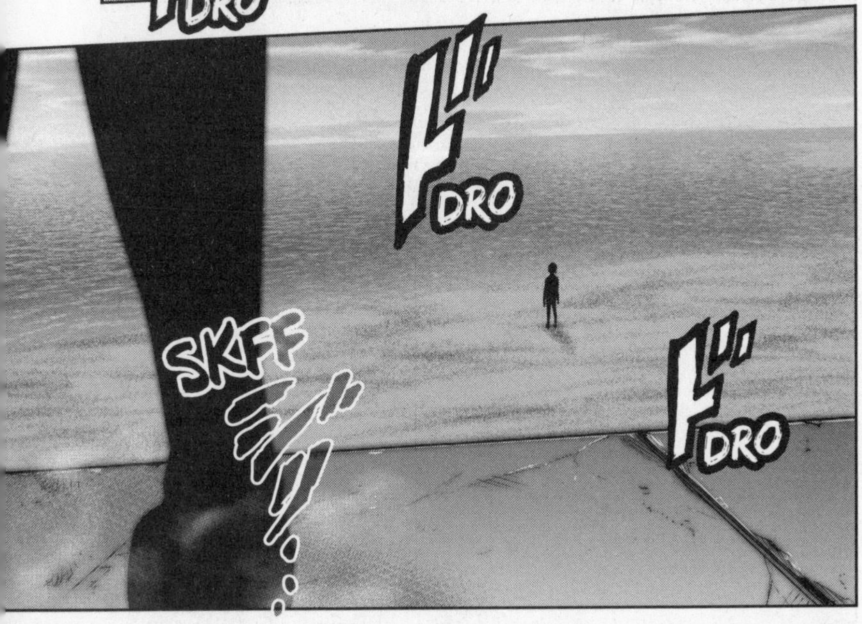
DRO
DRO
SKFF

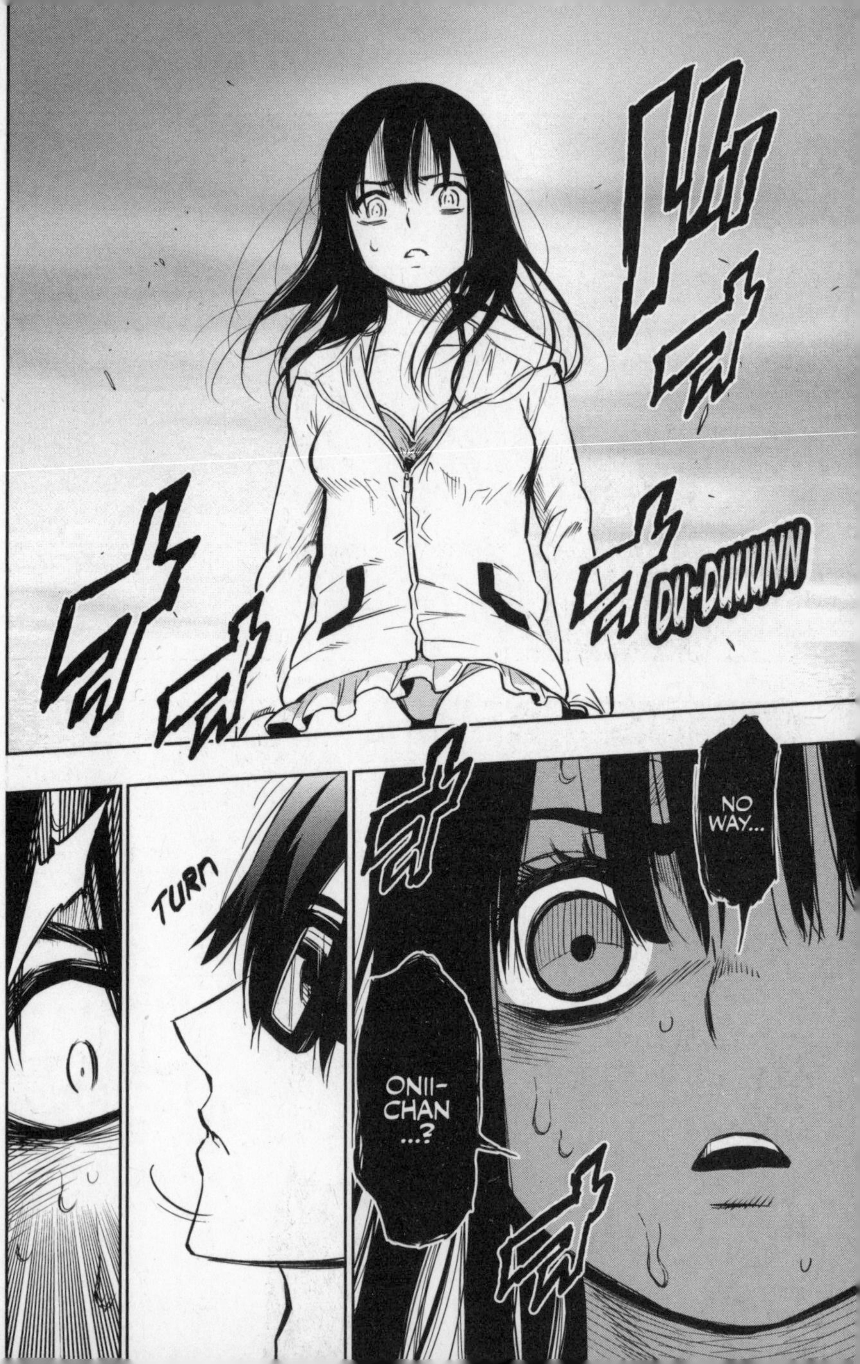
DU-DUUUNN
NO WAY...
ONII-CHAN ...?
TURN

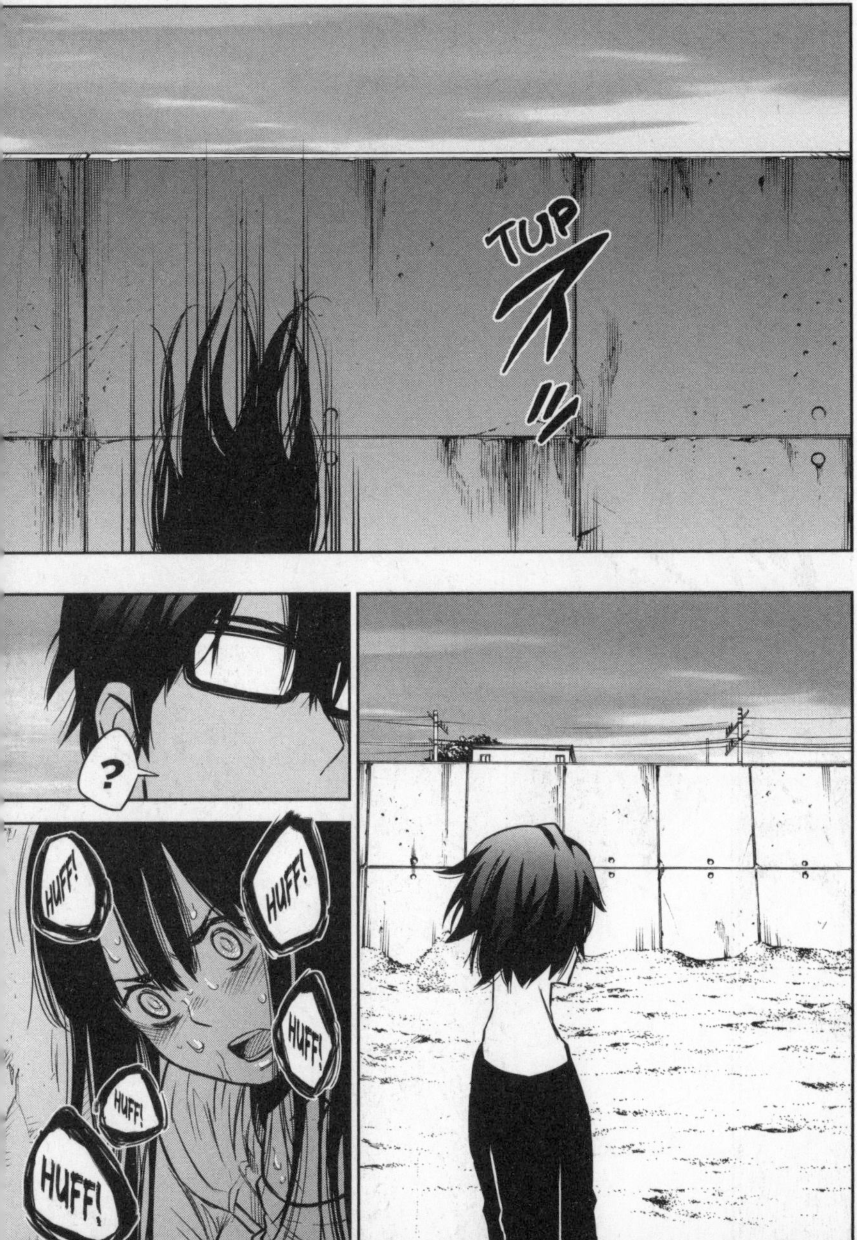
TUP
?
HUFF!
HUFF!
HUFF!
HUFF!
HUFF!

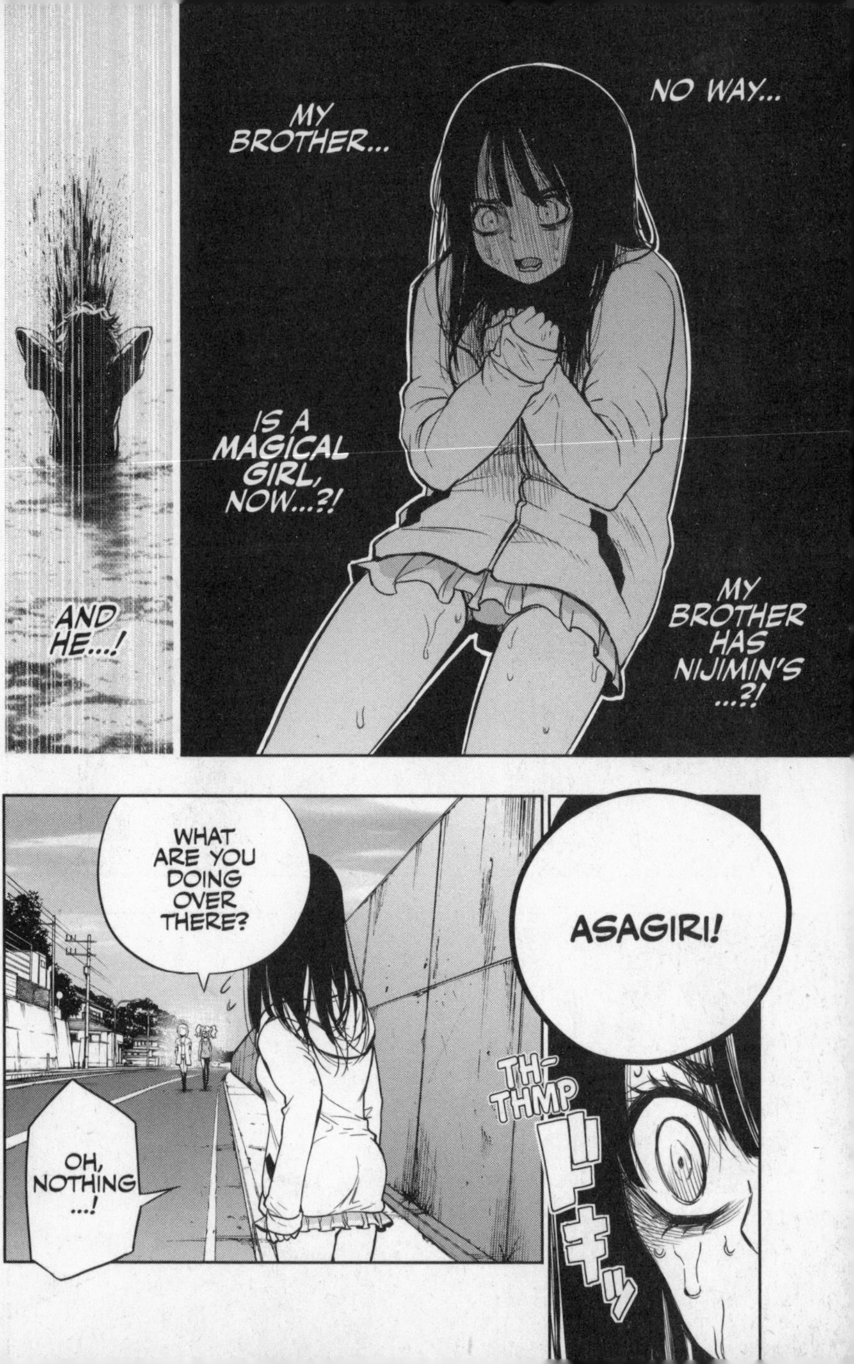
NO WAY...
MY BROTHER...
IS A MAGICAL GIRL, NOW...?!
MY BROTHER HAS NIJIMIN'S ...?!
AND HE...!
ASAGIRI!
TH-THMP
WHAT ARE YOU DOING OVER THERE?
OH, NOTHING ...!

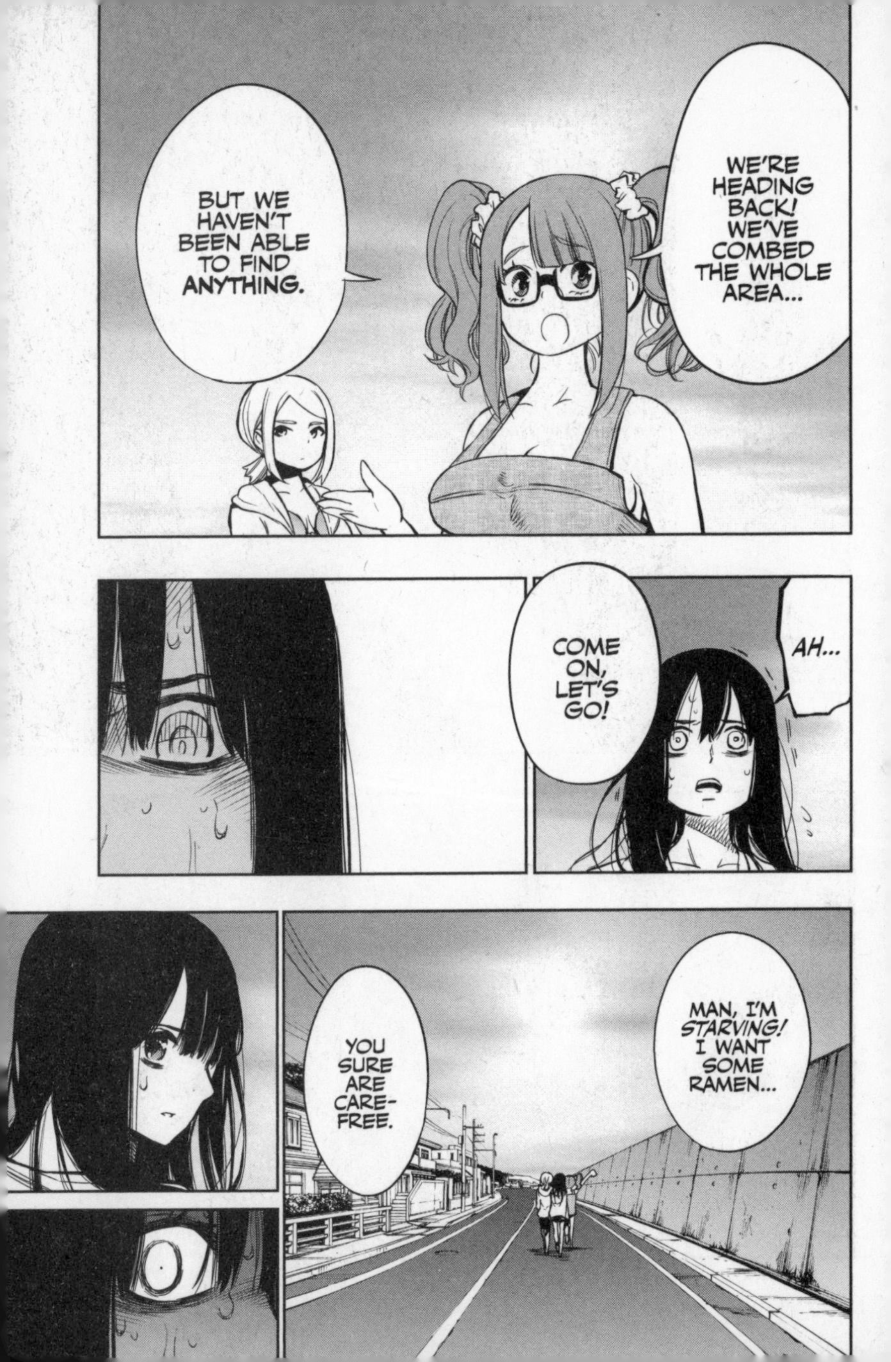
WE'RE HEADING BACK! WE'VE COMBED THE WHOLE AREA...
BUT WE HAVEN'T BEEN ABLE TO FIND ANYTHING.
AH...
COME ON, LET'S GO!
MAN, I'M STARVING! I WANT SOME RAMEN...
YOU SURE ARE CARE-FREE.

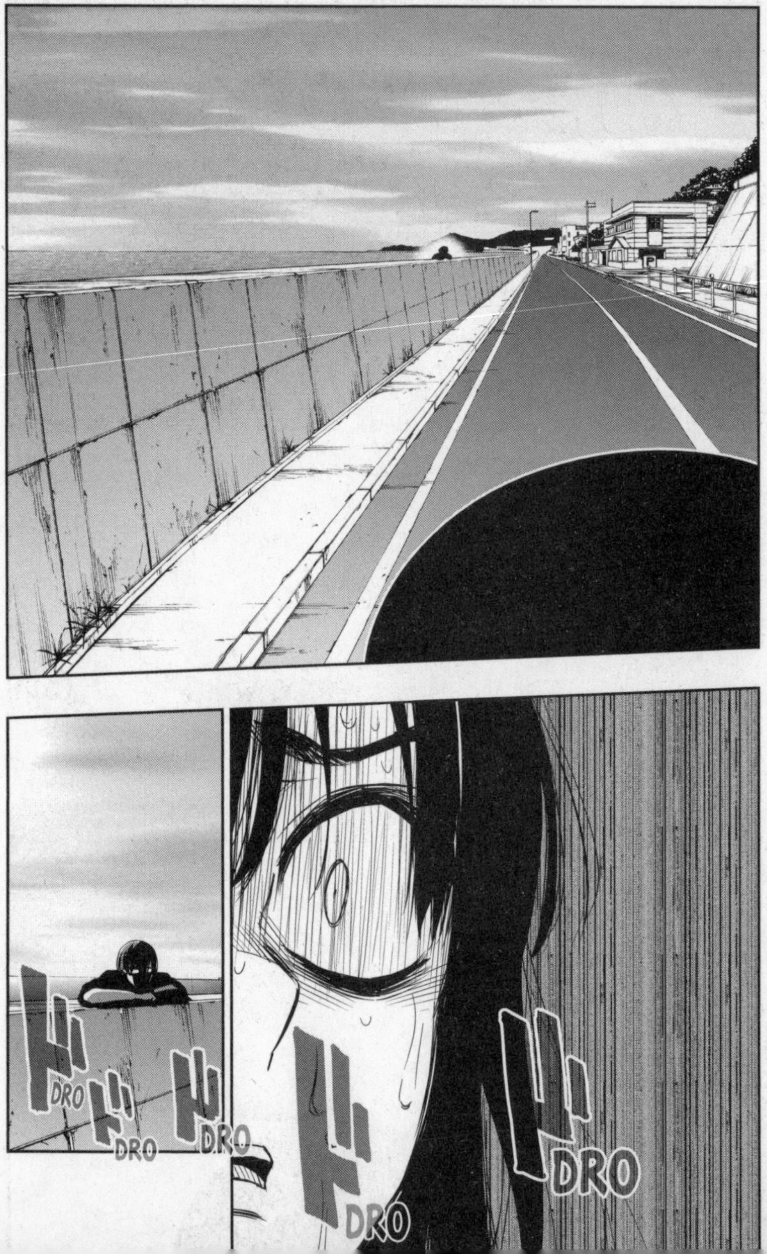
ド DRO
ド DRO
ド DRO
ド DRO
ド DRO

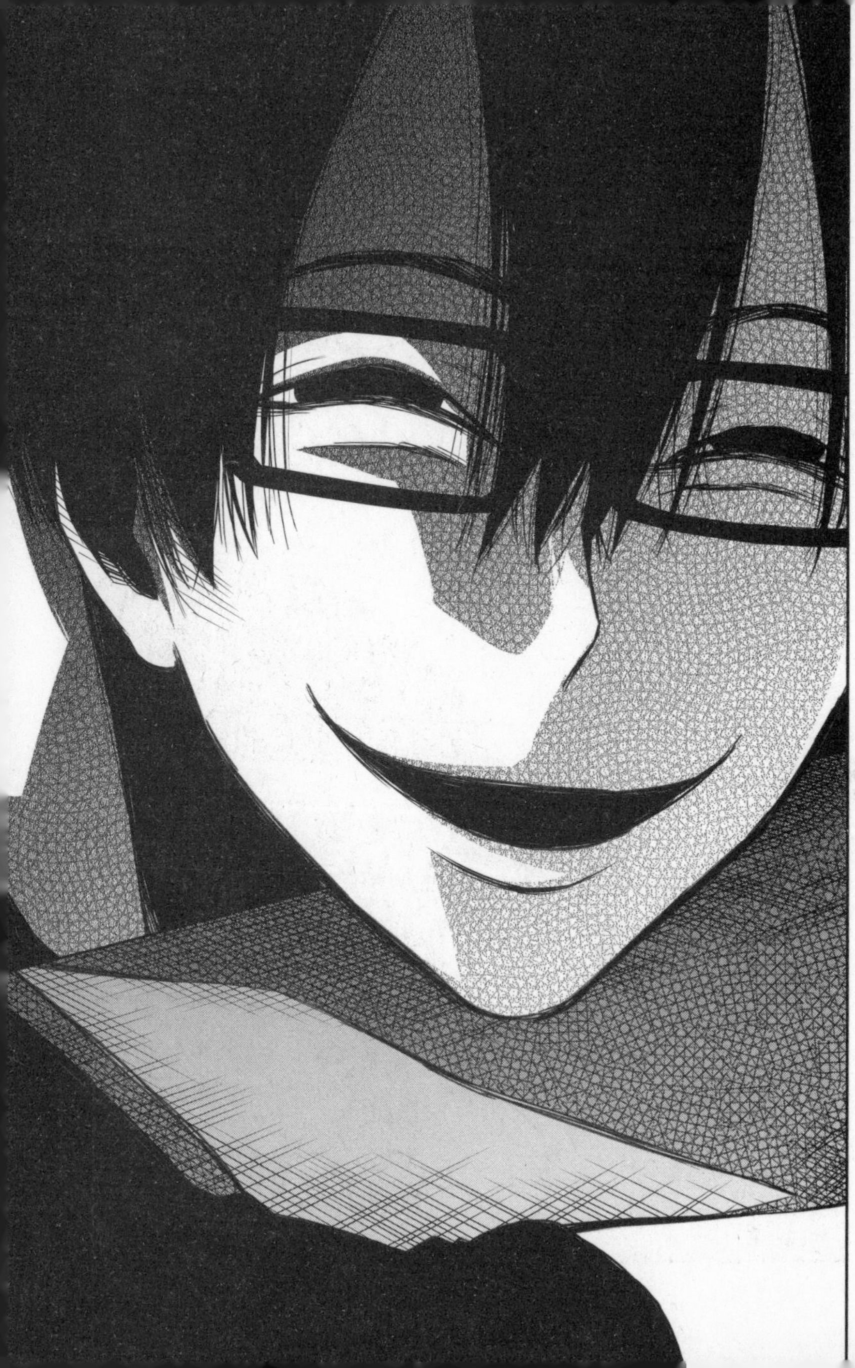

Oh, I see...

ENTER. 35 ARTICLES OF THE DECEASED

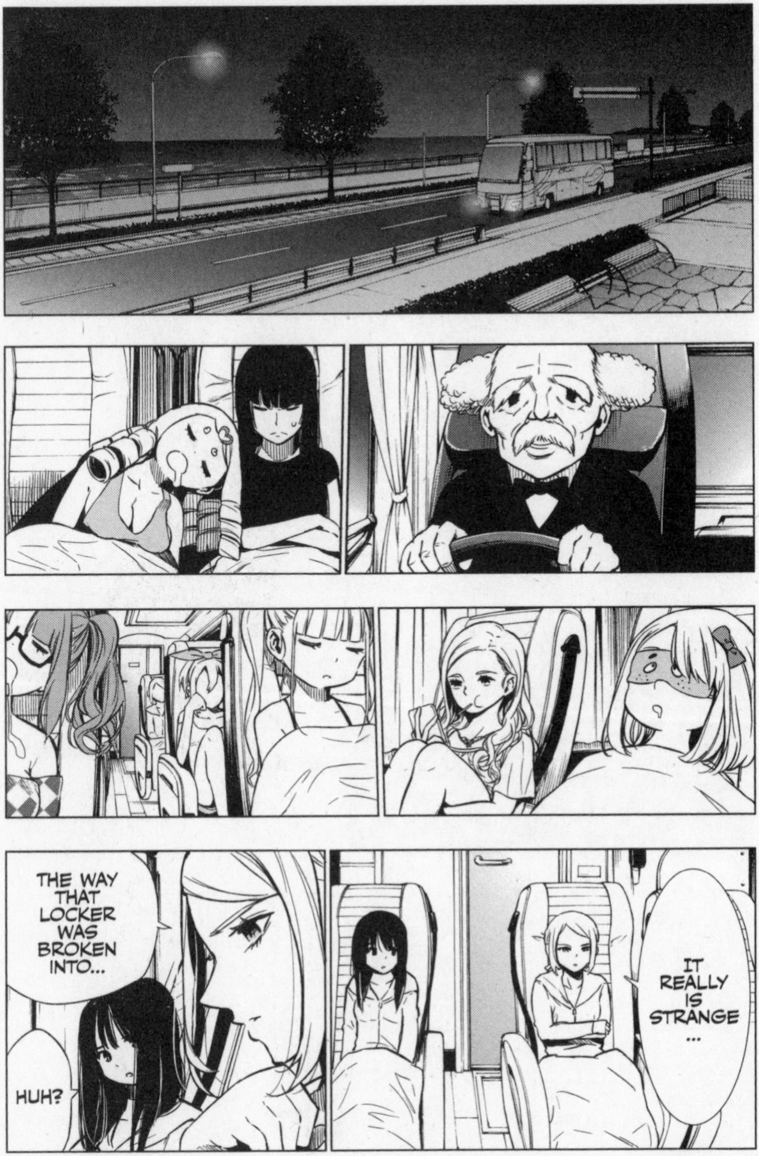
IT REALLY IS STRANGE ...
THE WAY THAT LOCKER WAS BROKEN INTO...
HUH?

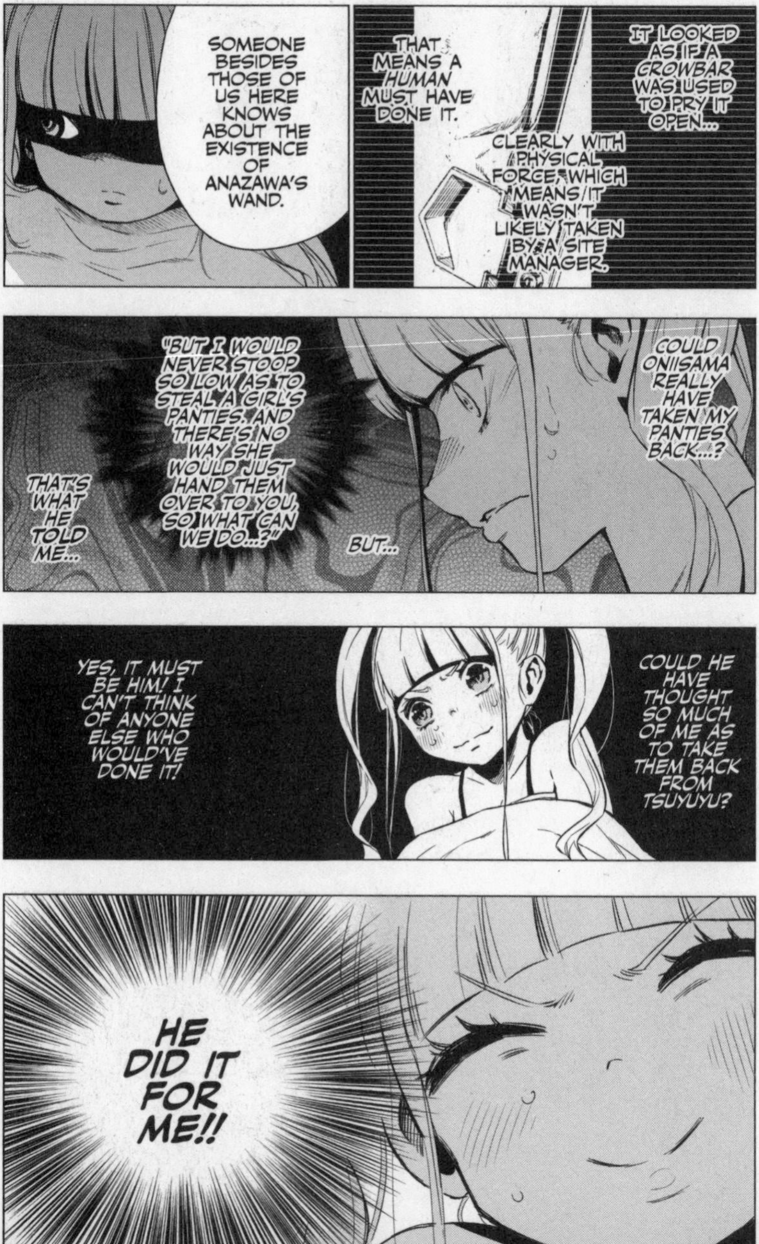
IT LOOKED AS IF A CROWBAR WAS USED TO PRY IT OPEN...
CLEARLY WITH PHYSICAL FORCE, WHICH MEANS IT WASN'T LIKELY TAKEN BY A SITE MANAGER.
THAT MEANS A HUMAN MUST HAVE DONE IT.
SOMEONE BESIDES THOSE OF US HERE KNOWS ABOUT THE EXISTENCE OF ANAZAWA'S WAND.
COULD ONIISAMA REALLY HAVE TAKEN MY PANTIES BACK...?
BUT...
"BUT I WOULD NEVER STOOP SO LOW AS TO STEAL A GIRL'S PANTIES, AND THERE'S NO WAY SHE WOULD JUST HAND THEM OVER TO YOU, SO WHAT CAN WE DO...?"
THAT'S WHAT HE TOLD ME...
COULD HE HAVE THOUGHT SO MUCH OF ME AS TO TAKE THEM BACK FROM TSUYUYU?
YES, IT MUST BE HIM! I CAN'T THINK OF ANYONE ELSE WHO WOULD'VE DONE IT!
HE DID IT FOR ME!!

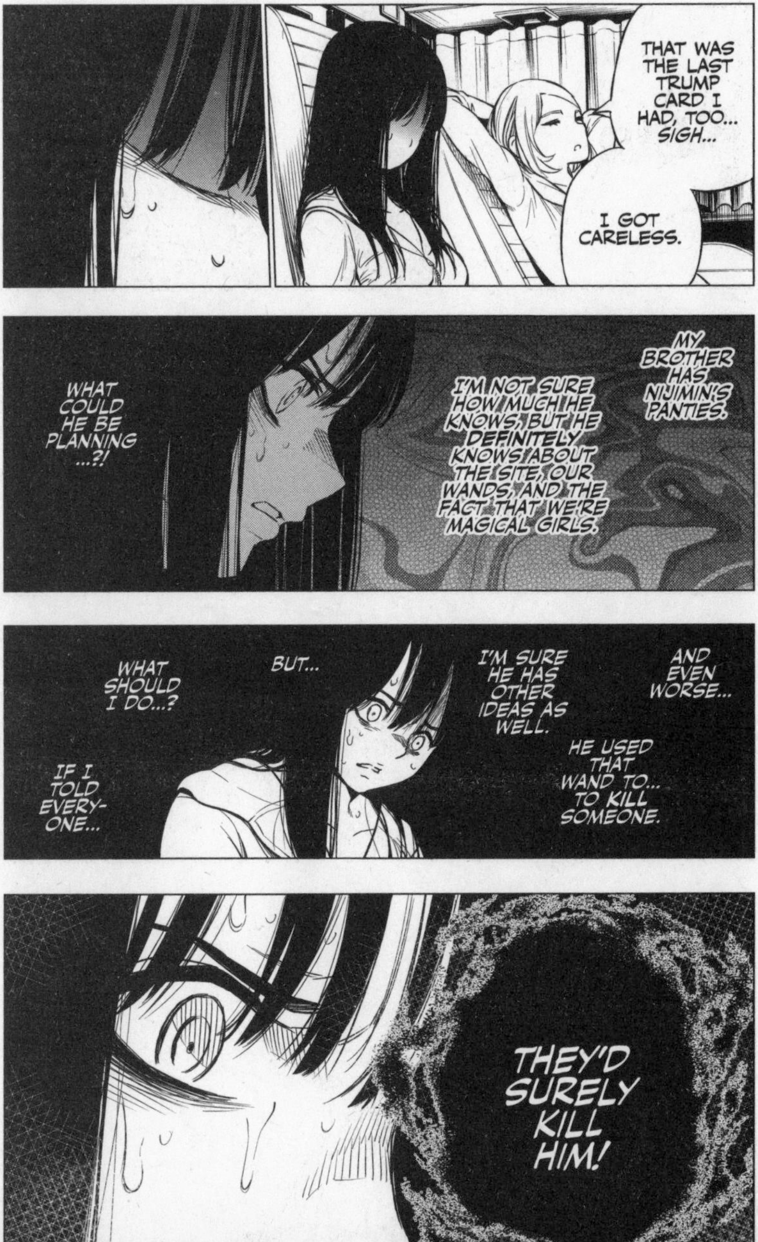
THAT WAS THE LAST TRUMP CARD I HAD, TOO... SIGH...
I GOT CARELESS.
MY BROTHER HAS NIJIMIN'S PANTIES.
I'M NOT SURE HOW MUCH HE KNOWS, BUT HE DEFINITELY KNOWS ABOUT THE SITE, OUR WANDS, AND THE FACT THAT WE'RE MAGICAL GIRLS.
WHAT COULD HE BE PLANNING ...?!
I'M SURE HE HAS OTHER IDEAS AS WELL.
AND EVEN WORSE...
HE USED THAT WAND TO... TO KILL SOMEONE.
BUT...
WHAT SHOULD I DO...?
IF I TOLD EVERY-ONE...
THEY'D SURELY KILL HIM!

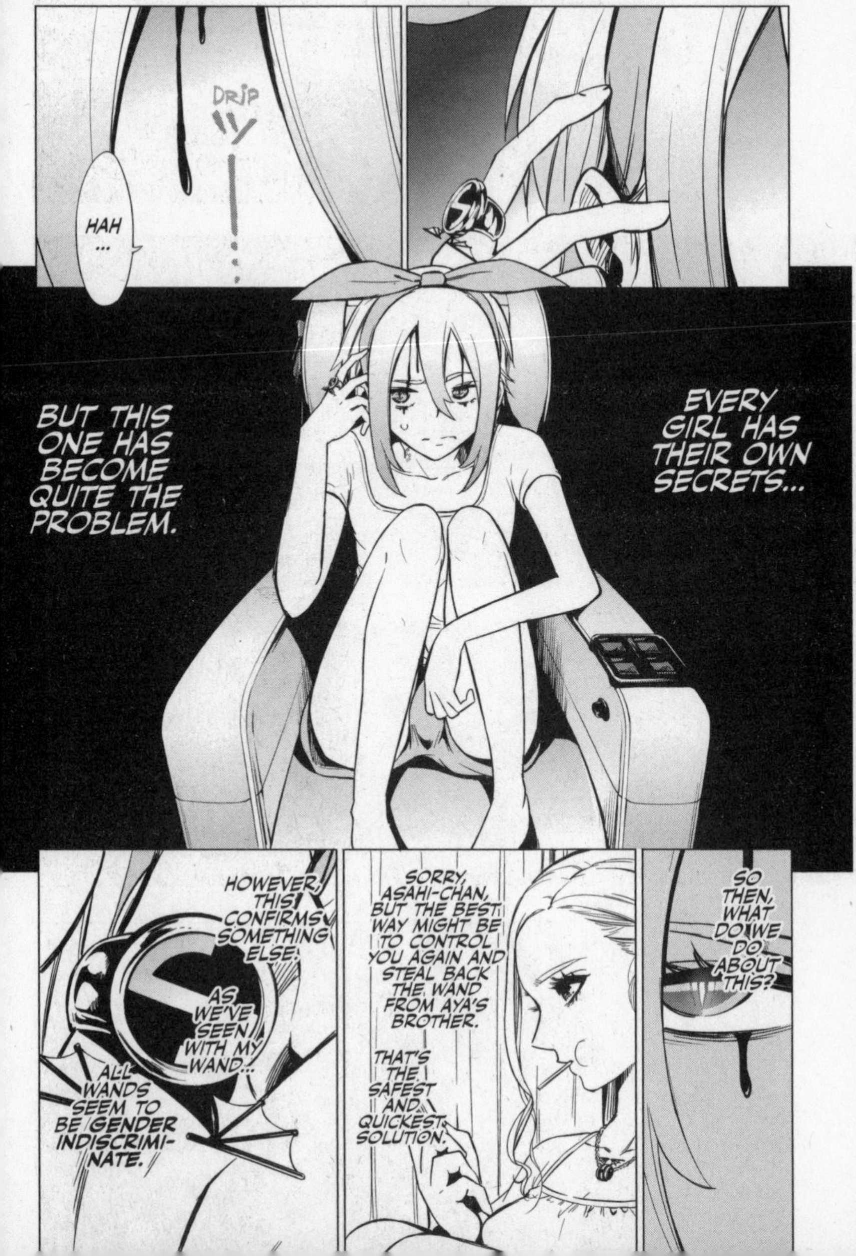
DRIP
HAH ...
EVERY GIRL HAS THEIR OWN SECRETS...
BUT THIS ONE HAS BECOME QUITE THE PROBLEM.
SO THEN, WHAT DO WE DO ABOUT THIS?
SORRY, ASAHI-CHAN, BUT THE BEST WAY MIGHT BE TO CONTROL YOU AGAIN AND STEAL BACK THE WAND FROM AYA'S BROTHER.
THAT'S THE SAFEST AND QUICKEST SOLUTION.
HOWEVER, THIS CONFIRMS SOMETHING ELSE.
AS WE'VE SEEN WITH MY WAND...
ALL WANDS SEEM TO BE GENDER INDISCRIMI-NATE.

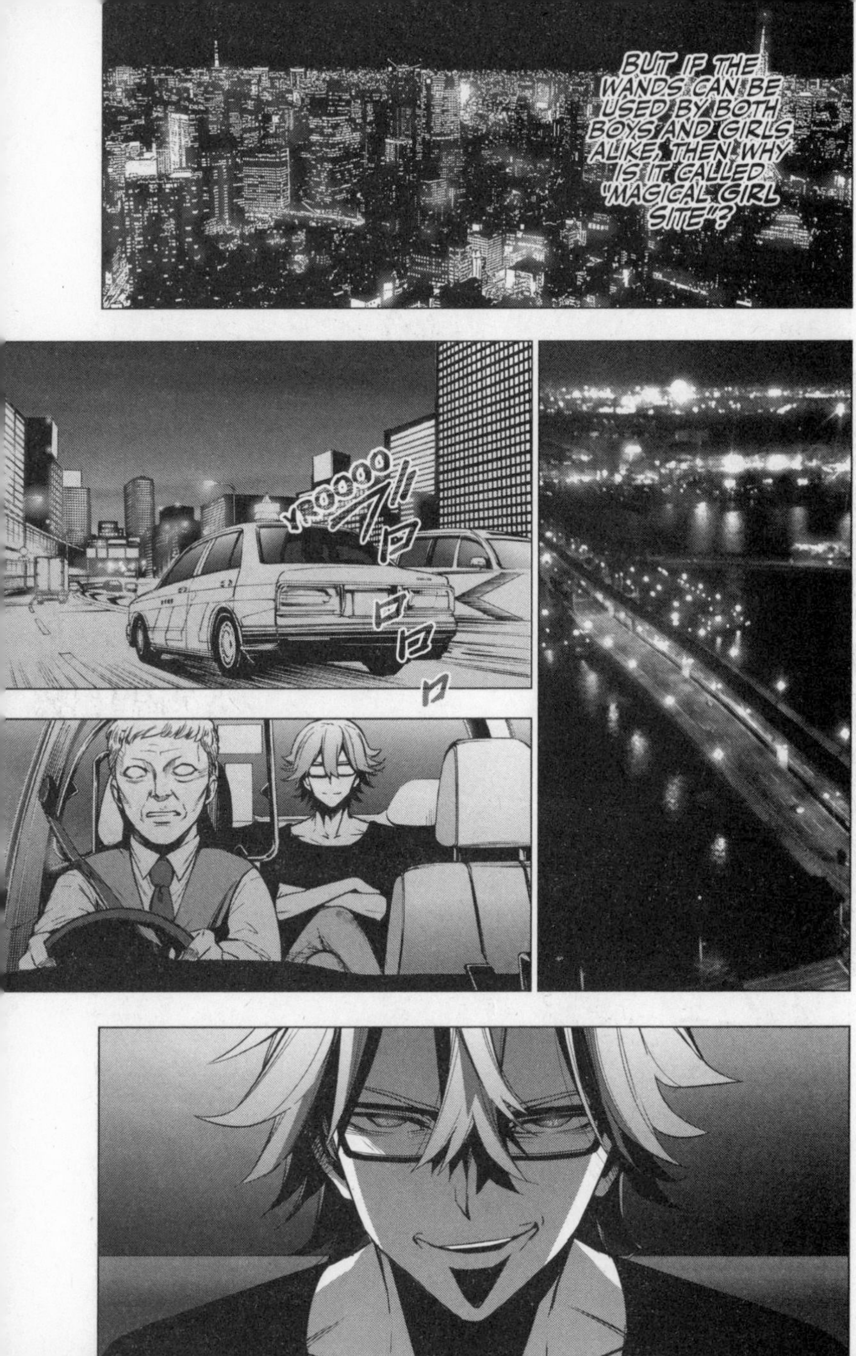
BUT IF THE WANDS CAN BE USED BY BOTH BOYS AND GIRLS ALIKE, THEN WHY IS IT CALLED "MAGICAL GIRL SITE"?
VROOOO

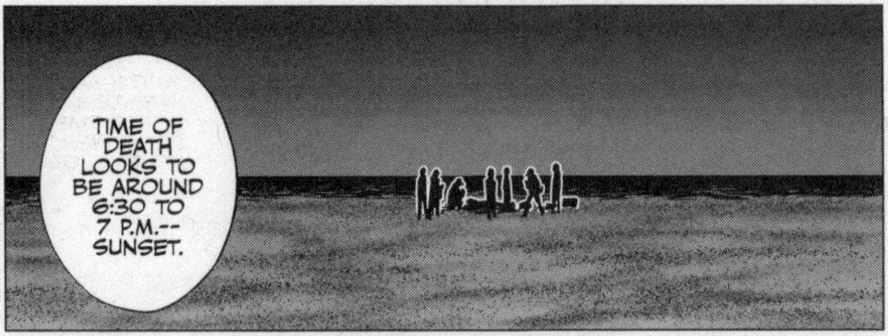
TIME OF DEATH LOOKS TO BE AROUND 6:30 TO 7 P.M.-- SUNSET.

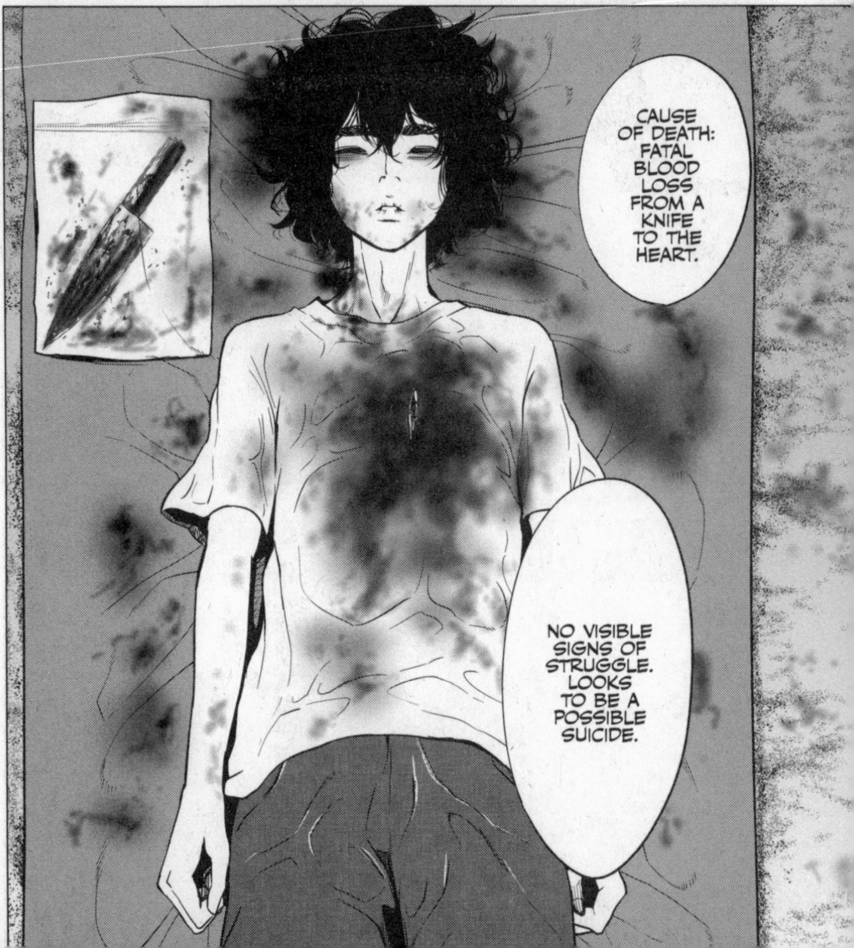
CAUSE OF DEATH: FATAL BLOOD LOSS FROM A KNIFE TO THE HEART.
NO VISIBLE SIGNS OF STRUGGLE. LOOKS TO BE A POSSIBLE SUICIDE.

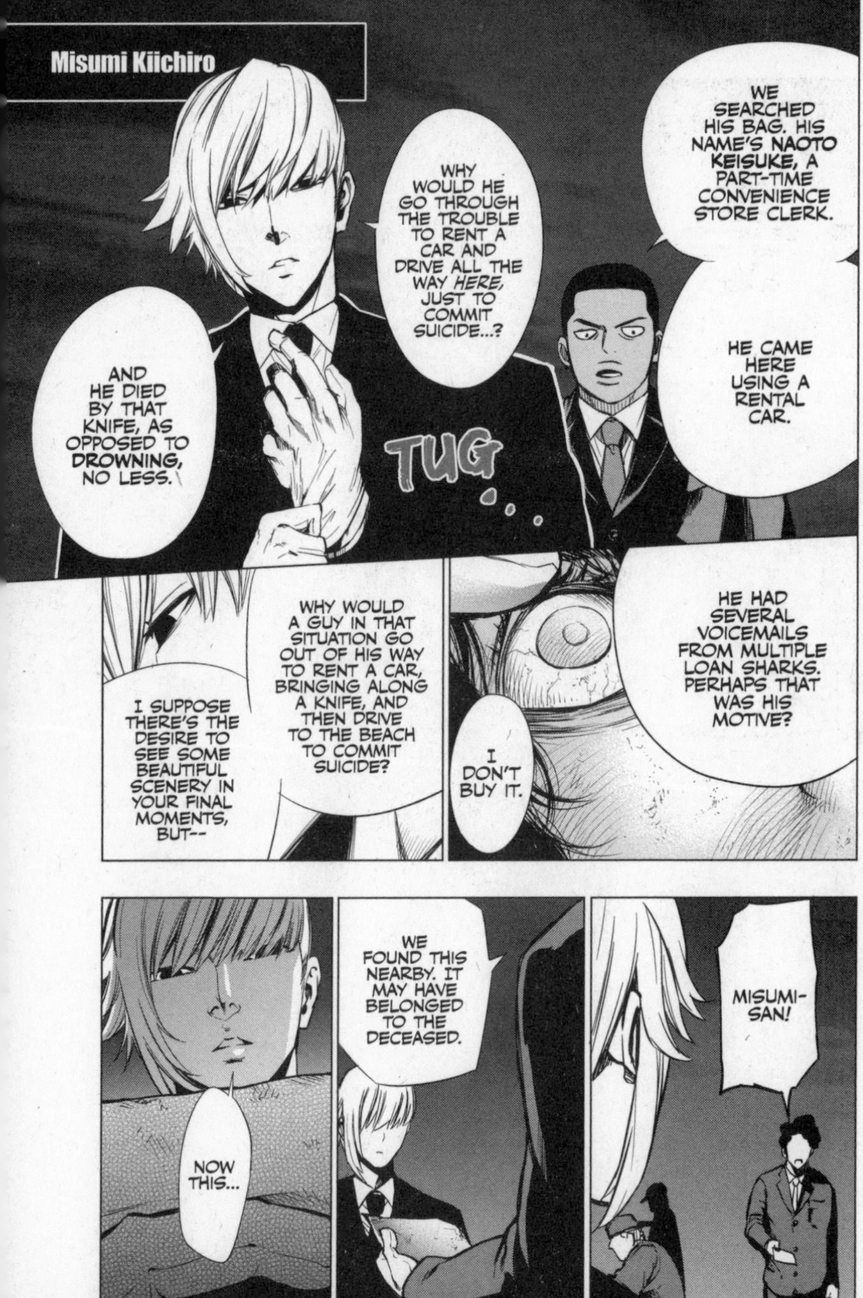
WE SEARCHED HIS BAG. HIS NAME'S NAOTO KEISUKE, A PART-TIME CONVENIENCE STORE CLERK.
HE CAME HERE USING A RENTAL CAR.
Misumi Kiichiro
WHY WOULD HE GO THROUGH THE TROUBLE TO RENT A CAR AND DRIVE ALL THE WAY *HERE,* JUST TO COMMIT SUICIDE...?
AND HE DIED BY THAT KNIFE, AS OPPOSED TO **DROWNING,** NO LESS.
TUG
HE HAD SEVERAL VOICEMAILS FROM MULTIPLE LOAN SHARKS. PERHAPS THAT WAS HIS MOTIVE?
I DON'T BUY IT.
WHY WOULD A GUY IN THAT SITUATION GO OUT OF HIS WAY TO RENT A CAR, BRINGING ALONG A KNIFE, AND THEN DRIVE TO THE BEACH TO COMMIT SUICIDE?
I SUPPOSE THERE'S THE DESIRE TO SEE SOME BEAUTIFUL SCENERY IN YOUR FINAL MOMENTS, BUT--
MISUMI-SAN!
WE FOUND THIS NEARBY. IT MAY HAVE BELONGED TO THE DECEASED.
NOW THIS...

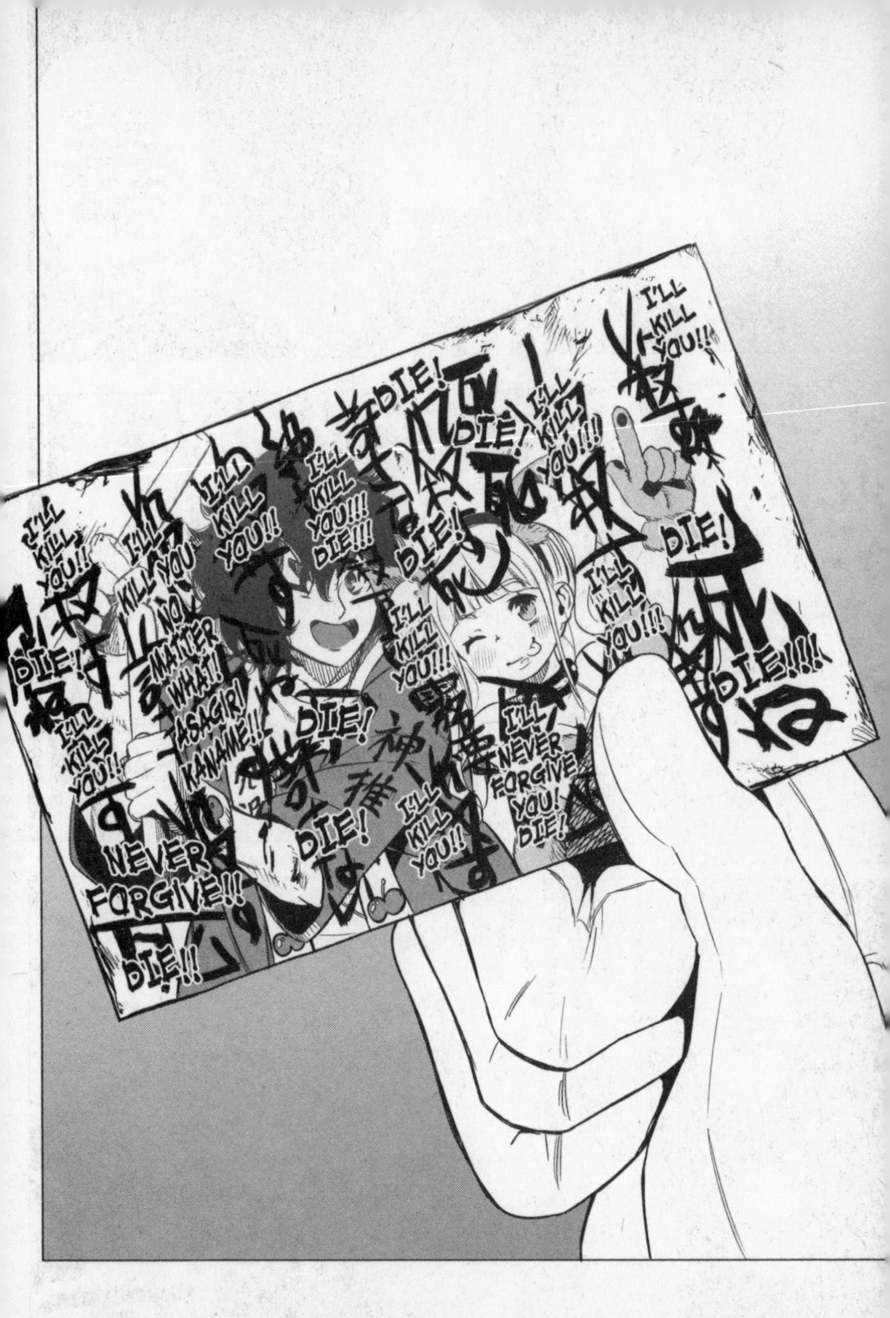
I'LL KILL YOU!!
I'LL KILL YOU!!!
DIE!
DIE!
DIE!
I'LL KILL YOU!!!
DIE!!!!
DIE!
I'LL KILL YOU!!! DIE!!!
I'LL KILL YOU!!
I'LL KILL YOU
I'LL KILL YOU!!
NO MATTER WHAT! ASAGIRI KANAME!!
DIE!
I'LL NEVER FORGIVE YOU! DIE!
I'LL KILL YOU!!!
DIE!
I'LL KILL YOU!!
DIE!
I'LL KILL YOU!!
NEVER FORGIVE!!
DIE!!

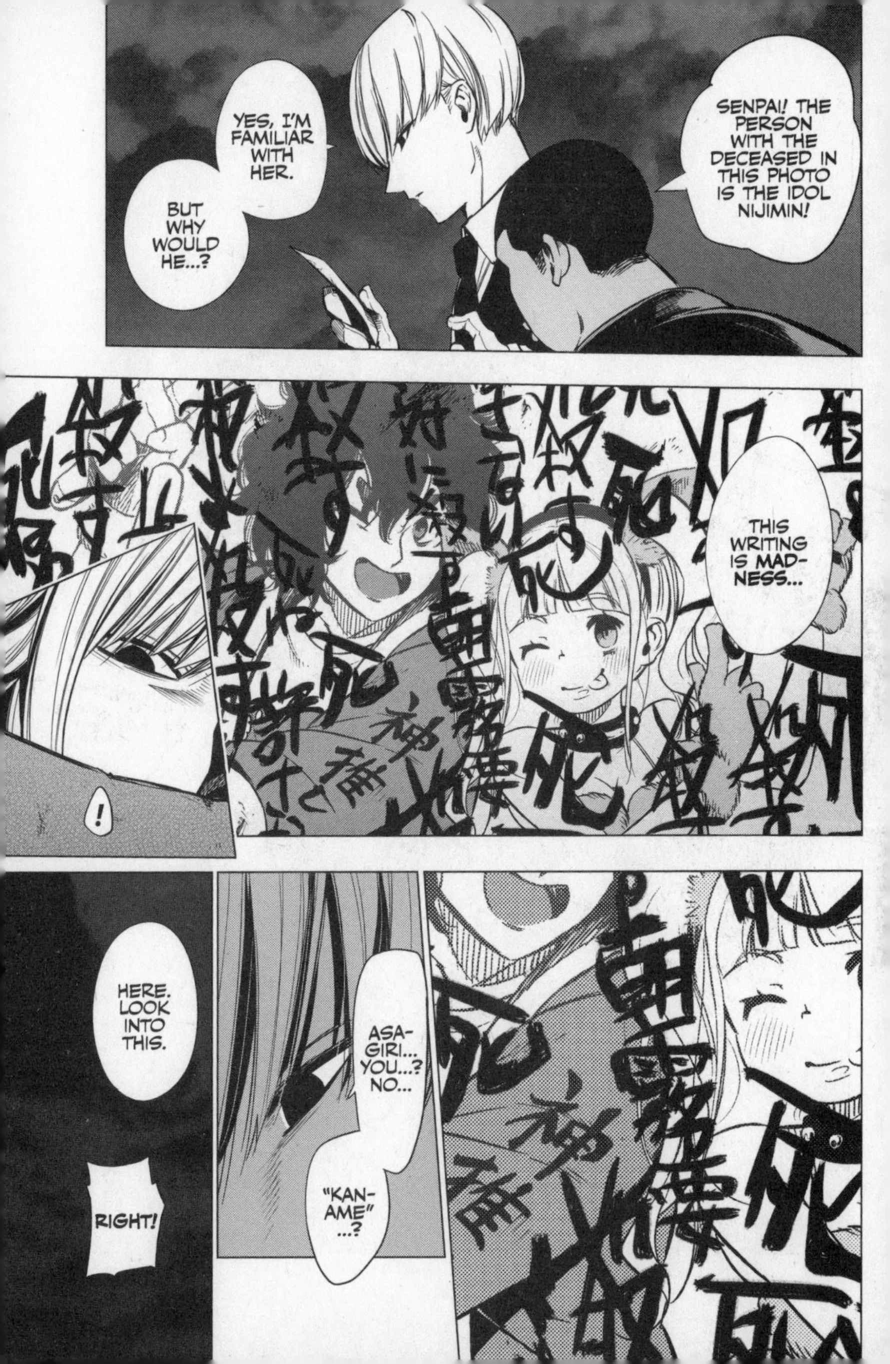
SENPAI! THE PERSON WITH THE DECEASED IN THIS PHOTO IS THE IDOL NIJIMIN!
YES, I'M FAMILIAR WITH HER.
BUT WHY WOULD HE...?
THIS WRITING IS MADNESS...
!
ASA-GIRI...? YOU...? NO...
"KAN-AME" ...?
HERE. LOOK INTO THIS.
RIGHT!

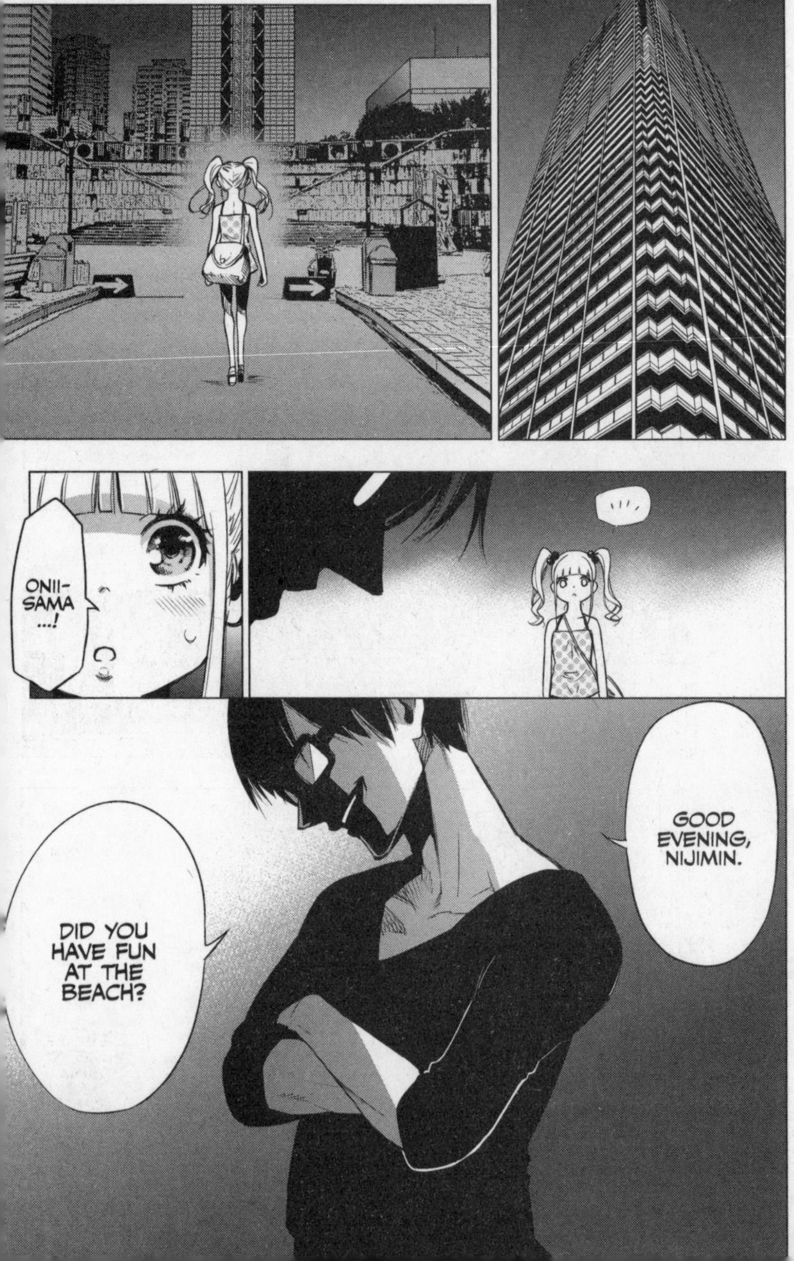
ONII-SAMA ...!
GOOD EVENING, NIJIMIN.
DID YOU HAVE FUN AT THE BEACH?

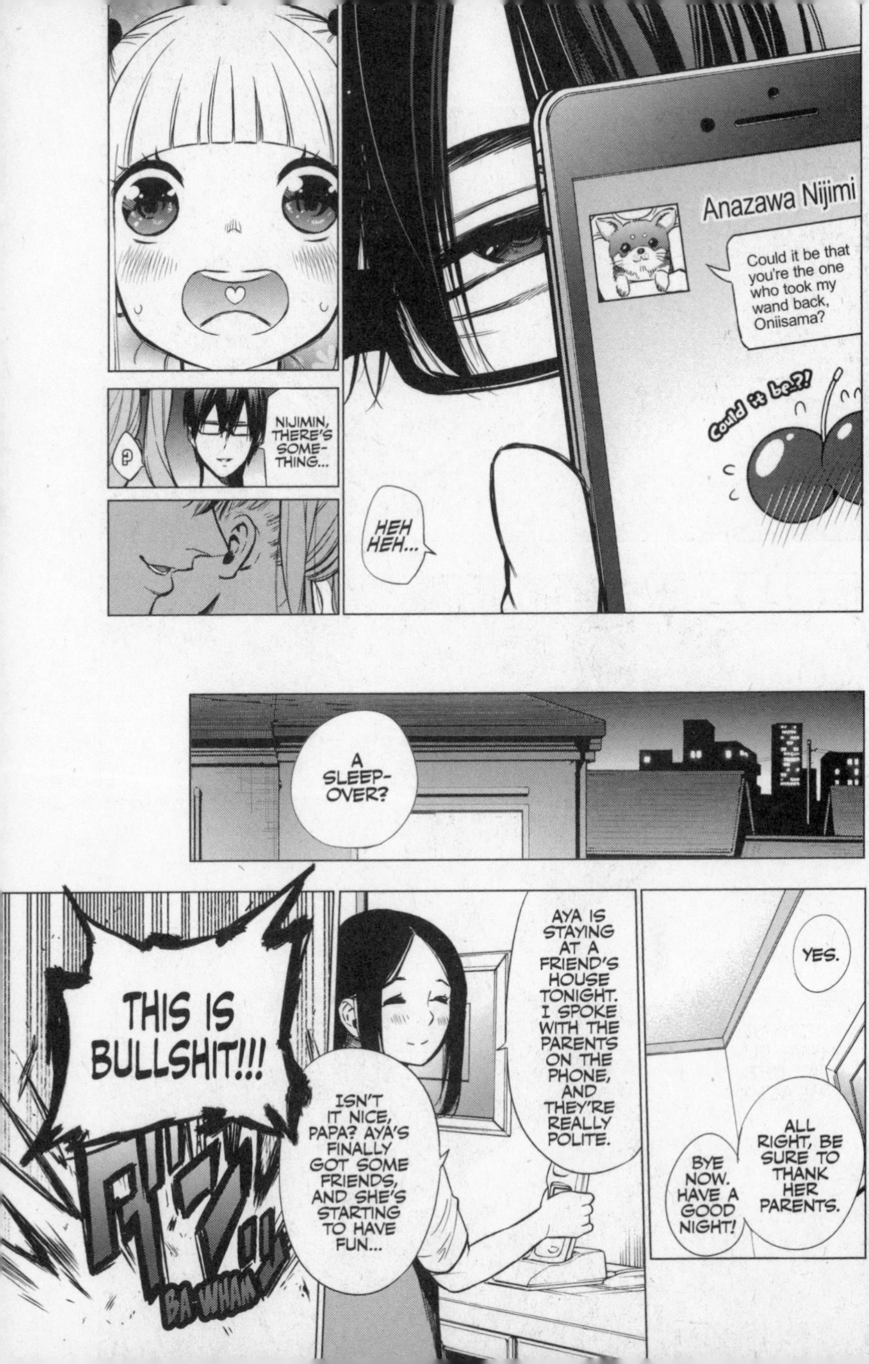
Anazawa Nijimi
Could it be that you're the one who took my wand back, Oniisama?
Could it be...?!
HEH HEH...
NIJIMIN, THERE'S SOME-THING...
A SLEEP-OVER?
YES.
ALL RIGHT, BE SURE TO THANK HER PARENTS.
BYE NOW. HAVE A GOOD NIGHT!
AYA IS STAYING AT A FRIEND'S HOUSE TONIGHT. I SPOKE WITH THE PARENTS ON THE PHONE, AND THEY'RE REALLY POLITE.
ISN'T IT NICE, PAPA? AYA'S FINALLY GOT SOME FRIENDS, AND SHE'S STARTING TO HAVE FUN...
THIS IS BULLSHIT!!!
BA-WHAM

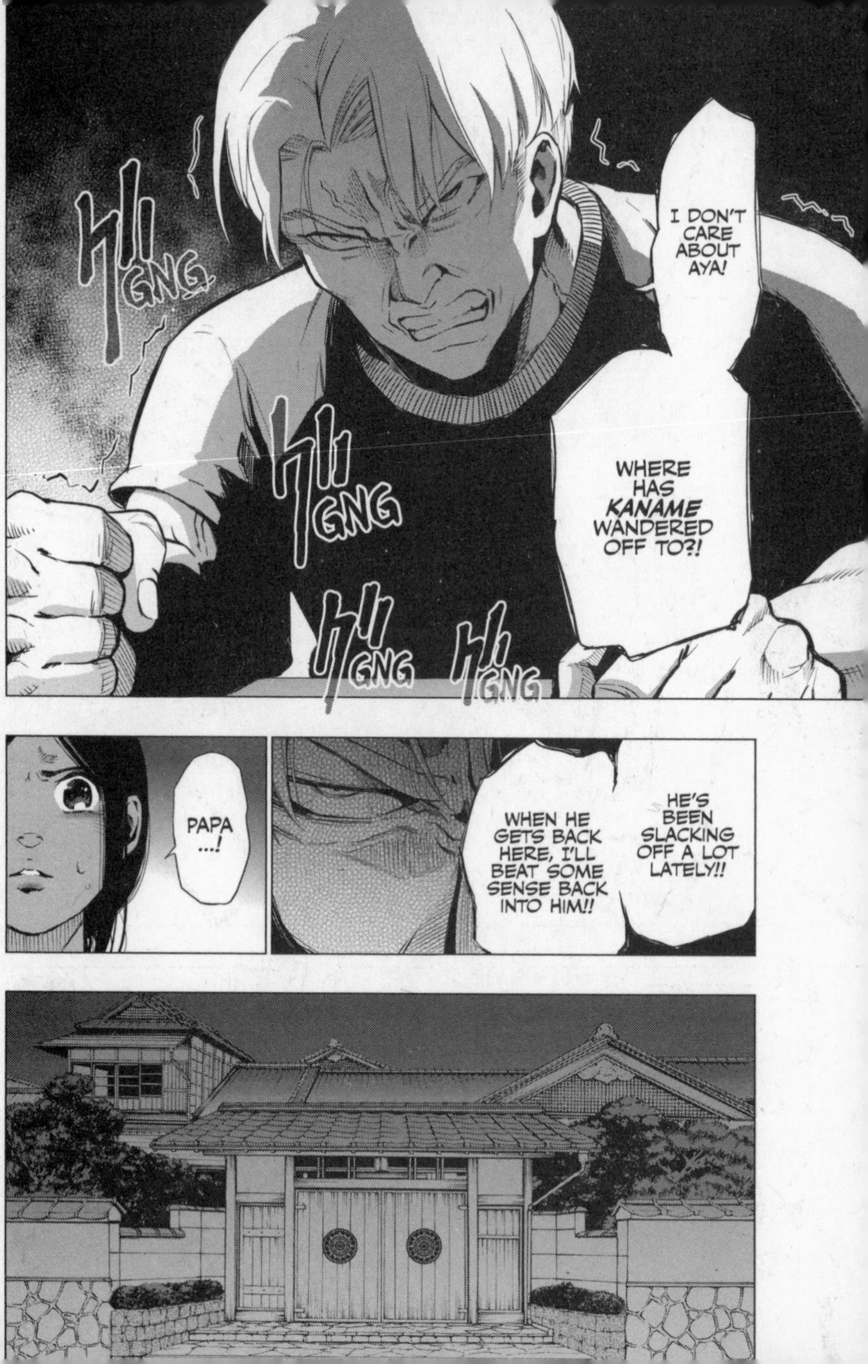
I DON'T CARE ABOUT AYA!
WHERE HAS *KANAME* WANDERED OFF TO?!
GNG
GNG
GNG
GNG
HE'S BEEN SLACKING OFF A LOT LATELY!!
WHEN HE GETS BACK HERE, I'LL BEAT SOME SENSE BACK INTO HIM!!
PAPA ...!

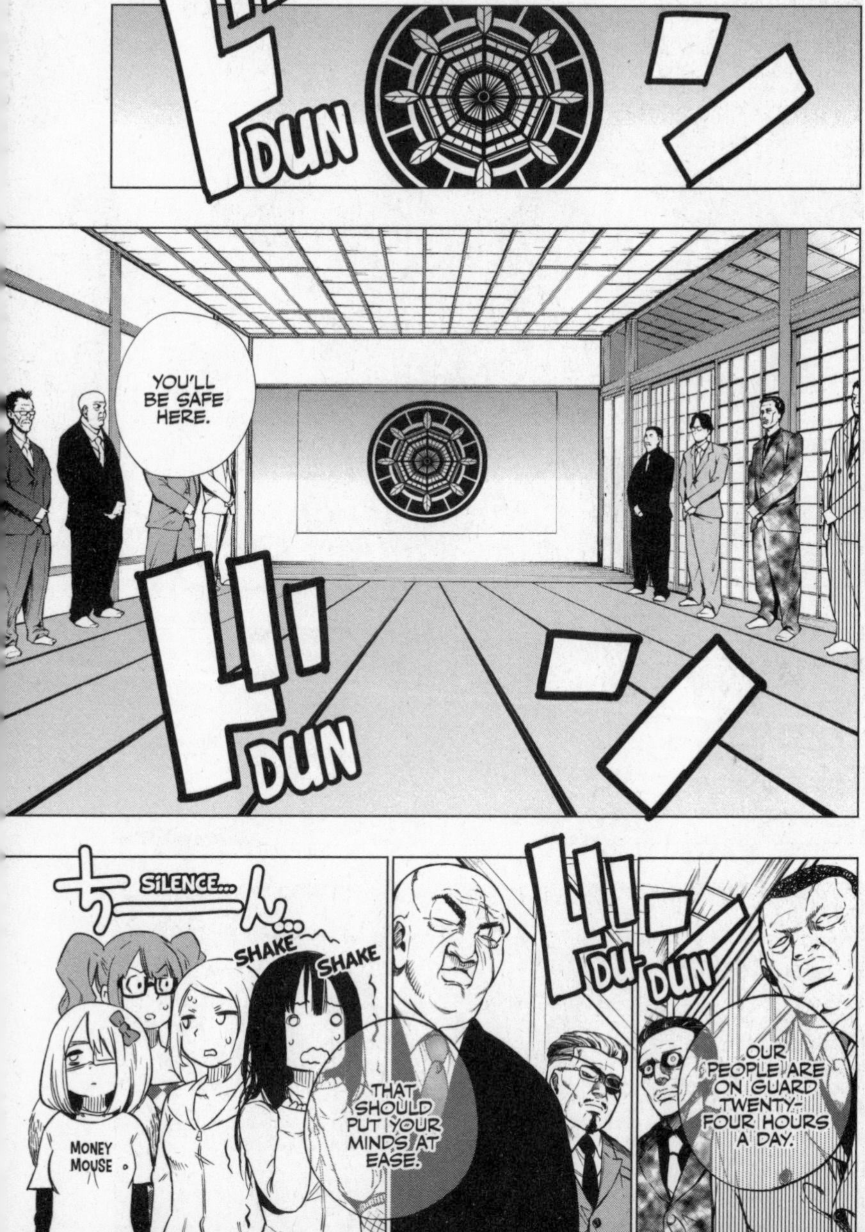
DUN
YOU'LL BE SAFE HERE.
DUN
DU-DUN
OUR PEOPLE ARE ON GUARD TWENTY-FOUR HOURS A DAY.
THAT SHOULD PUT YOUR MINDS AT EASE.
SILENCE...
SHAKE
SHAKE
MONEY MOUSE

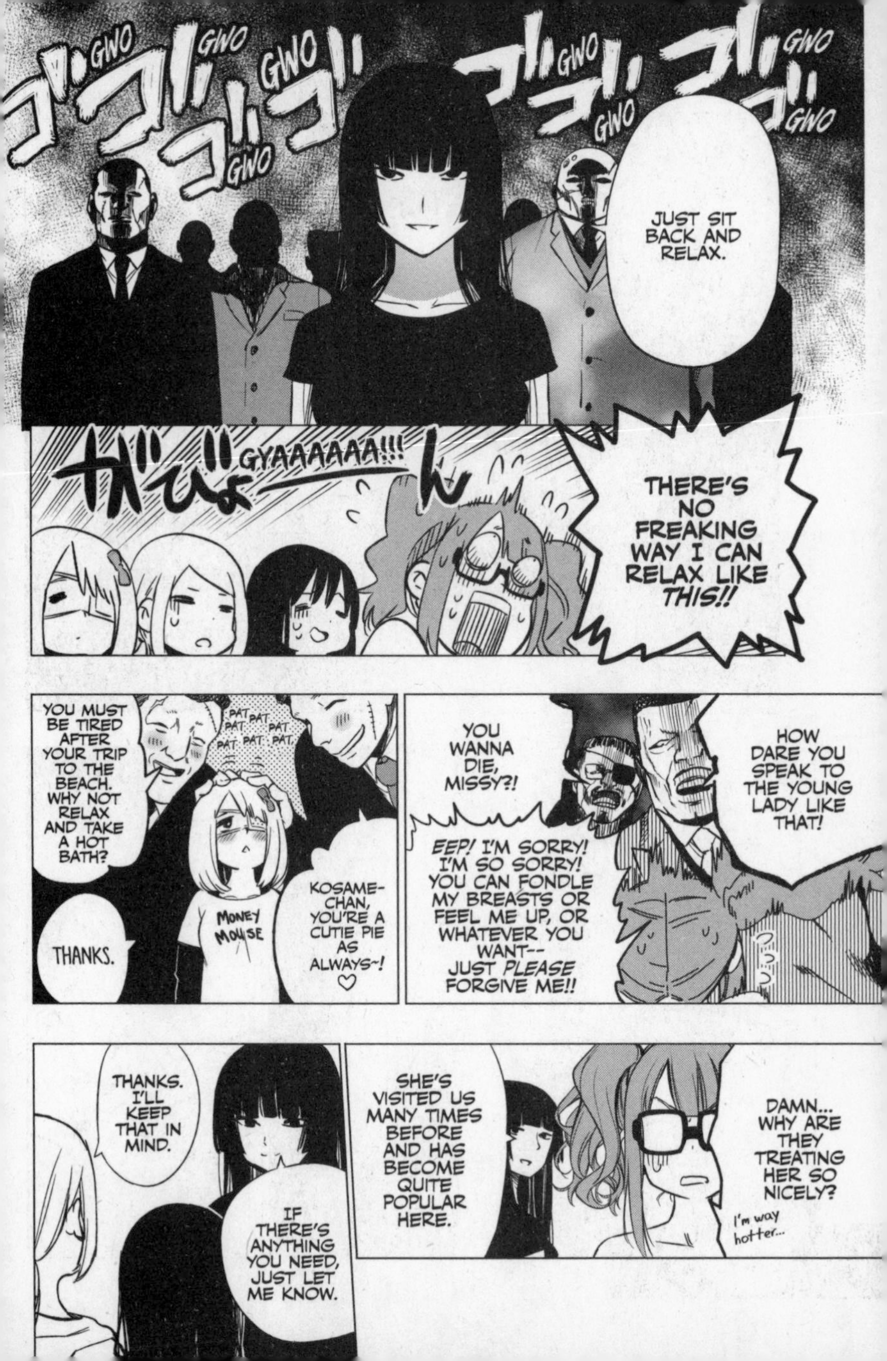
GWO GWO GWO GWO GWO GWO GWO GWO GWO
JUST SIT BACK AND RELAX.
THERE'S NO FREAKING WAY I CAN RELAX LIKE *THIS!!*
GYAAAAAAA!!!
HOW DARE YOU SPEAK TO THE YOUNG LADY LIKE THAT!
YOU WANNA DIE, MISSY?!
EEP! I'M SORRY! I'M SO SORRY! YOU CAN FONDLE MY BREASTS OR FEEL ME UP, OR WHATEVER YOU WANT-- JUST *PLEASE* FORGIVE ME!!
PAT PAT PAT PAT PAT PAT PAT
YOU MUST BE TIRED AFTER YOUR TRIP TO THE BEACH. WHY NOT RELAX AND TAKE A HOT BATH?
KOSAME-CHAN, YOU'RE A CUTIE PIE AS ALWAYS~! ♡
MONEY MOUSE
THANKS.
DAMN... WHY ARE THEY TREATING HER SO NICELY?
I'm way hotter...
SHE'S VISITED US MANY TIMES BEFORE AND HAS BECOME QUITE POPULAR HERE.
IF THERE'S ANYTHING YOU NEED, JUST LET ME KNOW.
THANKS. I'LL KEEP THAT IN MIND.

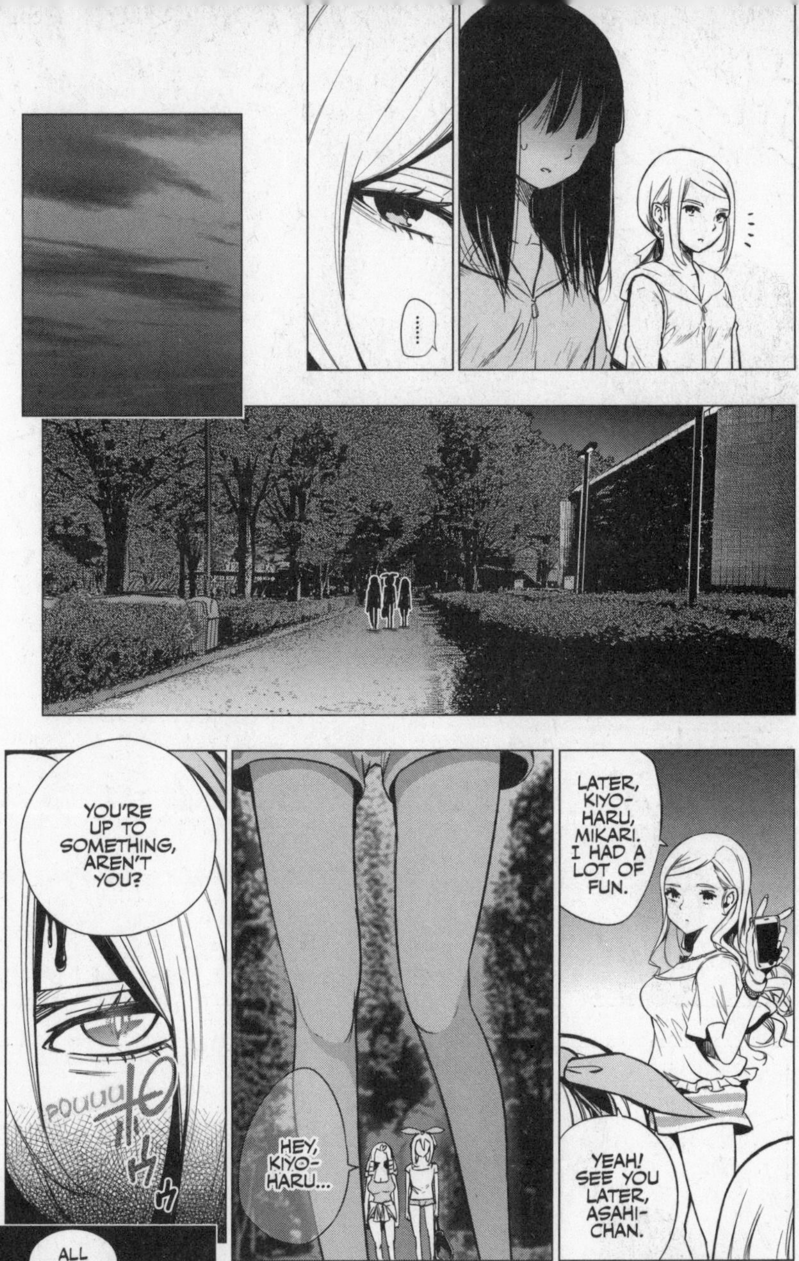
......
LATER, KIYO-HARU, MIKARI. I HAD A LOT OF FUN.
YEAH! SEE YOU LATER, ASAHI-CHAN.
HEY, KIYO-HARU...
YOU'RE UP TO SOMETHING, AREN'T YOU?
ALL RIGHT...

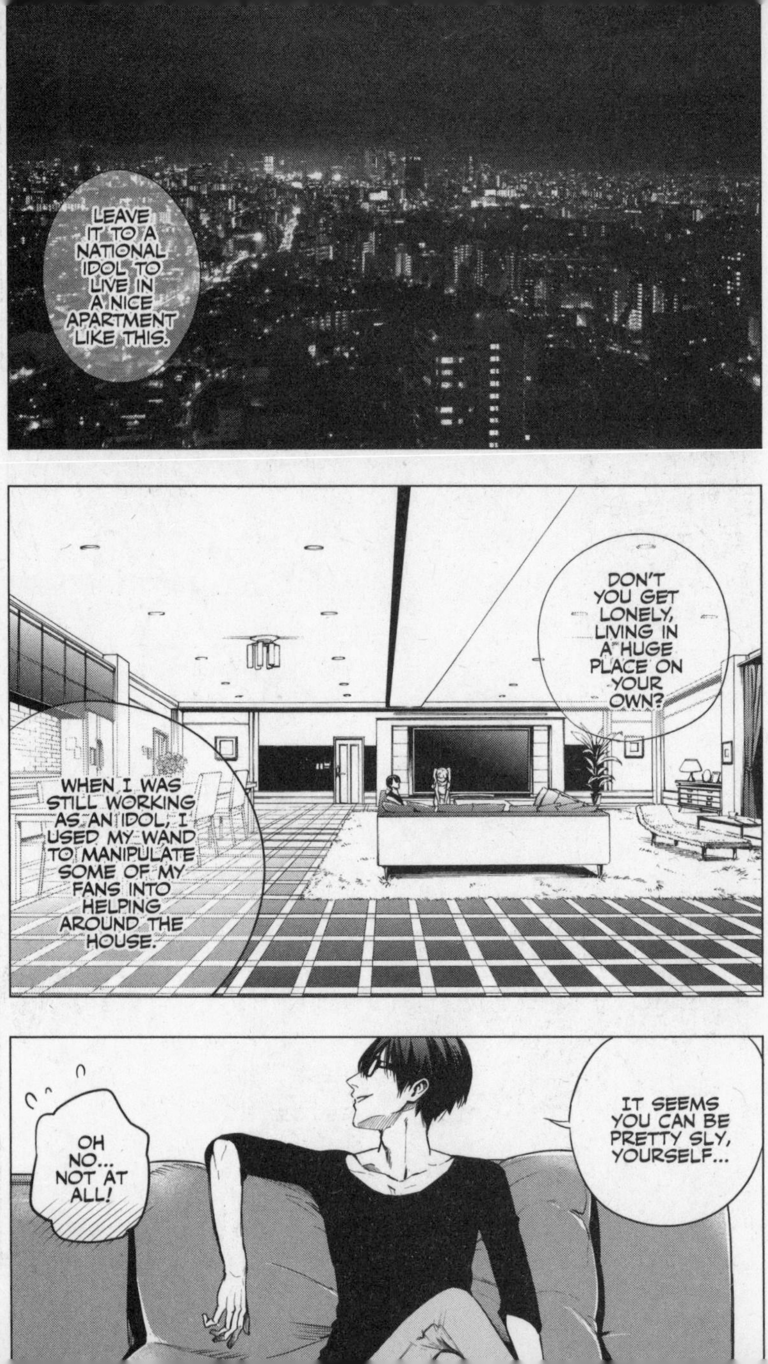
LEAVE IT TO A NATIONAL IDOL TO LIVE IN A NICE APARTMENT LIKE THIS.
DON'T YOU GET LONELY, LIVING IN A HUGE PLACE ON YOUR OWN?
WHEN I WAS STILL WORKING AS AN IDOL, I USED MY WAND TO MANIPULATE SOME OF MY FANS INTO HELPING AROUND THE HOUSE.
IT SEEMS YOU CAN BE PRETTY SLY, YOURSELF...
OH NO... NOT AT ALL!

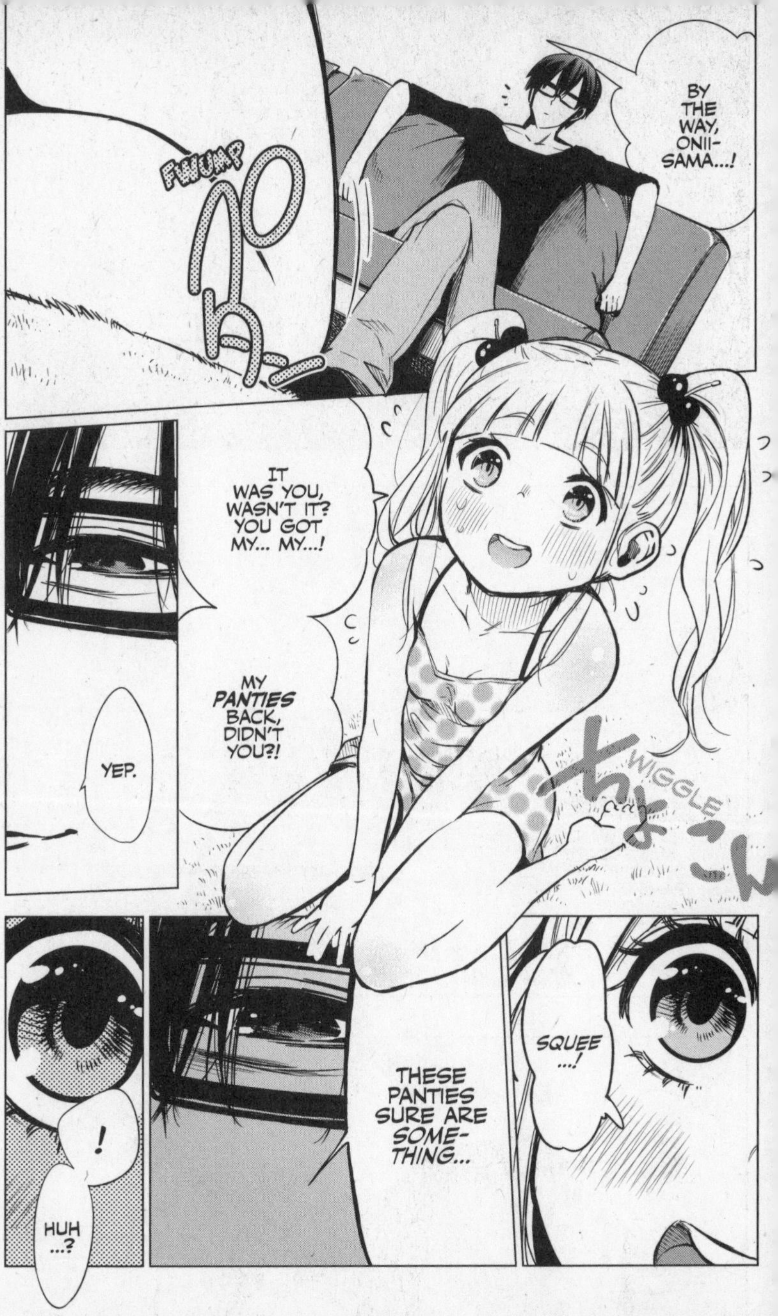
BY THE WAY, ONII-SAMA...!
FWUMP
IT WAS YOU, WASN'T IT? YOU GOT MY... MY...!
MY *PANTIES* BACK, DIDN'T YOU?!
WIGGLE
YEP.
SQUEE ...!
THESE PANTIES SURE ARE *SOME-THING...*
!
HUH ...?

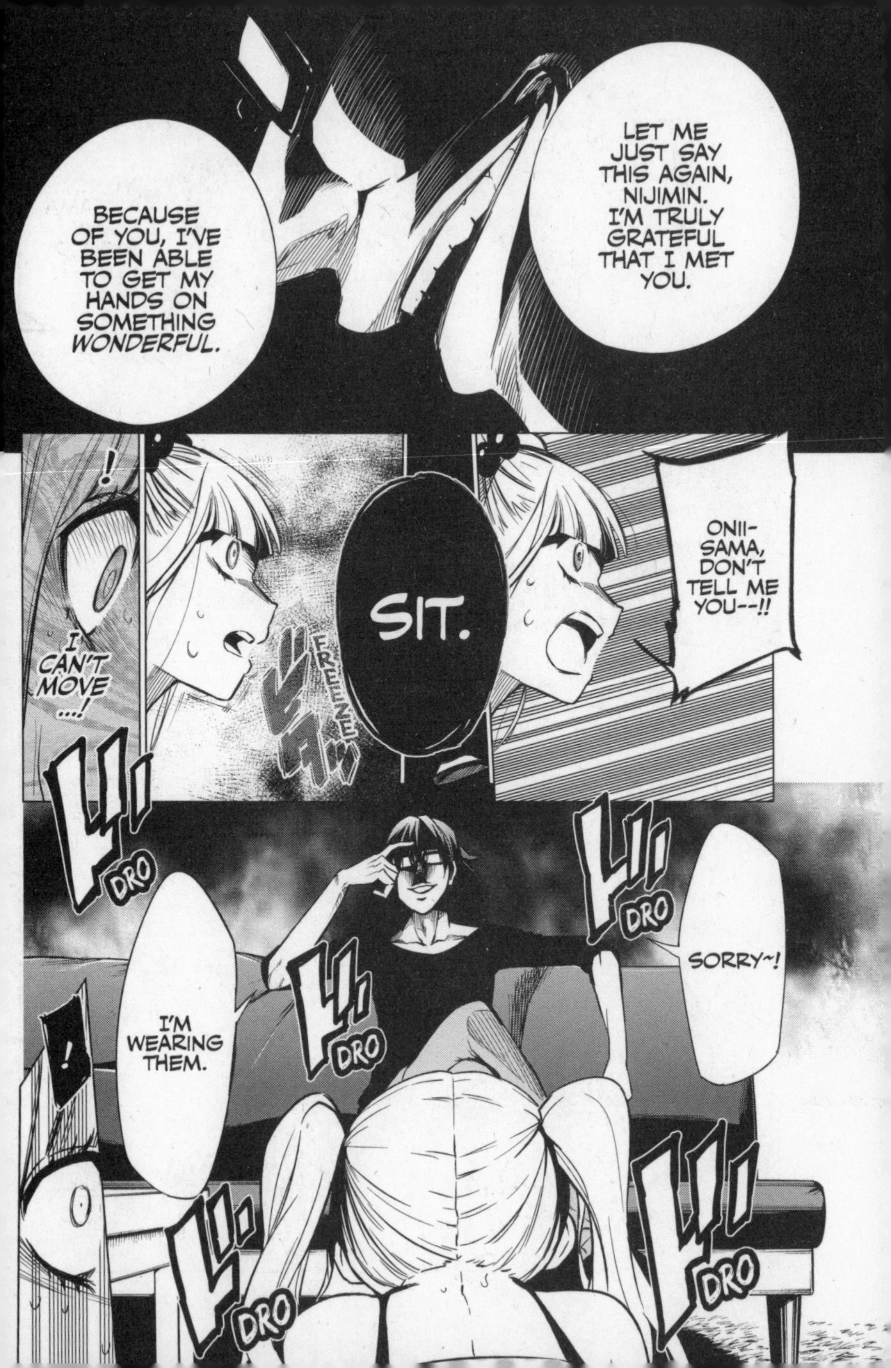
LET ME JUST SAY THIS AGAIN, NIJIMIN. I'M TRULY GRATEFUL THAT I MET YOU.
BECAUSE OF YOU, I'VE BEEN ABLE TO GET MY HANDS ON SOMETHING *WONDERFUL*.
ONII-SAMA, DON'T TELL ME YOU--!!
SIT.
FREEZE
!
I CAN'T MOVE ...!
DRO
DRO
SORRY~!
I'M WEARING THEM.
DRO
!
DRO
DRO
DRO

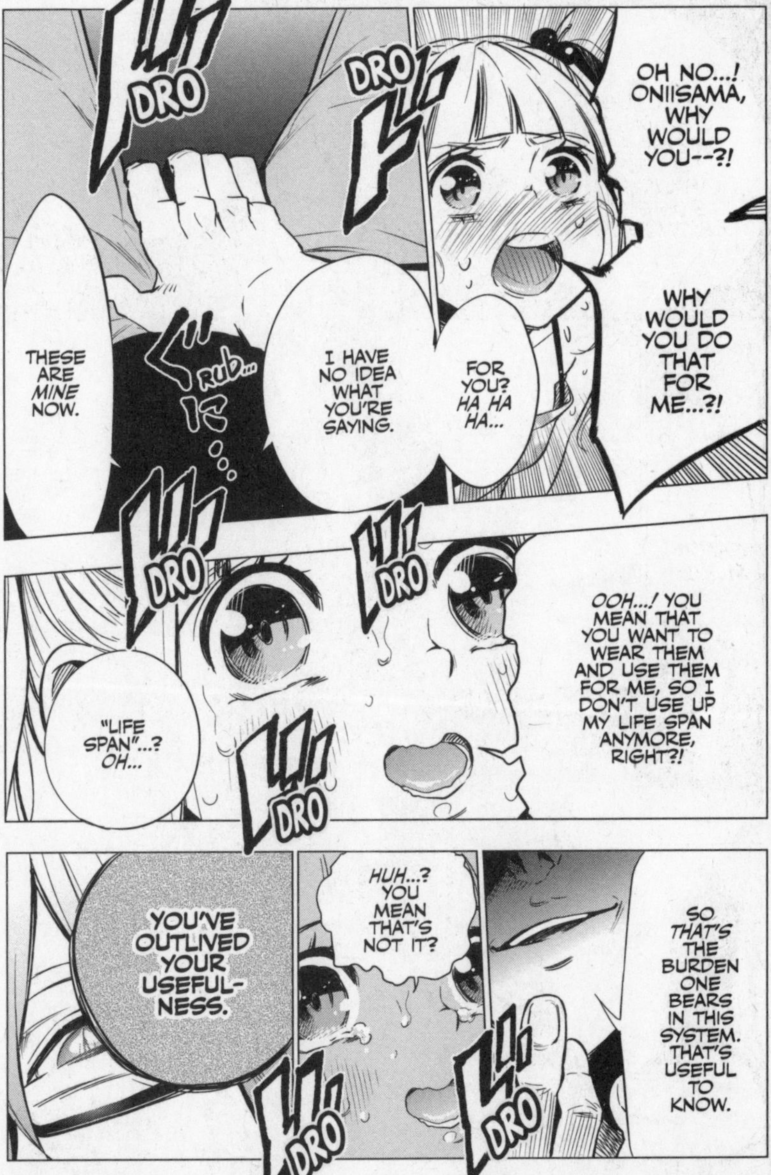
DRO
OH NO...! ONIISAMA, WHY WOULD YOU--?!
WHY WOULD YOU DO THAT FOR ME...?!
FOR YOU? *HA HA HA...*
I HAVE NO IDEA WHAT YOU'RE SAYING.
DRO
THESE ARE *MINE* NOW.
rub...
OOH...! YOU MEAN THAT YOU WANT TO WEAR THEM AND USE THEM FOR ME, SO I DON'T USE UP MY LIFE SPAN ANYMORE, RIGHT?!
DRO
DRO
"LIFE SPAN"...? *OH...*
DRO
SO *THAT'S* THE BURDEN ONE BEARS IN THIS SYSTEM. THAT'S USEFUL TO KNOW.
DRO
HUH...? YOU MEAN THAT'S NOT IT?
DRO
YOU'VE OUTLIVED YOUR USEFUL-NESS.

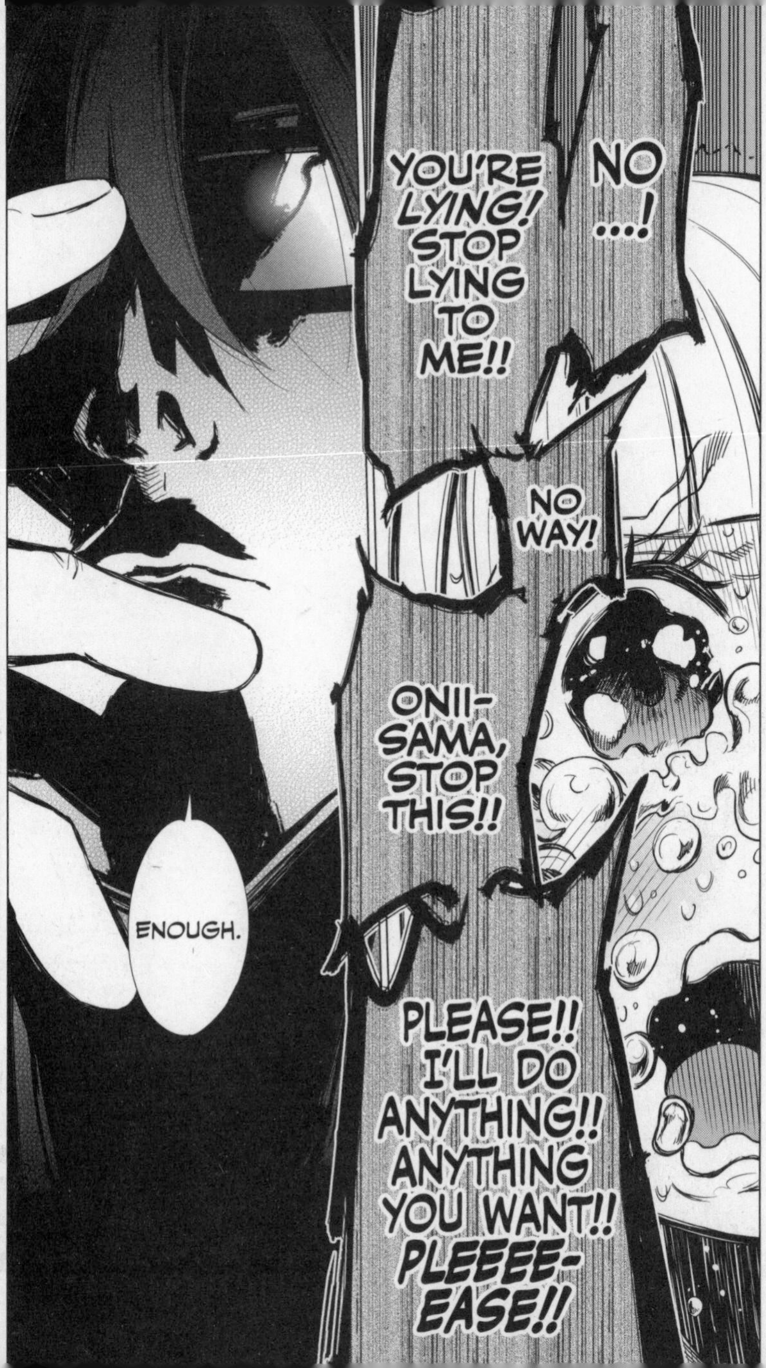
NO ...!
YOU'RE LYING! STOP LYING TO ME!!
NO WAY!
ONII-SAMA, STOP THIS!!
PLEASE!! I'LL DO ANYTHING!! ANYTHING YOU WANT!! PLEEEE-EASE!!
ENOUGH.

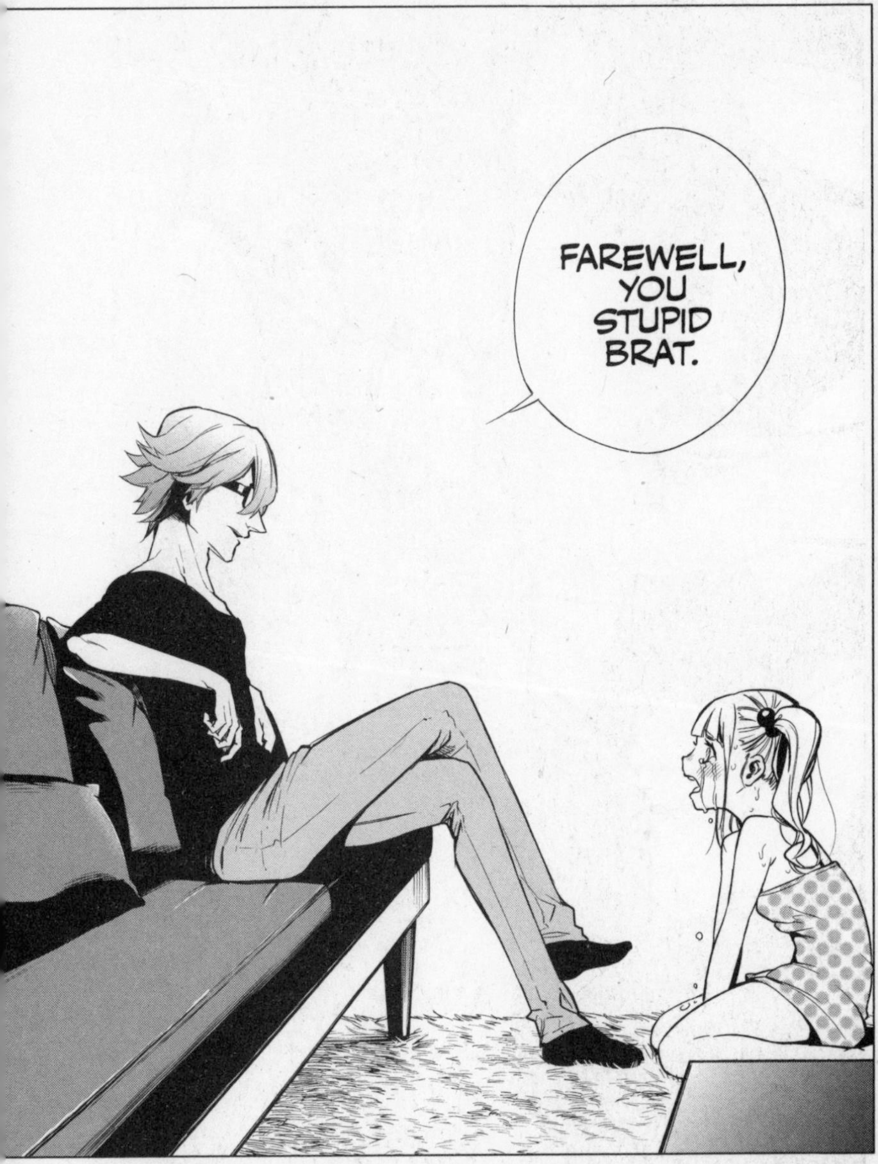
FAREWELL, YOU STUPID BRAT.

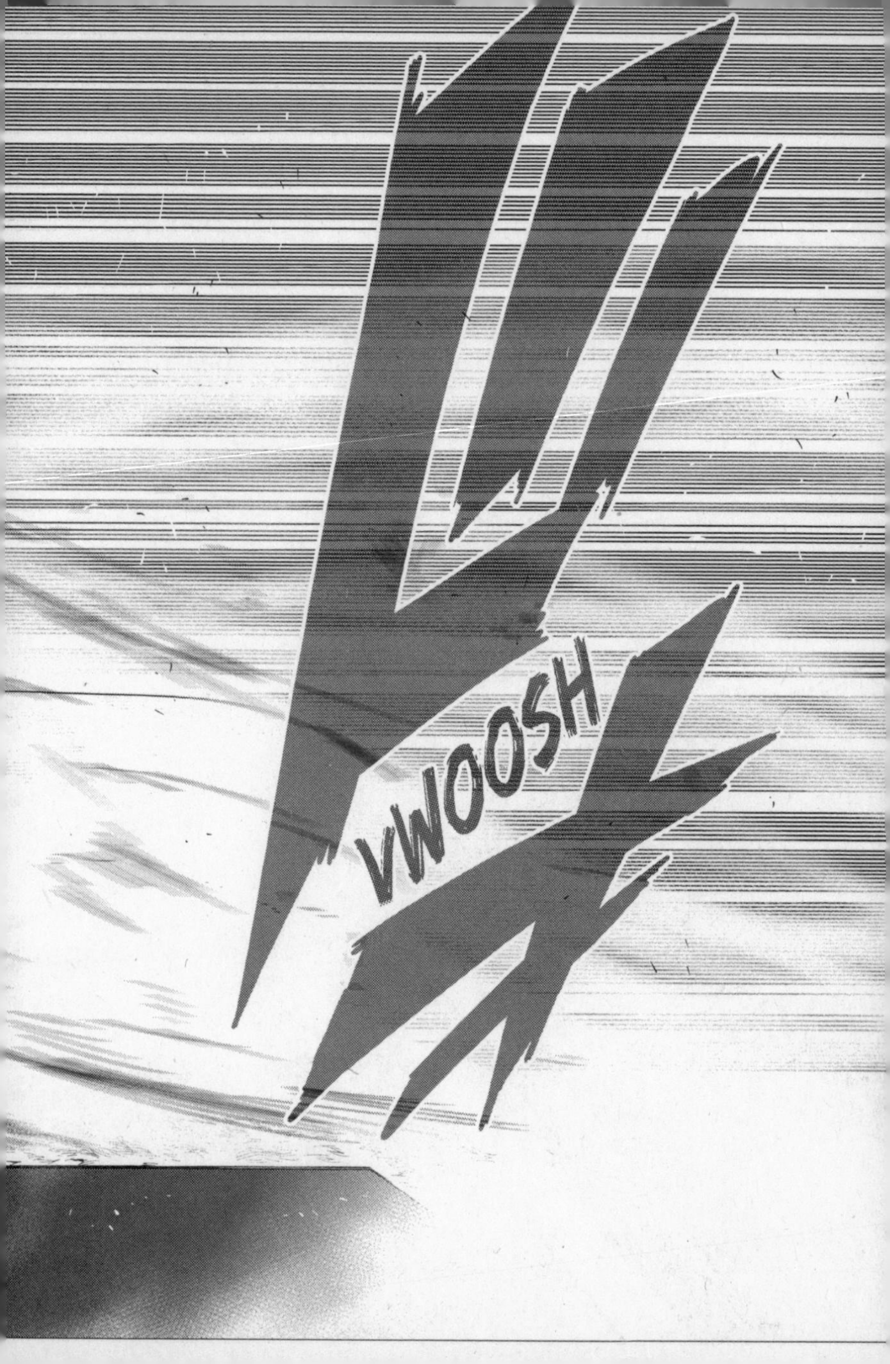
VWOOSH

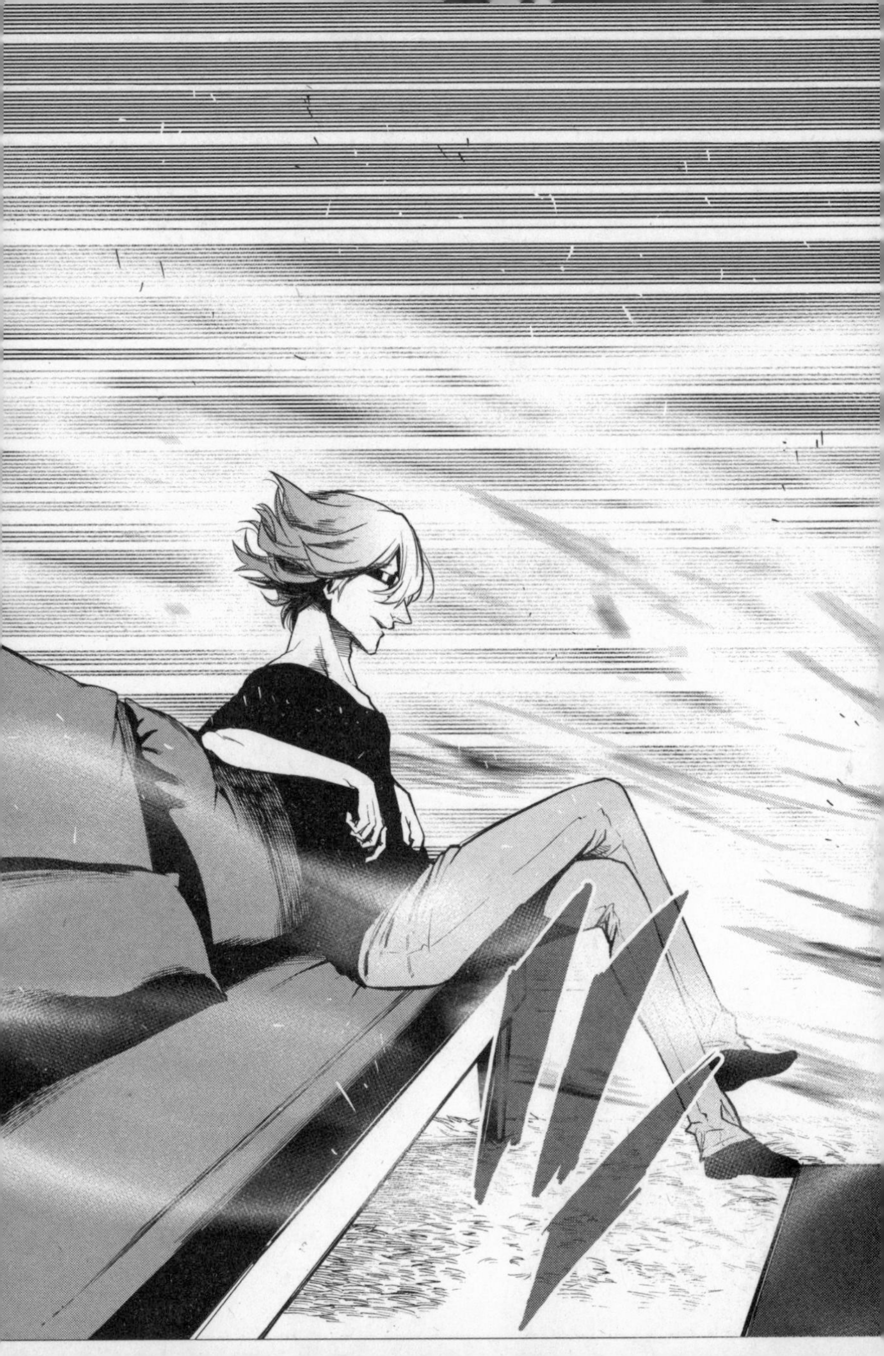

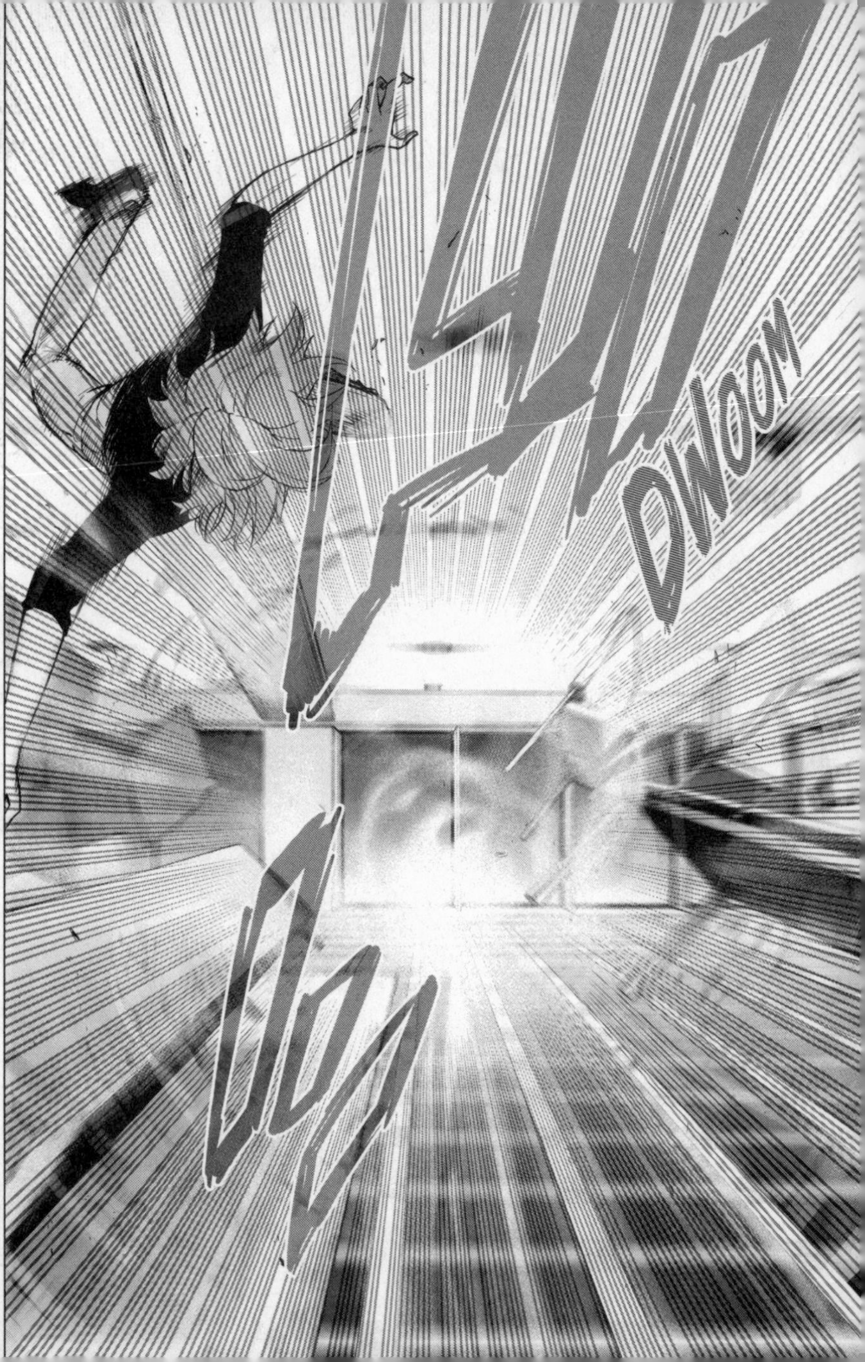
DWOOM

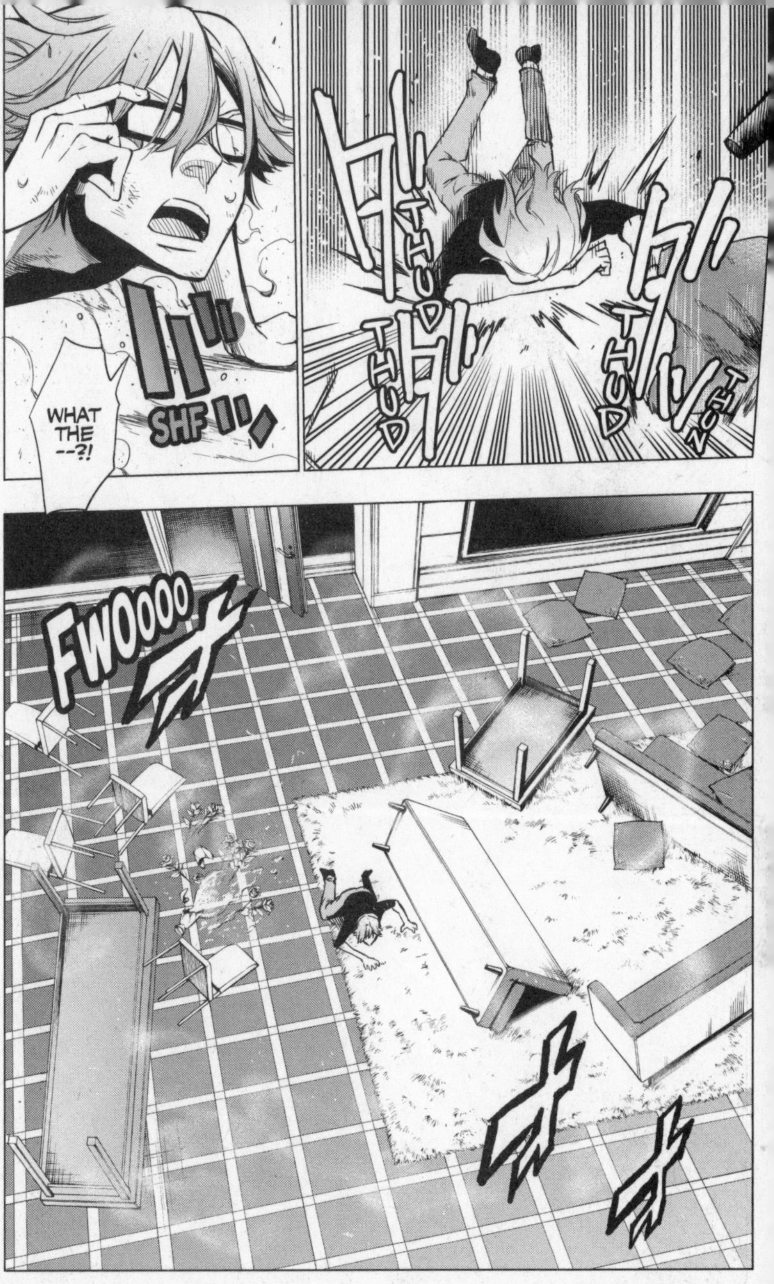
THUD
THUD
THUD
WHAT THE --?!
SHF
FWOOOO

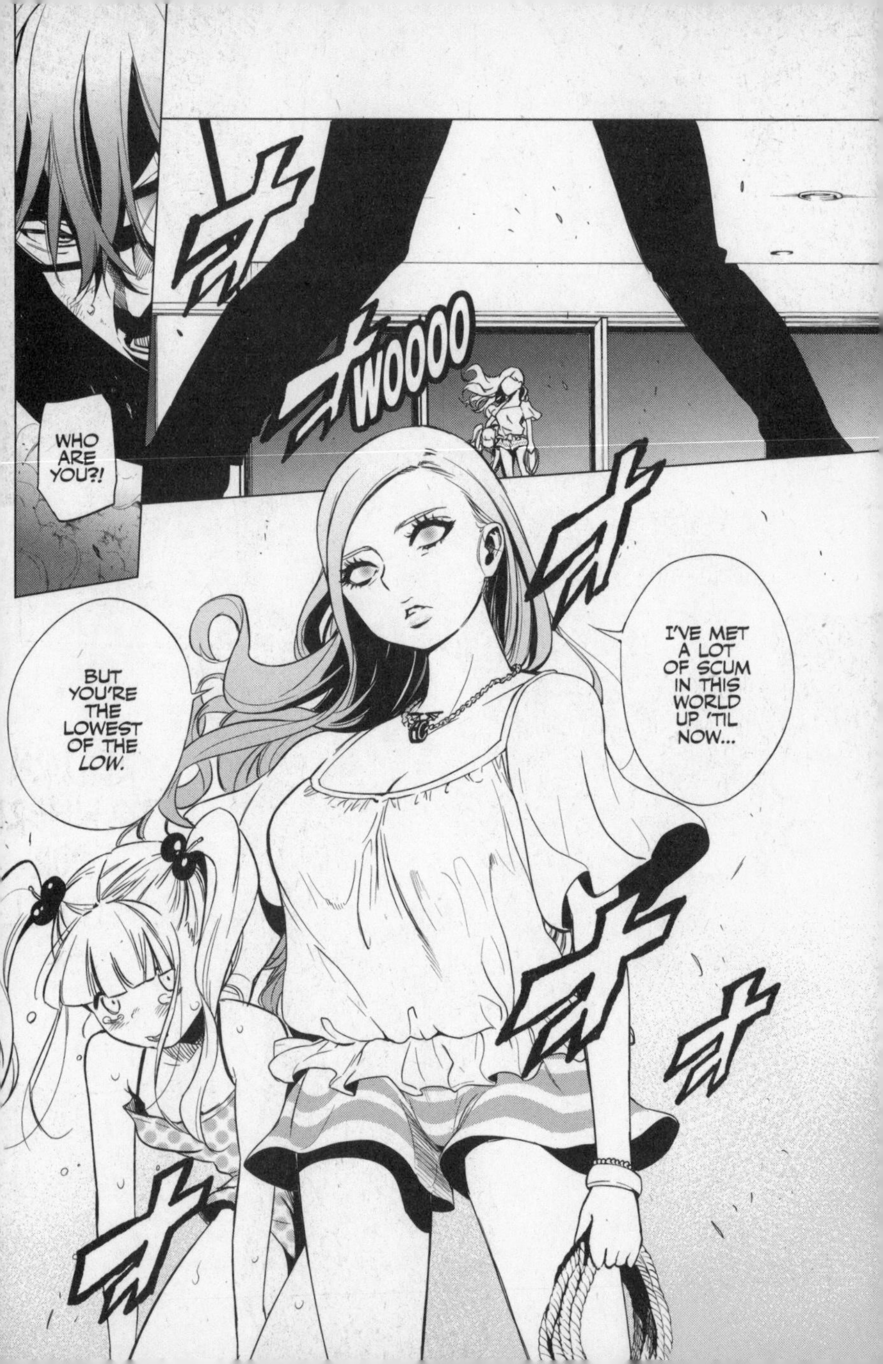
WOOOO
WHO ARE YOU?!
I'VE MET A LOT OF SCUM IN THIS WORLD UP 'TIL NOW...
BUT YOU'RE THE LOWEST OF THE *LOW*.

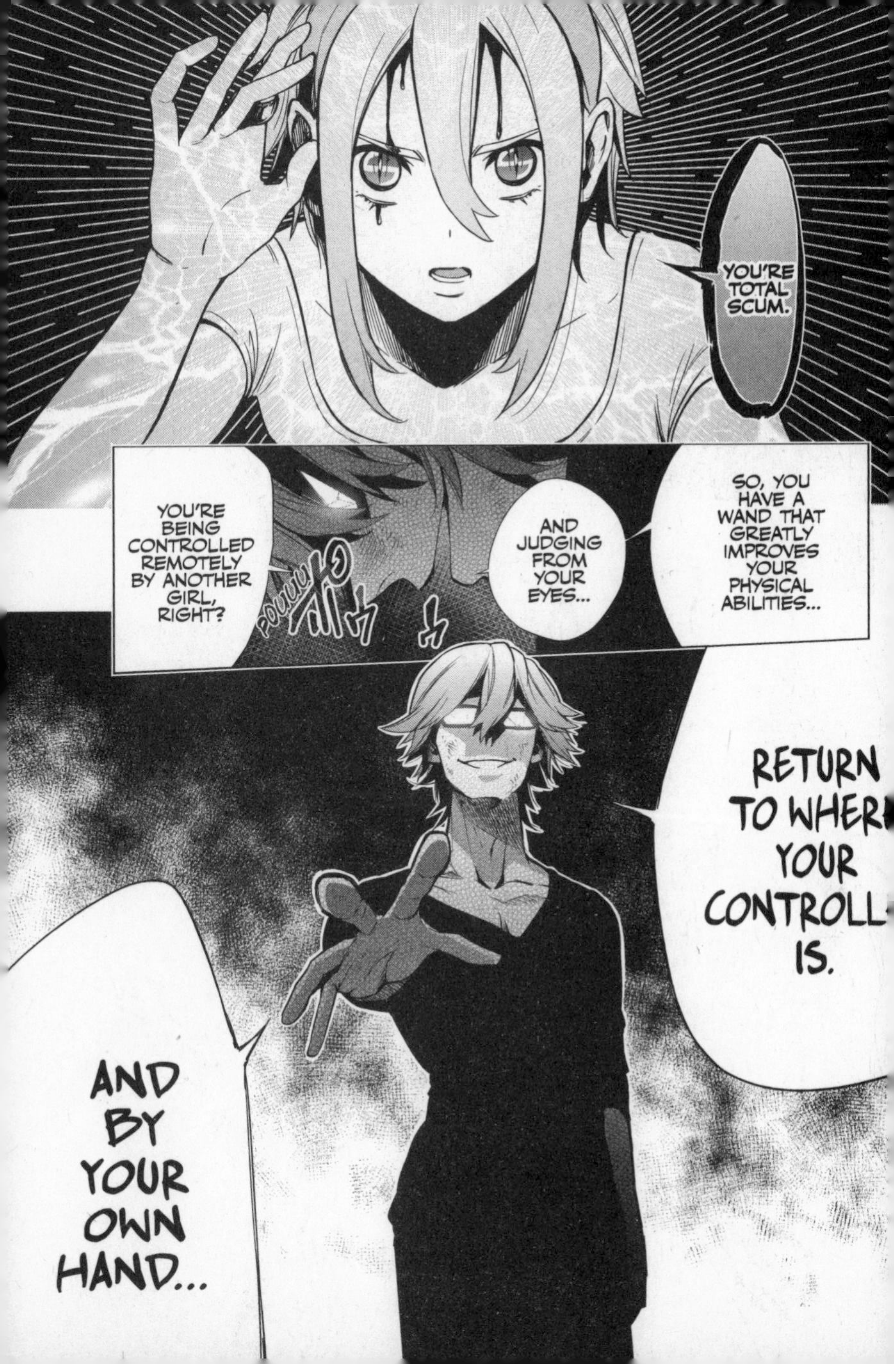
YOU'RE TOTAL SCUM.
SO, YOU HAVE A WAND THAT GREATLY IMPROVES YOUR PHYSICAL ABILITIES...
AND JUDGING FROM YOUR EYES...
YOU'RE BEING CONTROLLED REMOTELY BY ANOTHER GIRL, RIGHT?
RETURN TO WHER YOUR CONTROLL IS.
AND BY YOUR OWN HAND...

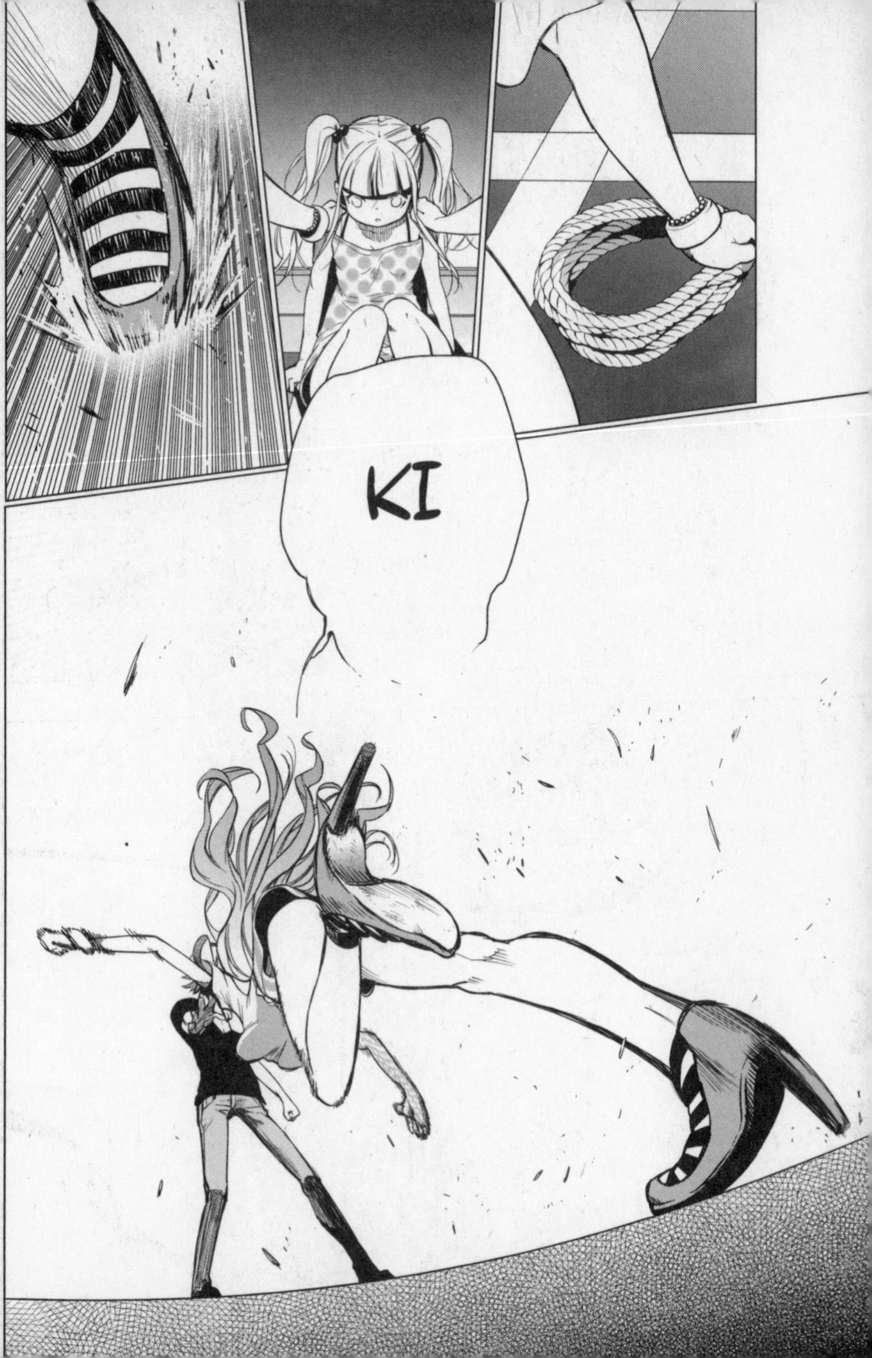
KI

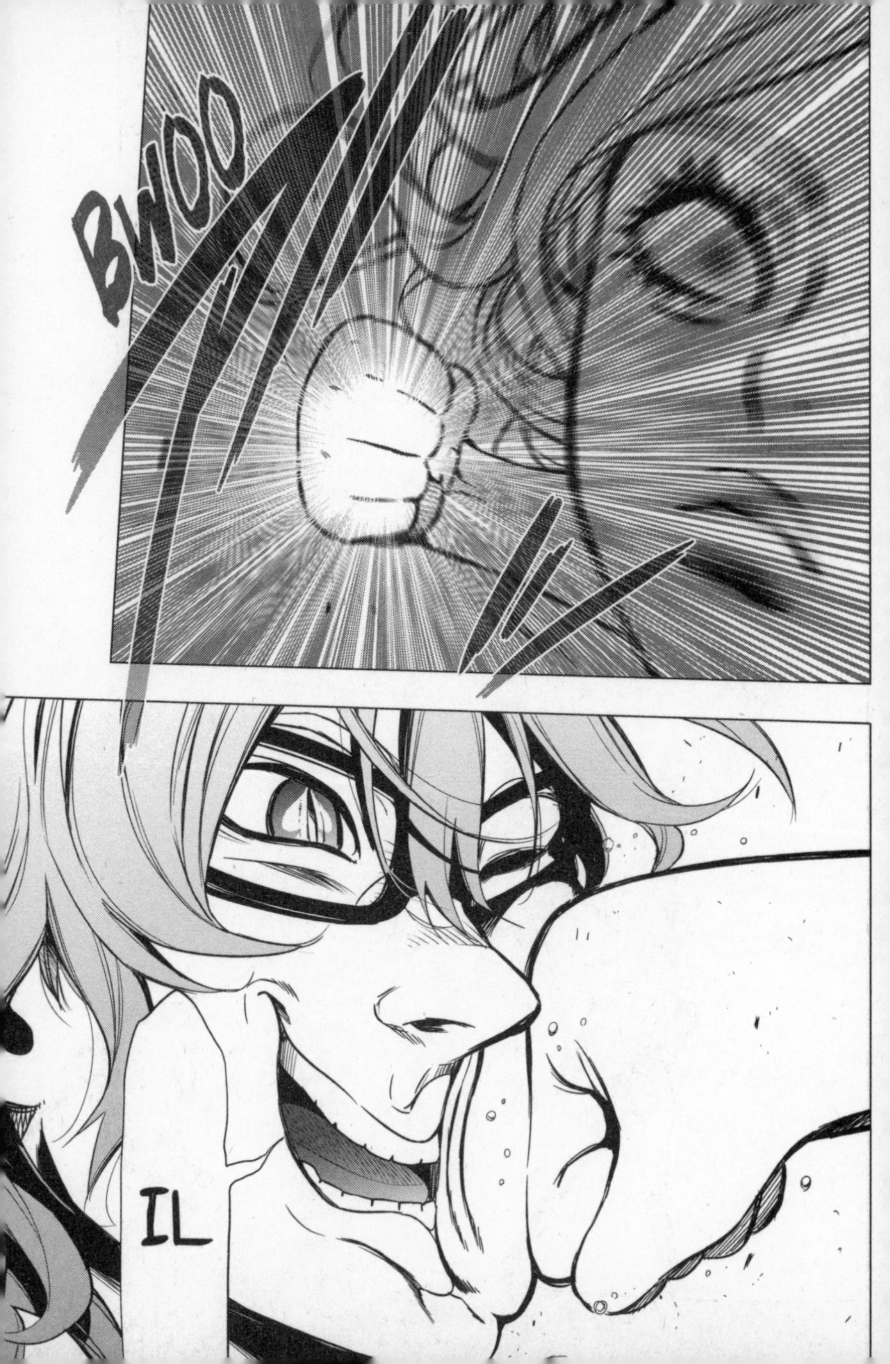
BWOO
IL

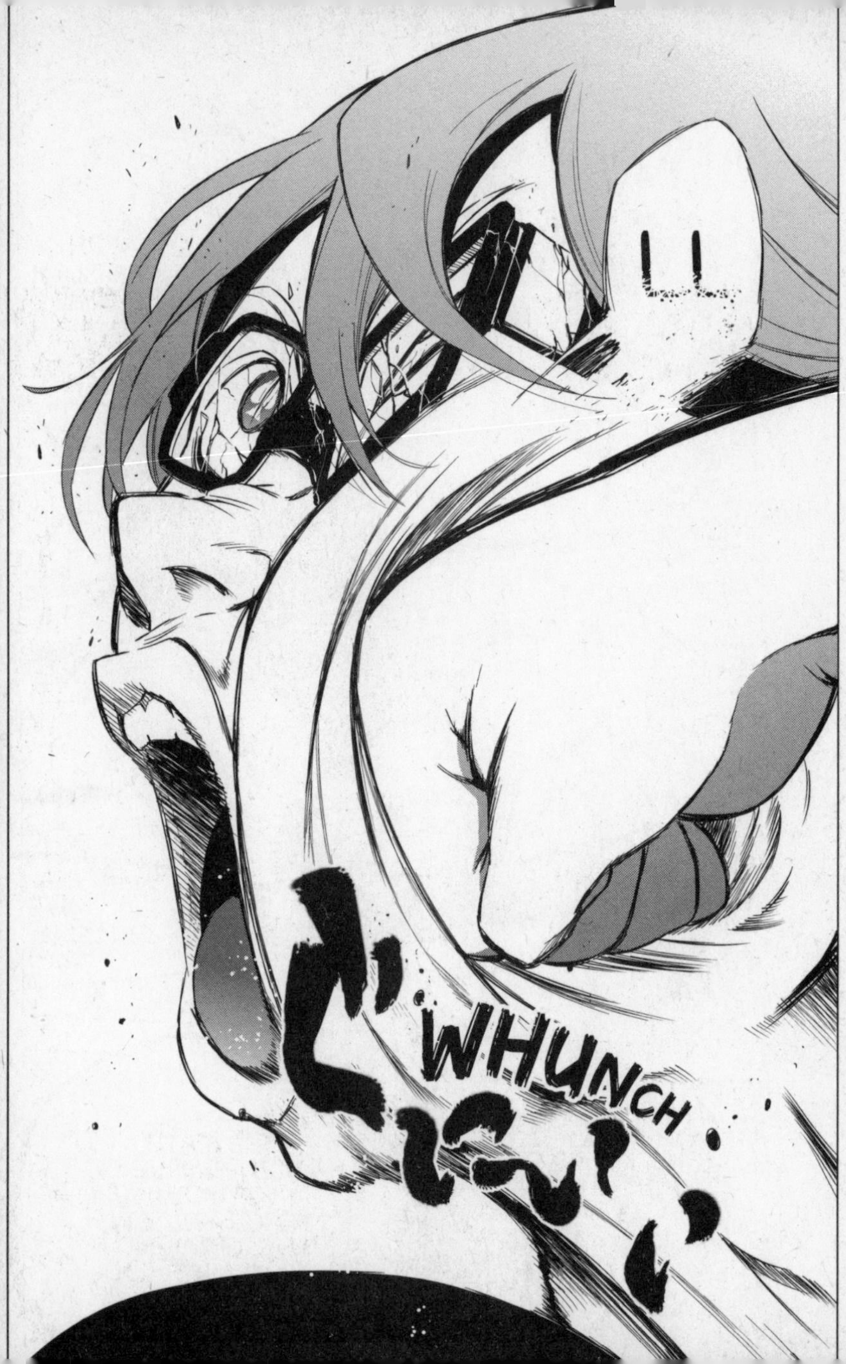
WHUNCH

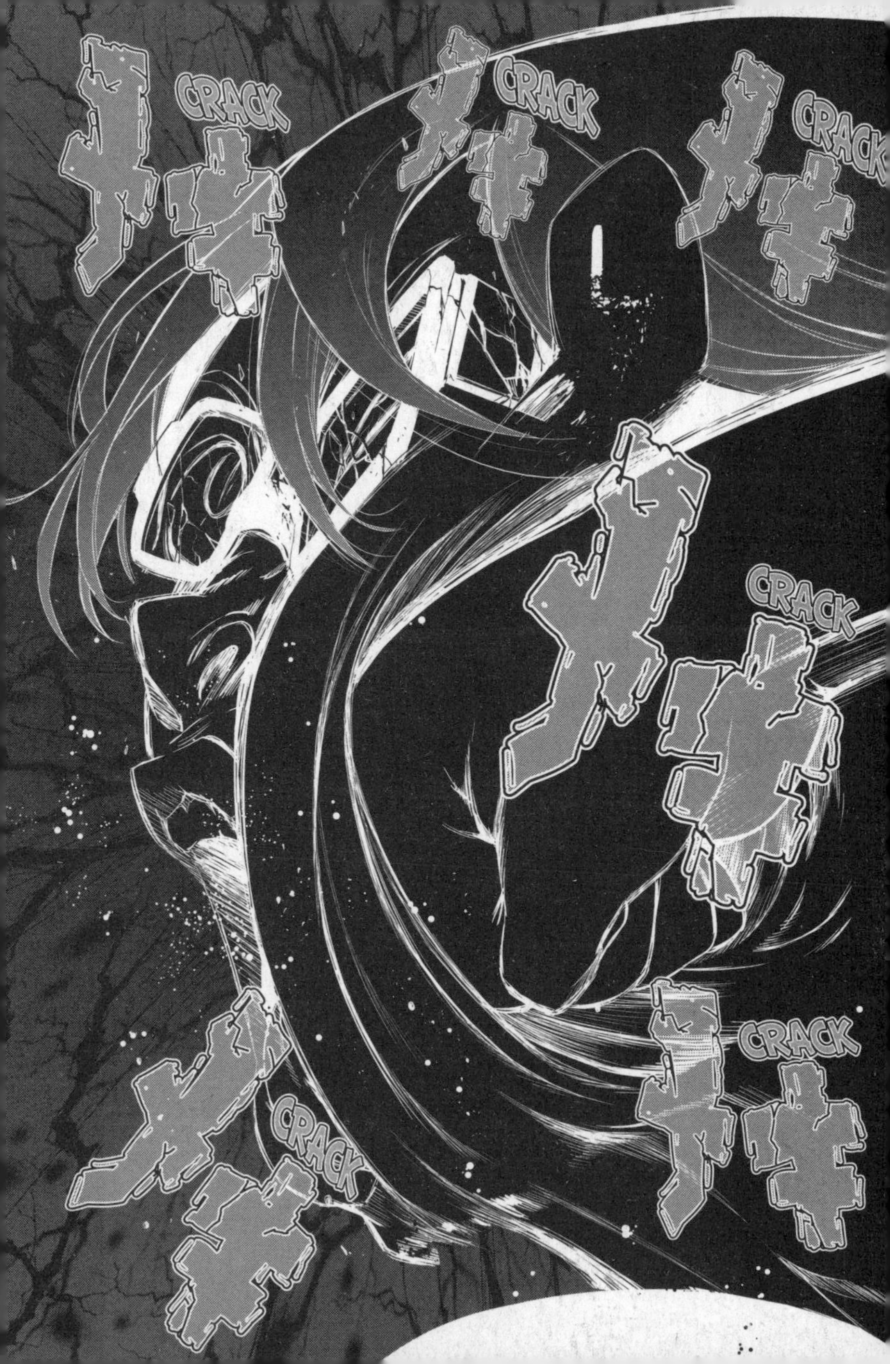
CRACK
CRACK
CRACK
CRACK
CRACK
CRACK

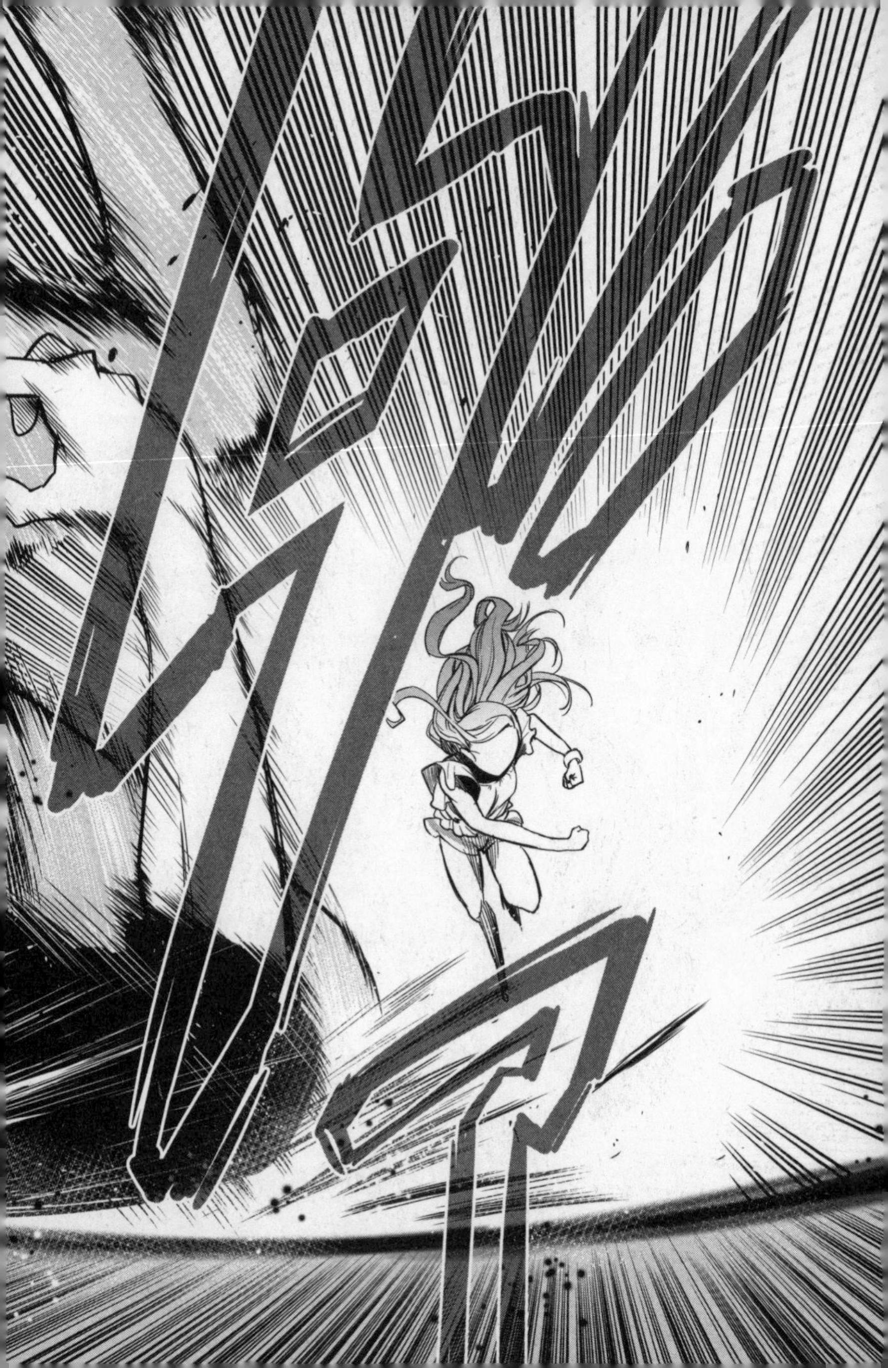

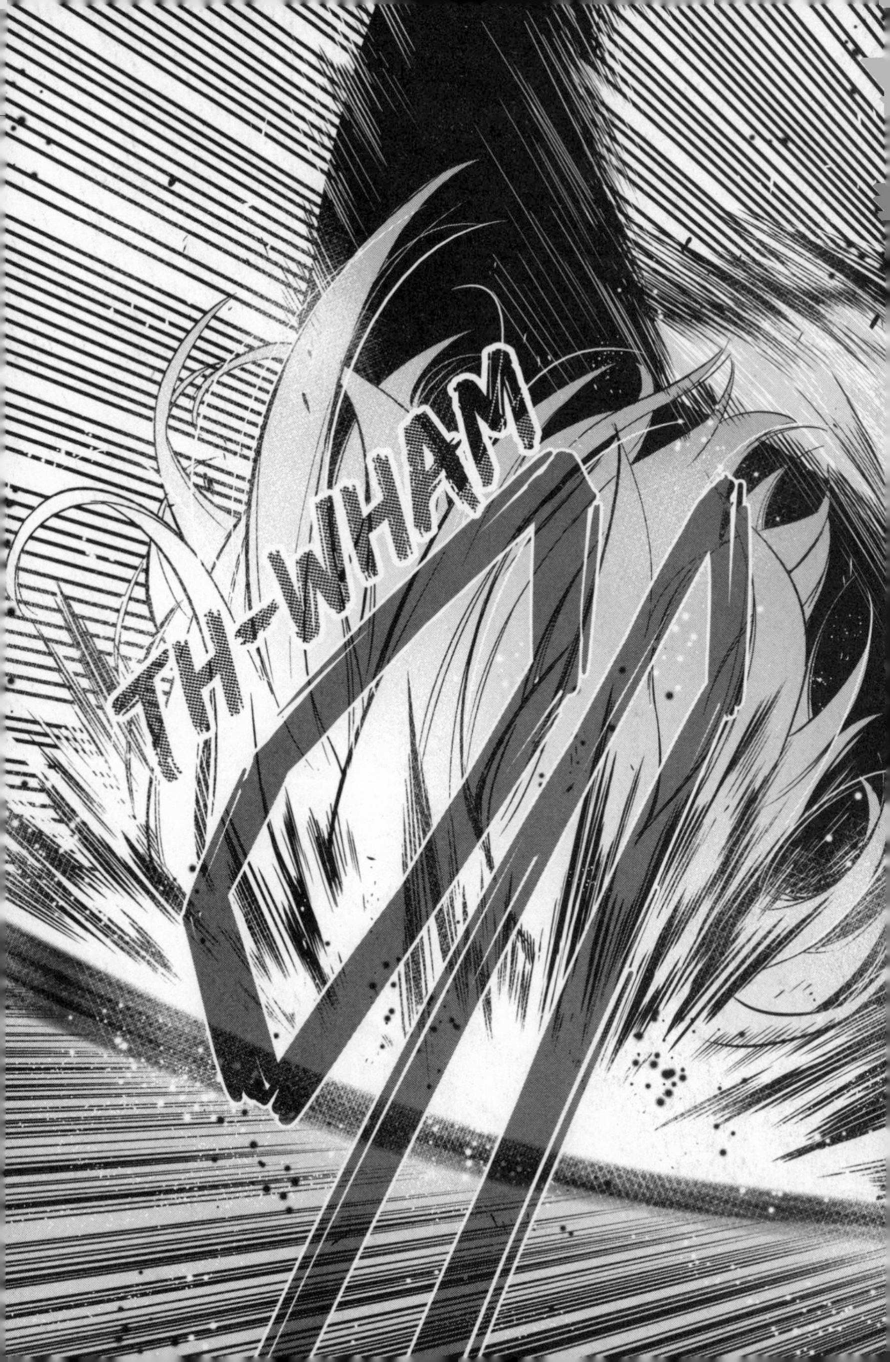
TH-WHAM

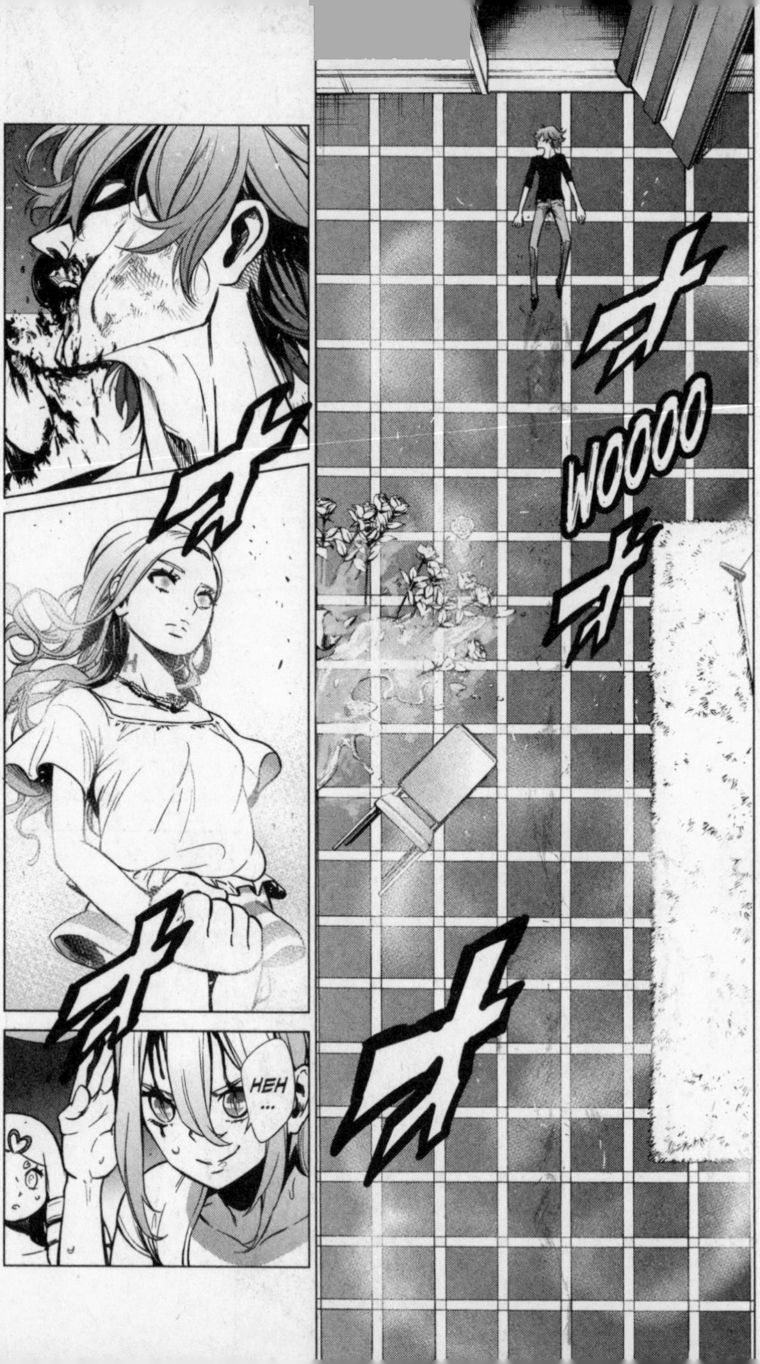
WOOOO
HEH ...

ENTER.36 MESSAGE

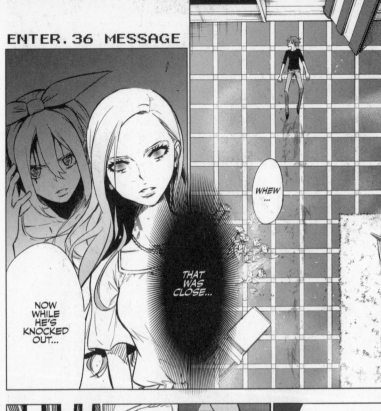

WHEW
...

THAT
WAS
CLOSE...

NOW
WHILE
HE'S
KNOCKED
OUT...

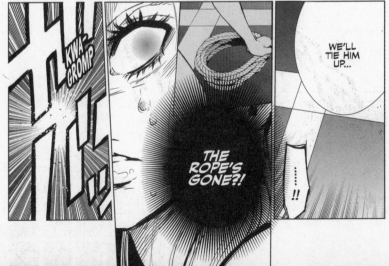

KWA-
CROMP

WE'LL
TIE HIM
UP...

THE
ROPE'S
GONE?!

......!!

!!

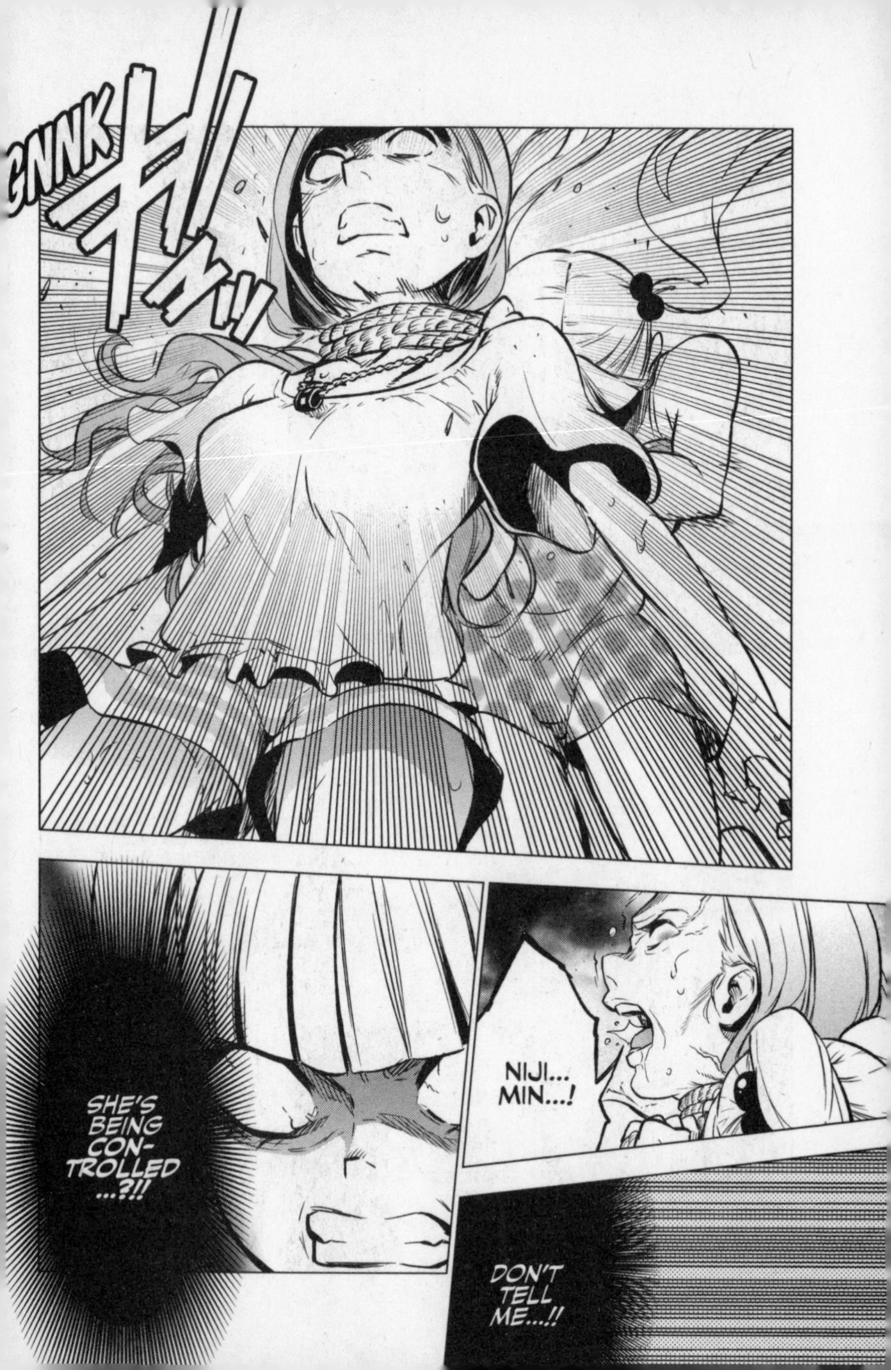
GNNK
!!
NIJI... MIN...!
SHE'S BEING CON-TROLLED ...?!!
DON'T TELL ME...!!

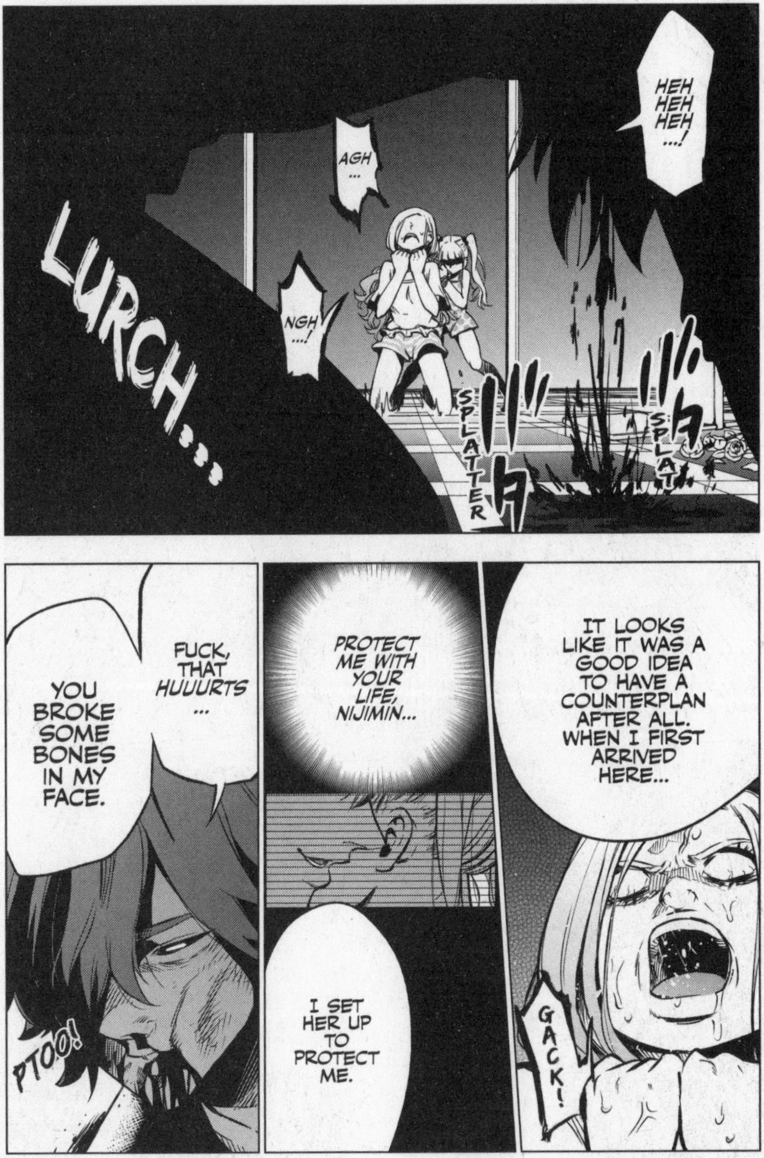
HEH HEH HEH ...!
AGH ...
SPLAT
SPLATTER
NGH ...!
LURCH...
IT LOOKS LIKE IT WAS A GOOD IDEA TO HAVE A COUNTERPLAN AFTER ALL. WHEN I FIRST ARRIVED HERE...
GACK!
PROTECT ME WITH YOUR LIFE, NIJIMIN...
I SET HER UP TO PROTECT ME.
FUCK, THAT HUUURTS ...
YOU BROKE SOME BONES IN MY FACE.
PTOO!

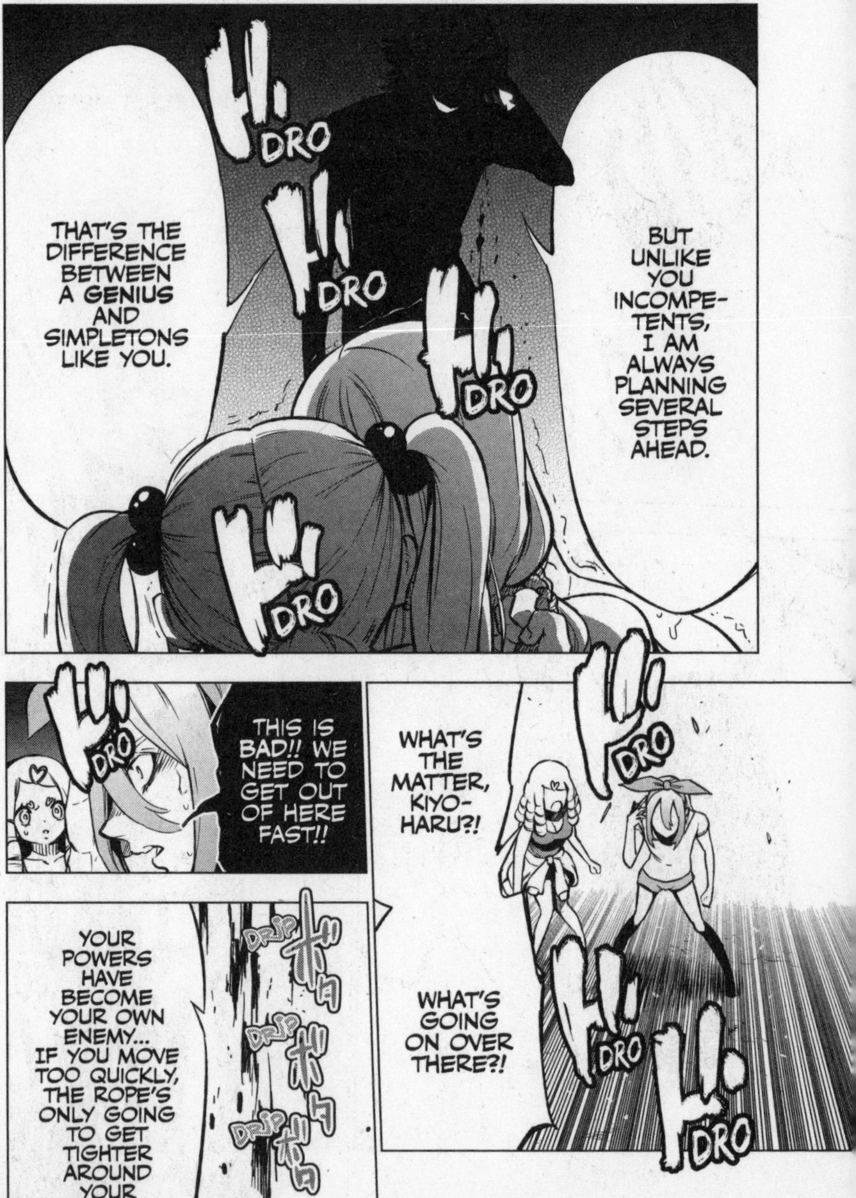
BUT UNLIKE YOU INCOMPETENTS, I AM ALWAYS PLANNING SEVERAL STEPS AHEAD.
DRO
DRO
DRO
DRO
THAT'S THE DIFFERENCE BETWEEN A GENIUS AND SIMPLETONS LIKE YOU.
DRO
WHAT'S THE MATTER, KIYO-HARU?!
WHAT'S GOING ON OVER THERE?!
DRO
DRO
DRO
THIS IS BAD!! WE NEED TO GET OUT OF HERE FAST!!
DRO
DRIP
DRIP
DRIP
YOUR POWERS HAVE BECOME YOUR OWN ENEMY... IF YOU MOVE TOO QUICKLY, THE ROPE'S ONLY GOING TO GET TIGHTER AROUND YOUR NECK.

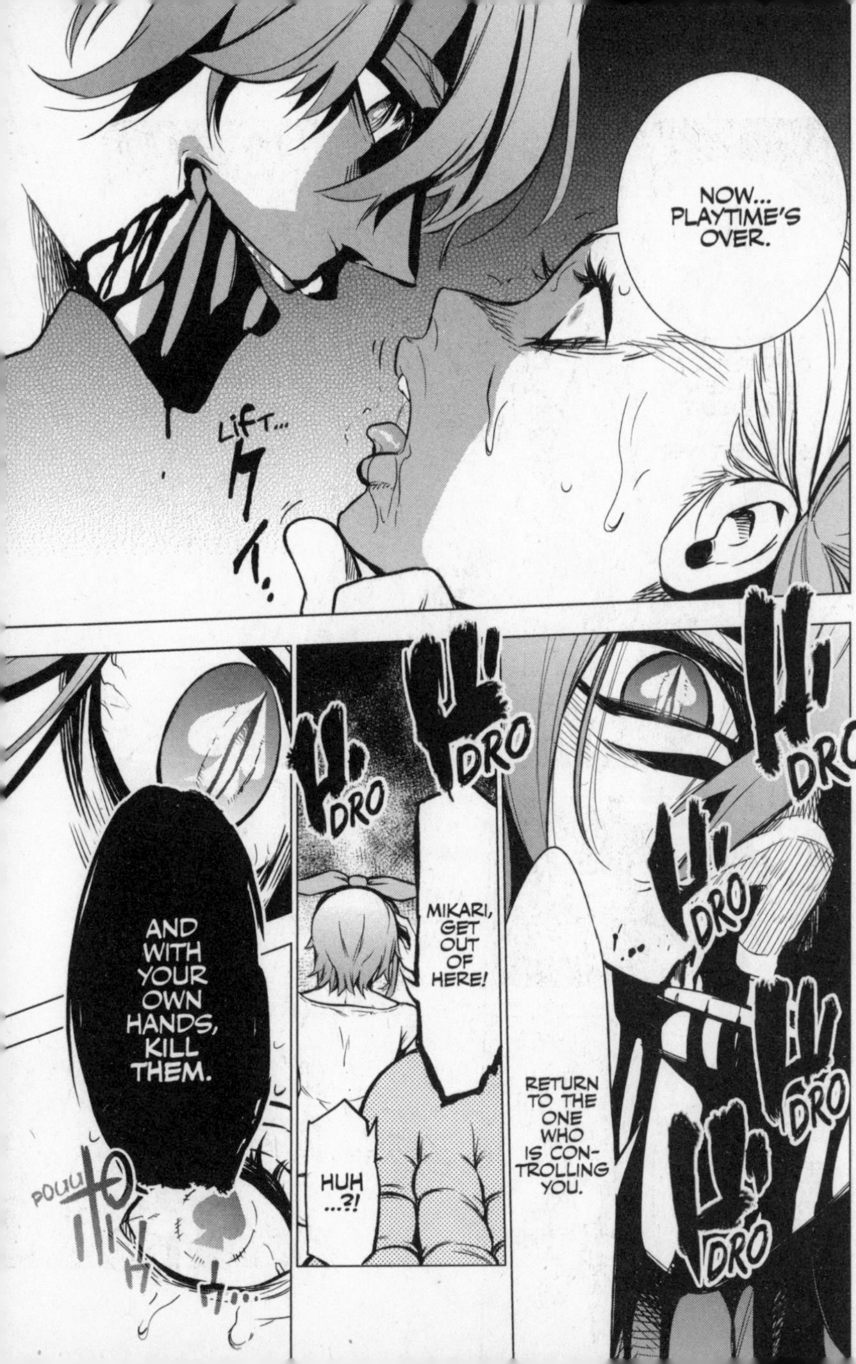

NOW... PLAYTIME'S OVER.
LIFT...
DRO
DRO
DRO
DRO
DRO
...
RETURN TO THE ONE WHO IS CON-TROLLING YOU.
DRO
DRO
MIKARI, GET OUT OF HERE!
HUH ...?!
AND WITH YOUR OWN HANDS, KILL THEM.
POUU

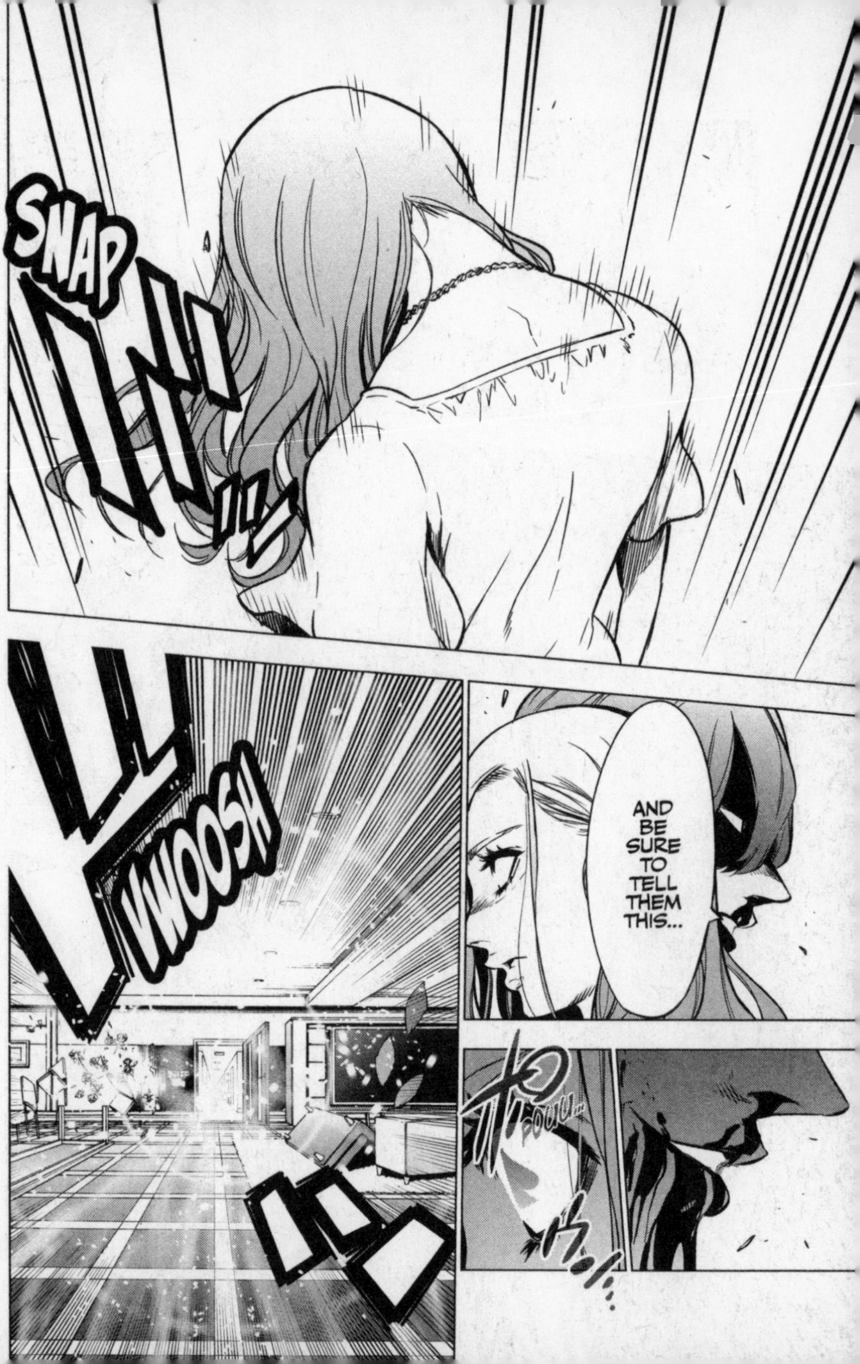
SNAP
AND BE SURE TO TELL THEM THIS...
VWOOSH

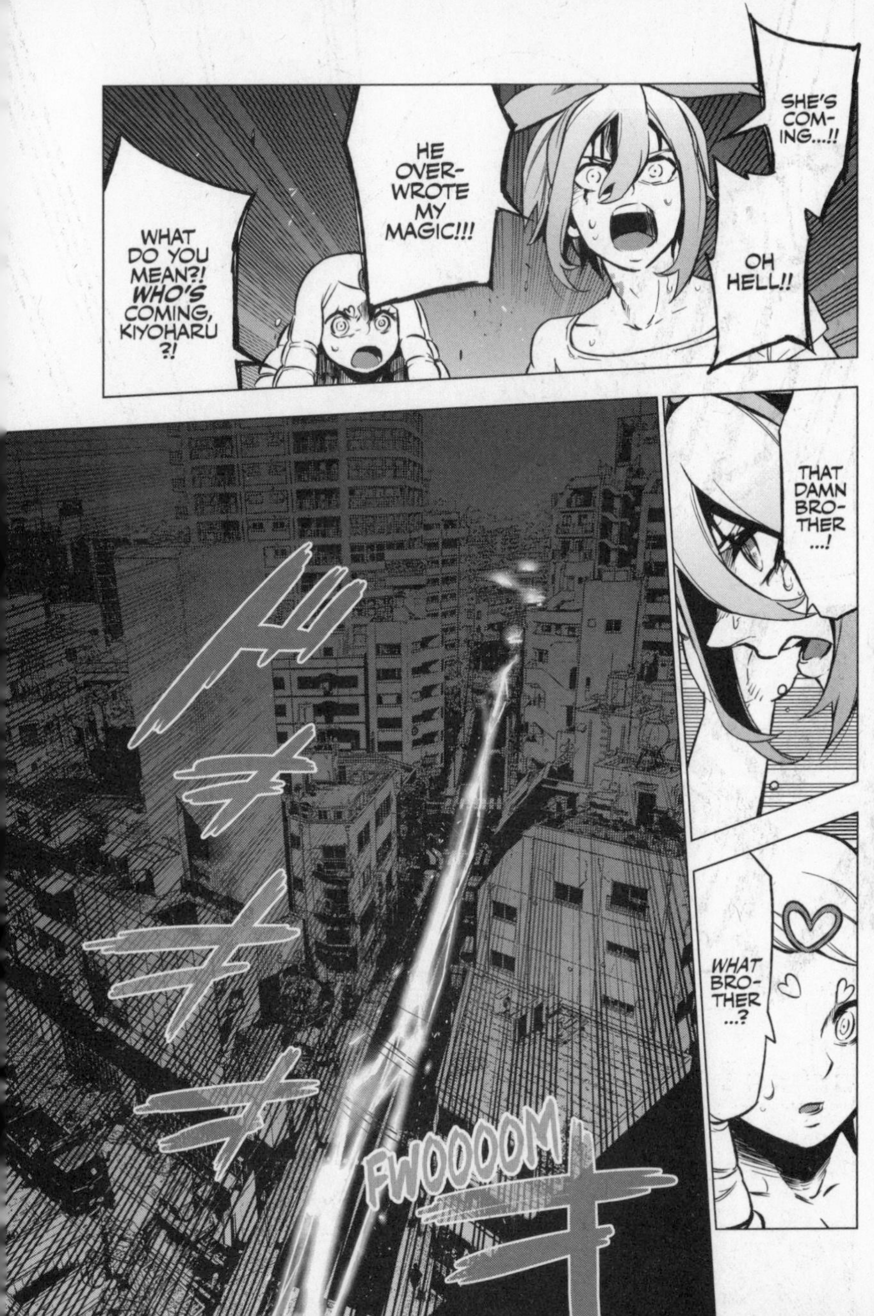
SHE'S COM-ING...!!
HE OVER-WROTE MY MAGIC!!!
OH HELL!!
WHAT DO YOU MEAN?! *WHO'S* COMING, KIYOHARU?!
THAT DAMN BRO-THER...!
WHAT BRO-THER...?
FWOOOOM

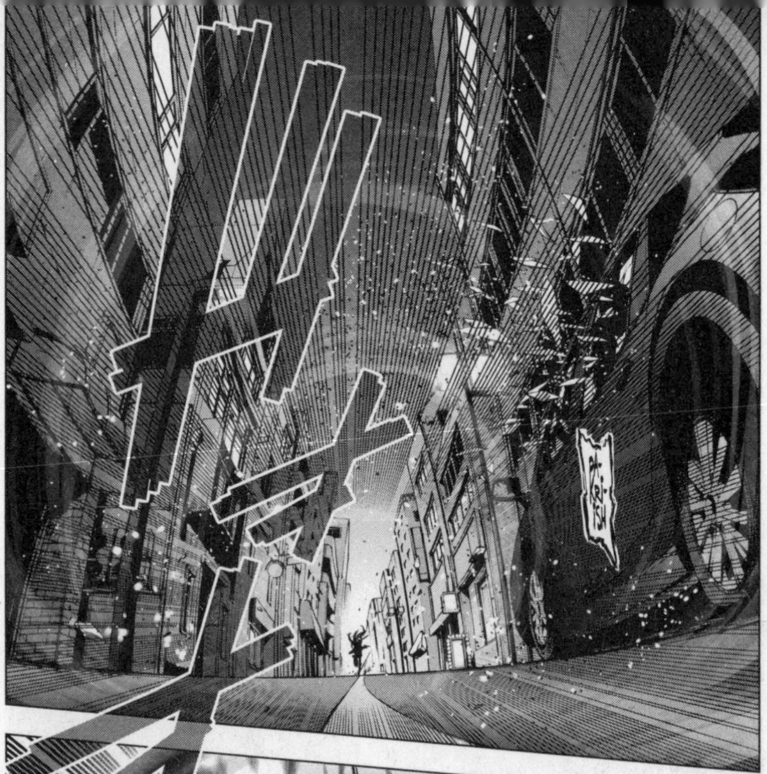
PA-KRI-ISH
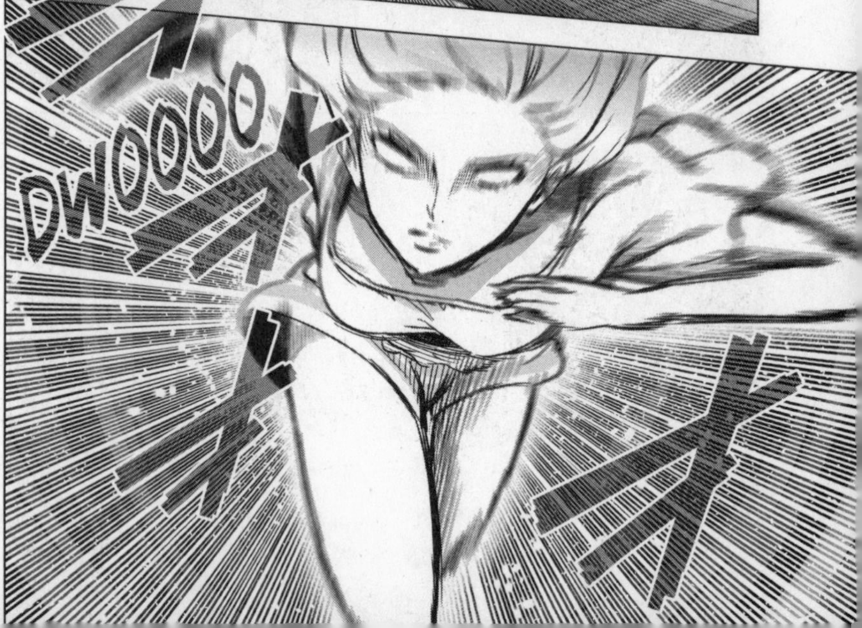
DWOOOO

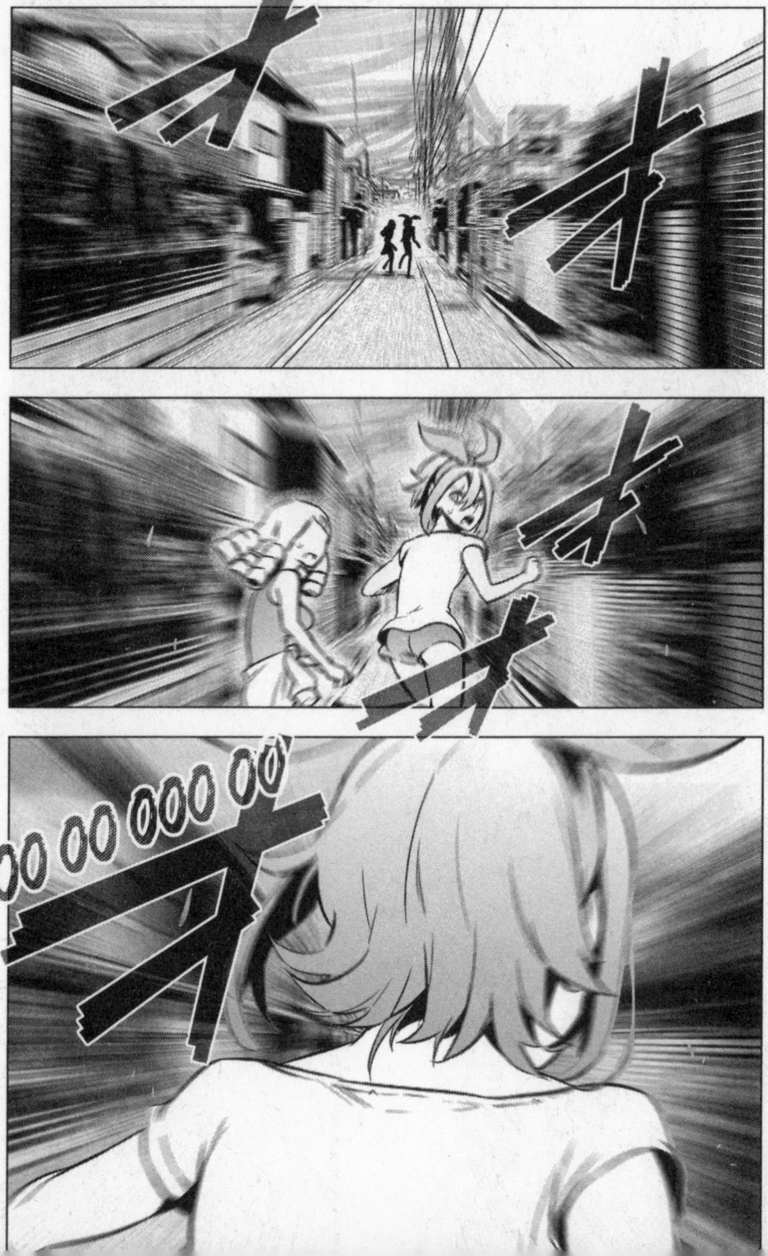

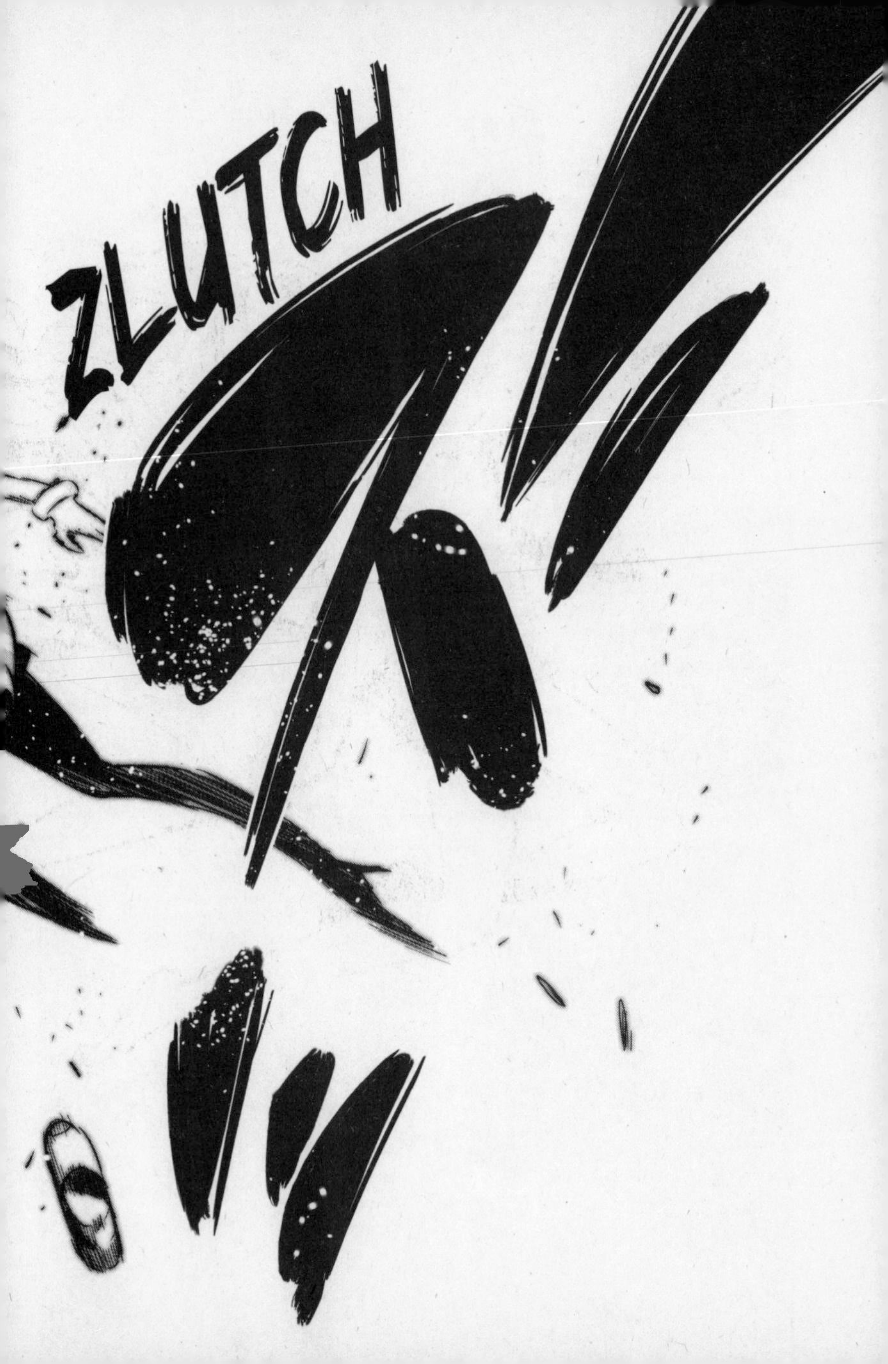
ZLUTCH

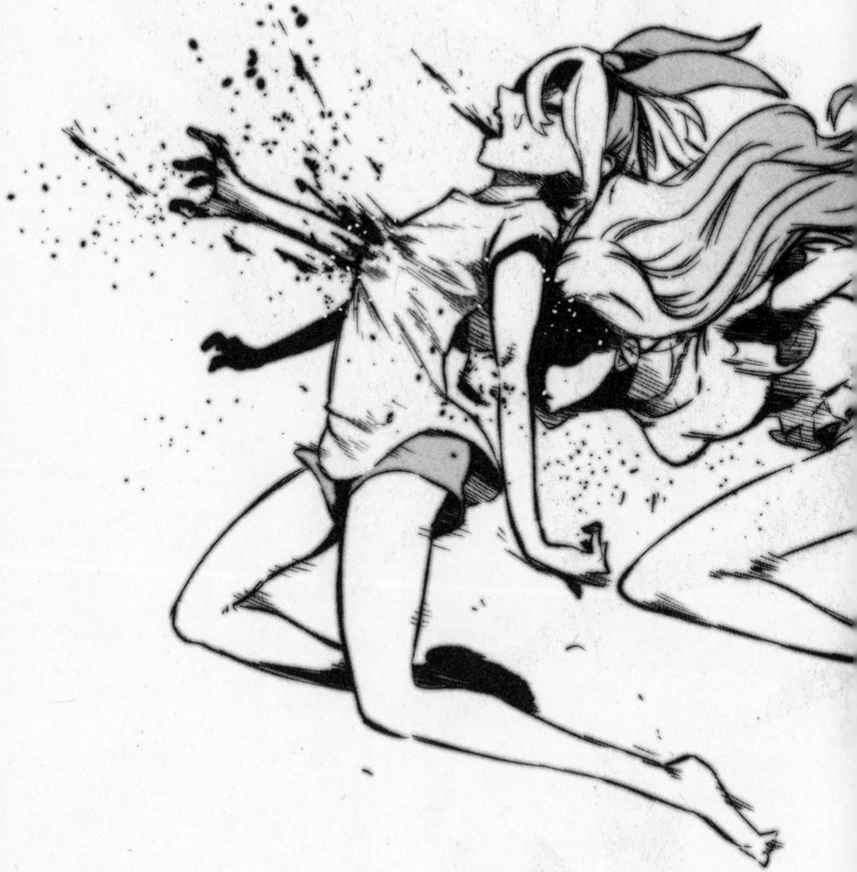

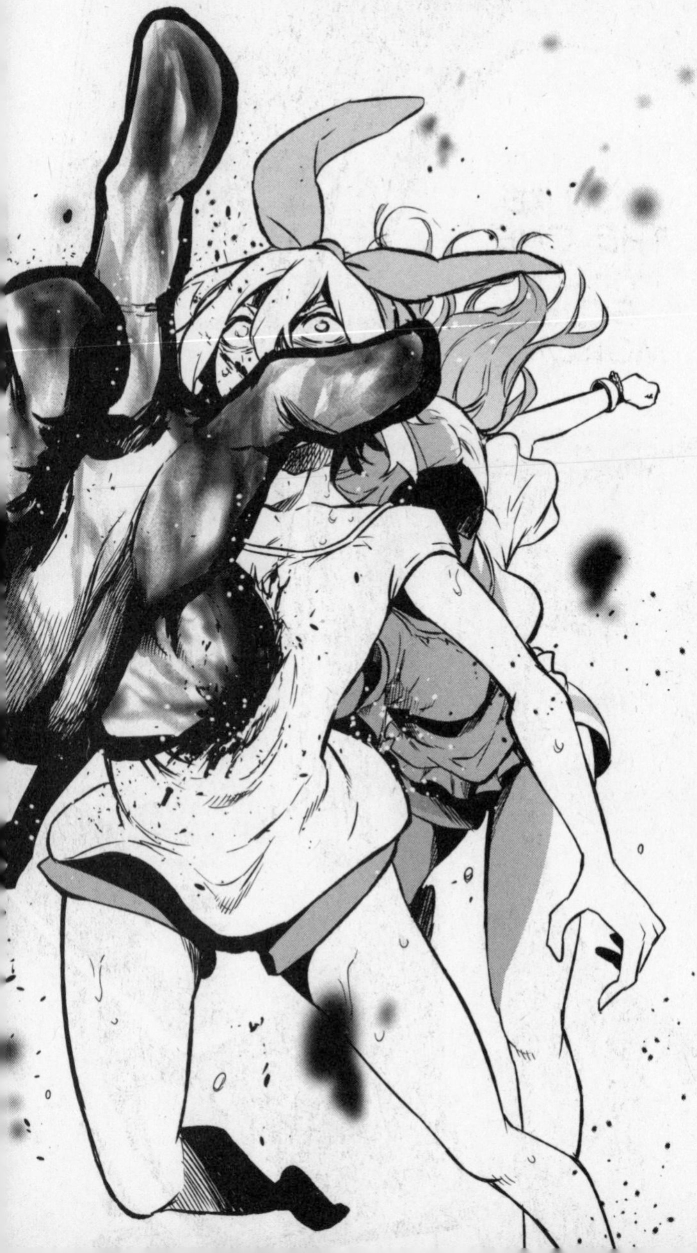

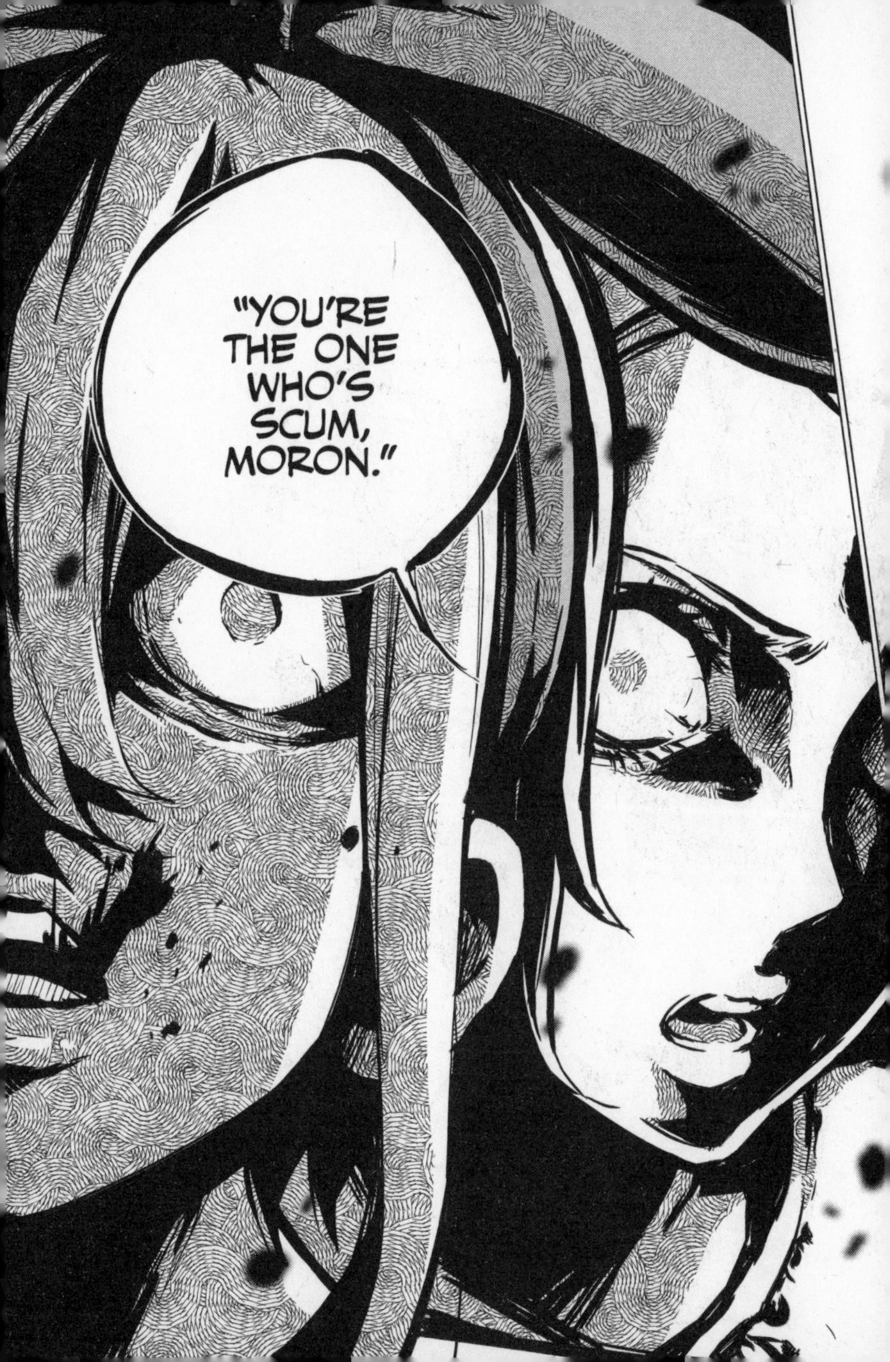
"YOU'RE THE ONE WHO'S SCUM, MORON."

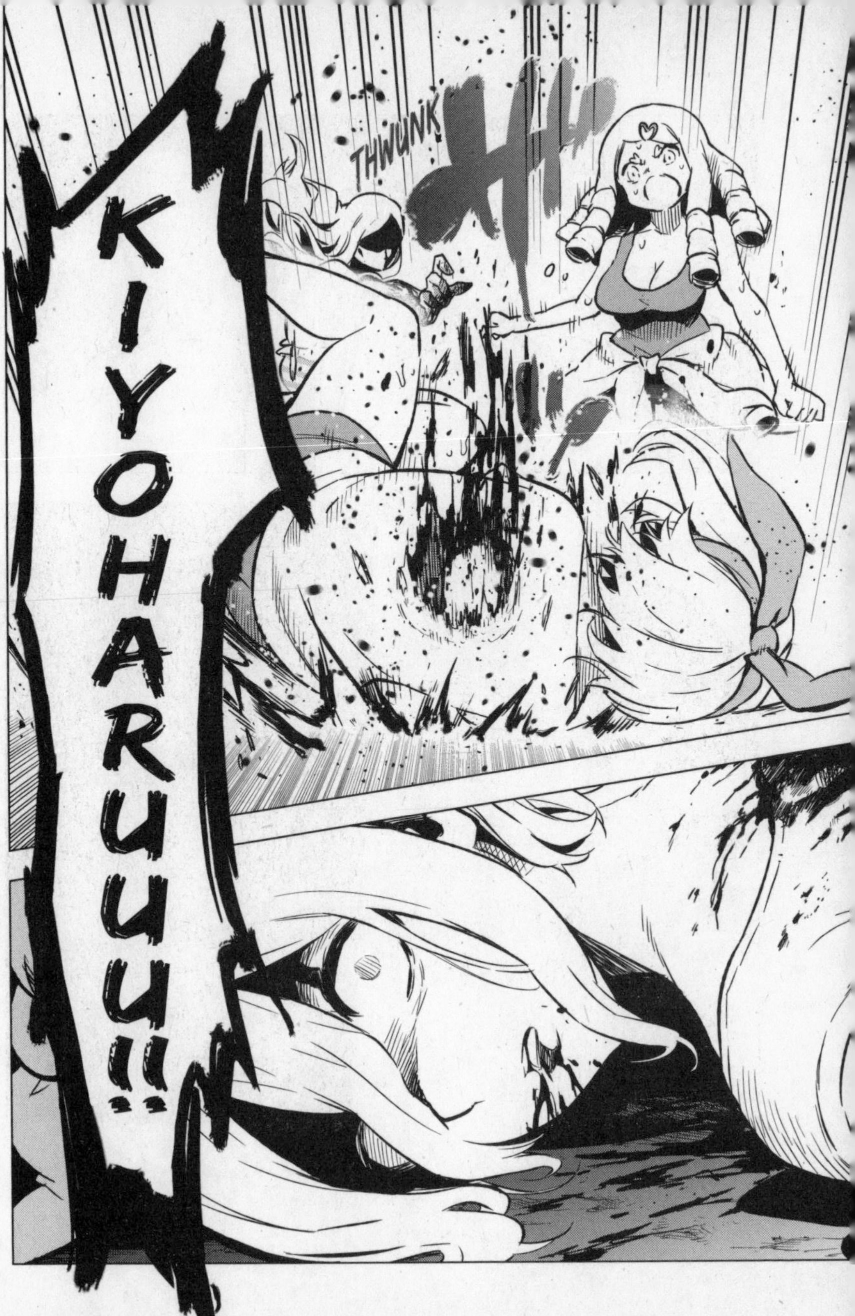
THWUNK
KIYOHARUU!!

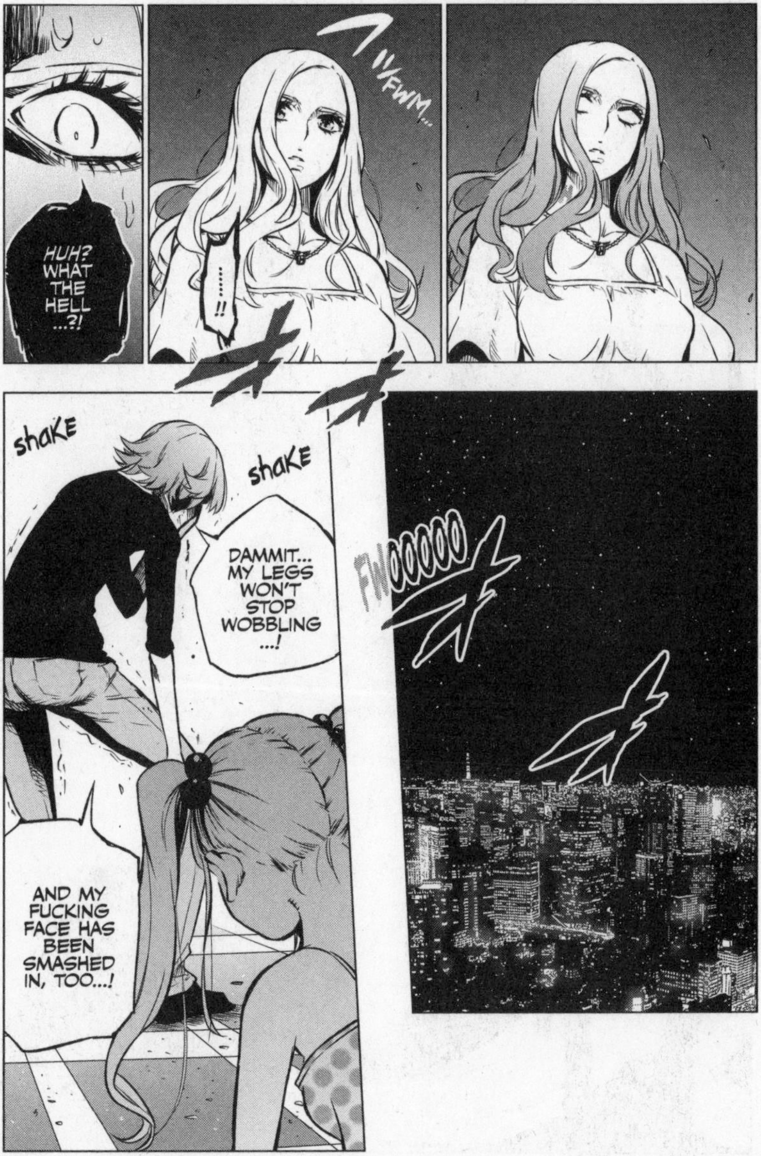
FWM...
......!!
HUH? WHAT THE HELL ...?!
FWOOOOO
shake
shake
DAMMIT... MY LEGS WON'T STOP WOBBLING ...!
AND MY FUCKING FACE HAS BEEN SMASHED IN, TOO...!

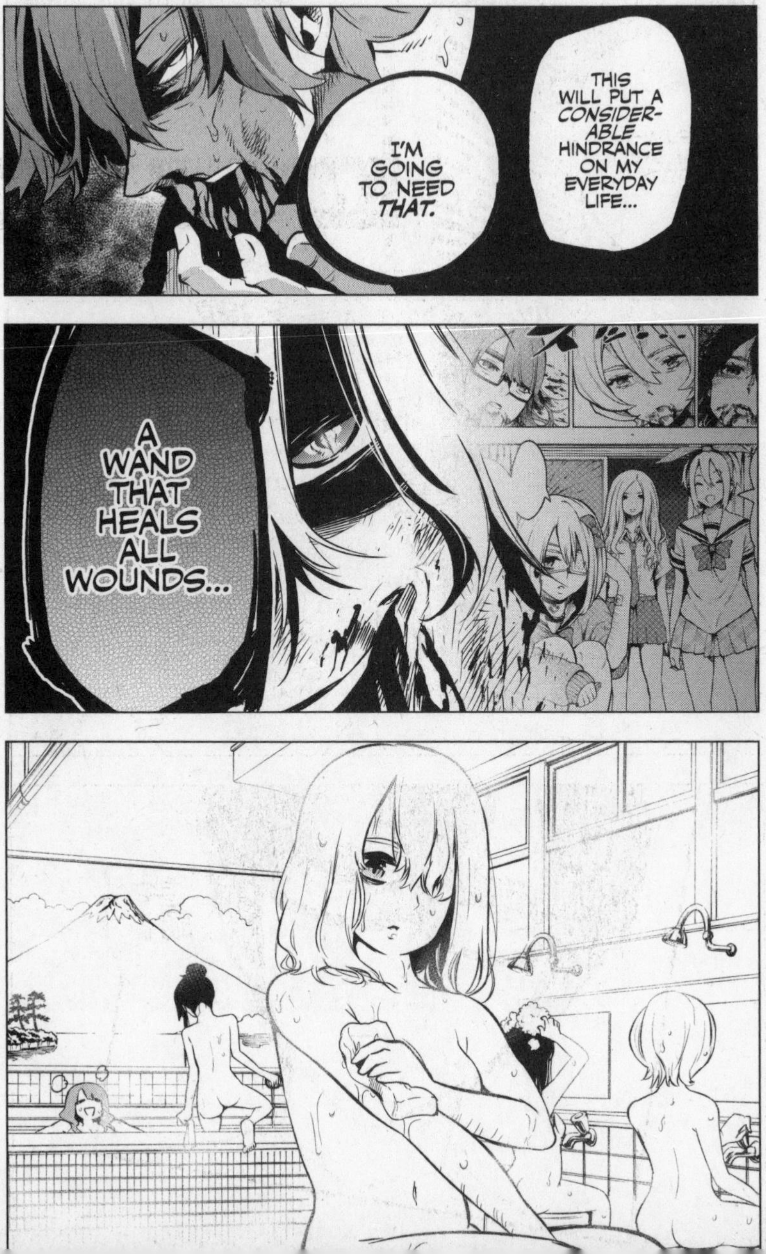
THIS WILL PUT A *CONSIDERABLE* HINDRANCE ON MY EVERYDAY LIFE...
I'M GOING TO NEED *THAT.*
A WAND THAT HEALS ALL WOUNDS...

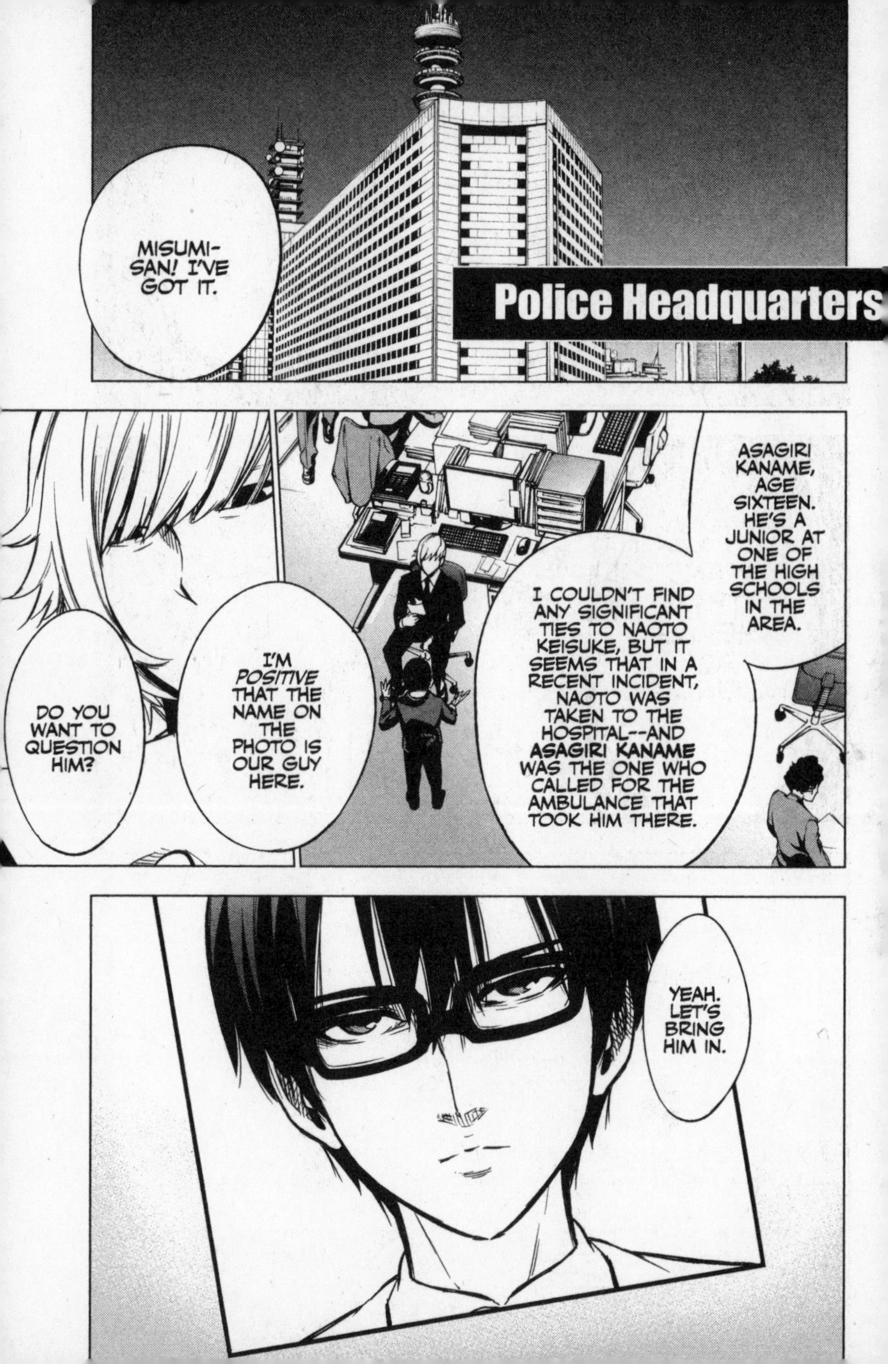
Police Headquarters
MISUMI-SAN! I'VE GOT IT.
ASAGIRI KANAME, AGE SIXTEEN. HE'S A JUNIOR AT ONE OF THE HIGH SCHOOLS IN THE AREA.
I COULDN'T FIND ANY SIGNIFICANT TIES TO NAOTO KEISUKE, BUT IT SEEMS THAT IN A RECENT INCIDENT, NAOTO WAS TAKEN TO THE HOSPITAL--AND ASAGIRI KANAME WAS THE ONE WHO CALLED FOR THE AMBULANCE THAT TOOK HIM THERE.
I'M POSITIVE THAT THE NAME ON THE PHOTO IS OUR GUY HERE.
DO YOU WANT TO QUESTION HIM?
YEAH. LET'S BRING HIM IN.

H

TAKIGUCHI ASAHI

Sex: Female
Age: 15
Date of Birth: September 28 (Libra)
Height: 155cm
Weight: 46kg
Blood Type: A
Birthplace: Saitama Prefecture

Hobbies/Interests: Painting her nails, shopping, tennis, pro wrestling, karaoke

Strong Points: Nice style, dancing, singing

Weak Points: Her face without makeup, Mondays

Favorite Things: Shibuya, exercising

- Freshman in high school.
- When she was in middle school, she got really tanned from all her club activities, but got rid of her tan in high school.
- She cannot bear letting people see her face without makeup on.
- Her favorite celebrity is the pro wrestler Hiroshi Tanahashi.

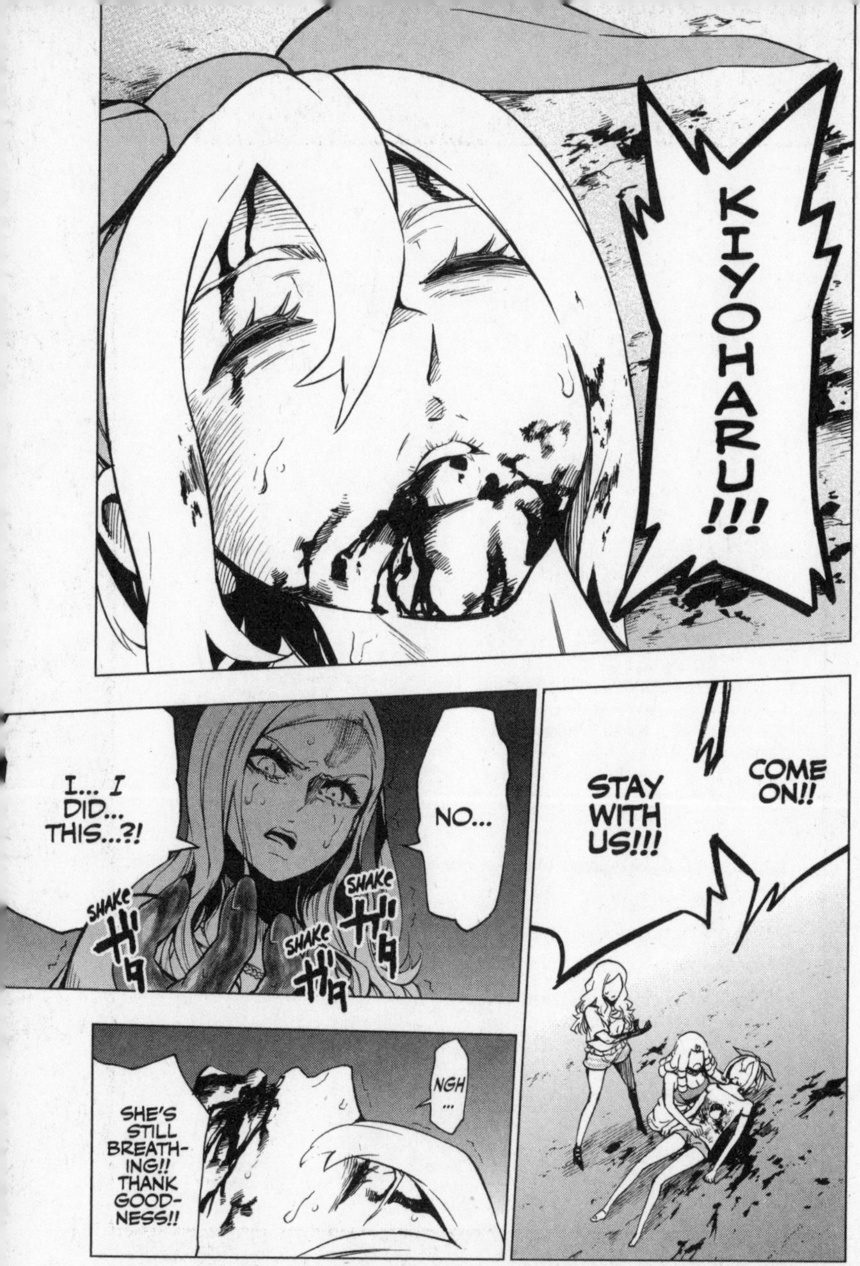
KIYOHARU!!!
COME ON!!
STAY WITH US!!!
NO...
I... I DID... THIS...?!
SHAKE ガタ
SHAKE ガタ
SHAKE ガタ
NGH ...
SHE'S STILL BREATHING!! THANK GOODNESS!!

ENTER.37 SHARING BLOOD

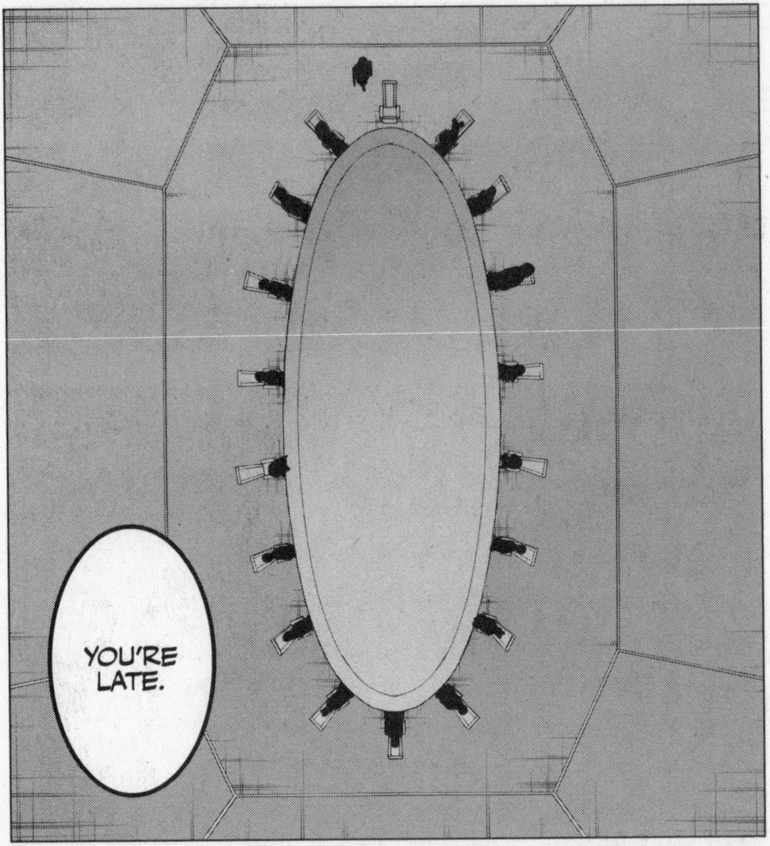
YOU'RE LATE.

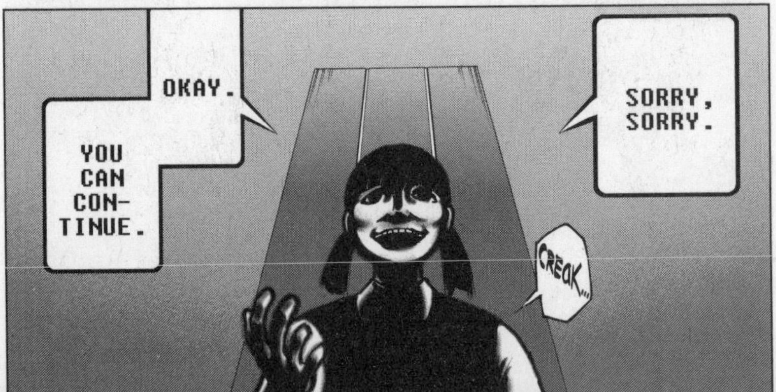
SORRY, SORRY.
OKAY.
YOU CAN CON-TINUE.
CREAK...

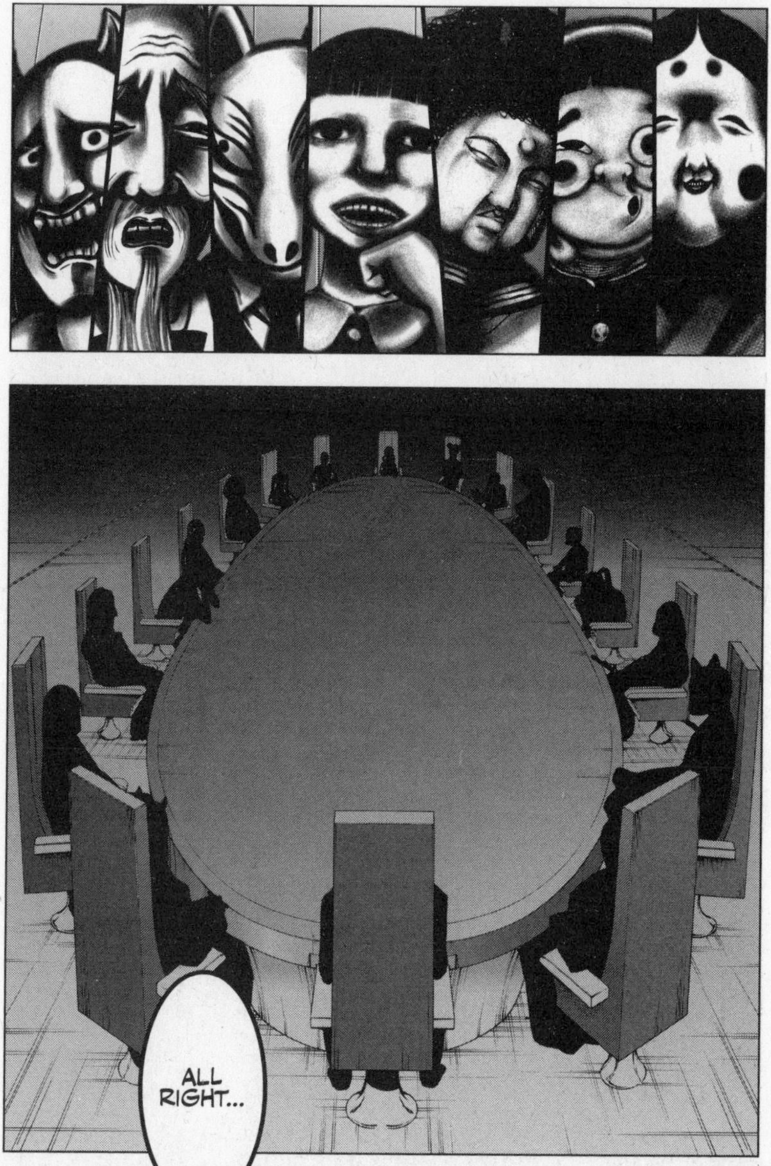
ALL RIGHT...

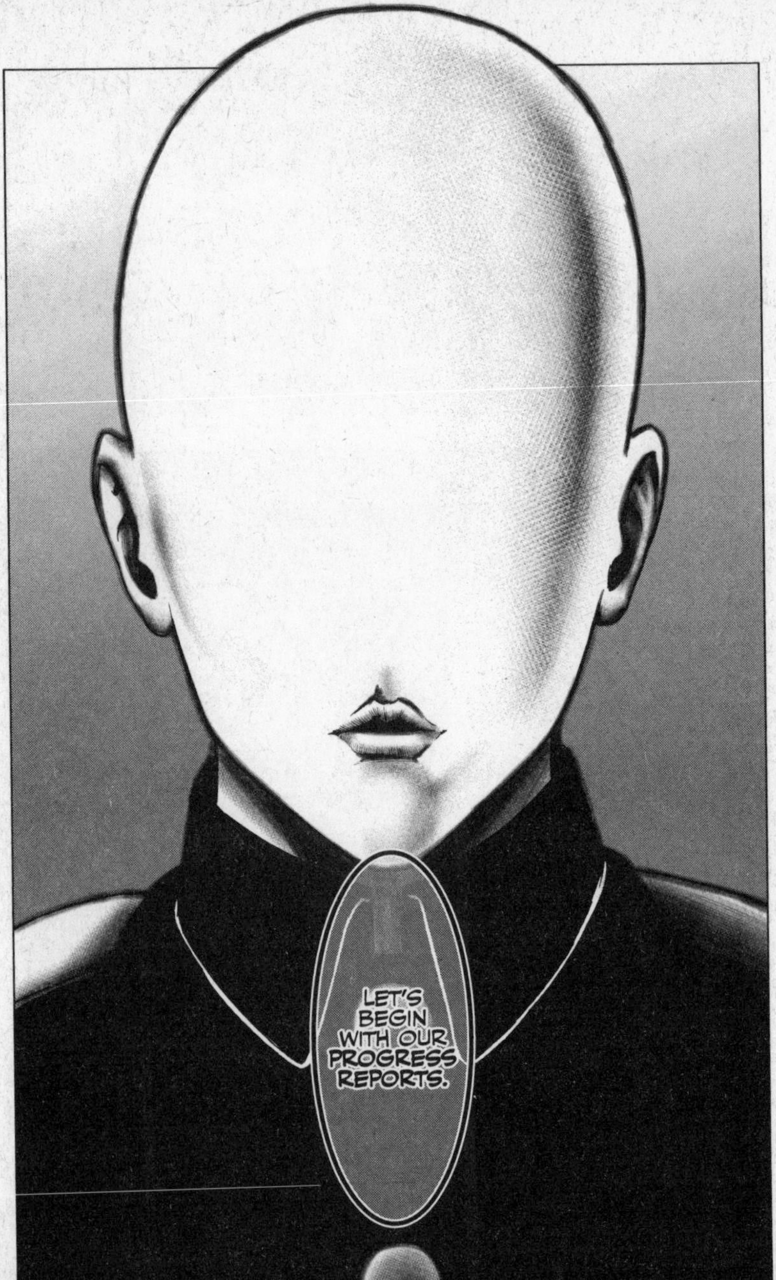
LET'S BEGIN WITH OUR PROGRESS REPORTS.

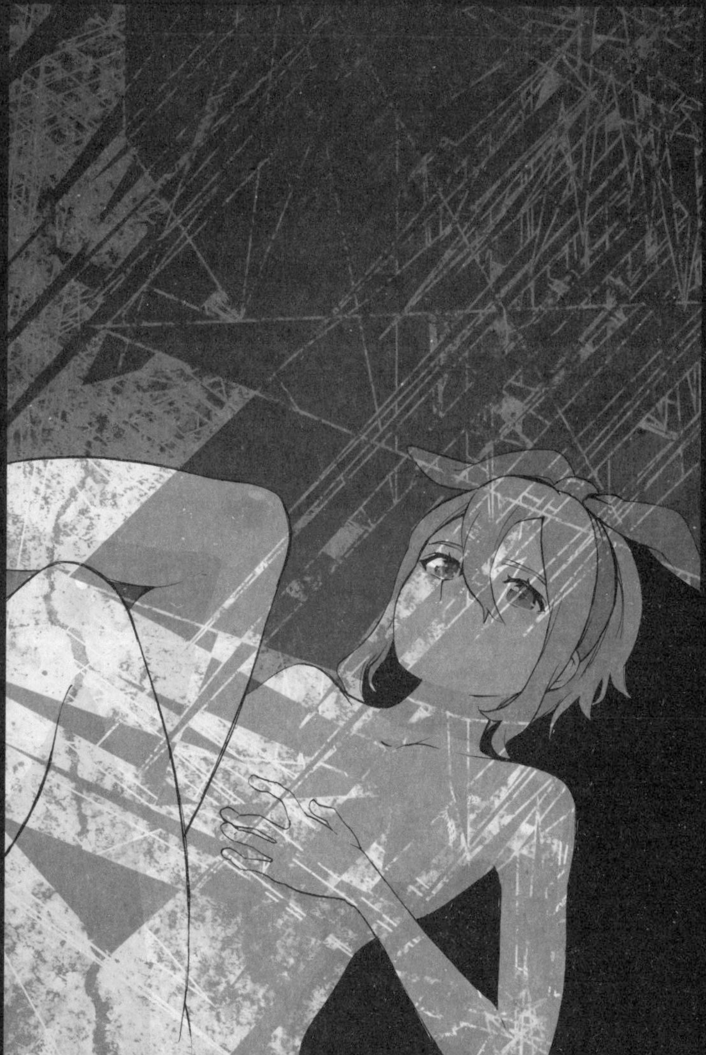

ENTER. 37 SHARING BLOOD

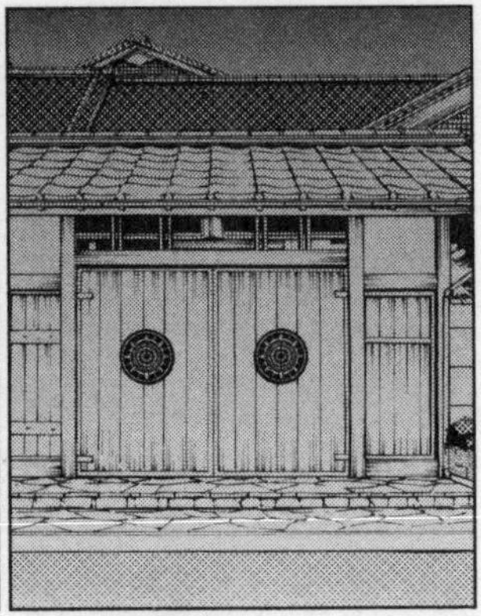

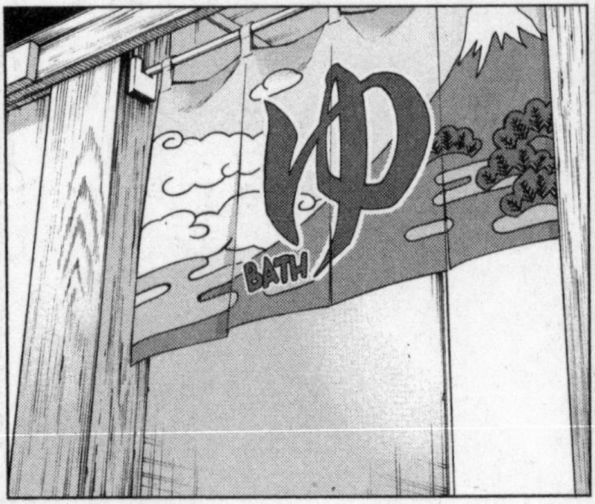
BATH

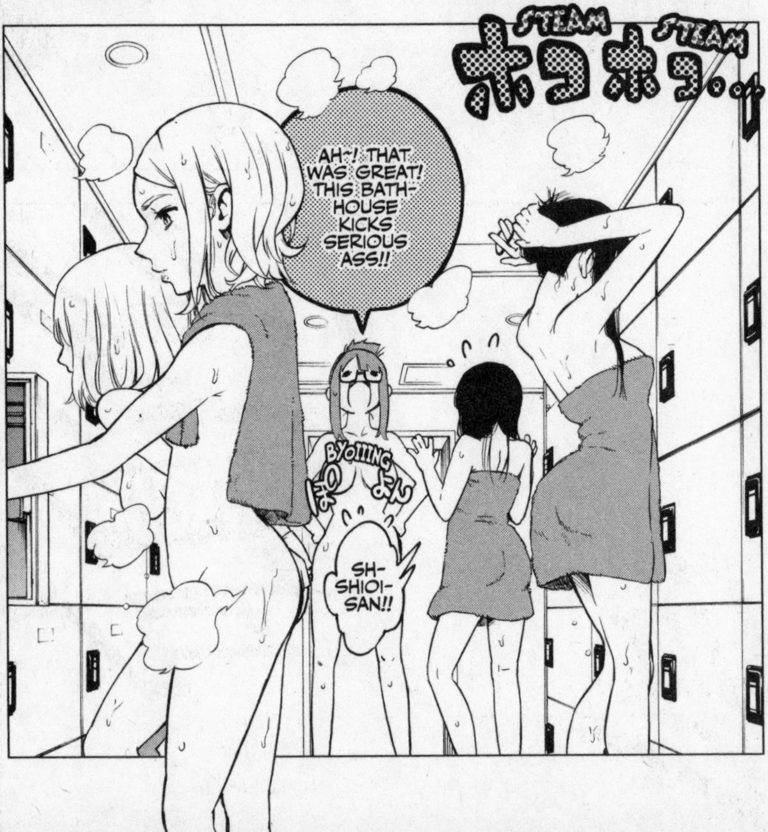
STEAM STEAM
ホコホコ..
AH~! THAT WAS GREAT! THIS BATH-HOUSE KICKS SERIOUS ASS!!
BYOIIING
ぼよん
SH-SHIOI-SAN!!

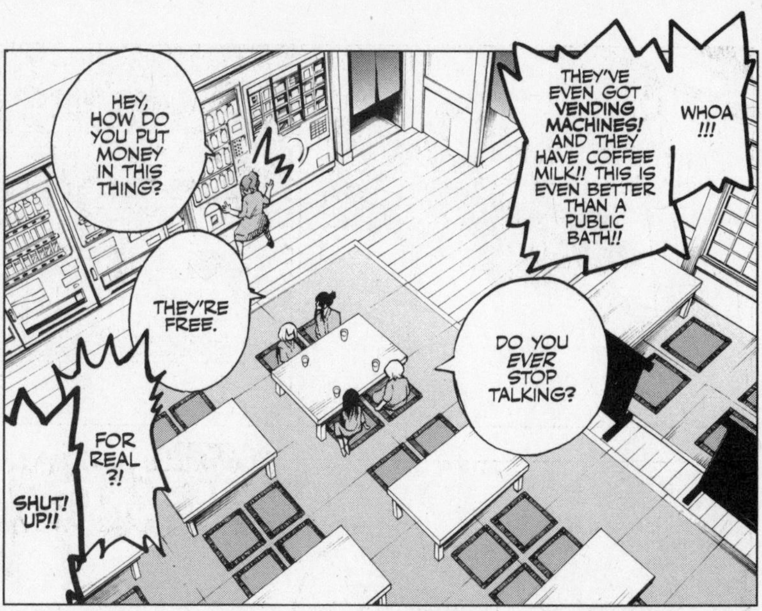
WHOA!!!
THEY'VE EVEN GOT VENDING MACHINES! AND THEY HAVE COFFEE MILK!! THIS IS EVEN BETTER THAN A PUBLIC BATH!!
HEY, HOW DO YOU PUT MONEY IN THIS THING?
THEY'RE FREE.
FOR REAL?!
DO YOU EVER STOP TALKING?
SHUT! UP!!

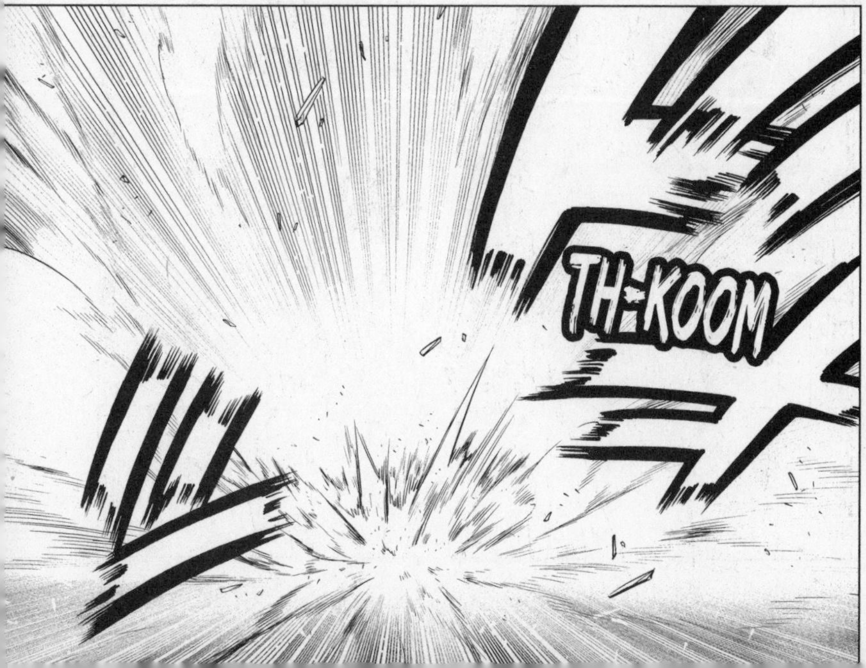
TH-KOOM

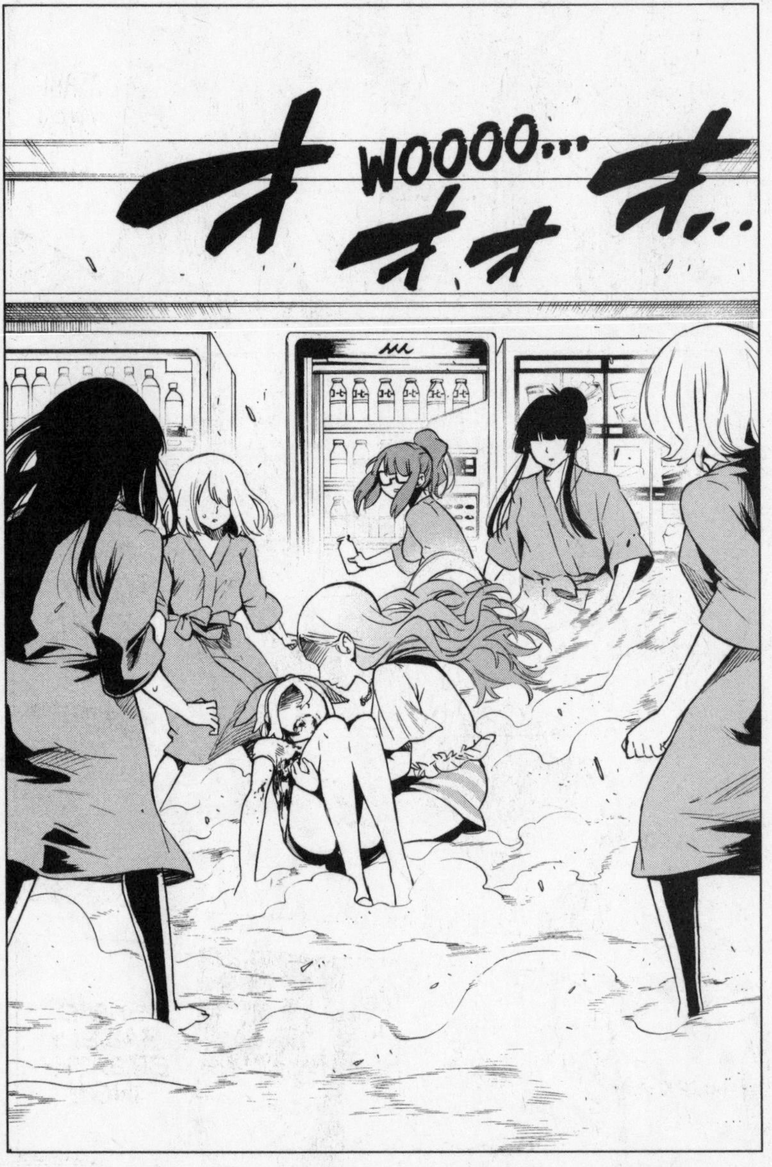
オオオオ…
WOOOO...

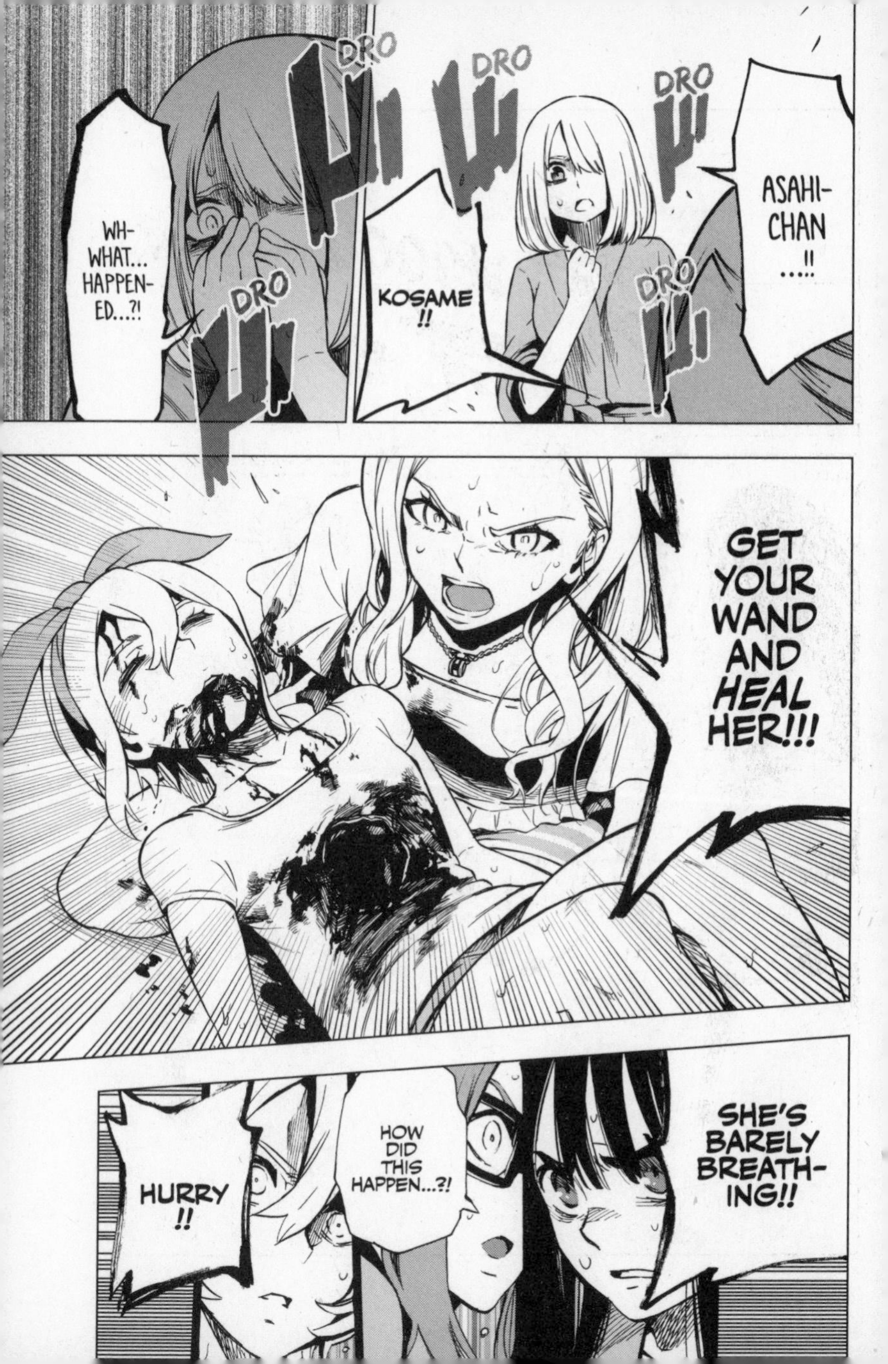
ASAHI-CHAN ....!!
DRO
DRO
DRO
KOSAME !!
WH-WHAT... HAPPENED...?!
DRO
DRO
GET YOUR WAND AND HEAL HER!!!
SHE'S BARELY BREATHING!!
HOW DID THIS HAPPEN...?!
HURRY !!

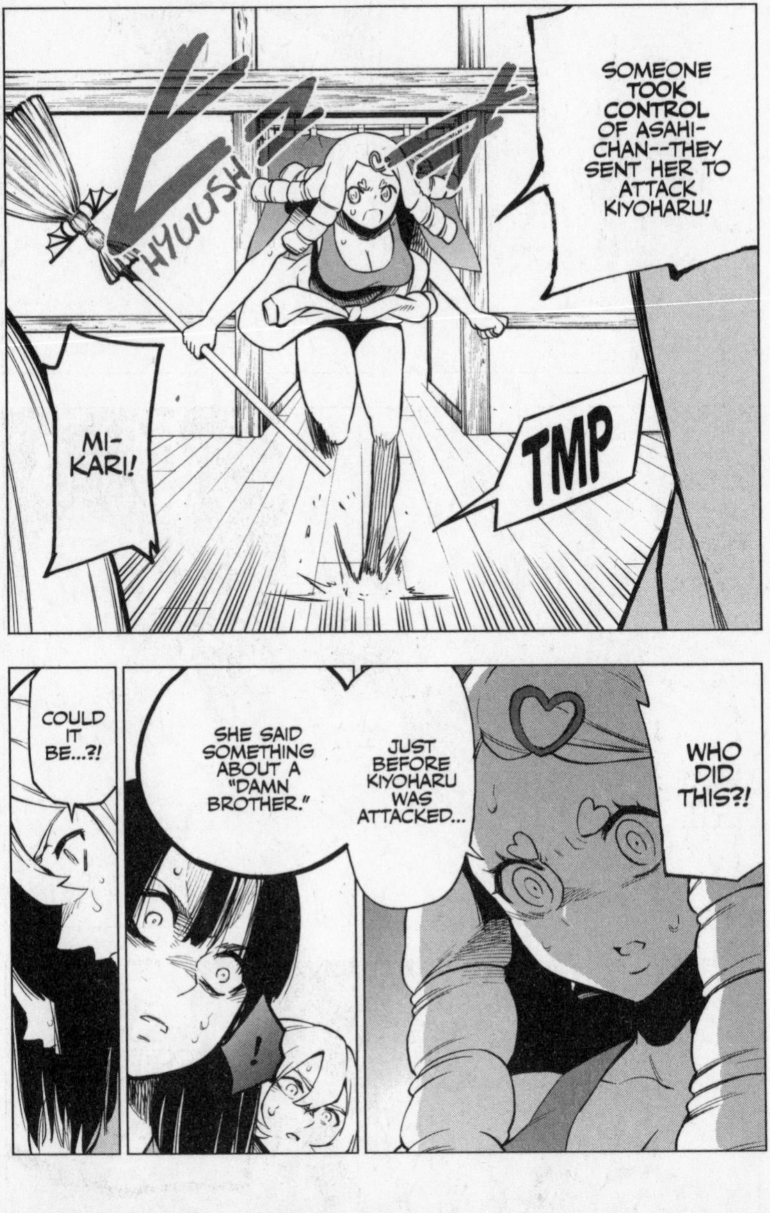
SOMEONE TOOK CONTROL OF ASAHI-CHAN--THEY SENT HER TO ATTACK KIYOHARU!
HYUUSH
TMP
MI-KARI!
WHO DID THIS?!
JUST BEFORE KIYOHARU WAS ATTACKED...
SHE SAID SOMETHING ABOUT A "DAMN BROTHER."
!
COULD IT BE...?!

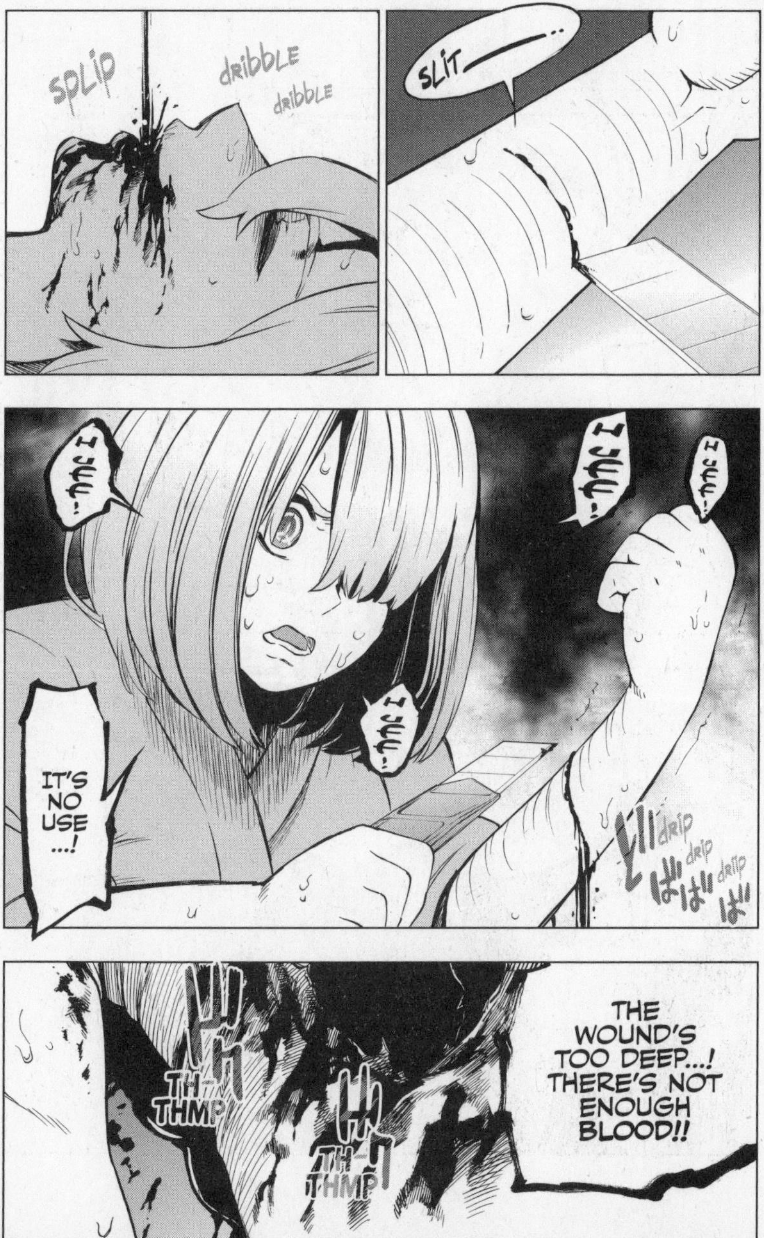
SLIT———..
SPLIP
DRIBBLE
DRIBBLE
HUFF!
HUFF!
HUFF!
HUFF!
IT'S NO USE...!
DRIP
DRIP
DRIP
THE WOUND'S TOO DEEP...! THERE'S NOT ENOUGH BLOOD!!
TH-THMP
TH-THMP

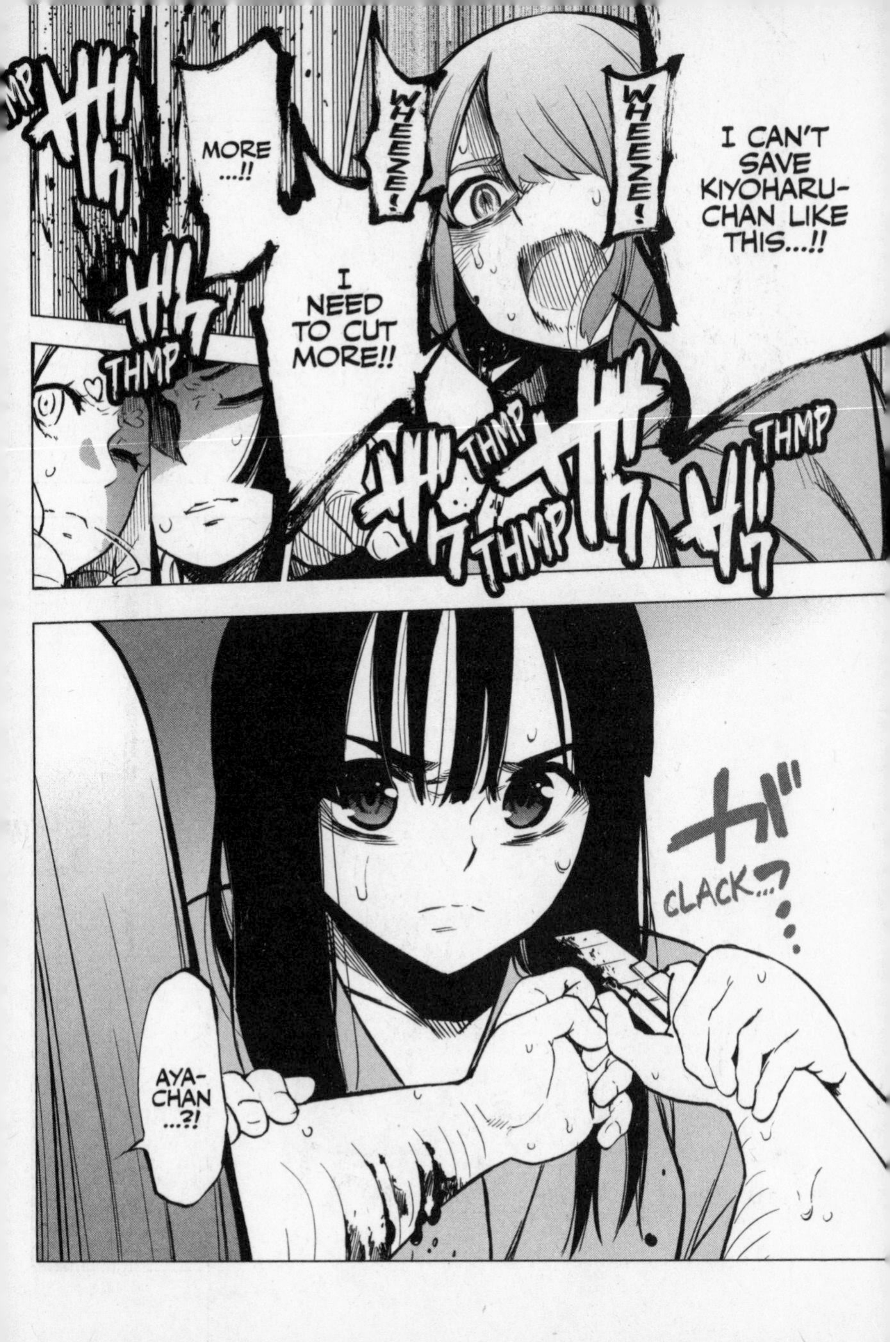
I CAN'T SAVE KIYOHARU-CHAN LIKE THIS...!!
WHEEZE!
WHEEZE!
MORE...!!
I NEED TO CUT MORE!!
THMP
THMP
THMP
THMP
THMP
CLACK...?
AYA-CHAN...?!

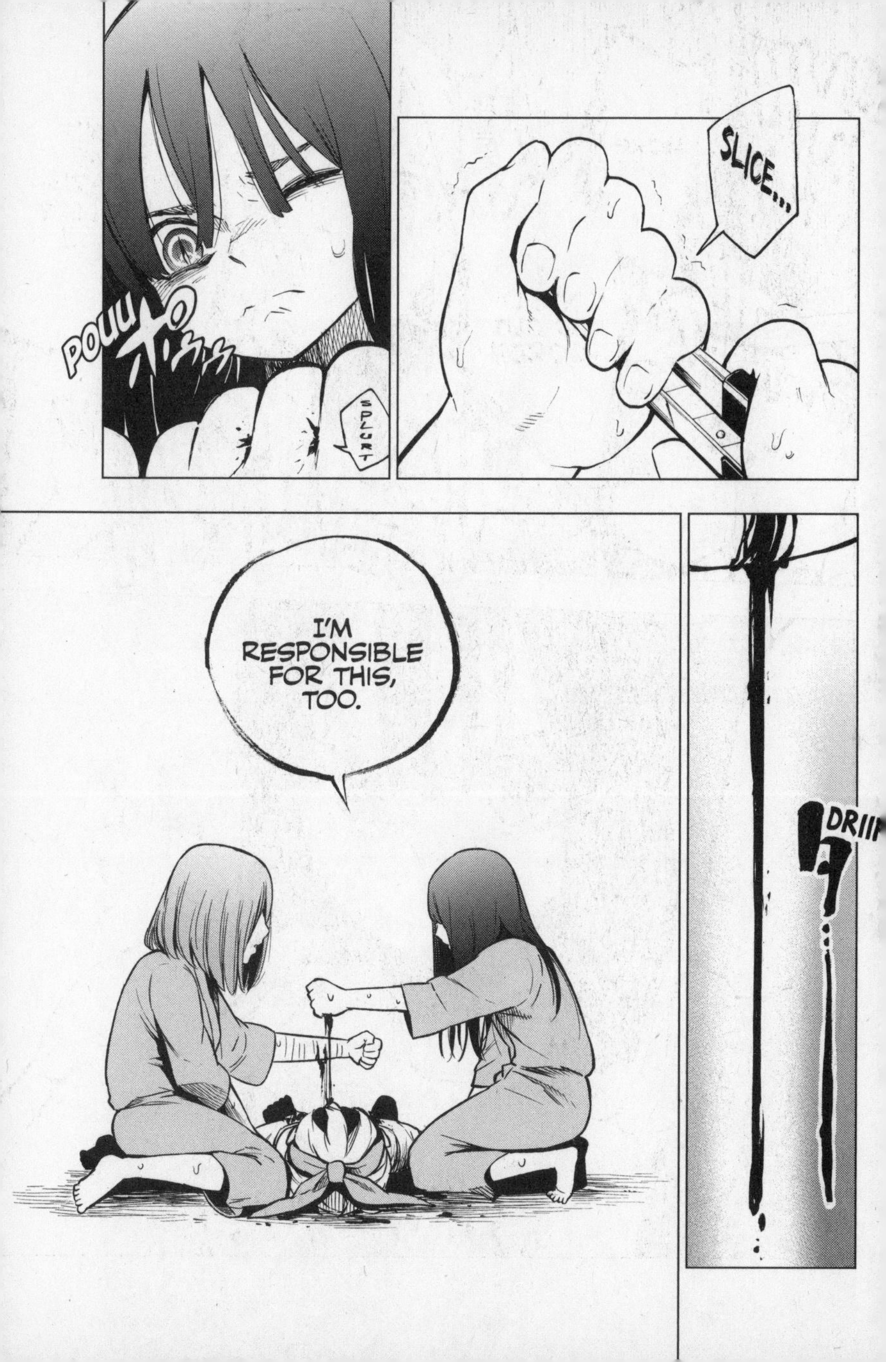
SLICE...
POUU
SPLURT
DRII
I'M RESPONSIBLE FOR THIS, TOO.

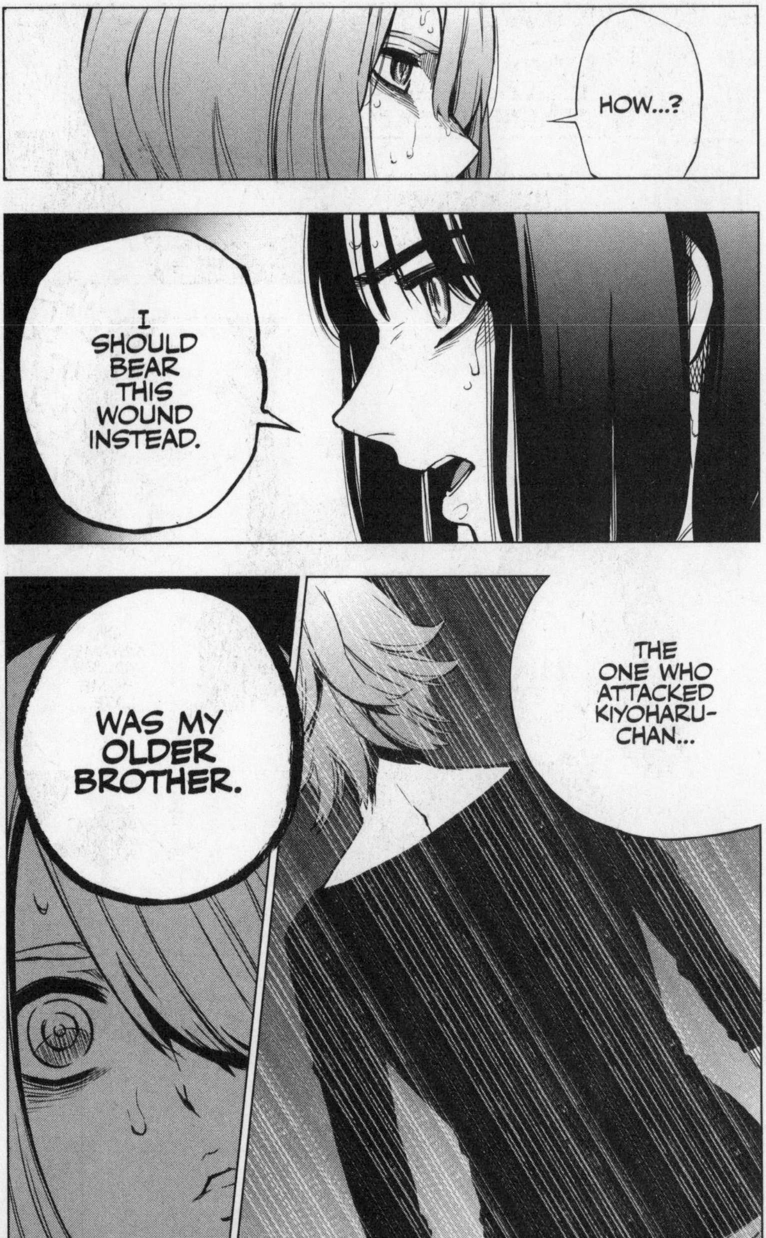
HOW...?
I SHOULD BEAR THIS WOUND INSTEAD.
THE ONE WHO ATTACKED KIYOHARU-CHAN...
WAS MY OLDER BROTHER.

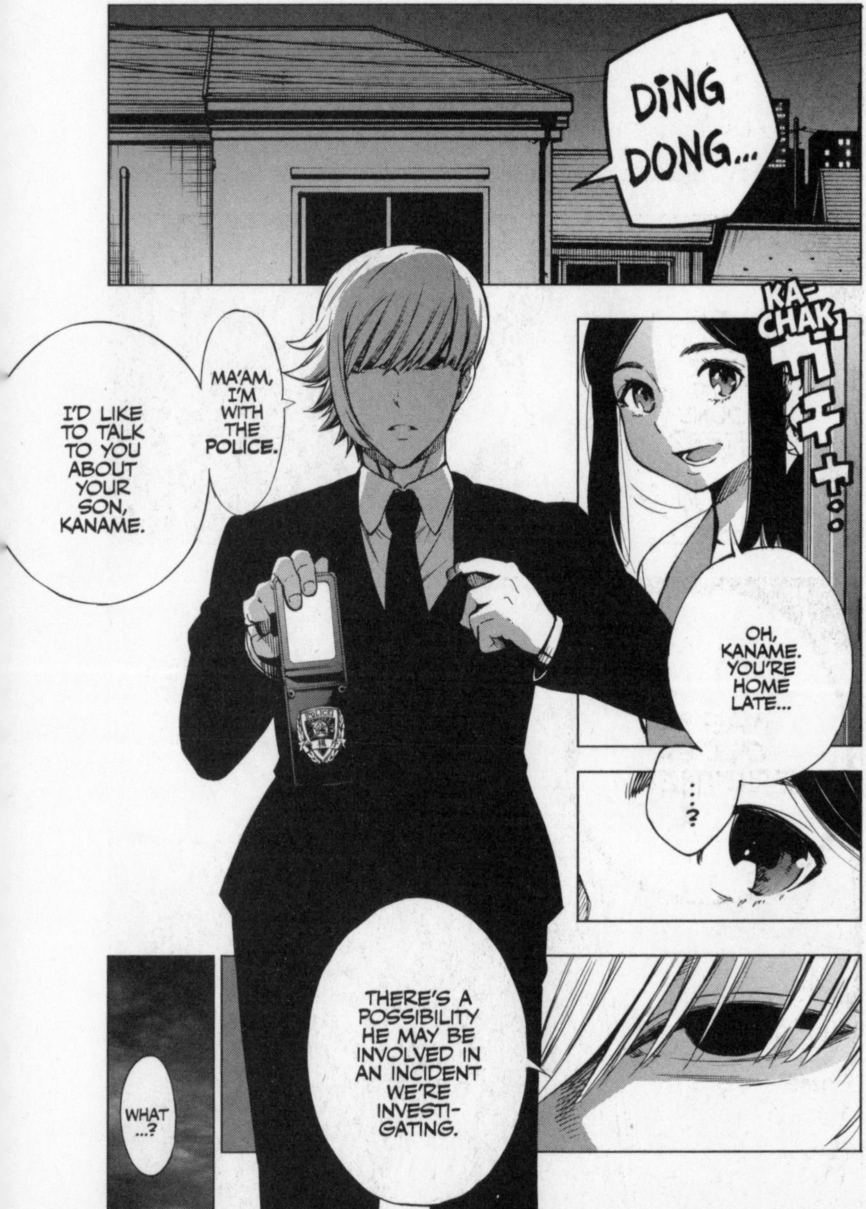
DING DONG...
KA-CHAK
OH, KANAME. YOU'RE HOME LATE...
...?
MA'AM, I'M WITH THE POLICE.
I'D LIKE TO TALK TO YOU ABOUT YOUR SON, KANAME.
THERE'S A POSSIBILITY HE MAY BE INVOLVED IN AN INCIDENT WE'RE INVESTIGATING.
WHAT ...?

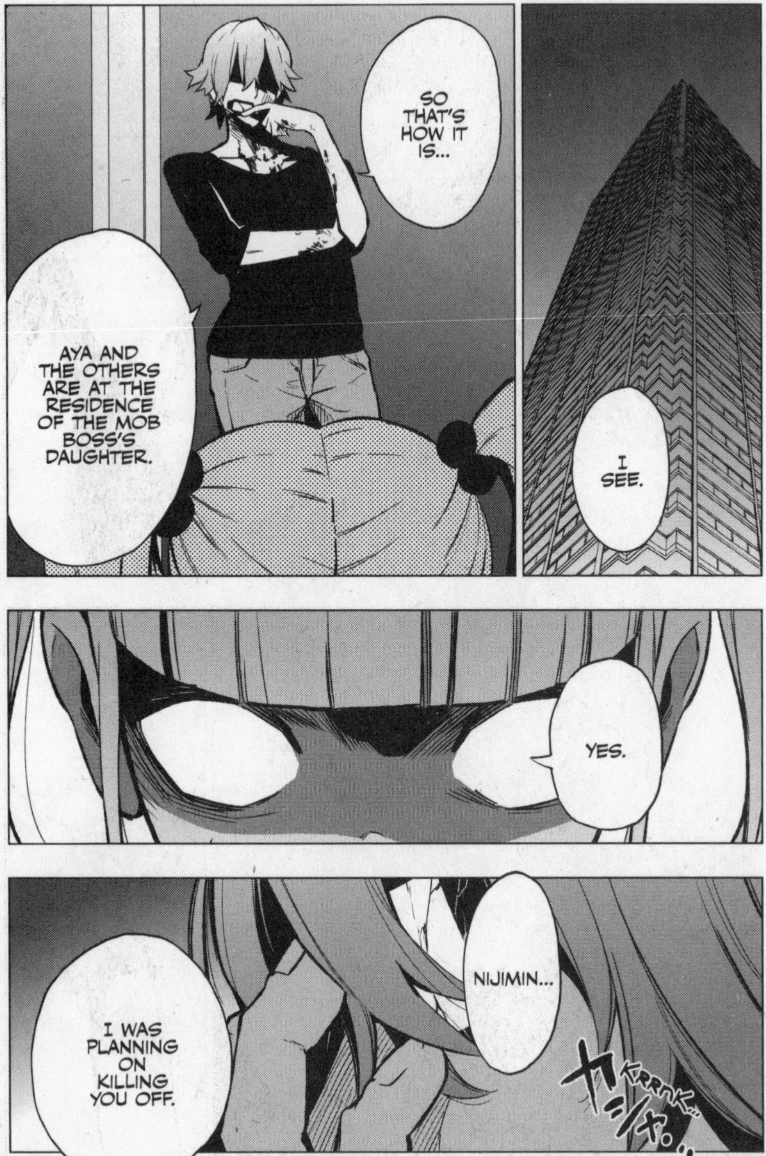
I SEE.
SO THAT'S HOW IT IS...
AYA AND THE OTHERS ARE AT THE RESIDENCE OF THE MOB BOSS'S DAUGHTER.
YES.
NIJIMIN...
I WAS PLANNING ON KILLING YOU OFF.
KRRNK...

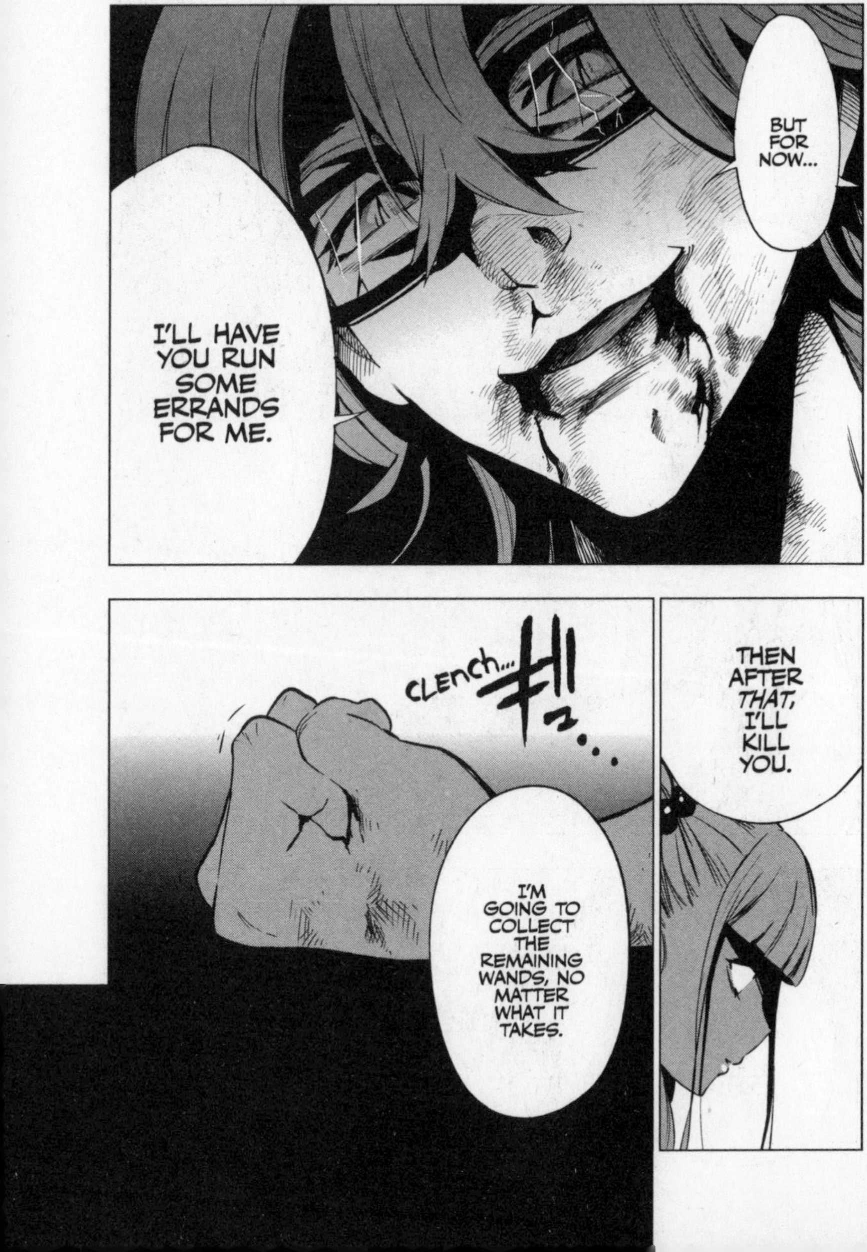
BUT FOR NOW...
I'LL HAVE YOU RUN SOME ERRANDS FOR ME.
THEN AFTER *THAT*, I'LL KILL YOU.
CLENCH...
I'M GOING TO COLLECT THE REMAINING WANDS, NO MATTER WHAT IT TAKES.

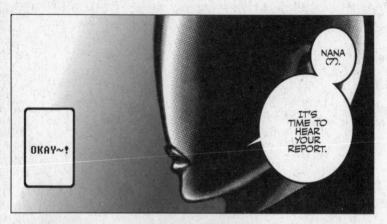

NANA (7).

IT'S TIME TO HEAR YOUR REPORT.

OKAY~!

I HAVE MADE AN ARRANGEMENT WITH A CERTAIN SOMEONE TO ENSURE THAT THE USE OF WANDS CONTINUES TO PROGRESS NICELY.

"SOME-ONE"?

A HUMAN?

YES.

To be continued...

NG ①

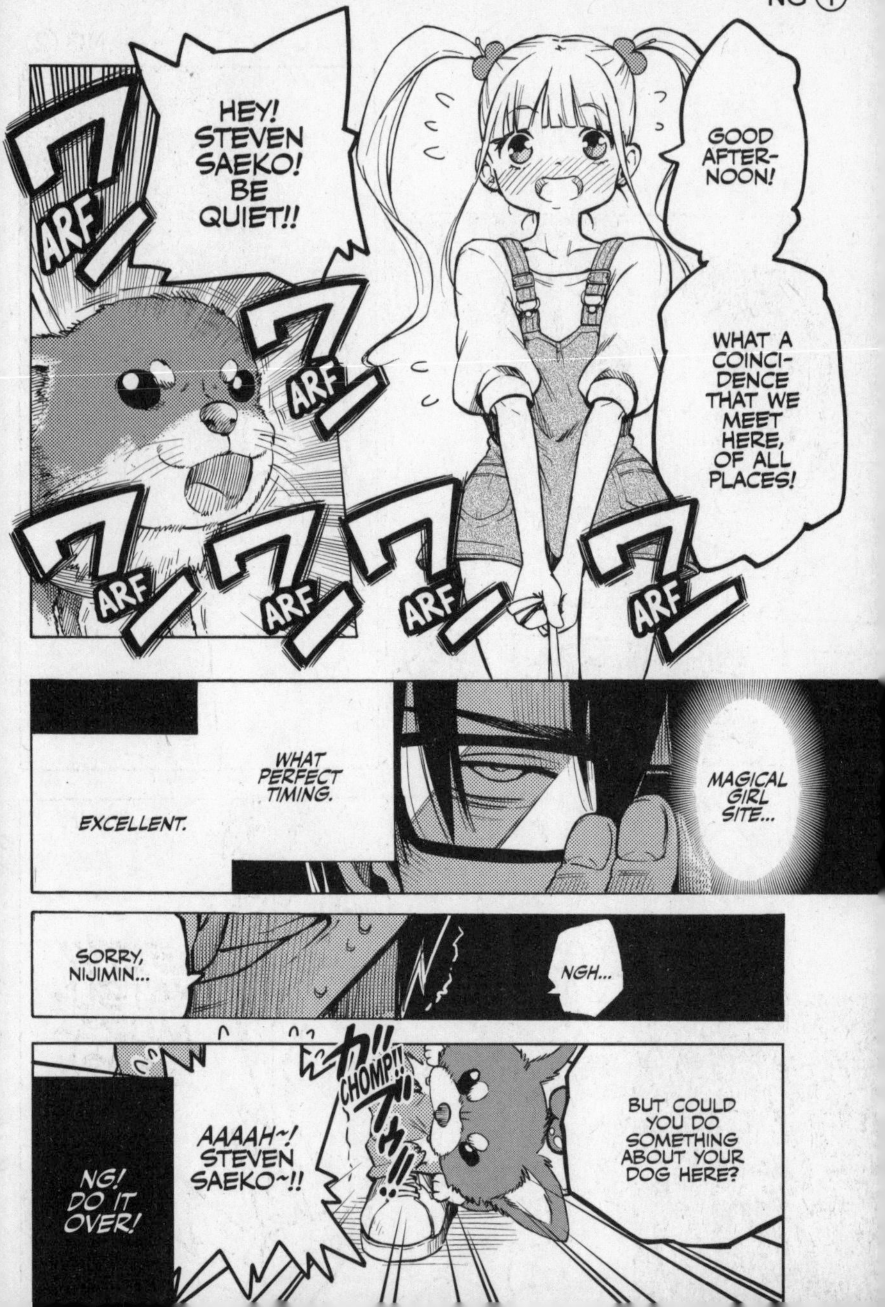
GOOD AFTER-NOON!
WHAT A COINCI-DENCE THAT WE MEET HERE, OF ALL PLACES!
HEY! STEVEN SAEKO! BE QUIET!!
ARF
ARF
ARF
ARF
ARF
ARF
MAGICAL GIRL SITE...
WHAT PERFECT TIMING.
EXCELLENT.
NGH...
SORRY, NIJIMIN...
BUT COULD YOU DO SOMETHING ABOUT YOUR DOG HERE?
CHOMP!!
AAAAH~! STEVEN SAEKO~!!
NG! DO IT OVER!

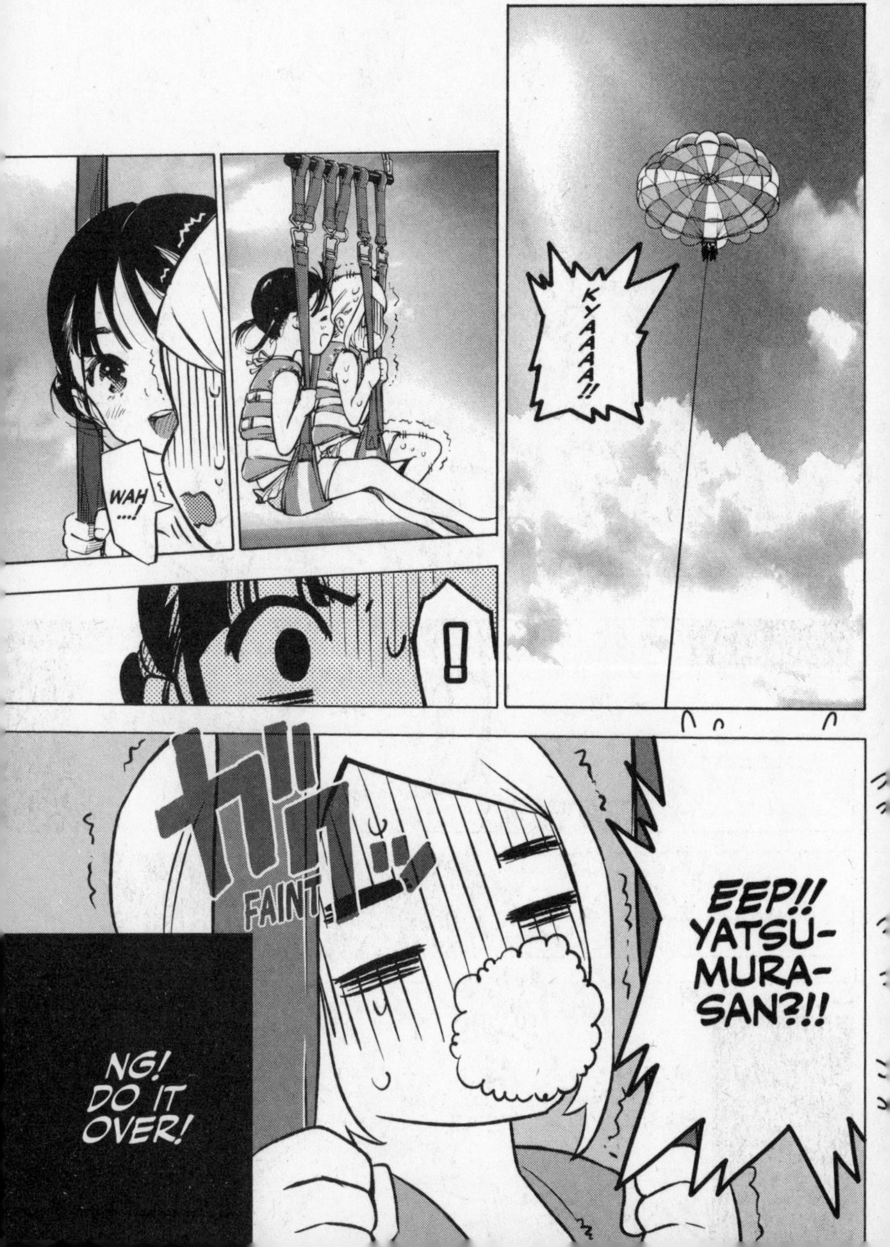
KYAAAAA!!
WAH ...!
!
EEP!! YATSÚMURA-SAN?!!
FAINT
NG! DO IT OVER!

NG ③

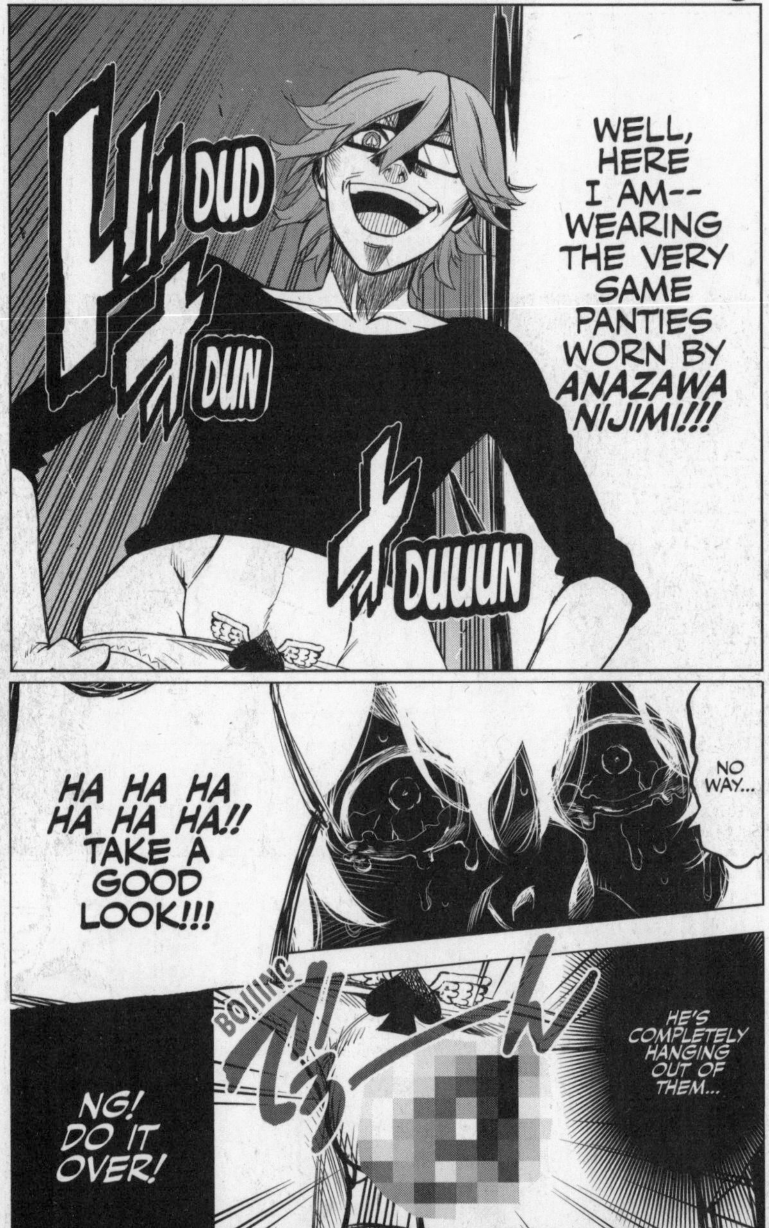

WELL, HERE I AM-- WEARING THE VERY SAME PANTIES WORN BY ANAZAWA NIJIMI!!!
DUD
DUN
DUUUN
NO WAY...
HA HA HA HA HA HA!! TAKE A GOOD LOOK!!!
HE'S COMPLETELY HANGING OUT OF THEM...
BOIIING
NG! DO IT OVER!

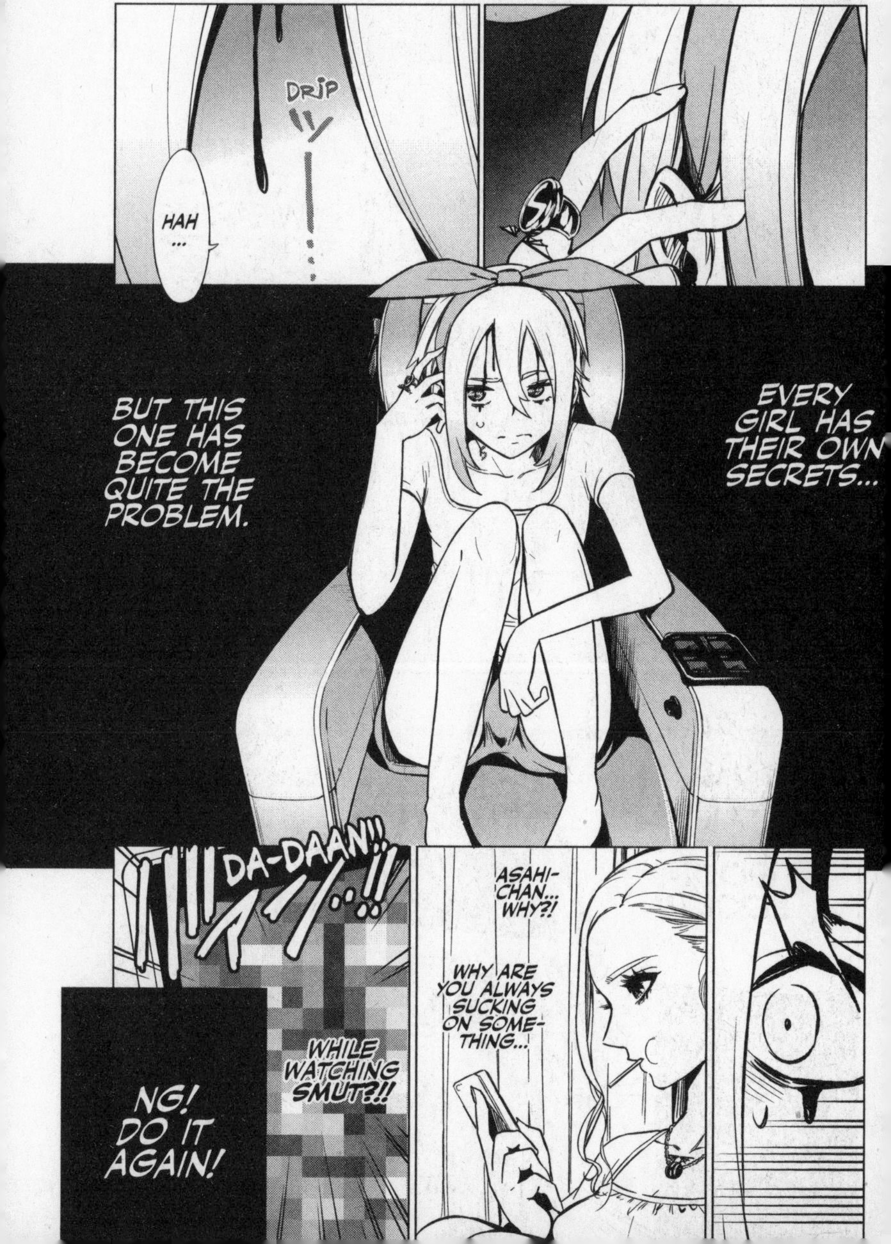
DRIP
HAH ...
EVERY GIRL HAS THEIR OWN SECRETS...
BUT THIS ONE HAS BECOME QUITE THE PROBLEM.
ASAHI-CHAN... WHY?!
WHY ARE YOU ALWAYS SUCKING ON SOME-THING...
DA-DAAN!!
WHILE WATCHING SMUT?!!
NG! DO IT AGAIN!

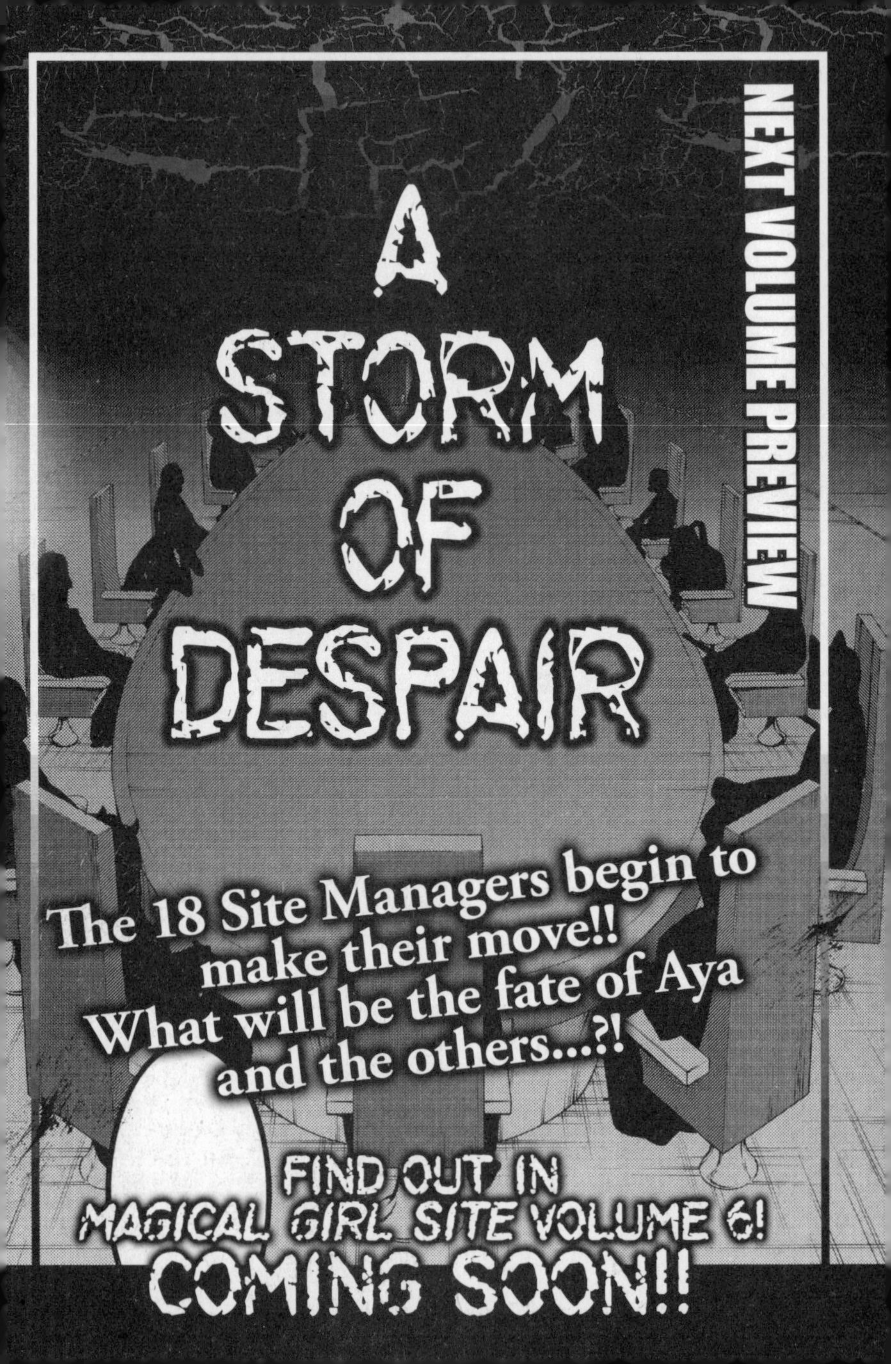
NEXT VOLUME PREVIEW
A STORM OF DESPAIR
The 18 Site Managers begin to make their move!!
What will be the fate of Aya and the others...?!
FIND OUT IN MAGICAL GIRL SITE VOLUME 6!
COMING SOON!!

Experience the thrills of HORROR from
SEVEN SEAS ENTERTAINMENT

LOVE IN HELL
THE COMPLETE TRILOGY

STORY & ART
REIJI SUZUMARU

STORY AND ART
TSUKASA SAIMURA

HOUR OF THE ZOMBIE

1

MAGICAL GIRL APOCALYPSE

1

KENTARO SATO

1-2

FRANKEN FRAN

KATSUHISA
KIGITSU

DEVILMAN
GRIMOIRE

VOL. 1

story by GO NAGAI
art by RUI TAKATO

TOKYO UNDEAD
THE COMPLETE COLLECTION

art by
TSUKASA SAIMURA

story by
SHIGEO NAKAYAMA

See all Seven Seas has to offer

gomanga

Seven Seas